Crime Scenery in Postwar Film and Photography

Henrik Gustafsson

Crime Scenery in Postwar Film and Photography

palgrave
macmillan

Henrik Gustafsson
The Arctic University of Norway
Tromsø, Norway

ISBN 978-3-030-04866-2 ISBN 978-3-030-04867-9 (eBook)
https://doi.org/10.1007/978-3-030-04867-9

Library of Congress Control Number: 2018966684

Cover image: Sarah Vanagt, 'Dust Breeding' (2013)
Cover design by Oscar Spigolon

This Palgrave Macmillan imprint is published by the registered company Springer Nature Switzerland AG.
The registered company address is: Gewerbestrasse 11, 6330 Cham, Switzerland

For Alfi and Elvis

Acknowledgements

According to John Constable, landscape is an artform that aspires to make something out of nothing. While the present study may be said to adhere to this credo, since it is concerned with scenes that on a cursory glance appear to have very little to offer, the project has not evolved out of nothing, but from a mass of notes, drafts and outlines amassed over the last decade. This material originates from my postdoctoral fellowship with *Nomadikon: New Ecologies of the Image*, an interdisciplinary research centre for the visual arts directed by Professor Absjørn Grønstad at the University of Bergen. I owe a debt of gratitude, first of all, to my friends and colleagues in this group and its vast network of collaborators, and to all those who, in one capacity or another, have contributed with inspiration, conversations or opportunities of various kinds. Too many to mention, I want here to extend my thanks in particular to Mark Ledbetter, Jennifer Swanson, Lars Sætre, Øyvind Vågnes, and James S. Williams.

The material gathered during my time in Bergen began to assume the contours of a realizable project in the fall of 2013 when I relocated to the University of Tromsø. First as a researcher with the group Border Culture, directed by Johan Schimanski and Stephen Wolfe, and later as part of the permanent staff of Media and Documentation Science. Among my colleagues in Tromsø, I am especially thankful for the friendship and support of Holger Pøtzsch, Andrei Rogatchevski, and Roswitha Skare, and to the staff at the Culture and Social Sciences Library for graciously putting up with my endless requests.

I am deeply grateful to all the exceptional artists who have generously granted permission to reproduce their work and provided the illustrations, many of whom went well beyond the call of courtesy to communicate on this and other matters. Sincere thanks to Yair Barak, Mikael Levin, Simon Norfolk and Jamie Marshall at Simon Norfolk Studio, Sophie Ristelhueber and Kari Astrup at BONO, and to the Department of Language and Culture at the University of Tromsø for financial support when needed. I want to extend a special thanks to Daniel Eisenberg and Sarah Vanagt, not only for providing me with copies of their films as well as illustrations, but also for graciously taking time to correspond with me and sharing invaluable insights into their work. During the last years of preparing the manuscript, I had a particular image in mind as the official "face" for this project, and I want to thank Sarah Vanagt who without hesitation gave permission to use this still from her film *Dust Breeding* as the book's cover.

It has been a pleasure to collaborate with Lina Aboujieb and Ellie Freedman at Palgrave Macmillan, who have been exemplary in all regards throughout the various stages of the process. I also want to thank the two anonymous readers of my book proposal and the clearance reviewer of the full manuscript draft for their careful readings and insightful comments, as well as their enthusiasm for the project.

Sections from two chapters have previously appeared in published form. A preliminary version of Chapter 5 was included in the anthology *Exploring Text, Media, and Memory*, edited by Lars Sætre, Patrizia Lombardo and Sara Tanderup Linkis (Aarhus University Press 2017). While substantially revised and expanded, this chapter has benefitted from the conscientious comments I received from Anders M. Gullestad and Ragnhild Evang Reinton, and the copy-edits of Mia Gaudren. Some sections from my article "The Cut and the Continuum: Sophie Ristelhueber's Anatomical Atlas," published in *History of Photography* (Vol. 40 No. 1 2016 © Taylor & Francis, available online: https://www.tandfonline.com/doi/full/10.1080/03087298.2015.1103458), have been developed and reframed for Chapter 3. These paragraphs therefore retain the improvements gained from the commentary of the journal editor Luke Gartlan and the two anonymous peer-reviewers. I would like to thank the publishers for granting me permission to draw on this body of material.

The opportunity to write this book would never have presented itself without the fortuitous interventions of two persons. First, Professor Astrid Söderberg Widding, who long ago encouraged me to pursue a Ph.D. in Cinema Studies at Stockholm University, and second, the aforementioned Asbjørn Grønstad, without whom I doubt I would have been able to continue this line of work. Moreover, if I had not crossed paths with Asbjørn, I would never have met Julie. For this, I am more grateful than I am for any of the above.

Tromsø
December 2018

Henrik Gustafsson

Contents

List of Figures

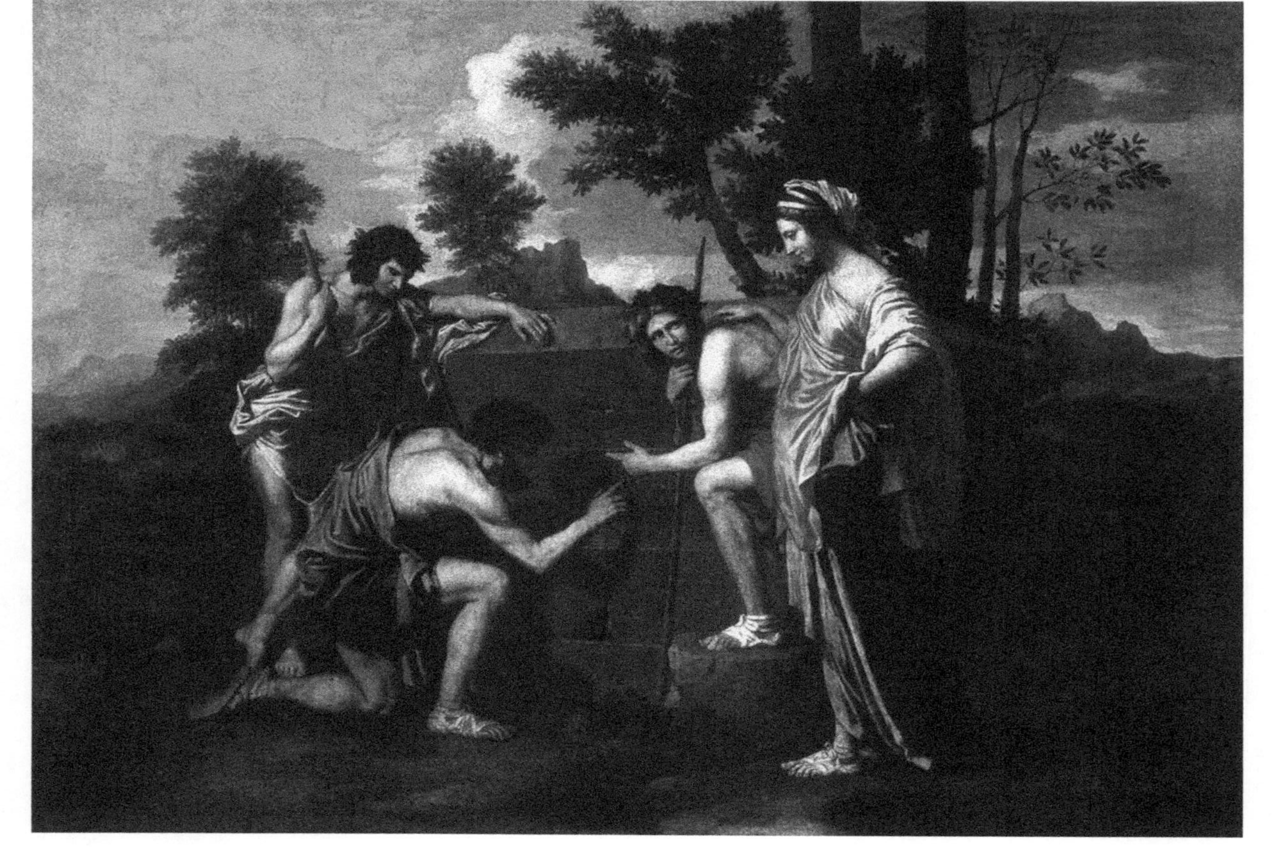

Fig. 1.1 Nicolas Poussin *Et in Arcadia ego* (also known as *The Arcadian Shepherds* 1637–1638) (*Source* Alamy)

CHAPTER 1

Imperfect Crimes

A few days after my mother died, my dad remarked: "She used to be all over the place, and suddenly she's nowhere." This is a commonplace, if bewildering, experience, as the places we inhabit or revisit tend to strike us as much for what is physically present before us as for what is palpably absent, no longer there to be seen, yet felt. This sensation also provides a point of entry into the conception of landscape and crime that informs the present study. Rather than promoting ideas of rootedness and belonging, inspiring community by tying a people to a place, landscape will be considered here as a means for reckoning with disappearances, with what has passed and vanished but nonetheless impinges on the present.

One of the primal scenes of landscape painting marks such an encounter: the discovery of a tomb in Arcadia painted by Nicolas Poussin in the late 1630s from Virgil's *Eclogues* where a small group of shepherds have gathered around a gravestone to study the Latin inscription "Et in Arcadia ego"—"I too once lived in Arcadia," or, "I, death, am also in Arcadia" (Fig. 1.1). Following art historian Christopher S. Wood, a notion of disappearance is endemic to the novel species of Western art that came into prominence sometime in the sixteenth century when the pictorial depiction of scenery began to gain autonomy as an artistic enterprise in its own right. "These pictures tell no stories," Wood asserts, "[i]nstead, they look like the settings for missing stories."[1] Disappearance is also at the heart of the reinvention of landscape as a

H. Gustafsson, *Crime Scenery in Postwar Film and Photography*,
https://doi.org/10.1007/978-3-030-04867-9_1

key pursuit of high modernism. Paul Cézanne, who during the last thirty years of his life made endless studies of the rockface of Mont Sainte-Victoire in Southern France, once remarked to a fellow painter: "You will have to hurry if you want to see anything. Everything is disappearing."[2] Turning to the alienated landscapes of postwar cinema, Cézanne's credo is echoed in a brief exchange from Michelangelo Antonioni's *The Passenger* (1975): "People disappear every day"/"Every time they leave the room." In Antonioni's films, this vanishing act is performed in moments of *temps morte*, of dead or inert time where the camera lingers on the locations long after the characters have exited the frame, sometimes never to return. Often, these desolate sites—the volcanic island in *L'avventura* (1960), Maryon Park in *Blow-Up* (1967), the Spanish courtyard in *The Passenger*—mark the scene of a crime that may or may not have taken place. Or, conversely, of a crime yet to be perpetrated, like the prospect of impending nuclear annihilation conveyed in the post-diegetic inventory of a deserted Roman suburb that concludes *L'Eclisse* (1962). In all cases, a disappearance takes place.

It has often been noted that the moments of suspension and standstill in Antonioni's films, when the story dissolves into the setting and narrative-driven time slips into a palpable sense of duration, entail an ontological blurring between the moving image and still photography. The opposite sensation has been attributed to Paris photographer Eugène Atget whose inventories of depopulated streets and urban peripheries have been described like film sets, as "stages for implied narratives" or "the natural theatre of violent death."[3] In common with the abandoned settings framed by Antonioni's camera, the first question these images provoke is not what they depict, but rather what compelled the photographer to minutely preserve, or dwell on, a site where nothing of apparent interest takes place. In Walter Benjamin's famous interpretation, the rationale could only be to mark the space for future investigation:

> It has quite justly been said of him that he photographed them like scenes of crime. The scene of a crime, too, is deserted; it is photographed for the purpose of establishing evidence. With Atget, photographs become standard evidence for historical occurrences, and acquire a hidden political significance. They demand a specific kind of approach; free-floating contemplation is not appropriate to them. They stir the viewer; he feels challenged by them in a new way.[4]

A crime scene thus solicits a specific form of attention. It is a look after the deed, in the wake of the event. It interpellates the spectator not as a disinterested or complacent viewer, but as a witness or bystander. The withdrawal of man augments the image's status as evidence, Benjamin says, "clearing the ground for the politically-trained eye."[5] This city devoid of people also alerted the surrealist imagination of André Breton and Man Ray, who praised Atget for his apprehension of a poetic yet sinister banality within the fabric of the everyday environment. Replete with illicit associations, the blind alleys, empty doorways and vacant windows suggest spaces where one could easily disappear, or secret passages through which a perpetrator might have fled the scene. For Atget himself, these documents served rather as portents of a crime to come, salvaging the overlooked and yet un-colonized remainders of an older Paris soon to be demolished by the onset of urban renewal. As Molly Nesbit has noted, the conspicuous absence of Haussmann's grand boulevards comes to function as indices of this crime, exerting "a subnormal pressure in the pictures as visible as a footprint."[6]

On the one hand, Benjamin's conception of Atget's uninhabited city as a crime scene ties in with ontological accounts of photography. Consider for example the prevalent metaphor of the photograph as equivalent to "a fingerprint left at the scene of the crime,"[7] or Roland Barthes's melancholic notion that mortality is already inscribed through the indexical trace as a premonition of "*a catastrophe which has already occurred.*"[8] On the other hand, it indicates an ontological ambiguity, as the crime scene may be said to constitute something like a threshold between still photography and moving images. Whereas the effect of *temps morte* in the films of Antonioni calls attention to the underlying presence of still photography in the celluloid strip, Atget's crime scenes mark the site of a latent narrative. As clues to something larger, they invite us to consider them, to borrow a phrase from Giorgio Agamben, as "stills from a film that is missing."[9] Photographers like Thomas Demand, John Baldessari, Clare Strand and Mac Adams have all pointedly highlighted this space of suspension between the still and the moving image, or what Adams' calls "the narrative void," in their meticulous reconstructions of real and fictive crime scenes.

The narrative voids instilled by the vacant expanses of rock, grass or concrete in Antonioni's enigmatic crime films have remained a salient trope of international art cinema. For some recent examples, we may consider the vast fields and monotonous plains of the provincial crime scenes in *Memories of Murder* (Bong Joon-ho, 2003), *The Night of the Sunflowers* (Jorge Sanchez-Cabezudo, 2006), *Once Upon a Time in Anatolia* (Nuri Bilge Ceylan, 2011) or *P'tit Quinquin* (Bruno Dumont, 2014). In all, landscape presents the inscrutable evidence of an unfathomable crime, a paradoxical signifier of that which exceeds a discursive frame or narrative logic. Rather than unlocking its secret, the characters and criminal investigators are exposed to the gaze that the land casts back upon them. In films like *Gerry* (Gus Van Sant, 2002) or *Twentynine Palms* (Bruno Dumont, 2003), there is nothing but the landscape and the crime, the vast, inert mineral expanses of the desert and a sudden outburst of senseless violence. Here, landscape serves as a visual corollary for the opacity of motif and explanation. It holds meaning at bay, lingering like a question mark.

* * *

The following pages will address the various facets of what the study proposes to call *Crime Scenery*, cross-referenced with a number of artistic works to delineate its two basic modalities as those of *coming-after* and *retracing*. While the visualization of affliction and atrocities tends to be synonymous with images of the human body, wounded and disfigured, the corpus of works to be considered here are noticeable instead for a conspicuous absence of bodies, showing neither perpetrators nor victims.

Instructive in this regard is an on-going series called *Fatescapes* (2009–) where the Czech photographer Pavel Maria Smejkal grafts the effect of *temps morte* onto a selection of iconic photographs of war, carnage and political assassinations by digitally removing the human figure from the image. What remains is a compilation of dates and locations: "1855 Crimea"; "1863 Gettysburg"; "1917 Passchendaele"; "1930 Marion"; "1936 Spain"; "1945 Berlin"; "1951 Nevada"; "1963 Texas"; "1968 Saigon"; "1970 Kent, USA"; "1972 Vietnam"; "1989 Beijing"; "1992 Somalia"; and so forth. The withdrawal of the human figure provokes a series of afterimages of *Pathosformeln*, the art historian Aby Warburg's coinage for a vivid or agitated gesture of shock or pain, like the outstretched arms of the Loyalist Militiaman at the moment of death, or of a child burnt by Napalm. Often, these afterimages appear immediately; in others, our gaze is left to scan an anonymous field or façade, unable to bring back the missing referent to the barren historical stage.

The omission of the injured or triumphant body entails a displacement of the historical index as the *here* and *now* is replaced by a confounding *where* and *when*: a green lawn or roadside curb, sand dunes or wooded slopes. Instead of the watershed event, *Fatescapes* offers an apparently random inventory of tarmac, grass, clouds, mud and rock. Smejkal's project raises questions about photographic inscription, collective memory and historical revisionism, as many of these iconic photographs were staged after the fact, like the flags raised at Iwo Jima and the Reichstag in Berlin, or the bodies of fallen soldiers that were rearranged for pictorial effect on a battlefield in Gettysburg. Contrary to the fatalistic tenor of its title, the series finally suggests the possibility of another history unfolding at these sites. In this sense, removing the figure restores the potential of ground.

Contemporaneous with *Fatescape* is *Trop tôt, trop tard (After Henri Cartier-Bresson)* (2007–2008) by the French photographer Isabelle Le Minh. From a selection of well-known photographs by Cartier-Bresson, Le Minh has digitally removed "the decisive moment," the defining act caught in the fraction of a second by the click of the shutter, like a pedestrian leaping over a flooded street, or a child rushing down a flight of stairs, leaving us with a portfolio of empty streets and dilapidated buildings reminiscent of the posthumous urban topographies of Atget and Antonioni.[10] Ironically, the voids instilled by Smejkal and Le Minh call to mind Cartier-Bresson's critique of the pristine scenes favored by his American colleagues during the height of the Great Depression and the rise of Fascism in the 1930s: "The world is going to pieces and people like Adams and Weston are photographing rocks!"[11] Cartier-Bresson's reproach proffers a basic question that undergirds and directs the present study: under what conditions may the activity of photographing rocks constitute a political or ethical gesture?

A tentative answer to this question was advanced in the film from which Le Minh borrowed the title for her project: *Trop tôt, trop tard* (Too Early, Too Late) made by Jean-Marie Straub and Danièle Huillet in 1981. The film unfolds as a land inspection divided into two sections. In the first part, excerpts from letters written by Friedrich Engels commenting on the harsh living conditions of the peasant population at the eve of the French Revolution are recited over static shots and slow-paced pans of the rural locations mentioned in the letters and revisited by the filmmakers. Counterpointing the scenes of hardship described by Engels, the present-day locations all appear to have been abandoned, conveying, in

Straub's phrase, the "science fiction, deserted-planet aspect" of the French countryside.[12] The second part is based on passages drawn from a more recent Marxist writer, Mahmoud Hussein's 1974 study *Class Struggles in Egypt, 1945–71*. This time, the camera traverses sites of the Egyptian resistance to the English occupation and the failed peasant revolution in 1952.[13] In the words of Serge Daney, the mission of *Trop tôt, trop tard* is to "identify a crime. Scene of the crime: the earth; victims: peasants; witnesses to the crime: landscapes. That is, clouds, roads, grass, wind."[14] Looking at these landscapes is thus to *bear witness to the witness* of the crime; to imagine what has already occurred there, and what may yet take place.

The untimely condition of being too early or too late, or what Hannah Arendt in similar terms has referred to as a "no longer and not yet," also pertains to the "historical no-man's-land" forged by Smejkal and Le Minh, as it remains uncertain whether these are places after an event or ones where something is about to happen.[15] Or, whether the photographer has arrived at the scene too late or too early. The patently anti-journalistic gesture of Smejkal and Le Minh's post-photographic projects resounds with a prolific tendency in contemporary photography to depict places devoid of human presence in the wake of violent encounters. What variously has been glossed as "aftermath photography," "post-reportage," or, most commonly, as "late photography," charts an almost complete inversion of the humanitarian stance of photojournalism.[16] Bringing together the post-conflict work of artists like Sophie Ristelhueber, Paul Seawright and Simon Norfolk, all of whom will be addressed below, David Campany notes that, "photography has re-engaged its forensic function, although none of these photographers make images that resemble police pictures. Instead, forensic attention to traces is spliced with an almost classical sense of place typical of traditional landscape photography."[17] Hence, they don't quite resemble landscape photographs either, many of them looking rather like images from a land survey, or of an archaeological dig.

In a memorable formulation, the artist duo Adam Broomberg and Oliver Chanarin have referred to such amalgamations of war reportage, forensics and landscape photography as a "post-mortem of photojournalistic representations of conflict."[18] This is also the dual implication intended by Campany in his coinage of late photography which not only refers to the artist's belated arrival to the place of the event, but also to the lateness of the medium of photography itself, as it has been outmoded by the speed of electronic and digital images. Along these lines, many commentators have identified the aestheticizing and anachronistic tendencies of late photography, with its amplified sense of stillness and muteness, as an elegiac response to sublimate or allegorize photography's double loss: first of its material support; then of its privileged relation to a singular and spectacular event.[19] But the gesture of turning away from instantly recognizable images of conflict may also be understood as an act of resistance against the rhetoric of immediacy and transparency propagated by news agencies and press photographers. In this sense, it seems to confound the very notion of the genre's eponymous "lateness" or "aftermath" as these terms imply a temporal continuum readily divided into a before and after the event by the opening and closing of the shutter. In common with the crime scenes of Atget, the effect of *temps morte* in the films of Antonioni, the deserted historical landmarks of *Fatescapes* and the indecisive moments of *After Cartier-Bresson*, late photography invokes not so much an aftermath as a sense of interrupted continuity.

The enigma of the missing body posed in all these works caters to a virtual dimension of the image. Challenging the viewer, as Benjamin noted, by revealing so little, they prompt us to ask what we are seeking. Put differently, they solicit a consideration of what it means that *events take place*. What is the relationship between what has taken place and the place that remains? Can a site hold the event *in place* so that it can be accessed or excavated after the fact? Or, does the impact of the event extract *from place* some essential characteristic? What constitutes an event in the first place, and how is it delimited from what comes before and after? These queries signal an epistemological shift toward the question of the trace, which is where forensic science, photographic theory and landscape art all converge.[20] The purpose of forensic photography is to provide a visual record of marks left on the scene, such as stains, disturbed dust, latent fingerprints and impressions of shoes or tires. The time-wrecked ruins, storm-blasted trees, rent clouds, rippled waters and ruffled fields in a landscape are also indexes of a passing energy that has acted upon the terrain. So are the inscriptions of war left upon it, whether they are Roman roads or pockmarked concrete, as well as the landforms themselves, shaped over eons by the slow forces of geomorphology. The landscape does not merely speak in the past tense, however, as shadows and ripples may also provide clues for unseen or pending presences.

In the semiology of Charles Sanders Peirce, the index is defined as a sign that maintains a physical relation with the object or force that has caused it. The light-sensitive film or the wet sand has been touched or impressed by something that has subsequently passed and disappeared. As Peter Geimer notes, "[w]hat matters is this brief moment of contact and the visible evidence that it leaves behind on the impressionable ground."[21] This is also the key premise, known as Locard's Exchange Principle, on which forensic science is based. According to the dictum attributed to the French criminologist Edmond Locard, "every contact leaves a trace."[22] While late photography elicits such an analogy between the imprints left by an external force on the photosensitive layer and on the physical terrain, this ground tends to be summoned less as a repository of traces than as a surface where they are susceptible to vanish. As Mary Ann Doane reminds us, however, the index did for Peirce not merely designate a trace of the past but also an event *taking place* in the present.[23] Significantly, the American semiotician found the exemplary form of indexicality not in the inscription of light on the photographic negative, but in the linguistic category known as the *deixis*. In linguistics, the deixis refers to the situation in which an utterance takes place, including demonstrative pronouns like "this" and adverbial locutions such as "here" and "now." Lacking any substance or content other than its function within a discourse, the deixis does not describe or explain anything, it merely calls attention to something. As incarnated by the index finger, or the viewfinder that frames and directs our attention, the deixis simply points and says "there!"—also when it points to what is no longer "there" to be seen.

The bifurcated temporality of the index as trace and gesture is highlighted in the photo-essay *On This Site: Landscape in Memoriam* (1996) where fine art photographer Joel Sternfeld tracks down a number of crime scenes across North America in what the introduction describes as "a memorial revisit to the site of the event."[24] We're given the date, place and circumstances of each crime in a matter-of-fact caption on one spread and the photograph of the location where it took place on the other. While the denotative pronoun "this" in the title reinforces the indicative function of the deixis to denote a single, physical site and to verify the immanence of the past, the quotidian and nondescript character of the locations themselves undermine this assurance. It is precisely by paying sustained attention to otherwise unremarkable scenes that *On*

This Site alerts the viewer, soliciting a gaze that is at once forensic and commemorative, so that the act of looking comes to constitute both an act of allocating guilt and of paying respect.[25] Notably, the first crime scene located by Sternfeld is the national memorial at Mount Rushmore, a site where the monumental figure and its elevated gaze literally obliterates the ground. Framed behind a rack of spotlights pointing toward the Founding Fathers, the image signals a shift of emphasis from the illuminated subjects of history to the ground as a surface of inscriptions as well as erasures. As the caption informs us, the memorial was chiseled into the rockface of the Black Hills of South Dakota; hallowed land stolen from the Sioux Nation after gold had been discovered in the area. The four presidents, who appear as natural outcroppings, are thus looking out over legally unsettled land. In all the counter-memorials to follow, the inconspicuous foreground will dominate the composition, with tracts of tarmac, snow, sand, grass or gravel randomly distinguished by the contingencies of season and light. In common with *Fatescapes*, *On This Site* gives us only the ground.

Refracting the clinical attitude of forensic photography through the contemplative mode of landscape art, Sternfeld's memorial revisits highlight the generic ambiguity that the titular notion of crime scenery attempts to paraphrase. Whereas the landscape gaze frames an expanse into a single view, the forensic gaze fragments space into a grid of systematic investigation and detection. The crime scene marks a site of disturbance and transgression that transforms the place by converting every object within its remits into a potential clue. Landscape, conversely, unfolds into a calm and composed vista, encouraging a cursory glance or the kind of "free-floating perception" that Benjamin deemed inappropriate for viewing the urban scenes captured by Atget. Hence, the commonplace critique against the euphemistic or escapist character of landscape, from Virgil's Arcadia to its contemporary lowbrow versions in postcards, advertisements and calendar art. Seeing the scenery together with the crime, therefore, prompts a double interrogation, not merely of a site but also of its status as an image, that is, its formation as an aesthetic artifact and exhibited object. Bringing together forensic fieldwork and fine arts, what distinguishes the artistic interventions under consideration in the subsequent chapters is precisely the proximity between these two fields, as they selectively map terrains of long-term conflict together with a panoply of landscape art.

A crime scene does not only compel a return; it also demands an intervention, urging the viewer to imaginatively reconstruct a scenario from scattered clues and circumstantial evidence. Summoning us as witnesses, it asks of us to consider what has been erased from the scene. To see forensically thus means to engage with the trace as an epistemic resource from which to construct invisible relations between events and places. *Crime Scenery* pivots on gestures of retracing that re-activate or re-inscribe a trace barely, or no longer, visible. While the past can never be recovered, it may nonetheless be retraced. To *re-mark* or *re-touch* the site, physically or figuratively, may therefore be understood as an ethical act against the epistemic violence of erasing traces through censorship, cover-ups and codenames, or simply through oblivion.

The prefix *re-* indicates a return or repetition, a going back to, or bringing back from, the original place. It finds its exemplary expression in the practice of re-photography as engaged by several of the artists to be considered below, whether by shadowing an artistic predecessor or by resuming the anonymous itineraries of military surveys, on the ground or in the air. Others return to make images that approximate an experience in the past of which no pictorial record exists, as when following in the footsteps of a previous generation along the routes of death marches and deportations. Here we may note the contiguity of retracing to concomitant terms such as reenactment or rememory. The latter is Toni Morrison's coinage from a famous passage in her novel *Beloved* (1987). In contrast to the condition of latency and relay that defines the labor of post-memory, rememory impels a search for, and a sensuous engagement with, the places of past events. Morrison thus conceives of rememory as a physical encounter in the present, a deictic event taking place at the crossroads of site and imagination:

> Places, places are still there. If a house burns down, it's gone, but the place—the picture of it—stays, and not just in my rememory but out there in the world. The picture is still there and what's more, if you go there—you who never was there—if you go there and stand in the place where it was, it will happen again; it will be there for you, waiting for you.[26]

There is slippage in these paragraphs from a place to a picture, at once conjured in the mind and remaining as an afterimage on the site itself. This suggests that images may be reactivated in the process of being relocated, as they are endowed with the concreteness, texture and there-ness of place. On the one hand, Morrison's notion of rememory latches back to the ancient art of memory, which relied on a dialectical play between *imagines*, the ability to form mental images, and *loci*, the location, real or virtual, where these images are stored and retrieved. On the other hand, Morrison reverses this formula, since images are not projected and impressed on space, as in the mnemonic architecture envisioned by Greco-Roman rhetoricians, but already linger there in a state of dormancy. Yet again, like the notorious cannonballs strewn in a ravine in Crimea, to which we will return shortly, this may also arouse the suspicion that evidence—traces, mnemonic cues—have been planted after the fact.

Retracing comprises strategies of doubling or shading, of seeking out and positioning oneself at a vantage point held by a former gaze. What is engaged in such works is as much a historically determined field of vision as the view that it encompasses. In this sense, the acts of retracing under consideration below may be said to reflect an abiding concern in the cultural critique of landscape, which has been committed to expose its "dark side" (John Barrell), its "duplicity" (Stephen Daniels) or "dreamwork" (W.J.T. Mitchell). However, in order to confront an image, rather than treating it as a code to crack, a spell to break, or a veil to tear, philosopher and art historian Georges Didi-Huberman has urged us, "to look at what remains (visible) while summoning up what has disappeared: in short, to scrutinize the visual traces of this disappearance."[27] Here, it is useful to recall the distinction that Ian Hacking has made between evidence and verisimilitude. Whereas the former "is a matter of inferring one thing from another thing," the latter, Hacking continues, "is a matter of one thing being, or not being, what it seems or pretends to be. The kind of evidence that I have in mind consists in one thing pointing beyond itself."[28] Such is also the nature of the evidence that will concern us here, which serves rather as evidence of how little there is to see by pointing to something that lies beyond the borders of the image, or buried in its midst. Furthermore, Hacking's definition implies that evidence evades the ontological question of being.

The notion of the trace left by an erasure or occlusion, but which nonetheless points to something that has departed from the scene, has its obvious precedent in the work of Emmanuel Lévinas. As construed in French post-structuralist thinking from the 1960s and onwards, the trace emerged as a highly potent trope to call into question the equation of being with presence in Western metaphysics. Whereas the sign reveals an absent signified, the trace, as understood by Lévinas, refers to what doesn't properly appear within the visible realm. Contrary to the common understanding of the trace as a mere imprint, a residue or reminder, Lévinas' trace marks an absence inscribed in the material present. Hence, if the trace does not immediately reveal or give access to the signified, Lévinas writes, it is because "the signifyingness of a trace consists in signifying without making appear."[29] The ethical obligation to engage with the traces of the historical Other postulated by Lévinas therefore also entails a critique of representation, as such non-phenomenal traces elude the binary divide of presence/absence on which mimesis rests. Following Lévinas, what has withdrawn from the world does not entirely disappear either, but remains as a passing.

The exemplary instance of the trace is for Lévinas therefore not the clues disclosed by the detective at the scene of the crime but, conversely, those of the criminal who covers his tracks and, "the fingerprints left by someone who wanted to wipe away his traces and commit a perfect crime."[30] These are not traces intentionally inscribed for us to find and interpret, but negative imprints that signify through their erasure and effacement, equivalent to a blocked memory or missing archival file. Landscapes proliferate with such shadows of the Other's passing, with what has been buried or removed, lodged in the soil, washed away or overgrown. As a privileged site of collective memory, it is a repository of vanished presences, and of events and experiences that have been silenced, neglected or denied appearance. This theme finds an emblematic expression already in Poussin's painting of the shepherds in Arcadia, as one of them kneels down before the tomb to retrace, with his index finger, the shadow projected by his body on the flat stone.

* * *

Predictably, Smejkal's iconoclastic revision of the photojournalist canon in *Fatescapes* begins in Crimea 1855. In Errol Morris' estimate, "the Crimean War is the 'perfect war.' It was started for obscure reasons, was hopelessly murderous, and accomplishing nothing."[31] It has also been described as the first modern war, not only for introducing new tactics and technologies of warfare, but for being covered by press photographers. In the Vorontsov ravine near Sevastopol in 1855, the British War Correspondent Roger Fenton made what is often considered the first icon of photojournalism, known as *The Valley of the Shadow of Death*. Before his foray into Crimea, Fenton had established himself as Great Britain's most prominent and widely exhibited landscape photographer, excelling in the picturesque template with images of misty gorges, gothic cathedrals and ruined monasteries clad in ivy. In common with his contemporaries in the United States, Timothy O'Sullivan and Eadweard Muybridge, Fenton transposed his skills as a landscape photographer to the battlefield. The stark monotony of the Crimean steppes, however, offered none of the tonal contrasts and delicate nuances of Tintern Abbey and the Lake District. *The Valley of the Shadow of Death* shows a landscape scraped of effulgence and embellishment: a meandering dirt road entices the gaze into the scene, but toward nothing; stretching across the barren slopes and abruptly cut off by the crest of

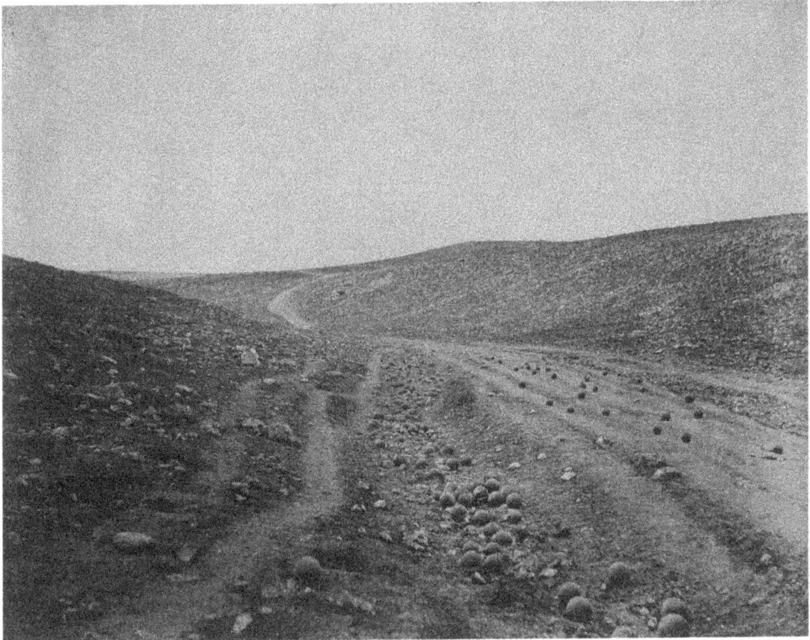

Fig. 1.2 Roger Fenton *The Valley of the Shadow of Death* (1855) (*Source* the Library of Congress)

a ridge and a blank sky (Fig. 1.2). Retouched by Smejkal, not even the Russian shells that overshot the British armies, rolled into the ravine and scattered in the furrows, remain.[32]

Fenton's footpath returns in *Hidden* (2002), a collection of photographs from Afghanistan made by Paul Seawright in the aftermath of the Coalition War, depicting the mine-infested terrain in muted sepia tones. This time, the sloping dirt road cuts through a ravine littered with spent casings of artillery shells from an Allied bomb attack. The photograph is laconically titled "Valley," acknowledging Fenton's valley as its generic template: the perfect image of the perfect war. In equal part self-reflexive homage and tragic irony, collapsing the distance between the Crimea in 1855 and Afghanistan in 2002, it suggests that the only thing that has changed is the military hardware. Hence, Seawright's dead ringer may be criticized for divesting the event of its political context. As a valley in the Crimea looks much like a valley in Afghanistan, or a landfill in California for that matter, as in Joe Deal's *Road Cut (Homage to Roger Fenton) Diamond Bar, California* (1984), the insistence on being at the scene paradoxically seems to blur out the specificities of historical causes and effects. From another perspective, the displacement from topicality to topography opens up a long-term view, invoking not so much an aftermath as an endurance of imperial incursions into the area.

At the time when Seawright was making *Hidden*, another late photographer traveled the Afghan–Pakistan borderlands, carrying a heavy wooden camera similar to that of Fenton. Trained as a photojournalist but turned into a landscape photographer due to the increasingly unphotographable nature of late modern warfare, Simon Norfolk reverses Fenton's career move in his two photographic albums *Afghanistan: Chronotopia* (2001) and *Scenes from a Liberated Baghdad* (2003). I want to consider here an image from the latter titled "The North Gate of Baghdad (After Corot)." It depicts the fake ornamental arch that Saddam Hussein had constructed along the entry roads into Baghdad to align his regime with the imperial grandeur of Babylon kings (Fig. 1.3). Mimicking the dictator's deceit, Norfolk has composed his image in the impressionistic style of Jean-Baptist-Camille Corot, with a eucalyptus tree majestically spreading against expansive cloud formations. The image distills several of the key features of Norfolk's work from this time, which usually includes some of the staple props of landscape painting (overgrown ruins, Arcadian shepherds, victory arches) while carefully emulating its formal arrangements (the golden section, atmospheric

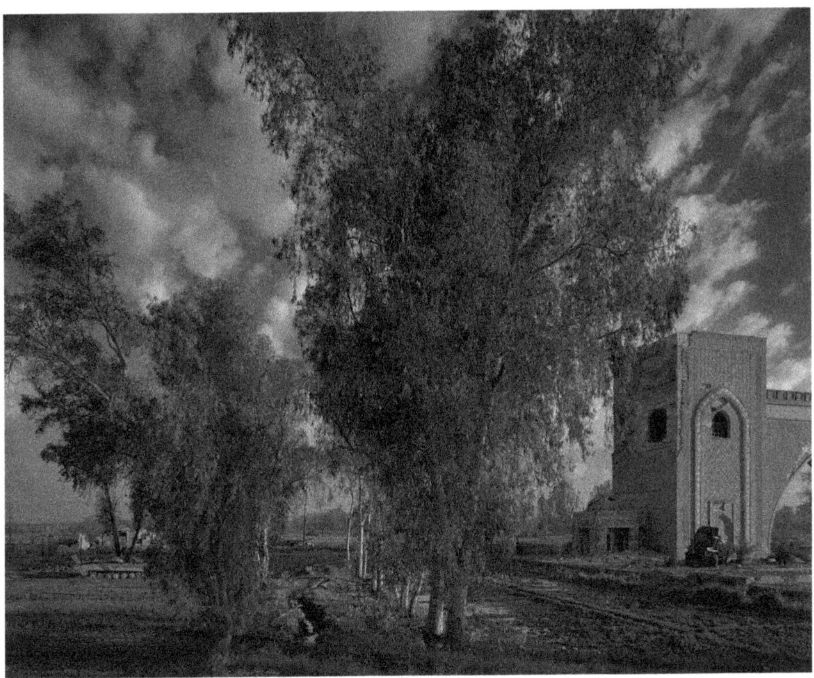

Fig. 1.3 Simon Norfolk "The North Gate of Baghdad (After Corot)" from *Scenes from a Liberated Baghdad* (2003). Courtesy of the artist

perspective) and the tonal range of oil painting, bathing the scenes in the delicate light at dawn or dusk. While steeped in this pictorial repertoire, Norfolk also introduces some element foreign to this tradition that disturbs the contemplative order. In "After Corot," a derelict rocket-launching system is discernable at the foot of the arch, a bombed Iraqi tank in the brushwood at the end of the avenue of trees and in the left middle ground, a ruined troop carrier.[33] Furthermore, the tiles have begun to crumble off the side on Hussein's archway, exposing the gray concrete beneath. With its deliberate anachronisms, "After Corot" implies that the artist has not only arrived in the aftermath of battle but also in the aftermath of landscape art.

In the conclusion of his iconographic study *Political Landscape—The Art History of Nature*, Martin Warnke elegiacally proclaims that the natural landscape's, "rich reservoir of motifs and experiences that once guided human action has run dry."[34] This ending has been proclaimed so frequently that it arguably has come to constitute the master-plot of landscape art in the twentieth century, which has been narrated as a series of death throes wrought by the onset of industrial-scale warfare and manmade environmental disasters. Significantly, landscape shares this moribund fate with the genre of history painting. Maybe we should take this as an intimation, as the works from Afghanistan by Seawright and Norfolk suggest, both of which infuse the scale and subject matter of history painting with the deceptive calm of landscape art, that these two pictorial modes have not, in fact, died, but rather, that they have merged.

If landscape began with the advent of perspectival painting and the formation of the nation-state and its sovereign subject, its demise coincides with an inflation of proclaimed aftermaths: the end of the grand narratives of enlightenment and emancipation, and our present state of posterity circumscribed by the overlapping categories of the post-modern, post-historical, post-national, post-racial, post-colonial, post-political, post-human, post-medial and post-factual. The prefix *post-* doesn't so much mark an end as a return, however, for by proclaiming the end of something one inadvertently elicits its afterlife. Ideologically and aesthetically stigmatized, inflated by the heritage of empires and settler nations, landscape may therefore also provide a mnemonic tool for working through the atrocities of a century of killing fields, blitzed cities and mass graves. While early practitioners and theorists of landscape extolled its potential to convey moral lessons that ennobled the viewer, the genre now seems more adapted to implicate the viewer in the violent legacies of land grabs, forced deportations and ethnic cleansings.

"After Corot" is symptomatic of what Hal Foster in 2002 diagnosed as our current cultural condition "of coming-after and living-on."[35] After modernist invention and postmodernist deconstruction have both run their course, Foster asks, what else is there to do than to return? Among such "versions of this living-on," Foster notes that a "strategy in the condition of coming-after is the staging of *nonsynchronous* forms."[36] To reengage antiquated genres and to mine their forms of a new content may further serve to remind us, Foster continues, "that 'form' is nothing but 'content' that has become historically sedimented."[37] In the present context, this strategy entails a venture into the shadows and blind corners of landscape as a scopic regime endemic to modernity, and complicit in its dramatic failures, in order "to haunt these outmoded spaces,"[38] as Foster writes, as if reopening a closed case.

Traditionally, landscape has been an art of tonal contrasts and chiaroscuro. While it suspends our disbelief through its lucid depiction of details and depths, shadowy lairs and things unseen are required in order to create an effect of immersion. It is precisely these obscured areas of the canvas that John Barrell called attention to in his landmark study *The Dark Side of the Landscape* from 1980.[39] Idealizing the beauty of the landscape while occluding the labor that had produced it, the contrasts between the lit and dimmed areas on the canvases painted by someone like John Constable sustained a social hierarchy, Barrell argues, as the rural proletariat was banished to the shady margins of the frame. J.M. Coetzee reiterates this assessment in his study of the landscape imagery of South African literature which is marked, Coetzee writes, by a constitutive "occlusion of black labor from the scene," a consequence of the judicial dictate that labor equals property by right.[40] In both cases, the "dazzling" light of power projected by the landed gentry utilizes, as Michel Foucault noted in a 1976 lecture, "a divisive light that illuminates one side of the social body but leaves the other side in shadow or casts it into darkness." Consequently, any history of class or race struggle must "speak from the side that is in darkness, from within the shadows."[41] It is, then, only through a critical engagement with these murky fringe areas that landscape may lead us back to the conflicts from which it allegedly provided a respite.

Following from Foster and Barrell, and the counter-histories called for by Foucault, I want to consider here three versions of "coming after" Constable. The first two in brief, beginning with Peter Kennard's photomontage *Haywain with Cruise Missiles* (1980), where three cruise missiles have been mounted in the eponymous farm cart of Constable's most well-known painting, *The Hay Wain* (1821), to comment on the placement of nuclear missiles in the British countryside of East Anglia during the height of the Thatcher–Reagan era. Second, John Kippin's photographic triptych *After Constable*, showing a sky suffused with dramatically gilded and swirling plumes towering above a thin strip of land, invoking the *plein air* studies of Constable, the supreme cloud painter in John Ruskin's estimate. The billowing formations photographed by Kippin, however, are in reality a manmade smokescape, an index caused by the burning of heather on moorland. More menacing than mocking in tone, and more pertinent to our present concerns, a third revisit to

Constable Country was paid by Robert Priseman in a series of five small oil paintings called *SUMAC* (2011). They show innocuous views of the countryside south of Ipswich, each approximately the size of a Post-it note and ornamentally framed in antique Indian shrines. The work was named after "Operation Sumac," a police investigation into a series of brutal murders that was committed in Suffolk in the fall of 2006. Each miniature depicts a deposition site of the Ipswich serial murders: a brook with a sewage pipe, a forested roadside and a grove of bare trees. While their intimate scale beckons us to look closer, as if peering into another world, they leave the viewer clueless as nothing in the pictures themselves, other than the close scrutiny that they call for, indicate that something of gravity has occurred there. In common with the barren views of Atget, Antonioni, Smejkal and Sternfeld considered above, something is conspicuously missing from the picture. It is this impression of lack or dearth that marks their forensic character, as the image appears to conduct some sort of investigation that not only puts the site in question, but also the nature of vision itself.

Priseman has cited Constable's painting *The Cornfield* (1826), a reproduction of which hung in his childhood bedroom, as the inspiration for the series. Hence, the *SUMAC* series bears a structural similarity to what Sigmund Freud termed a screen memory. According to Freud, a screen memory is distinguished by two conflicting characteristics: on the one hand, by its trivial appearance, containing no manifest information that would reveal its significance; on the other, by its vividness and compulsion to return. While a screen memory covers up the past, it also retains some vital clue or connection that obliquely points out the direction toward the primal scene. Along these lines, independent of the viewer's knowledge of the Ipswich murders, Priseman insists that the deposition sites remain, "scarred by some kind of residual energy attached to violence." Once *touched* by violence, the artist suggests, the site remains *in touch* with the event. Another Freudian concept thus also seems to be pertinent in this context, that of *Nachträglichkeit*, meaning after-effectiveness, or what Lévinas referred to as "[t]he posterity of the anterior."[42] Returning to landscape as if returning to the scene of a crime, Constable Country becomes retroactively haunted by acts committed two centuries after its inception on the canvas.

How, then, does the temporal sensibility that informs the strategies of coming-after and living-on under consideration in *Crimes Scenery* distinguish themselves from a more conventional scheme of before-and-after?

As a final case in point, let us compare two projects that have followed in the footsteps of the Irish landscape painter Paul Henry. Salvaging scenes of rural life rapidly falling fallow with the drift to the cities in the interwar period, Henry is foremost known for his romantic depictions of the primeval bogs and turf stacks in the West and Midlands of the Emerald Island. The collaborative re-photography and re-painterly project *After Paul Henry* (2013–2015) revisited these locations in order to take note of the effects of modernity that the painter had sought to keep at bay. The result is a heritage trail equally informed by rediscovery and lament, depicting the countryside in a state of oscillation between permanence and progress, tradition and transition. Around the same time, the boglands eulogized by Henry came to provide a more oblique point of entry into the past for the Irish multimedia artist Willie Doherty. In common with photographers like Paul Graham, Paul Seawright and David Farrell, Doherty frequently steers away from the stock imagery of sectarian violence in the urban centers of Belfast and Derry to seek out more subtle traces of disorder—freshly turned soil, scrubby grass or recently planted saplings—in the rural parts of the North. In his video installation *Ancient Ground* (2011), shot on the location of a bog in Ulster, Doherty invokes at once the distinct national topos popularized by Henry and the ancient practice of disposing bodies deemed undeserving of a proper burial in the bogs. While the camera patiently examines the marshy soil in static long shots, close-ups and tracking shots, an off-screen voice announces that it is, "looking for a sign, some disturbance, something shifted, revealed, given up, leaking."[43] A quest for such disturbances propels the trilogy of films on the post-conflict landscape of Northern Ireland that *Ancient Ground* concludes. In the first, *Ghost Story* (2007), the presence of disappeared and discarded bodies is invoked by a long Steadicam shot tracking down a forested path in the province of Derry, occasionally venturing into the undergrowth, while the voiceover cautions the viewer that, "the surface of the road was no longer thick enough to conceal the contents of the tomb that lay beneath." Filmed in the same location, *Buried* (2009), the middle part of this trilogy, dispenses with the spoken narrative altogether. Instead, close-ups of plant species, fungus and mold are interspersed with forensic clues scattered in the topsoil, such as a latex glove, a shotgun cartridge and a metal noose.

The acts of coming-after Cartier-Bresson, Fenton, Corot, Constable and Henry considered above reinforce the latently uncanny position that we assume before any landscape. Whether occupying the perceptual field of a national subject or an innocent abroad, our sightline is aligned with that of a former witness to the scene. Refuting the modernist myth of a clean break with the past as well as the postmodern myth of the end of history, this diachronous gaze summons a present overshadowed by the past. While all works discussed in the present study were made after the Second World War, and all bear the stigma, in one way or the other, of its atrocities, the label "postwar" is to be understood in the present context less as a periodizing category, dramatizing the course of history into a series of discrete epochs, than as a ubiquitous condition. In other words, it compels a consideration of how the after-effects of old alliances and animosities, promises and disappointments, bear down on and govern the present, and of aftermaths as the breeding ground of new conflicts.[44] Poised between two national imaginaries, that of the Jewish homeland in the Middle East and the *Heimat* of Greater Germany, the ensuing chapters actualize a specific trajectory that emphasizes the historical stratification of sites of violence and erasure. Turned from an art of auspicious beginnings, broadening horizons and expanding frontiers to one of residual energies and half-lurking presences, landscape is here consigned to a posthumous and spectral life, conjured forth as a framework no longer capable of retaining the view, nor of keeping at bay that which has been denied appearance.

* * *

The penultimate of the nine theses on landscape listed by W.J.T. Mitchell at the outset of his highly influential essay "Imperial Landscape" states the following: "Landscape is an exhausted medium, no longer viable as a mode of artistic expression."[45] The second claim, however, doesn't automatically follow from the first. Instead, my argument proceeds from the counter-assumption, that landscape has assumed a new critical role precisely because its time has passed. As Gilles Deleuze has suggested, exhaustion may in itself be a productive condition, as it facilitates an opportunity for unthinking given categories.[46] Visual culture theorist Irit Rogoff has recently brought Deleuze's notion to bear on geographies of long-term conflict, or what she calls "Exhausted Geographies."[47] To acknowledge the exhaustion of geography and its operative principles of division and containment entails for Rogoff a recognition of the arbitrary nature of such strictures and an unwillingness to grant them the authority that they demand. Against the disciplinary effects of geography, Rogoff posits an active practice of un-belonging and self-excommunication. From this perspective, the exhaustion of the spiritual and moral basis that traditionally has undergirded landscape art, and its visions of sacred homelands, divinely sanctioned returns and new beginnings, is not so much a cause for lament as an occasion for something new to emerge.

Over the last decade, landscape has taken on a renewed currency in contemporary art, evident in group-exhibitions such as *Ecotopia* (2006), *Loaded Landscapes* (2007), *Badlands* (2008), *After Nature* (2008), *Topographies of War* (2011), *Unsettled Landscapes* (2014–2015), *Suspended Spaces* (2016), and countless others. In the academy, it has launched what Lesley Head already in 2004 described as "an explosion of landscape studies."[48] Moreover, it was precisely at a historical moment of disillusionment and exhaustion that landscape came to gain momentum as a vehicle for formal and conceptual innovation and for the critical examination of categories such as natural beauty, nationhood and art history. Out of the failed political movements of the 1960s and their debased utopian aspirations emerged what in retrospect may be termed a "landscape turn" in the visual arts. Whether impelled by blunt irony or aggressive iconoclasm, landscape no longer appeared as the pastoral refuge envisioned by the counter-culture, but as the epitome of a fictitious and deceitful image. For artists like Anselm Kiefer and Gerhard Richter, it provided a focal point for probing the intertwined legacies of German Romanticism and Nazi politics. In the words of Richter: "Every beauty that we see in landscape—every enchanting color effect, or tranquil scene, or powerful atmosphere, every gentle linearity or magnificent spatial depth or whatever—is our projection; and we can switch it off at a moment's notice, to reveal only the appalling horror and ugliness."[49] Switching off this projection became an abiding concern in the burgeoning fields of environmental art and conceptual photography in the wake of the decade's progressive thrust.

Notably, this exhaustion spurred a vogue of manuals and manifestos. In his 1967 "A Tour of the Monuments of Passaic," Robert Smithson superimposed the template of picturesque tourism onto his sightseeing of a depleted, postindustrial construction site in New Jersey. Two years later, the Austrian artist Hermann J. Painitz called for a total vanquishing of the natural landscape in his manifesto *On the Designs for Leveling the Alps*. Also in 1969, the Canadian artist Jeff Wall published his *Landscape Manual*, a handbook for reading "a defeatured landscape" mapped in a series of artless black-and-white snapshots taken through the windshield on a road trip.[50] Lavishing attention to locations usually considered unworthy of interest, Wall's manual encapsulated the concerns of a group of photo-conceptual artists based in Vancouver from the late 1960s until the mid-1970s whose images appeared as flat and featureless as the monotone stretches of suburban sprawl that they depicted. In the United States, the vernacular landscape allowed artists like Ed Ruscha and Lewis Baltz to develop a detached and understated formal approach most famously associated with the taxonomies and typographical charts featured in a landmark 1975 group exhibition called "New Topographics: Photographs of a Man-Altered Landscape." In a phrase that calls to mind the uninhabited scenes of Atget and Antonioni, Allan Sekula referred to the new topographic surveys of industrial parks, tract houses and mobile homes as, "the 'neutron bomb' school of photography: killing people but leaving real estate standing."[51]

One of the least known, but perhaps most instructive, exponents of this tendency is the Japanese discourse on *Fûkeiron*, literally meaning "landscape theory," which evolved out of the production of a brief cycle of experimental films made in the late 1960s and early 1970s while the militant protest movement was on the wane.[52] Most notable of these is an enigmatic topographical crime film called *A.K.A Serial Killer* (Masao Adachi, 1969) that follows in the footsteps of Nagayama Norio, an illiterate migrating worker who committed four homicides in the fall of 1968. The following year, a small film crew retraced Nagayama's vagrant itinerary across the Japanese archipelago to record the locations he had seen. Clinically devoid of characters and drama, *A.K.A Serial Killer* charts the homogenous environment produced by the economic recovery and reconstruction of postwar Japan in static long takes, tracking shots and lateral pans. Not drawn into an action or argument, the spectator remains resolutely outside the views that unfold, in the words of the film's director Masao Adachi, as a series of "picture postcards" whose distinguishing feature is their "stifling" and "suffocating" uniformity and lack of local flavor.[53]

In his 1970 essay "City as Landscape," the leftist film critic Masao Matsuda states that "Nagayama must have shot the bullets in order to tear the landscapes apart." Here, Matsuda also expounds the guiding methodological principle established in the film. "In the process of encountering this landscape, we may be following an exact inverse cycle from that of Benjamin appreciating Atget," Matsuda explains: "In inverse of Atget, we shot the scenes of crime like landscapes."[54] Avoiding the topical images of police violence and student riots that dominated mainstream news as well as militant documentary filmmaking at the time, the *Fûkeiron* critics' sought to turn the landscape against itself in order to make it reveal its complicity with regimes of power and surveillance. "Landscapes as they appear in these films are more than documentary images," film theorist Yuriko Furuhata explains, as "their political significance lies in their ability to indirectly point to—or index—what remains invisible."[55] These quotidian scenes of construction, commerce and communication thus convey an idea of landscape as crime, an anonymous and ubiquitous crime dispersed over the networks through which bodies and spaces are governed, and discernable only to what Benjamin called "the politically-trained eye."

Several vectors converge, in embryonic form, in the *Fûkeiron* movement's program for studying the relation between the built environment and social power structures. First, it heralded some of the key tenets that would inform the broad convergence field of Anglo-Saxon landscape studies first to be articulated by British cultural critics including John Barrell, Stephen Daniels and Denis E. Cosgrove from the early 1980s and onward. Second, the formal and thematic concerns advanced by the *Fûkeiron* theorists anticipated the work of filmmakers like Chantal Akerman, James Benning, Patrick Keiller and Eric Baudelaire, all of whom have reengaged the template of the pre-documentary actuality film, with its static tableaux, traveling shots and phantom rides, as an exploratory toolbox for probing the sociocultural strata embedded in the vernacular environment.

In his second book on cinema, Gilles Deleuze has remarked that while classical cinema, whether American or Soviet, was always a cinema of peoples, of individuals and masses, the political dimension of the work of filmmakers such as Alain Resnais or Straub-Huillet seemed to derive instead from a conspicuous absence of people. This led Deleuze to the following speculation: "if there were a modern political cinema, it would be on this basis: the people no longer exist, or not yet … *the people are missing*."[56] Rather than representing or interpellating the people as a pre-given entity, always already in place, such a cinema would cater to an absent population, summoning a people to come. Maybe, then, the turn to landscape may also constitute a search for the political and ethical agency of the image.

* * *

"Were it not for appearances, the world would be a perfect crime," Jean Baudrillard asserts at the outset of his 1995 essay *The Perfect Crime*.[57] The goal of this crime is to cleanse reality of its imperfections and to eliminate all negativity so as to create a perfectly positive, transparent and rational world. Hence, it constitutes nothing less than, "*the murder of reality*."[58] The vanishing act that this program entails, however, is never complete, nor is the crime perfect, for the world continues to give itself away through appearances. It is by allowing itself to be sensed, Baudrillard says, that "the world betrays its secret."[59]

The French philosopher and photographer here resorts to a metaphor that will provide us with a final occasion to ponder the efficacy of the gestures of coming-after and retracing: "Just like we cannot plumb the first few seconds of the Big Bang, so we cannot locate those few seconds in which the original crime took place either. It is a fossilized crime, then, like the 'fossilized' background noise scattered about the universe."[60] The Big Bang, furthermore, is an event that has never ceased to take place, as the gravitational waves emitted from the blast are still rippling through space-time.[61] Since the universe is expanding, the echo of the violence continues to act in the present. Properly speaking, the universe does not expand through space; rather, it is perpetually *creating* space. While the mass of dark energy increases as the expansion accelerates, its density remains constant. Dark matter, then, does not exist *in* space but is rather a property *of* space itself; by estimate seventy-five percent of the universe is invisible, a phantom-like presence that can only be inferred through its repercussions in the visible world.

The belated arrival of the fossilized waves of light that reach us from celestial bodies that may long since have ceased to be, itself a metaphor for the photographic image,[62] is not merely a cause for melancholy, but also for hope. For Baudrillard, it is precisely because the universe is not perfectly synchronized that we may be able to retrace what has vanished, so that disappearance may "remain a living disappearance, and the trace of the crime a living trace."[63] This is also the basic tenet that spurs the three acts of retracing on which these introductory notes will conclude. More specifically, we are dealing in all three cases with a gesture of charting the crest of a distant mountain ridge as a means to expose the dark matter of a violent past. All these projects are concerned with the question of historical legibility, or, to quote Hugo von Hofmannsthal's motto, with developing strategies for learning "to read what was never written."[64] And all, finally, create a form of diachronic montage: in the first example, through long exposure times; in the second, through the historical ellipsis between two images; and in the final case, through the duration of a series of glacially paced panning shots.

The first project is also the one that evinces the most literal implementation of Baudrillard's metaphoric notion. For the American artist, activist and geographer Trevor Paglen, dark matter cognates the sprawling "dark geography" of the Pentagon's military and intelligence community in the vast hinterland of the desert southwest.[65] Just like dark matter can only be deduced and documented indirectly, Paglen argues, we need to develop new ways of looking askew in order to catch a glimpse of the clandestine infrastructure of mass-surveillance, preemptive strikes and extraordinary renditions. In his ongoing photographic project *The Other Night Sky*, started in 2007, astronomy does not only provide a metaphor but also the technical apparatus for seeing secrecy, re-tooling astronomic imaging equipment designed to observe remote galaxies to make a record of extra-terrestrial activities invisible to the unaided eye.

In *The Other Night Sky*, Paglen strategically positions himself at the vantage points previously held by the first explorers of the Great American Desert, such as Eadweard Muybridge, Carlton Watkins and Timothy O'Sullivan, on the military and geological surveys following the Civil War. While the wet plate collodion process used by his predecessors required very long exposure times, which meant that moving objects failed to register and that the sky bleached out into a uniform blank surface, the long exposures of Paglen's re-photography engender the opposite effect. Seen through telescopic lenses used for astrophotography, hidden presences emerge above the summits of the canyons and mesas, like the glowing flash of a classified spacecraft or an eavesdropping satellite that bisect the curved lines of the star trails. Through this procedure, the iconic profiles of the Half Dome in Yosemite Valley, the Tufa Domes in Nevada and the soaring sandstone formations of Monument Valley pull the contours of the black world into historical relief. It is through the calibration of focal ranges and exposure times that covert operations "show through" or "squint out through appearances," as Baudrillard puts it, to provide the clues through which we may recover "the imperfection of the crime."[66] The resulting telescoping effect elides two frontiers into one image: the colonization of the continental interior and the New Frontier of outer space. Returning the gaze of the surveillance satellites, *The Other Night Sky* also presents a record of how the infrastructure of military reconnaissance has continued to expand over the course of one and a half centuries.

For our second example, we turn once more to the work of Simon Norfolk. Ten years after his first foray into Afghanistan, Norfolk came back to the war-torn territories of Kabul, this time following in the footsteps of the Irish war correspondent John Burke who under the auspices of the British army took the first photographs in Afghanistan. *Burke+Norfolk: Photographs from the War in Afghanistan* was conceived as a collaborative project over time and exhibited as a series of diptychs that juxtaposed images from the second Anglo-Afghan War (1878–1880) with its fourth incarnation following the terrorist attacks on the World Trade Center.[67] The singular "War" in the title highlights this continuity, corroborating the proposal made by geographer Derek Gregory that the misnomer "post-colonialism" should be replaced with the "colonial present."[68]

Covering the same ground as Burke, Norfolk was only able to relocate the vantage points held by his predecessor by retracing the rugged skyline of the Hindu Kush Mountains that surround Kabul. Ravaged by invasions and civil war, the crest of these mountains was the single element in Burke's photographs that remained unchanged. Norfolk has described his first encounter with Burk's photographic albums as a rediscovery of "a piece of forensic evidence of a crime," and his own gesture of re-photographing these sites as an effort, "to chisel something out of the rock face and blow the dust off it."[69] In common with *The Other Night Sky*, the rockface serves as an interface where the past and the present are aligned to reveal the longevity of imperial campaigns into a desert hinterland on the fringes of the empire.

The third and final ridgeline to be considered here is that of the Apuan Alps in northern Tuscany that was charted in a series of panning shots by Jean-Marie Straub and Danièle Huillet in their film *Fortini/Cani* (1977), based on the Italian-Jewish communist, critic and poet Franco Fortini's 1967 novel *The Dogs of the Sinai*. Part autobiography, part pamphlet, Fortini's book critically reflects upon the identitarian politics of the Israeli state and its role for the power balance in the Middle East against the backdrop of the rise of Fascism in Europe and the recent events of the Six-Day War. Early in the film, Fortini recites a brief passage from his book that mentions the massacre that took place in the hillside village of Marzabotto in August 1944 when the *Wehrmacht*, aided by local Fascists, killed more than five hundred civilians. What then follows is a sequence of slow panning shots that circle the hillside villages along the so-called Gothic Line, the German defensive line of gun pits, bunkers and trenches that stretched from coast to coast along the high crests and peaks of the northern part of the Apennines.

Continuing for almost fifteen minutes, and accompanied only by synchronous natural sound, these long takes firmly inscribe and envelope Fortini's passing reference to the blood spilled in 1944 in the present tense. The syncopation of past and present along the gently rolling hills further implies a vacillation between the inscription and the erasure of memory.[70] Softened by aerial perspective, the soaring mountains and terraced valleys of Tuscany conform to a conventional landscape aesthetics, subtly counterpointed when the camera pauses on a memorial plaque in a village square that reminds its present population of the destructive flames "enclosed in the marble of your mountains." In a note to the filmmakers, Fortini reflects that, "[t]he absence of man … affirms *the enormous presence of the dead*; but not only of *those* dead, of the victims of Nazi massacres. When the present is seen from outside the present, it becomes a place onto which past and future spirits can be projected."[71] It is the spoken text, read by the author with ten years hindsight, which facilitates this position of seeing "outside the present" in the film. Fortini continues: "The pan of the Apuan Alps does not say 'only' what happened there and how calmness now covers the sites of massacres both ancient and modern. It also 'says' that *this* land is the place inhabitable by human beings, that we *must* inhabit it."[72] The placid land inspection in *Fortini/Cani* thus marks a terrain of the already dead and the yet unborn, of passing and becoming. In their patient and minute study of the countryside, Straub and Huillet may thus be said to resume the pedagogical legacy of landscape as an artform committed to retrain perception, teaching the spectator to discern what is not immediately visible.

Fortini/Cani returns us to our beginnings, Poussin's tomb in Arcadia and Cézanne's rockface. Whereas the subject of Paglen's *The Other Night Sky* hovers above the desert mountain ranges, and *Burke + Norfolk* hones in on the valley wedged between them, the subject of the panning shots of *Fortini/Cani* resides within the mountains. The visual image in the films of Straub-Huillet has been described alternatively as a "tomb" or a "rock," its content being, in the words of Serge Dancy, "what is concealed in it, the corpses under the ground."[73] It was Jacques Rivette who after a screening of *Fortini/Cani* first called the filmmakers' attention to the structural affinity between their approach and the method pursued by Cézanne.[74] In two subsequent films devoted to the painter, Straub-Huillet would retrace Cézanne's excursions into the Provençale countryside and through the collections of the Louvre. While it has often been said that Cézanne, a self-declared disciple of Poussin, painted Provence as a Virgilian Arcadia, his work was also informed by an intimate knowledge of the region's geological and cultural strata of Mesolithic caves and Greek and Roman colonizers.[75] Rather than presenting the indigenous landscape as a timeless bucolic bliss, the genres of history and landscape painting seamlessly merged: most strikingly in the fulcrum of Cézanne's later work, the *Mountain of Victory*, a former volcano that was named after the battle that spared Rome from invasion.[76] From the 1870s to his death in 1906, Cézanne depicted the mountain from various viewpoints and in various mediums and moods: sometimes mirage-like and ethereal, other times bulky and opaque, but always with the intention of exposing its geological structure in the striated flames of his brushstrokes, conjuring the forces of the earth that continue to shape it.

Hence, Deleuze reference to Cézanne as "the Straubs' mentor," founding a template for their historical-materialist filmmaking in *Plein air*.[77] Stressing the isomorphic relation between the processes of geomorphology and of long-term political struggle, and the manner in which such anonymous forces shape places as well as populations, Deleuze consistently draws from the earth sciences when he reflects upon the work of Straub-Huillet. Like the mineral strata painted by Cézanne, the discrete layers of present and past are rendered, in Straub's phrase, as "geological blocks."[78] In *Fortini/Cani*, audible blocks of words and sound are stacked together with visible blocks of light and color not only to expose, as Deleuze writes, the "geological strata or foundations" of the image,[79] but also to chisel out from the rocky mass what Baudrillard referred to as "a fossilized crime" entombed in the summits of the Apennines.

In closing, let us once more consider Benjamin's appraisal of the crime scenes photographed by Atget. The "hidden political significance" that he confers to these documents precisely corresponds to the sedimented historical indexes exhumed in the meandering inventories of *Das Passagen-Werk*. On one occasion, Benjamin notes that Paris possesses "the kind of beauty that is proper to great landscapes—more precisely, to volcanic landscapes. Paris is a counterpart in the social order to what Vesuvius is in the geographical order: a menacing, hazardous massif, an ever-active hotbed of revolution."[80] Cézanne concisely expressed this conflation of political and geological upheaval in a formula that came to be adopted by Straub-Huillet as the credo of their project: "Look at that mountain; once it was fire."[81] In their first film on the painter, *Cézanne* (1989), Huillet reads these lines while the static camera lingers on a long shot of Mont Sainte-Victoire. It is with such fires congealed and concealed in the land that the artists to be considered in the following chapters imaginatively engage.

* * *

Before we proceed, I would like to draft a brief synopsis to show how the set of inquiries and propositions concerning the relation between trace and landscape raised above will be developed and expanded over the arc of ensuing chapters. Fleshing out the methodological underpinnings of the project, the argument of Chapter 2, "From Dreamwork to Earthwork," orbits around two motifs. The first is a pastoral mural painted on a defensive wall bordering the Israeli settlement of Gilo outside Jerusalem, which returns as a paradigmatic instance of landscape as the "dreamwork of imperialism" in the writings of W.J.T. Mitchell. Drawing on a host of artistic engagements with Gilo Wall, the chapter offers a critical appraisal of dominant approaches for the interpretation of landscape, polarized between the hermeneutics of memory and myth that Mitchell labels the "depth model" and his own "surface model." Whereas the former understands landscape as a repository of collective memories, the latter seeks to expose it as a medium for distorting and screening out historical realities. The second motif is Poussin's *Shepherds in Arcadia*. Here, the discussion turns to a series of artistic and theoretical speculations on the significance of the enigmatic "Ego" inscribed on the tomb, all of which suggest that landscape from its inception has been riddled by traumatic scars.

Further expounding on the notion of a fossilized crime presented above, the chapter introduces Aby Warburg's atlas of pictorial memory from the late 1920s as a heuristic model for rethinking the binarism of a surface or depth approach to landscape. While the fulcrum of Warburg's project pivots on the human gesture, his *Mnemosyne* atlas was conceived in geoscientific metaphors, intended both as a map of Western visual culture from pagan antiquity to the present, and as a seismic station to pick up signals of the distant and impending disasters that rumble beneath this terrain. Refracting Warburg's morphology of memory traces through Freud's notion of dreamwork, Georges Didi-Huberman significantly expands upon this geological and tectonic discourse. With Mitchell, Warburg and Didi-Huberman as its primary interlocutors, read together with a miscellany of works by artists including William Kentridge, Simon Norfolk and Robert Smithson, the second chapter presents a theoretical exposition for an eminently dialectical understanding of landscape as a series of ongoing tensions, perched between surface and sediment, scenery and symptom, dreamwork and earthwork.

The third chapter, "Intruders in the Dust," continues to explore the epistemological gains of bringing Warburg's atlas of mnestic traces to bear on landscapes in the wake of violent upheavals. Closely engaging with the vast body of work created by the French artist and photographer Sophie Ristelhueber, renowned for her rigorous examinations of geographies scarred by long-term conflict, from Beirut and Kuwait to the Balkans and the West Bank, the analysis pursues the proposition that the terrain, in common with the body, can suffer from recollections. The post-operative fields charted by Ristelhueber are further considered together with Jananne Al-Ani's aerial archaeology of the Jordanian desert in her two *Shadow Sites* films, as well as two experimental films by Sarah Vanagt, *Dust Breeding* and *The Wave*, which follow forensic exhumations of mass burial sites in the aftermath of civil war. This comparison of images of disturbed earth queries two interrelated phenomena: on the one hand camouflage, which blurs the distinction between foreground and background, subject and surround; on the other, the transfigurative effects of airborne reconnaissance and its capacity to turn tracts of land into a set of clues to be deciphered.

As a matrix for the arcane semiotics of traces probed by these three artists, the latter part of the chapter draws on the discourse surrounding Man Ray's enigmatic 1920 photograph *Dust Breeding*, which frames the dust-laden surface of Marcel Duchamp's sculpture *The Large Glass* as a miniaturized landscape seen from the air. Advancing a notion of the artwork as a receptor of accidental marks and imprints, *Dust Breeding* foreshadowed a forensic turn in the arts. Acknowledged by Ristelhueber as a formative influence on her work, and examined here as an expressive form that continues to resurface across the domestic and geopolitical spaces traversed by her camera, the chapter considers *Dust Breeding* through the analytical lens of Warburg's concepts of *Pathosformel* and *Nachleben*. This investigation also raises a series of questions concerning the "lateness" of aftermath photography, and the manner in which the earthbound approach adopted by Ristelhueber, Al-Ani and Vanagt invites us to reconsider how traces relate to time, aftermaths to events and bodies to territories.

Chapter 4, "A Murder of Crows," announces a change of scenery: from the conflicted terrains of the Middle East to the concentrationary universe of Greater Germany. The trace under investigation here is not etched into the earth, however, but suspended in flight: initially above a wheatfield in Arles where Vincent van Gogh according to common lore painted his final canvas. In his 1947 rumination on *Wheatfield with Crows*, apocryphally known as the artist's "suicide note," Antonin Artaud calls attention to how the painting blurs a series of conceptual categories: between the still and the moving image, portrait and landscape, life and death. The following year, Alain Resnais invoked van Gogh's late canvas in similar terms as the coda for his experimental film on the painter, and once more in the opening shots of *Night and Fog*, made a decade after the Liberation. As the camera cranes down from a high-angle view of a field with crows to frame it behind the barbed wire fence, the voiceover cautions the viewer that any landscape may take us into a concentration camp. The chapter tracks the many afterlives of van Gogh's auspicious birds, proposing that the skein of crows operate according to the convoluted logic of Warburg's *pathosformel*.

From the anachronistic vantage points of *Nachträglichkeit* and *Nachleben*, the analysis then proceeds by considering the recurring yet enigmatic presence of van Gogh's painting in the late cinema of Jean-Luc Godard. Introduced in reference to the Nazi camps in the first part of *Histoire(s) du Cinema*, the carrion birds spread across the remaining chapters of Godard's videographic archaeology of the moving image, and migrate further into a series of his feature films from this period. Undergoing constant transformations, the slashes of black paint and the screeching call of crows here accrue the overdetermined force of a symptom around which a miscellany of motifs cluster. Linking the Nazi extermination campaigns to the airstrikes on Guernica, Germany and Japan, and Étienne-Jules Marey's chronophotographic studies of aerial locomotion to the predatory birds unleashed Alfred Hitchcock, van Gogh's telltale flock of crows are conscripted by Godard into a dire genealogy of cinema. Not merely an index of the artist's hand, or of the gun blast that startled the flock, they ultimately emerge as an elementary form for the shadows coming to life on the screens and battlefields of the last century, but also as an elegiac reminder of the unfulfilled promises of cinema itself.

The penultimate chapter, "Persistence of Vision," investigates a series of artistic reencounters with the former territories of the Third Reich and the Soviet Bloc performed by second-generation survivors of the camp and gulag systems. With recourse to the dynamics of *imagines* and *loci*—the ability to form mental images and the location from where they may be retrieved—stipulated by ancient mnemotechnics, the analysis draws on Warburg's thesis on the surviving image in order to develop an understanding of memory that is at once imagistic and site-specific. This reciprocal process of recollection and relocation is further facilitated with regard to Toni Morrison's notion of rememory, according to which mnestic residues linger like "pictures" on the sites of former events, and to the concepts of post-memory, trauma and secondary witnessing that pervade the field of cultural memory studies. Here, the discussion turns to three semi-autobiographical road trips that aspire to resuscitate the past by retracing the itineraries of a former generation: Chantal Akerman's film *D'Est*, Mikael Levin's photo-essay *War Story*, and Ori Gersht's photographic project *The Clearing*. Together, these works establish an assemblage of strategies for how to utilize the camera as a mnemonic tool, including traveling shots, prolonged exposures, re-photography and montage. They also introduce us to an allegorical trope for the belated witness, and thus for the melancholic condition that they seek to overcome: the brooding *rückenfigur* of Caspar David Friedrich's romantic sublime, a figure who will emerge as the protagonist of the second half of the chapter.

The taxonomy of mnemotechniques identified in these eastbound travelogues provides a launching pad for an in-depth analysis of three films made by Daniel Eisenberg. The first, *Displaced Person*, is comprised of newsreel footage of Hitler's tour through the monuments of Paris in 1940. The second, *Cooperation of Parts*, retraces the early life of the filmmaker's parents from their birthplaces in Poland to their deportation to Dachau. The third, *Persistence*, meditates on the two *Stunde Null* of postwar German history by juxtaposing the rubble of Berlin in 1945 with the demolition and reconstruction sites of formerly East Berlin in 1991. Closely attending to the particular art of memory crafted in each film, the analysis considers the duplicitous nature of the topography of memory sites trailed in Eisenberg's Postwar Trilogy, which at once alerts us to the risk of consolidating the past into a series of stable landmarks, and to the possibilities of its redemption.

The final chapter unfolds as a cross-reading of two attempts "to read what was never written," undertaken by Georges Didi-Huberman in his photo-essay *Écorces* (Bark), and by Claude Lanzmann in his monumental film *Shoah*. During a visit to the compound of Auschwitz-Birkenau, now converted into a state museum, Didi-Huberman collects pieces of bark in the surrounding birch forest and ponders how these fragments may compel a work of memory on the events that they witnessed and outlived. The chapter situates this apparently futile attempt to interrogate trees within a long lineage of latecomers to the scene of the crime, including Lanzmann, who have all called upon the forest to act as a witness; not merely as a survivor of the event, but also as an agent of its erasure. By unpacking the series of ideas that Didi-Huberman pursues in his essay, which actualizes a number of motifs that inform his work on the image, such as survival, symptom, contact-image, and visual archaeology, the analysis sheds new light on the theological framework that has galvanized his polemical conversation with Lanzmann.

Within this context, the chapter further investigates the multifaceted role that trees and forests play across the vast geographies charted by Lanzmann over the course of four decades of filmmaking. From his debut *Pourquoi Israël* to his final film *The Last of the Unjust*, trees are imbricated in a struggle over memory that is as much symbolic as it is strategic, not merely serving as an index and a metaphor for the destruction of European Jewry, but also for the resurrection of the lost world of the Jewish nation. Hence, the shreds of bark collected by Didi-Huberman offer a nodal point where the various vectors and geographies of *Crime Scenery* all converge, thereby preparing the ground for a concluding reflection on the dialectical structure of the trace as both index and deixis, as a vestige of the past and an event taking place in the present. Seeking to overcome the binary ontologies that have undergirded the cultural critique of landscape, the study as a whole explores the distinct modes of ethic, aesthetic and epistemological address that the deep surface of landscape engenders by soliciting us as witnesses to the silences and disappearances that it hides and harbors.

Notes

1. Christopher S. Wood *Albrecht Altdorfer and the Origins of Landscape.* Revised and Expanded Second Edition (London: Reaktion Books 2014) 9 and 13.
2. Ulrike Becks-Malorny *Cézanne* trans. Phil Goddard (Cambridge: Taschen 2004) 20.
3. Wolfgang Brückle "Almost Merovingian: On Jeff Wall's Relation to Nearly Everything" *Photography After Conceptual Art* eds. Diarmuid Costello and Margaret Iversen (Malden: Wiley-Blackwell 2010) 153–171, 160. Albert Valentin "Eugène Atget (1857–1927)," originally published in *Variétés* (Brussels, December 1928), quoted in Molly Nesbit *Atget's Seven Albums* (New Haven and London: Yale University Press 1992) 196.
4. Walter Benjamin "The Work of Art in the Age of Mechanical Reproduction" [1936] *Illuminations: Essays and Reflections* trans. Harry Zohn (New York: Harcourt, Brace & World, Inc. 1968) 217–251, 226.
5. Walter Benjamin "A Short History of Photography" [1931] trans. Stanley Mitchell *Screen* Vol. 13 No. 1 (Spring 1972) 5–26, 21.
6. Nesbit 135.
7. William J. Mitchell *The Reconfigured Eye: Visual Truth in the Post-Photographic Era* (Cambridge, MA: MIT Press 1992) 24.
8. Roland Barthes *Camera Lucida: Reflections on Photography* [1980] trans. Richard Howard (New York: Farrar, Straus and Giroux 1982) 96.
9. Giorgio Agamben "Difference and Repetition: On Guy Debord's Films" *Guy Debord and the Situationist International: Texts and Documents* ed. Thomas McDonough and trans. Brian Holmes (Cambridge: MIT Press 2002) 315.
10. The term was coined by Cartier-Bresson's publisher Tériade for the 1952 portfolio *Images à la sauvette* ("images on the run" or "stolen images"), a title that was translated for the English edition into *The Decisive Moment.*
11. Cartier-Bresson quoted in Estelle Jussim and Elizabeth Lindquist-Cock *Landscape as Photograph* (New Haven and London: Yale University Press 1985) 140.
12. Jonathan Rosenbaum "Jean-Marie Straub and Danièle Huillet" *Film: The Front Line* (Denver: Arden Press 1983) 187–199, 193.
13. From the mid-1970s and onward, Straub and Huillet frequently staged their films in rural or pastoral locations, occasionally amidst the ruins and shepherds of the Roman *Campagna.* Refuting the commonplace assumption of the innocuous and apolitical character of landscape as a concern merely for aloof and reclusive romantics dodging the call to political struggle, Barton Byg understands the historical-materialist

cinema of Straub-Huillet as "landscapes of resistance" where the counter-pointing of texts and locations mobilize the ground to challenge the "conventional definitions of the cinema's relation to nature, myth, and history." Barton Byg *Landscapes of Resistance: The German Films of Danièle Huillet and Jean-Marie Straub* (Berkeley, Los Angeles, and London: University of California Press 1995) 3.

14. Serge Daney "Cinemeteorology." Daney's text was originally published in *Libération* February 20–21 (1982) and translated by Jonathan Rosenbaum in a catalogue for a Straub-Huillet retrospective curated by Rosenbaum on November 2–14, 1982 at New York's Public Theater. The translation is available at https://www.jonathanrosenbaum.net/2018/03/cinemeteorology-serge-daney-on-too-early-too-late/ (accessed 1 August 2018).
15. Hannah Arendt "No Longer and Not Yet" [1946] *Reflections on Literature and Culture* ed. Susannah Young-ah Gottlieb (Stanford: Stanford University Press 2007) 121–125, 121.
16. See David Campany "Safety in Numbness: Some Remarks on Problems of 'Late Photography'" *Where Is the Photograph?* ed. David Green (Brighton and Kent: Photoforum, Photoworks 2003) 123–132; and Ian Walker "Desert Stories or Faith in Facts?" *The Photographic Image in Digital Culture* ed. Martin Lister (London and New York: Routledge 1995) 236–253. The label "aftermath photography" derives from two prolific, yet very different, photographic works. First, Sophie Ristelhueber's images of the desert of Kuwait in the wake of the First Gulf War originally titled *Fait* and, against the artist's wishes, translated into English as *Aftermath*. Second, *Aftermath* was also the title of a photo book by Joel Meyerowitz who was commissioned by the Museum of the City of New York to photograph the ruins of the World Trade Center after the terror attacks on September 11.
17. David Campany *Photography and Cinema* (London: Reaktion Books 2008) 45–46.
18. Adam Broomberg and Oliver Chanarin "The Day Nobody Died" presented at the Barbican Art Gallery (8 December 2008) http://www.broombergchanarin.com/new-page-4/ (accessed 1 August 2018).
19. See for example John Roberts "Photography After the Photograph: Event, Archive, and the Non-Symbolic" *Oxford Art Journal* Vol. 32 No. 2 (2009) 281–298.
20. Forensics has in recent years crystalized as a potent nexus of academic research, artistic intervention and political activism. Most notable is perhaps the work of Eyal Weizman, director of the Center for Forensic Architecture at Goldsmiths College. With recourse to etymology, the stated ambition of Weizman's project has been to retrieve the original

significance of *forensis*, Latin for "pertaining to the forum," the space where the Roman Senate gathered, and to reverse the forensic gaze and deploy it as a tool, "to challenge and resist state and corporate violence and the tyranny of their truth." Eyal Weizman "Introduction: Forensis" *Forensis: The Architecture of Public Truth* (Berlin: Sternberg Press 2014) 9–32, 9 and 11. Forensics thus stakes out a space between the field where evidence is gathered and the forum where it is demonstrated. This requires the intervention of what Weizman has dubbed a "forensics aesthetics" that seeks to yoke from bones, dust and rubble the violence that they have endured: "It is in the gestures, techniques, and turns of demonstration, whether poetic, dramatic, or narrative, that a forensic aesthetics can make things appear in the world." Thomas Keenan and Eyal Weizman *Mengele's Skull: The Advent of a Forensic Aesthetics* (Berlin: Sternberg Press 2012) 67. Rather than the hardcore positivism of CSI entertainment, forensic aesthetics charts a field of partial, multiple and conflicting truths. Evidence, then, does not exist prior to the act of disclosure before the public eye.

21. Peter Geimer "Image as Trace: Speculations About an Undead Paradigm" trans. Kata Gellen *Differences* Vol. 18 No. 1 (2007) 7–28, 10.
22. Lisa Yount *Forensic Science: From Fibers to Fingerprints* (New York: Chelsea House Publishers 2007) 64.
23. Mary Ann Doane "Indexicality: Trace and Sign" *Differences* Vol. 18 No. 1 (2007) 1–6.
24. Joel Sternfeld *On This Site: Landscape in Memoriam* (San Francisco: Chronicle Books 1996) n.p.
25. Along these lines, Matthew G. Kirschenbaum notes that, "forensics is commemorative as well as juridical, and fundamental to the arts as well as the sciences." Matthew G. Kirschenbaum *Mechanisms: New Media and the Forensic Imagination* (Cambridge and London: The MIT Press 2008) 250.
26. Toni Morrison *Beloved* [1987] (London: Vintage 2007) 43.
27. Georges Didi-Huberman *Confronting Images: Questioning the Ends of a Certain History of Art* [1990] trans. John Goodman (University Park: The Pennsylvania State University Press 2005) 50.
28. Ian Hacking *The Emergence of Probability: A Philosophical Study of Early Ideas About Probability, Induction and Statistical Inference* (Cambridge: Cambridge University Press 1975) 34.
29. Emmanuel Lévinas "The Trace of the Other" [1963] *Deconstruction in Context* ed. Mark C. Taylor (Chicago and London: Chicago University Press 1986) 345–359, 356.
30. Ibid. 357.
31. Errol Morris *Believing Is Seeing (Observations on the Mysteries of Photography)* (New York: The Penguin Press 2011) 36.

32. Smejkal's manipulation holds an additional irony, since the photograph of the valley in Crimea exists in two versions, one with cannonballs and one without. Hence, Fenton has been accused of arranging the image for pictorial effect. For an illuminating discussion and field study, involving a reenactment and re-photography on site, see Errol Morris' essay "Which Came First, the Chicken or the Egg?" in *Believing Is Seeing* 3–71.
33. "Simon Norfolk's best shot" Norfolk interviewed by Leo Benedictus in *The Guardian* 23 October 2008 https://www.theguardian.com/artanddesign/2008/oct/23/photography-iraq (accessed 1 August 2018).
34. Martin Warnke *Political Landscape—The Art History of Nature* [1992] (Cambridge: Harvard University Press 1995) 146.
35. Hal Foster "This Funeral Is for the Wrong Corpse" *Design and Crime (and Other Diatribes)* (London and New York: Verso 2002) 123–143, 143.
36. Ibid. 130 and 137.
37. Ibid. 137.
38. Ibid. 139.
39. John Barrell *The Dark Side of the Landscape: The Rural Poor in English Painting 1730–1840* [1980] (Cambridge: Cambridge University Press 1998).
40. J.M. Coetzee *White Writing: On the Culture of Letters in South Africa* (New Haven and London: Yale University Press 1988) 5.
41. Michel Foucault *Society Must Be Defended: Lectures at the Collège de France, 1975–76* eds. Mauro Bertani and Alessandro Fontana and trans. David Macey (New York: Picador 2003) 70.
42. Emmanuel Lévinas *Totality and Infinity: An Essay on Exteriority* trans. Alphonso Lingis (The Hague, Boston, and London: Martinus Nijhoff Publishers and Duquesne University Press 1979) 54.
43. As Terry Eagleton has noted, "if bogs have haunted the Irish imagination, it may be partly because they reveal the past as still present. With a bog and its buried contents, the past is no longer behind you, but palpably beneath your feet." Terry Eagleton *The Truth About the Irish* (New York: St. Martin's Press 1999) 30–31.
44. See, for example, Robert Gerwarth *The Vanquished: Why the First World War Failed to End* (New York: Farrar, Straus and Giroux 2016) and Gregor Dallas *1945: The War That Never Ended* (New Haven and London: Yale University Press 2005).
45. W.J.T. Mitchell "Imperial Landscape" *Landscape and Power* ed. W.J.T. Mitchell (Chicago: The University of Chicago Press 1994) 5–34, 5.
46. Gilles Deleuze "The Exhausted" trans. Anthony Uhlmann *SubStance* Vol. 24 No. 3 Issue 78 (1995) 3–28.
47. Irit Rogoff "Exhausted Geographies" keynote lecture at *Crossing Boundaries Symposium*, INIVA London 2010 https://www.youtube.com/

watch?v=PJOP910_nbI&feature=player_embedded (accessed 1 August 2018).

48. Lesley Head "Landscape and Culture" *Unifying Geography: Common Heritage, Shared Future* eds. John Anthony Matthews and David T. Herbert (London and New York: Routledge 2004) 243.
49. Gerhard Richter "Notes 1986" *The Daily Practice of Painting, Writings 1962–1993* (Cambridge: MIT Press 1995) 124.
50. Jeff Wall *Landscape Manual* (1969–70). Artist book published by the University of British Columbia Fine Arts Gallery, 1.
51. Allan Sekula "Translations and Completions." Exhibition notes for *California Stories* (Santa Monica, CA: Christopher Grimes Gallery 2011) n.p.
52. For a discussion, see Yuriko Furuhata "Diagramming the Landscape: Power and the *Fûkeiron* Discourse" *Cinema of Actuality: Japanese Avant-Garde Filmmaking in the Season of Image Politics* (Durham and London: Duke University Press 2013) 115–148. See also the round-table discussion "On Landscape (1970): Nakahira Takuma, Adachi Masao, and Nakahara Yūsuke (Moderator)" *From Postwar to Postmodern: Art in Japan 1945–1989: Primary Documents* eds. Doryun Chong, Michio Hayashi, Kenji Kajiya, and Fumihiko Sumitomo (Durham: Duke University Press 2012) 233–238.
53. Masao Adachi quoted in Furuhata 134.
54. An excerpt from Masao Matsuda's "City as Landscape," from which this quote is derived, is available at http://www.bordersphere.com/events/adachi9.htm (accessed on 1 August 2018).
55. Furuhata 170.
56. Gilles Deleuze *Cinema 2: The Time-Image* [1985] trans. Hugh Tomlinson and Robert Galeta (Minneapolis: University of Minnesota Press 1989) 216. Deleuze's emphasis on the phrase "*the people are missing*" is a reference to Paul Klee's lecture "Uns traegt kein Volk" held at the Kunstverein Jena in 1924. In the concluding paragraphs of "What is the Creative Act?" Deleuze writes: "What relationship is there between human struggle and a work of art? The closest and for me the most mysterious relationship of all. Exactly what Paul Klee meant when he said: 'You know, the people are missing.' The people are missing and at the same time, they are not missing. The people are missing means that the fundamental affinity between a work of art and a people that does not yet exist is not, will never be clear. There is no work of art that does not call on a people who does not yet exist." Gilles Deleuze *Two Regimes of Madness: Texts and Interviews 1975–1995* [2001] ed. David Lapoujade and trans. Ames Hodges and Mike Taormina (Cambridge and London: The MIT Press 2007) 312–324, 324.

57. Jean Baudrillard *The Perfect Crime* [1995] trans. Chris Turner (London and New York: Verso 1996) 1.
58. Ibid. n.p. (ingress of *The Perfect Crime*).
59. Ibid. 1.
60. Ibid. 2.
61. In the spring of 2014, scientists announced that they had detected traces of the gravitation waves emanating from the Big Bang. The claim was denounced a year later but reassumed again on February 11, 2016 when a sound file recording of the collision and merger of two black holes was released to the public.
62. "The photograph is literally an emanation of the referent. From a real body, which was there, proceed radiations which ultimately touch me, who am here; the duration of the transmission is insignificant; the photograph of the missing being, as Sontag says, will touch me like the delayed rays of a star." Roland Barthes *Camera Lucida* trans. Richard Howard (New York: Farrar, Straus and Giroux 1981) 80–81.
63. Baudrillard 3–4.
64. Hugo Van Hofmannsthal as quoted in Walter Benjamin *The Arcades Project* [1927–1940] trans. Howard Eiland and Kevin McLaughlin (Cambridge, MA and London, England: The Belknap Press of Harvard University Press 1999) 416.
65. For a close reading of Paglen's work, see Henrik Gustafsson "Foresight, Hindsight and State Secrecy in the American West: The Geopolitical Aesthetics of Trevor Paglen" *Journal of Visual Culture* Vol. 12 No. 9 (April 2013) 148–164.
66. Baudrillard 3 and 15.
67. Simon Norfolk *Burke+Norfolk: Photographs from the War in Afghanistan by John Burke and Simon Norfolk* (Stockport: Dewi Lewis 2011).
68. Derek Gregory *The Colonial Present: Afghanistan, Palestine, Iraq* (Malden: Blackwell 2005).
69. Artist quoted from the short video-documentary introducing the exhibition *Burke+Norfolk: Photographs from the War in Afghanistan* at Tate Modern https://www.youtube.com/watch?v=XXrmBhpRG2U (accessed 1 August 2018).
70. In his commentary on this sequence, Gilberto Perez delineates the vacillation between the inscription and the erasure of memory that the act of retracing entails: "In *Fortini/Cani* the camera inspects the landscape of the Apennines near Florence in a series of slow, prolonged panning shots around places where the Germans massacred large numbers of Italian partisans during the Second World War, pretty landscapes where no trace can be seen now of the blood that once was spilled here. That blood may have left no mark in these places but the camera marks them

with its deliberate panning, marks them but does not appropriate them, lets us know but lets them be, for people died in these places but people go on living here too. When the last of these panning shots, taken at the village of Marzabotto where hundreds were killed, goes around full circle and keeps going over the same ground we have just seen, enough time has passed since we saw it, owing to the slowness of the panning, that we have to make an effort of recognition: after only a few moments we have already started to forget." Gilberto Perez *The Material Ghost* (Baltimore and London: The Johns Hopkins University Press 1998) 232.

71. Franco Fortini "A Note for Jean-Marie Straub (1978)" *The Dogs of the Sinai* [1967] trans. Alberto Toscano (London, New York, and Calcutta: Seagull Books 2013) 74–82, 77–78.
72. Fortini 78.
73. Serge Daney quoted by Gilles Deleuze in *Cinema 2: The Time-Image*, footnote 39, 325. As Jacques Aumont further notes: "In almost every one of their films, the landscapes are immense tombs, cenotaphs, or monuments to some anonymous martyrology." Jacques Aumont "The Invention of Place: Danièle Huillet and Jean-Marie Straub's *Moses and Aron*" *Landscape and Film* ed. Martin Lefebvre (New York and London: Routledge 2006) 1–18, 5.
74. Sally Shapiro "Artistic Encounters: Jean-Marie Straub, Danièle Huillet, and Cézanne" *Film, Art, New Media: Museum without Walls?* ed. Angela Dalle Vacche (Houndmills, Basingstoke, Hampshire: Palgrave Macmillan 2012) 199–220, 202.
75. For a discussion, see chapter five, "Arcadia," in Nina M. Athanassoglou-Kallmyer *Cézanne and Provence: The Painter in His Culture* (Chicago and London: The University of Chicago Press 2003) 187–231. For a comparative analysis, see the exhibition catalogue *Cézanne and Poussin: The Classical Vision of Landscape* (London: Lund Humphries Publishers 1990).
76. The second film on Cézanne by Straub-Huillet is called *Une visite au Louvre* (2004). The film retraces the painter's excursions into the museum collections and concludes with a 360-degree pan of a lush and shaded hillside grove.
77. Deleuze *Cinema 2: The Time-Image* 255.
78. Jean-Marie Straub quoted from "A Thousand Cliffs. Interview with Elke Marhöfer and Mikhail Lylov" *Point of View* ed. Tobias Hering (Berlin: Archive Books 2014) 333–354, 350.
79. Deleuze *Cinema 2: The Time-Image* 246.
80. Benjamin *The Arcades Project* 83.
81. Straub "A Thousand Cliffs" 345. As first cited by Cézanne's friend and biographer Joachim Gasquet, whose memoir provided the text for

the two films made by Straub-Huillet: "These rocks were made of fire and there's still fire within them." Joachim Gasquet *Joachim Gasquet's Cézanne: A Memoir with Conversations* trans. Christopher Pemberton (London: Thames & Hudson 1991) 153. Originally, this line seems to derive from William Wordsworth's poem "Lines Composed a Few Miles Above Tintern Abbey" *Lyrical Ballads* (1798): "These boulders were made of fire. There is still fire in them."

CHAPTER 2

From Dreamwork to Earthwork

During the Second Intifada in 2001, a barrier was erected to protect the Israeli settlement of Gilo east of Jerusalem against gunfire from the nearby Palestinian village of Beit Jala. The defensive wall came to serve as a support for a mural painted by Russian immigrant artists, making the gray concrete dissolve into the meandering panorama of a peaceful countryside oblivious to refugee camps, checkpoints and curfews. The mural not only replaced the missing view, it also subtly retouched flora, fauna and architecture: the hills are more sparsely populated and dotted by cypress trees, and the buildings undamaged by shelling and modified according to the style of settler housing developments.[1] Embellished with occasional features of the Roman *Campagna*, with its staple ruins and shepherds, it offers at once a nostalgic fantasy about the past and a prophecy about the future.

The mural on Gilo Wall returns as an exemplary case in W.J.T. Mitchell's work on landscape and power, reproduced in several of his essays, on his website, and on the cover of his 2012 book *Seeing Through Race*.[2] The cover photograph, taken by the Israeli artist Miki Kratsman in 2001, frames the wall frontally in broad daylight. The composition is bisected by a horizontal and a vertical axis. First, along the upper edge of the wall that marks the almost seamless transition from the painted pine tree to the living branches of the tree that grows behind it. Second, along the last section of the row of concrete slabs that marks the point where the fictive space abruptly ends and reality begins. To the right the propaganda; to the left the truth that it screens out.

H. Gustafsson, *Crime Scenery in Postwar Film and Photography*,
https://doi.org/10.1007/978-3-030-04867-9_2

A greater variety of vantage points on this motif can be found in Shai Kremer's *Infected Landscape* (2008).[3] Following its titular medical analogy, Kremer's photo book unfolds as a symptomatology of the militarized landscape, broken by minefields, caterpillar tracks, tank shelters, firing zones, security barriers, missile launching ramps and nuclear silos.[4] *Infected Landscape* is bookended by Gilo Wall, which appears on its front and back cover. The cover image frames the same section of the mural as Kratsman's, but at a further remove. A frail, barren tree cast against the winter sky stands next to the wall, augmenting the contrast between pastoral make-believe and crass reality. Two children appear on the sidewalk, captured by the camera slightly out of focus at the moment they pass the wall's edge. The book concludes with three photographs of Gilo Wall. The first brings together a close-up with a long-distance view. Easily mistaken for a photomontage, the pastel brushwork on the mural is framed up front on the right-hand-side while Beit Jala spreads out on the left. An elevated Israeli viaduct, facilitating safe transport between the settlements and Jerusalem, spans the valley floor with a narrow Palestinian road winding its way below it. In the penultimate photograph of *Infected Landscape*, a lush branch spills over from the other side of the wall, as if in an effort to overcome the division. The last page shows Gilo Wall in profile. To the left, the painted side that faces the hill casts its shadow; to the right, two young men rest on the foundation of the last unit of unpainted concrete overlooking the gorge, facing the sun while sharing a cigarette. Moving from front to profile, *Infected Landscape* is framed by a forensic gaze, borrowing the device of Alphonse Bertillon's famous mug shots used for identifying criminals. Bisected between "the dark side of the landscape" and the enlightened view, the book nonetheless concludes on a note of optimism. By exposing the physical screen that splits the land, it suggests that the architecture of ethnic division may be overcome, or overturned, by a shift of viewpoint. In 2010 Gilo Wall was indeed dismantled, replaced with the Separation Wall that made no attempts to disguise its crude material support on either side of the dividing line.

In common with the genre of *trompe l'oeil* painting, the reward offered by these portrayals of Gilo Wall derives from the viewer's recognition of the labor of deception. In this sense, the *trompe l'oeil* ("deceive the eye") is an intrinsically pedagogical genre that stages lessons in mimicry and perception. The juxtaposition of mural and milieu in the photographs by Kratsman and Kremer further alludes to the formal technique of the *mise en abyme*, in which an image contains a smaller version of itself. Such ironic or playful conjunctions are prevalent in late landscape art. Consider, for instance, René Magritte's *La condition humaine* where a canvas on an easel set up in front of a high window replaces the view it depicts, or Stephen Shore's photograph of a wayside billboard painting of Mount Hood that simultaneously blends into and blocks out the Oregon countryside.[5] Considerably grimmer is Susan Meiselas' recourse to this device in her reframing of the landscape of Nicaragua twenty-five years after the Sandinista insurrection, screening back the past by installing her photographs as mural-sized billboards on the sites where they had originally been taken.[6] There is a glitch or slippage between the two landscapes framed by Kratsman and Kremer, however, noticeable in the fissures and shadows that delineate each panel of reinforced concrete, like disjunctions between the film frames of a panning shot. By showing the edges of the mural or turning it off-kilter, these images sharpen our attention to what the landscape within the landscape deliberately leaves out or forgets. The contrasts advanced to make the illusion unmask itself and yield its true and brutal nature may also alert us to something else, I want to argue, as they invite us to reflect on some of the epistemological assumptions that have underpinned the critical analysis of landscape.

Splitting the territory and suturing over the scar, Gilo Wall shows us landscape at work. Following Mitchell's proposition that we should consider landscape as a verb rather than a noun, asking what it *does* or *wants* rather than what it is, the mural palpably demonstrates his thesis on landscape as "the 'dreamwork' of imperialism."[7] This thesis merits further elaboration, beyond its initial implication of the depopulated vista as an instance of wish fulfillment. The process of dreamwork (*traumwerk*) described by Sigmund Freud proceeds through displacements, condensations and inversions, as a dormant, and usually dangerous or disturbing, material is translated and distorted into something pictorial. Latent dream-thoughts are thus worked-over into a manifest content that effectively buries the affects associated with it. The images considered above at once display and dispel this dreamwork, corroborating Mitchell's notion of landscape as a medium that veils and naturalizes "the violence and evil written on the land, projected there by the gazing eye."[8] In other words, Gilo Wall exhibits the double logic of the screen, serving both as a material support for projecting images, and as a physical object used to protect, divide and conceal. Like dreamwork, the mural on Gilo Wall performs a series of interlaced operations. It projects a picture perfect world that is both retrospective and prospective, invoking a time that was and a time to come, corroborating the divine match between "a land without people and a people without a land."[9] The mural thus effects a double vanishing act, making the Palestinians disappear along with the medium that renders them invisible.

Whether Constable Country, suburbanized California, or Israeli settlements, the art of landscape, following a dominant strand of cultural criticism, is one of deception and disguise. Rather than an object of vision, landscape is a technology for relegating what is opened up and occluded within a perceptual field. Despite its vocation for overview, landscape hides, deceiving the eye by luring the gaze into an imaginary depth. In this sense, Mitchell writes, "landscape is all about forgetting, about getting away from the real."[10] Screening out the labor and property relations that went into its making, it entices us to overlook social and political realities on the ground. Consequently, every landscape is a crime scene, a cover-up replete with erasures and repressions.

Moreover, Mitchell contends that the discourse of modernist abstraction has been subservient to this dreamwork by conscripting the Western landscape tradition into its dominant telos of "a quest for pure *painting*, freed of literary concerns and representation."[11] According to this plotline, the genre has been impelled by a vocation to turn physics into metaphysics, matter into spirit, and natural resources into supernatural resources. Or, to use Mitchell's terms, to turn "real estate" into "ideal estate."[12] A lineage may then be drawn from the Northern Romantic of Caspar David Friedrich via J.M.W. Turner's ethereal visions to the "atmospheric pressure" of Mark Rothko's color-fields.[13] Seeking to harness primeval energies through a process of gradual abstraction, reduction and distillation, the transparent depths of the Baroque era can be construed as continuous with the "paint-theism," to use Robert Rosenblum's term, of the flat and copious canvases of Abstract Expressionism.[14] In light of the geographical imagination under consideration here, Larry Abramson has brought Mitchell's claim to bear on the first artistic movement to emerge after the founding of the state of Israel. Established in 1948, the "New Horizons" group of landscape painters rendered the newly opened frontiers in bright pastels, bold brushstrokes and dazzling Mediterranean light. The selective filter of lyrical abstractionism is defined by Abramson as "the ultimate Israeli 'scopic regime,' an 'Art of Camouflage'" that facilitated a peaceful coexistence of cosmopolitan modernism and ancestral homeland.[15]

The "New Horizons" school demonstrates the paradoxical rootlessness of landscape's scopic regimes. Aided by optical devices such as Claude glasses, outlook platforms and picturesque manuals, distinct national topographies were cultivated through transnational templates, migrating from the canvasses of Claude Lorrain to English gardens and parks, from the Romantic Movement's haunt in the Lake District to the Alps and the Rocky Mountains, and along the waterways of the Wye, the Rhineland and Hudson Valley. Etymology further indicates that landscape is preeminently about seeing, or "a way of seeing."[16] The suffix *scape*, from the Greek verb *skopein*, means to behold, contemplate, examine or inspect. Adopted from the Dutch *Lantscap*, which was a painter's term before it came to designate a section of land, the English *scape* denotes an aesthetic intervention of framing or shaping. From this perspective, seminal titles such as the New Topographics movement's *Manmade Landscape* (1975) or Edward Burtynsky's *Manufactured Landscapes* (2003) appear tautological.

A related tautology is addressed by Mitchell when he points out that the expression "to look at the view" implies that we are, in fact, "looking at looking," becoming spectators to our own act of beholding.[17] Consequently, landscape posits an ideal test case for visual studies, a discipline whose distinct task Mitchell has defined as devoted to "showing seeing."[18] Another prolific voice in the field of visual culture, art historian James Elkins, instead asserts that, "the moments I spend looking at the view are not looking at all: they are the gaps between looking."[19] But do these gaps denote a pacified, mindless, and disinterested stare, as Elkins suggests, or, conversely, a heightened and self-reflexive perception? Maybe in experiencing such gaps, we also become sensitized to the phenomenology of appearing and disappearing, and to our ability to see, and to oversee? Mitchell again: "Of all the media and genres of imagery, landscape is the one that makes the constitutive blindness and invisibility of the visual process the most evident … Looking at the view is like looking at the grammar of a sentence, while forgetting what it is saying."[20] Like the "gaps between looking" identified by Elkins, to forget what language is saying also makes it possible to discern language as such. By preventing language from disappearing into its act of mediation, or the landscape to withdraw into its desaturated depths, I propose, we may be able to touch the threshold where language and looking takes place.

This chapter will develop and expand upon, by way of a series of detours, the Freudian-inflicted notion of landscape as dreamwork. Taking its cue from the mural on Gilo Wall as a literalization of the concept of screen memory (protecting the minds, bodies and eyes of the settlers from the Palestinians), the images addressed above all postulate a landscape *behind* the illusion. The metaphor of the wall or veil is cognate with that of the window, as walls can be toppled over and veils torn apart.[21] The mural does not only bisect the land, then, it also implies a binary divide of fantasyland and sobering disillusionment, virtual and real, absence and presence. Truth, in this scenario, is hidden, lurking behind or beneath the manifest pictorial content and secondary disguises. Yet, according to Freud, our sole entry point into the dreamwork is the screen memory, as we can only access what it shields through what it shows. The analyst thus has to reconstruct something forgotten, he explains, like an archaeologist at the site of a buried ancient dwelling.[22] Following this convoluted logic of showing and shielding, we may infer that the physical landscape approximates evidence in two contradictory ways. On the one hand, the landscape presents itself to our senses; unfolding before our eyes it renders itself manifest in its own self-evidence. On the other, the landscape conceals its evidence beneath a cloak of green or shifting sands. It is this oscillation between surface and depth, screen and strata, that is to say, between the lateral and vertical extension of any given landscape, which the present chapter seeks to grasp. My argument will proceed by aligning a string of theorists and artists: moving from Mitchell's analysis of the deceptive dreamwork of landscape to William Kentridge's charcoal animation films; from Aby Warburg's *Mnemosyne* atlas to Nicolas Poussin's Arcadian shepherds; and from Jean-Luc Nancy's notion of displacement (*dépaysement*) as the founding event of landscape to the earthworks of Robert Smithson.

Desert Bloom

In 2005, the London-based artist duo Adam Broomberg and Oliver Chanarin gained access to Chicago, a mocked-up Arab village constructed in the Negev desert for urban combat training. Originally built to resemble a Lebanese village, Chicago has been continuously modified over the last four decades to meet the current demands of the Israeli Defense Forces (IDF) and expanded to encompass parts of Beirut, Gaza city and Ramallah. This malleable set-piece city, complete with minarets, refugee camps and graffiti-sprayed walls, and with false fronts made from the same T-shaped concrete modules deployed for Gilo Wall, is the first in a series of thematically arranged artifacts assembled by Broomberg and Chanarin under the title *Chicago*.[23] As a pendant to the Arab ghost town, another series explores the tourist attraction "Mini Israel," a miniature park shaped like the Star of David featuring scale models of all the famous landmarks and holy sites, along with hotels, beaches and housing projects.

Taken as a whole, *Chicago* unfolds as a compendium of screening techniques implemented to divide, disguise and deceive. It is not merely the physical terrain that is managed and modulated, but also vision itself, as the architecture of separation enforces an intricate system of looking relations and blind spots. Another dialectical pair brings together the unobstructed 360-degree view from an Israeli hilltop settlement on the West Bank with the network of walled-in bypass roads that connect the settlements in the occupied territories. These highways serve a twofold purpose: blocking access to Palestinian vehicles and blocking out the view of the occupied territories. The elevated panorama and the tunnel vision of the roads burrowing through the mountains thus achieve the same goal through contrary means: to efface the Palestinian population from the scopic environment. In its final suite of images, *Chicago* assumes the viewpoint from inside a series of surveillance outposts and IDF strongholds overlooking the Lebanese border. Framed by narrow firing slits, the bunker's visual field is commensurate to the elongated rectangular layout colloquially referred to as the "landscape" format. Amendable to a range of manipulations, landscape and vision are strategically imbricated with armature, ballistics and camouflage, but also, as we shall see, with the mutually contingent processes of inscription and erasure.

One set of images from *Chicago* is of particular interest in the context of our present epistemological deliberations. Generically titled "Forest," the series consists of five eye-level shots of rustic, arboreal scenes depicted in the pristine light at daybreak. It is only the slender shapes of the pine trees that indicate their recent origin. These wooded reserves around Jerusalem—national parks, camping grounds and picnic areas—were planted under the auspices of the Jewish National Fund and inspired by David Ben-Gurion's idiom "to make the desert bloom."[24] Financed by worldwide donations to plant saplings, the afforestation campaigns subsequently taking place in the Ottoman Empire, the British Mandate and the Occupied Territories were promoted as a ritualistic homecoming. Redeeming the stereotype of the Wandering Jew, diasporic, rootless and cosmopolitan, the tree-planting ceremonies inaugurated a new national subject bound to the soil of the ancestral Zion.

In the first pages of his epic study *Landscape and Memory*, the art historian Simon Schama fondly recalls participating in the donation programs organized by the Jewish National Fund while attending Hebrew school in London. "[W]e were never exactly sure what all the trees were *for*," Schama admits: "All we knew was that to create a Jewish forest was to go back to the beginning of our place in the world, the nursery of the nation."[25] The anecdote serves as an entry point into the hermeneutics of memory and myth pursued by Schama throughout his three-part volume, sifting through the cultural strata deposited in wood, water and rock, "digging down through layers of memories and representations toward the primary bedrock."[26] Contradicting Schama's notion of such a primary bedrock, Broomberg and Chanarin instead refer to the forest reserves as "re-enactments of an imaginary Eden," and as "places of erasure of amnesia." Hence, the woodland scenes are congruous with the string of miniatures and monuments, stage-sets and scale models scrutinized in *Chicago*, and the various operations through which "the rocks, trees and riverbeds are engaged in telling a story."[27]

Framed in a narrative of return and renewal, the labor of reforesting, with its concomitant notions of rootedness, genealogies, origins and natural order, sought to restore the proper depth to the land. The redemptive gesture of "recreating that garden in the new Zion," as Schama puts it, was premised on the notion of the Biblical land left fallow during the Diasporas, and an old Ottoman land law that provided the judicial basis for entitlement to undeveloped tracts of land.[28] Due to its rapid growth in acid and sandy soil, the pine tree, also known as the "pioneer species," has dominated the efforts to reforest the land. Considered as a mnemotechnique, the historical and geographical reference of the monocultural pine forestations remain ambiguous, however, as they more accurately conjure a composite landscape or double projection. Rather than the new Zion, Irus Braverman remarks, "the pines construct a distinct, European-type landscape" that invokes a "lost European homeland."[29]

Though the forest scenes photographed by Broomberg and Chanarin yield little evidence, the ground of these images is materially dense. Outcompeting other plants for nutrients and water, the coniferous woods effectively blanketed the grounds of former Palestinian homesteads, orchards, mosques and cemeteries, deserted and destroyed during the war. Razed first from the ground and then from the map, the Government Naming Committee assigned cartographers, historians and archaeologists to create Hebraized maps of these areas. The names listed for the five scenes depicted in *Chicago*—the Saints Forest, Independence Park, Rabin Park, Canada Park, and Ben Shemen Forest—are indicatory of the interlaced practices of arboriculture and nomenclature, as new forests were raised as memorials to Jewish victims of the Nazi genocide, terrorist attacks and territorial wars, or named after founding fathers like Theodore Herzl and Lord Balfour. While toponyms have been replaced or erased on the map, however, the scattered rubble of the demolished villages still remains lodged in the forest floor.

Early in an essay called "Holy Landscape," which examines the prominent yet paradoxical iconography of landscape in Zionist rhetoric, W.J.T. Mitchell explicitly takes issue with Schama's recollection of the fund-raising campaigns in order to make a methodological distinction between two antithetical methods for the interpretation of landscape. Mitchell designates these as the "surface model" and the "depth model."[30] Whereas the latter aspires to exhume the strata of memories and myths accrued over the ages, the former hones in on the very superficiality of the landscape in order to display its "false depths, selective memories, and self-serving myths."[31] Following Nietzsche's advice in *The Twilight of the Gods*, Mitchell advocates the tuning fork, rather than the shovel or the hammer, as the instrument to make these "specular surfaces," rather than their illusive depths, resound in their hollowness.[32]

A landscape may also be veiled by digging in a literal sense. In his study *Hollow Land: Israel's Architecture of Occupation*, Eyal Weizman, director of the Center for Forensic Architecture at Goldsmiths College, considers how the discipline of archaeology implements yet another version of landscape as screen:

> The existing landscapes of Palestine were seen as a contemporary veil under which historic biblical landscapes, battlegrounds, Israelite settlements and sites of worship could be revealed by digging. The national role assigned to archeology was to remove the visible layer and expose the ancient Israelite landscape and with it the proof of Jewish ownership. The subterranean strata was thus perceived as a parallel geography akin to a national monument.[33]

Impelled by the conviction that the deeper you dig the closer you get to the historical truth, to scrape away the imperial strata of Roman, Christian and Arab conquerors constituted an act of purging the land and of disclosing its true identity. The depth model thus legitimizes a violation of the surface, as digging, whether literally or metaphorically, inevitably disturbs and destroys the higher stratum. These divergent methods for interpreting the landscape, scanning its surface or mining its depths, are respectively commensurate to the lateral gaze of the surveyor and the vertical descent of the archaeologist. Rather than dichotomizing these two vantage points as mutually excluding epistemologies, however, I propose that we recast them in dialectical terms. Pursuing such a notion of the landscape as a deep surface, the next section will consider the conflicting axes of the surveyor and the archaeologist, or geologist, through the lens of the stop-animation charcoal projections created by the South African artist William Kentridge.

Incomplete Erasures

At the time of the foundation of the Jewish National Fund in 1901, another manmade forest began to spread on the pavements, sidewalks and private gardens of Johannesburg, planted there, a penny a tree, by the city's demobilized soldiers in the wake of the Second Boer War (1899–1902). In the third of his six drawing lessons, called *Vertical Thinking: A Johannesburg Biography*, given at Harvard University in the spring of 2012, William Kentridge refers to this artificial forest as an instance of wish fulfillment, creating a pastoral shelter from the arid scrubland surrounding the city. I want to quote here at some length a section from Kentridge's lecture, which establishes the ethical and epistemological stakes of the gesture of retracing as the basis for an artistic project predicated on an eminently dialectical poetics of landscape, trace and memory:

> The land is an unreliable witness. It is not that it effaces all history, but events must be excavated, sought after in traces, in half-hidden clues. There is a similarity to the land and what it does, and our unreliable memory. Things which seemed so clear and so embedded in us, fade; a shock, an outrage that we should live by, becomes dull. We have to work to find that first, true impulse. A forest we know contained mass killings is filled with wind in the leaves. Only a section where the trees are shorter, in a

> straight line, marks the spot of the mass grave. A change of color in the vegetation marks where there were once foundations of a prison block. What should be proclaimed clearly—HERE THIS HAPPENED, let us not forget—becomes ever thinner, ever harder to see, the landscapes and our memory push it farther away, until we get lost in the undergrowth.
>
> Even our outrage is lost. We are left with something closer to regret. Regret at what happened, but also regret at our inability to hold onto our feeling. We are deceived by the landscape. Not only deceived, but disappointed, betrayed. The landscape, and our memory, should be that much stronger.[34]

Confronted with this unreliability, how are we to assume the responsibility of remembering? The dulling and diminishing prospect of the past, Kentridge continues, calls for a recalibration of our sense of geography: "We need the terrain of the half-solved, the half-solvable riddle, the distance between knowing and not knowing," acknowledging "the limits of our memory, but prodding the memory nonetheless."[35]

Contrary to the forests reminisced in the prologue of Schama's *Landscape and Memory*, Kentridge remarks that the irrigated suburban garden of his childhood was merely a "miniaturized copy."[36] His first artistic impulse, to make charcoal drawings tracing the derelict infrastructure of civil engineering in the Highveld, recording its culverts, pipelines, storm drains and slag heaps, was provoked by the discord, what Kentridge calls an "impasse" or "non-meeting,"[37] between these verdant enclaves and the city's scorched and stagnant surroundings. Bereft of water, vegetation and spatial cues (shaded shelters, clearings, footpaths, outlook points), the veld was incompatible not only with "the Baroque theater set" of the Claudian schema, "moving from the depth of the painting to the foreground of the canvas,"[38] but also, it seems, with the cultural layers unfolded by Schama.

A process of erasure is innate to the two media, landscape and charcoal drawing, amalgamated by Kentridge. In two essays, "Memory and Geography" and "Landscape in a Stage Siege," he reflects on the correlation between the means of obliteration and oblivion constitutive of each media.[39] Let us begin with the genre of landscape painting. As the African continent was conquered the colonial vistas became increasingly depopulated, absented of tribal props and wildlife. It was only after the process of colonization was completed that a "pure landscape" could emerge on the canvas in edenic visions of a pristine and majestic country. Kentridge refers to the embellishment of the botanic and geological features of South Africa by artists like Jan Ernst Abraham Volschenk and Jacobus Hendrik Pierneef as "documents of disremembering."[40] Thus far, his account corroborates Mitchell's understanding of "landscape as a place of amnesia and erasure, a strategic site for burying the past and veiling history with 'natural beauty.'"[41] Such becalmed and oblivious surfaces may, however, themselves become sites of excavation. Determined to recuperate an image of his native land, Kentridge turned to the industrially depleted hinterland spreading on the edges of Johannesburg:

> [T]he drawings started out as revenge. However non- the landscape was, however null, the drawing could track and trace it. However bleak, parched, the view was, it could be put down on paper. However unstructured by the dictates of the picturesque, in the drawing I could record this non-landscape.[42]

The discord between landscape and non-landscape is narrated by Kentridge as a formative experience perched between two childhood memories, respectively commensurate to a screen memory and a primal scene. The first was a gift from his grandfather, a picture book called *Great Landscapes of the World* containing reproductions of paintings from Bruegel and Hobbema to Courbet and Rousseau. The second, a traumatic encounter with a crime scene when, at the age of six, coming upon a Kodak box in his father's study.[43] Instead of the anticipated chocolates, the yellow box contained glossy, black-and-white photographs showing the victims of a massacre that took place in the black township of Sharpeville in March 1960 when the South African Police opened fire against a crowd of anti-apartheid demonstrators, killing sixty-nine protestors. The artist's father, the attorney Sir Sidney Kentridge, represented some of the families of the victims at an inquest where the photographs were used as evidence, but failed to convince the judges. Kentridge recaps, "this too I had seen—the violence, the bodies in the veld. Not only the Cézanne, the Poussin."[44]

Almost forty years later, Kentridge made the fifth film in his *Drawing for Projection* series, which I want to discuss here in more detail as exemplary of the surface and depth oscillations that inform his work. Completed in February 1994, *Felix in Exile* preceded the first free democratic election in South Africa by a mere two months, soon to be followed by the publicly broadcast proceedings of the Truth and Reconciliation Commission (1995–2002) which staked the claims of a post-Apartheid state on the grounds of the absolved crimes of the old regime. *Felix in Exile* is an animation film made from forty large-scale charcoal drawings. Each drawing contains a single scene that is altered through a series of erasures and redrawings while a stop-motion movie camera records the successive stages of rubbings and re-inscriptions on the bruised and battered paper. At the beginning of the film, an African woman, Nadi, conducts a land survey of the derelict minefields of the East Rand. She studies the veld with the aid of a sextant and a theodolite, a surveying instrument used to frame and divide land into a grid of straight lines. As she begins to mark a blank sheet of paper with some preliminary dots and diagonals, the survey chart transforms into a site of atrocity. Bodies with leaking wounds appear on her drawings, dark stains spread on the ground and dissipate. In an instant, Nadi's activity shifts from charting the land to unearthing the evidence that it has absorbed, circling the bullet wounds and outlining the contours of the bodies scattered in the veld with crimson chalk marks.[45] Wind-tossed newspapers flutter in the wind and settle over the slain bodies that morph into mounds of earth.[46]

A second character, the eponymous Felix Teitelbaum, appears naked and isolated in a sparsely furnished hotel room, brooding over Nandi's drawings that fill his suitcase, cover the walls, and lay scattered around the room. At this point, another geo-instrument is introduced, an old-fashioned seismograph. The needle inscribes a red graph on the rotating paper-covered drum. In light of the film's forensic imagery, the seismograph brings to mind a polygraph test, as if the land itself was being subjected to a criminal interrogation. Nadi is also shot and falls to the ground, her body covered with paper first turns into a slagheap and then into a sinkhole. The hotel room is flooded with blue water and the film ends with Felix standing naked waste deep in the sinkhole, positioned like a *rückenfigur* facing the decimated flatlands.

The crude, low-grade medium of stop-animation charcoal drawing, or what Kentridge calls "stone age filmmaking,"[47] begets a landscape in constant metamorphoses, transforming like a time-lapse film. Steel beams jut out of the ground and tire tracks appear as if on their own accord; a constellation of stars turns into a water tap; corpses wrapped in paper turn into piles of earth; a mirror turns into a lake; drawings turn into reality and reality back into paper. “The imagery unfolds not as events do in the world, but as thoughts might do in a dream,” Joseph Koerner has remarked.[48] Relating the film’s fluid iconography to Freud’s notion of dreamwork, Koerner further observes that the “images condense and displace meanings, and meanings are overdetermined because partly concealed.” This amorphous scenery not only evokes Mitchell’s notion of dreamwork, but also his first thesis on landscape, namely that it “is not a genre of art but a medium.”[49] Kentridge’s landscape is a medium in the original sense of the word, in Latin the *middle*, *midst* or *interval.* Facing a sheet of paper pinned to the wall opposite a stop-motion camera, shooting frame-by-frame, repeatedly crossing the space of the studio floor, “stalking the drawing” as Kentridge puts it,[50] the landscape evolves in the middle-ground of place and perception, inscription and projection.

Instead of preserving the porous carbon, which is easily obliterated “with an eraser, a cloth, even with a breath,” through the application of a fixative, Kentridge continually rubs it out.[51] The cellulose ground of the paper retains a trace of the former drawings, however, discernable as a trail of dusty afterimages ingrained in the rough fiber. In analogy to the terrain explored, the erased granular marks remain, the artist comments, as “evidence of some disturbance. But this is easily overgrown and incorporated in the drawing.”[52] The technique of “imperfect erasure”[53] utilized by Kentridge thus has a tripartite designation, referring to the land, its embellishment on the canvas, and his own practice of marking, erasing and remarking.[54] In this way, the procedure of stop-animation facilitates an archaeological and geological articulation of the landscape, both as artistic legacy and material stratum.

At the most rudimentary level, the charcoal sketch is the substrate of oil painting, the medium through which the luminous distances of the classical landscape was conjured. In a concrete sense, a subsoil of charcoal dust is unearthed from the polished glaze of oil and varnish. Beneath the harmonizing atmospheric unity of the Claudian “magic hour” lays a more primal, monochrome landscape, smeared, stained and sooty. Kentridge’s urge to develop an antidote to the “plague of the picturesque”[55] is consistent with the fundamental distrust of nineteenth-century pastoralism that J.M. Coetzee has singled out as a key characteristic of South African landscape poetry. This shift from a botanical to a geological disposition toward the land, Coetzee argues, was provoked by the suspicion “that vegetation *disguises* landscape, that traditional landscape art, the art of the prospect, is superficial by nature, cannot tell the true story of the land, the story that lies buried, or half-buried, beneath the surface."[56]

The socioeconomic landscape finally posits an additional layer in the stratified ground of the image. Johannesburg rests on the deepest mine shafts in the world, plunging down toward the impact site where a meteor struck some two billion years ago, leaving a thin streak of golden ore in the rock. In order to access the mineral deposit, water had to be pumped out of the earth, creating sinuous cavities in the stratum. "The rumblings of the earth," Kentridge ruminates, "as the earth readjusted itself to its excavations. A message from the dark underground caves, stopes, and passageways of the mines below."[57] On the one hand, water held the promise of lush gardens and forestations; on the other, by driving it out, the ground upon which the city had been installed became "vulnerable to collapse," instilling a terrifying awareness that "you could be drowned in the earth itself."[58] This invisible vertical axis had its horizontal equivalent in the urban grid of high walls and barbed wire fences, which segregated White miners, Afrikaners, tribesmen and migrant workers from the irrigated suburbs.

Felix in Exile thus provides us with a different optics for the interpretation of landscape, neither as a screen or wall blocking vision, nor as a window through which we can peer into its depths, but as palimpsest. Like Medieval parchments, earth is repeatedly scribbled and scraped, yet retains faint traces of its previous inscriptions. Devoured but never completely disappeared, dreamwork evolves here in tandem with the metaphor of the *Wunderblock* through which Freud sought to grasp the transience and resilience of traces that, despite the incessant work of erasure and overwriting, never vanish completely. In *Felix in Exile*, erasure itself remains as evidence. The term palimpsest, we should further note in light of the multiple-layered images created by Kentridge, is also part of the vocabulary of forensic science, where it refers to a method for reconstructing a sequence of events at a crime scene by placing objects, or a sequence of photographs, over one another.

The multifarious ensemble of motifs in *Felix in Exile*—the surveyor lens and the seismograph, the apparition and absorption of bodies in the veld, the gardens and mineshafts, the rumblings and floods caused by mnestic and seismic tremors—provide us with a rich context for the next section, which will address these dialectical pairings through the analytical lens of the pictorial memory atlas constructed by the Jewish-German cultural historian Aby Warburg in the late 1920s.

Scenery and Symptom

Let us begin with a final consideration of Gilo Wall, this time as seen through the viewfinder of Simon Norfolk's large format, mahogany and brass field camera. Framed obliquely from above, the wall recedes along the ridgeline at a slanting angle. Neither the *trompe l'oeil* effect of the rigorously frontal composition, nor the unmasking effect of the profile shot, the mural and Beit Jala meander side by side as two parallel realities. Bathed in the mellowing haze of the low sun, Beit Jala appears like a fairytale city, duplicating the soft tonalities on the mural. Instead of highlighting the contrast between pastoral artifice and political reality, Norfolk's photograph directs our attention to the torn surface of the earth where the wall has carved its way, leaving a trail of shattered rock along its winding trail, piled up against the mural's foundation (Fig. 2.1).

The image is part of a suite of photographs from Israel-Palestine called *Mnemosyne* (2003), named after the goddess of memory in Greek mythology who gave birth to the nine muses. The title merits critical development, for what does Mnemosyne designate in this context? In the first instance, it refers to the physical terrain of Israel-Palestine as a malleable memory atlas in a one-point-one ratio replete with commemorative markers (regimental museums, memorial forests, roadside shrines and recreated battlefields). Second, Mnemosyne invokes the memory of landscape art, which is the medium and mnemonic tool through which Norfolk frames and filters his picture, aligning his work with early ruin photographers and the painters and poets of the Roman *Campagna*.

The name Mnemosyne, finally, was also engraved in capital letters above the entry door to the library in Hamburg where Aby Warburg created his *Mnemosyne* atlas. Utilizing the atlas format's propensity for making bold connections and comparisons across time and territory, Warburg continually rearranged a plethora of iconic material—including postcards, postage stamps and geographical maps, reproductions of sculptural friezes, frescos and reliefs, newspaper clippings and commercial ads—on wooden boards stretched with black cloth without regard to medium or artistic merit. Cut loose from the conventional criteria of art history (epoch, canon, oeuvre, influence), the expressive forces embedded in vivid or agitated gestures were isolated and suspended against the black fabric. This spatial constellation of images, laterally displayed across the panels provisionally arranged in the oval reading room of his library, constituted at once a topographical and stratigraphical configuration of time.

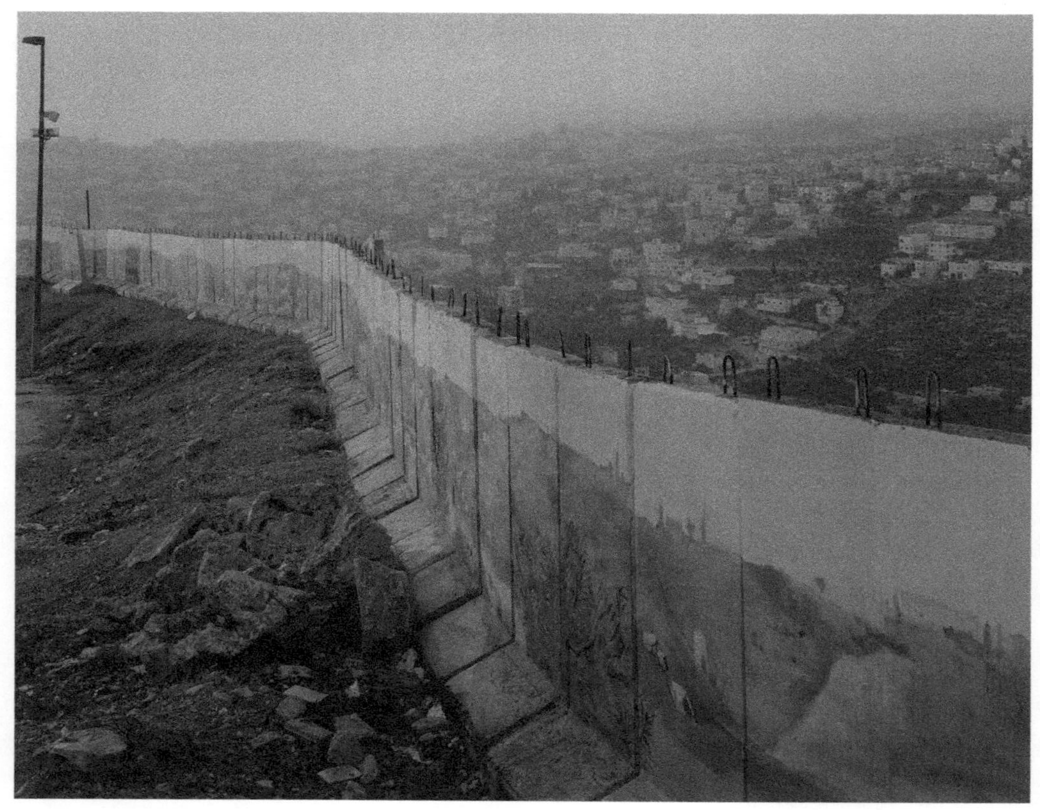

Fig. 2.1 Simon Norfolk *Israel-Palestine: Mnemosyne* (2003). Courtesy of the artist

Rather than an iconographic chart, Warburg designed his atlas as a diagnostic tool for mapping the migrations and survival of what he termed *Pathosformeln*, psychic states of passion or suffering deposited in the image from pagan antiquity to the present. Hence, the topic of Warburg's research was not the image as such, conceived as a stable formal unit, but rather the migratory routes and subterranean passages through which the mnestic charges "fossilized" in images are transmitted across time and territory.[59] In other words, Warburg's was a theory of the index rather than the image, where the latter served both as a storage facility, preserving traces of life in a fragmentary and suspended form, and as a vehicle enabling their migration and eruption into unexpected times and places. In analogy, Warburg understood the human body as a host to primeval fears and anxieties erupting in involuntary spasms and convulsions. With a term borrowed from social psychologist Richard Semon, Warburg referred to such mnestic traces, imprinted in the past and reactivated in the present, as engrams.[60]

While the fulcrum of Warburg's investigations was the human figure, the metaphors through which he envisioned his project derived from the earth sciences. The *Bilderatlas* was a seismic station, a tool for monitoring disturbances in the earth, picking up signals of impending disasters and shockwaves emitted by catastrophes in the past. Highlighting the political dimension of Warburg's project, which materialized in the interim between two world wars and in the wake of Warburg's recovery from a mental breakdown, Georges Didi-Huberman has described the atlas as "a tool for 'sampling,' by means of juxtaposed images, the chaos of history."[61] Although Warburg never dealt with landscape as such, as it was unknown to the pagan world whose afterlife he sought to trace, the concept of *Pathosformel* did not exclusively pertain to corporeal expressions of extreme emotions, but to life in motion (*bewegtes Leben*) more generally, or what Warburg at the beginning of his lecture on the snake dance ritual performed by the Pueblo Indians of New Mexico described as "the boundless communicability between man and environment."[62] While only tentatively explored by Warburg in regard to drapery or foliage stirred by a gust of wind, the domain of life-in-motion may thus be extended to encompass disturbances in the earth and sky as well: rent clouds, ruined buildings, jagged rocks, distressed leaves and chopping waves.[63] But also, as Kentridge's charcoal animated landscapes demonstrate, the residual traces that jut through terrain, like "an underlying prehistoric form threatening to erupt back into history."[64]

What, then, are the epistemological gains for exploring how Warburg's unfinished, and unfinishable, atlas may contribute to our understanding of landscape and the recurring forms that spread and disappear across its surface? Briefly addressed in the introductory chapter, such a project has been undertaken, but also prematurely foreclosed, by the German art historian Martin Warnke, founder of the Research Center for Political Iconography at the Warburg-Haus in Hamburg.[65] While Warnke's iconographic study *Political Landscape* concludes that landscape was drained of its mnemonic potential in the twentieth century, this exhaustion and obsolescence, I want to argue, may instead be thought of as a condition for the possibility for renewal. In common with Kentridge's charcoal animated drawings, where projection becomes a method for excavation, Warburg's morphology of memory traces straddles the surface/depth dichotomy posited by Mitchell. As we shall see, it also casts the notion of landscape as dreamwork, and its affiliated concepts of symptoms, screens and survivals, in a different light.

A deterritorializing impulse pervades Warburg's cartographic model of memory, the goal of which was to facilitate "an iconological analysis that can range freely, with no fear of border guards."[66] The epistemological implications of Warburg's project appear in sharper relief when compared to the topographies of memory charted by the French sociologist Maurice Halbwachs, who coined the term "collective memory" at the very moment Warburg began amassing the material for his engrammatic atlas. In his posthumously published essay *The Legendary Topography of the Gospel in the Holy Land*, Halbwachs investigates how Christian pilgrims and crusaders came to graft images conjured from the Gospels onto the terrain of Palestine.[67] Through the consecration of sacred sites, beliefs struck root. When animated by faith, conversely, visible landmarks summoned "invisible truths."[68] In common with Warburg, Halbwachs thus conceived of the transmission of memory in imagistic terms, arguing that "[t]hese reconstructed images provide the group with an account of its origin and development and thus allows it to recognize itself through time."[69] Ultimately, however, the *Mnemosyne* atlas inverts the territorializing logic of Halbwachs' mnemonic map. Instead of establishing the common ground of a social framework (Halbwachs' *cadres sociaux*), it designated a non-place or atopia, a phantasmatic space that Warburg termed a *Zwischenraum* out of which memories rise and fade. For the German iconologist, memory was neither the contemplative work of an individual, probing the inner recesses of the psyche, nor the collective projection of "a singularly vivid image on the screen of an obscure and unclear past"[70] as understood by the French sociologist, but the recursive passages and transmissions through which affective energies are charged and discharged. Hence, Warburg's insistence that the historian should develop the sensibility of a seismograph, receptive to the seismic waves and tremors that ripple through the social fabric.

Refracting Warburg's model of memory through Freud's notion of dreamwork, Georges Didi-Huberman significantly expands upon Warburg's geological and tectonic metaphors. The experience of recollecting a dream upon awakening, he argues, is analogous to that of confronting an image. In both cases there is a material substratum, what Didi-Huberman describes as the "*nocturnal remains*," that have sunken beneath the threshold of consciousness and perception.[71] Freud's dream-image, whereby a latent material has been transformed into a manifest picture, is "the *vestige*: the sole survival, simultaneously a sovereign remainder and the trace of an erasure. A visual agent of disappearance."[72] This oblivion constitutes the ground upon which dreams and images, seen or conjured in the mind, rests, and from which symptoms are prone to surface and spread. Compatible with Freud's account of the symptom as a manifestation of a repressed impulse or anxiety ignited by the conflict between the Ego and the Id, Warburg understood the agitated or manic gestures of ecstasy or pain as an eruption of the conflict between humanist enlightenment and ancient paganism, as intolerable memories and primitive emotions buried in the "cultural soil"[73] welled up to contort and distort the civilized surface. Warburg's view of antiquity thus stands in stark opposition to the becalmed perfection eulogized by art historians of the eighteenth century. For Warburg, the afterlife of antiquity is equivalent instead to a return of the repressed, and antiquity itself what art history has wished to forget.

The concept of the symptom is crucial to Didi-Huberman's critique of the idealist and humanist legacies of the discipline of art history. Driven toward synthesis and sublimation, the interpretation of the work of art has tended to skirt along "the lowlands of the symptom" in order to arrive at unity and closure.[74] The hermeneutic of the symptom contrarily opens up the image to multiple causes and meanings. Symptoms are "slippages in the terrain,"[75] Didi-Huberman writes, an unintentional escaping or incursion of the past into the present. The symptom is what rents the fabric of representation, disturbing the formal unity of the work of art and displacing it from any fixed or stable provenance within the oeuvre of an individual artist or epoch. In other words, Didi-Huberman's concept of the symptom serves not only as a master-trope and nodal point for the plethora of neologisms coined by Warburg—*Zwischenraum*, *Dynamogram*, *Leitfossil*, *Nachleben*, *Pathosformel*—but also for the pseudo geo-scientific discourse spun around the *Mnemosyne* atlas. In analogy to the fault lines and eroded shatter zones of randomly fissured or cracked rock caused by the movement and friction of tectonic plates, the symptom, Didi-Huberman writes, "manifests itself—extricates itself from the earth—only at the cost of *a ripping apart* of the ground, that is to say, of an earthquake."[76] But from where, more exactly, do these subterranean movements rise and plummet?

The *Mnemosyne* atlas conflates two apparently discordant spatial tropes. While the latter invokes geography's disciplinary compulsion to bound, divide and contain, the former suggests osmosis, seepage and saturation. For Mnemosyne was not only the name of a goddess, but also of a mythical river in Hades flowing parallel to Lethe, the river of oblivion from which the souls of the newly dead would drink to lose all recollections of their earthly existence. Those initiated who drank instead from the Mnemosyne would attain a total recall, thereby bringing the transmigration of the soul to an end. In the final pages of *The Surviving Image*, Didi-Huberman aligns the murky waters in the infernal regions of the earth with the black intervals of the atlas itself, which he understands as a "milieu of appearance" or "a *background*" that is "located physically *under the images*."[77] The interval or *Zwischenraum*, Didi-Huberman writes, is "a corridor formed by erosion," an "opening created by the seismic faults, the fractures in history."[78] Warburg thus understood the image in dialectical terms: as both surface and depth, screen and sediment, present and ancient. While the image has a genealogy, it is reanimated in our time. "[T]he Freudian concept of the symptom as a *moving fossil* accounts for Warburg's pathos formula and its distinct temporality of oblivion and return from oblivion," Didi-Huberman concludes, since "the movement it opens up comprises things that are *at once* archeological (fossils, survivals) and current (gestures, experiences)."[79]

The exemplary manifestations of the intrusive and fracturing force of the symptom, following Didi-Huberman's *Confronting Images*, occur when "the event of the flesh has rent the ideal appearance of the body."[80] In the canon of art history, where the French coinage of the Italian Renaissance had gained currency a mere decade before Warburg was born, this ideal was epitomized by the marble statues of Ancient Greece, bodies poised in a state of grace and balance.[81] In analogy, the first school of landscape painting, inaugurated by French painters residing in Rome, was popularized as the "Ideal Landscape." Subordinated to academic laws of harmonized proportions, landscape painting dealt with perspectival lines, spatial planes and delicate nuances of shades and chiaroscuro, that is to say, with skin. Landscape imposed a formula, with its side screens and staffage-figures framing the central plain like a floodlit stage, on the earth and all that lies lodged within it. The smooth surface of emerald pastures, luxuriant foliage and glassy lakes turned the physiognomy of the earth into a sculptural vessel for mood and atmosphere. "Before 1420 you don't see territory, civilization's hinterland, but rather *terra*," Jacob Wamberg reminds us. Prior to its domestication by perspectival differentiation, tonal gradations and atmospheric depth, "the pre-modern rocky grounds are overtly terrestrial, almost uncovering the underworld with its ravines and chaos" and thus consonant with "ancient ideas of the wilderness as being part of the underworld."[82] As the next section will demonstrate, however, the Ideal Landscape was always riddled by traces of that chthonic domain.

Let us now return to Norfolk's golden hour rendition of Gilo Wall. It is an image, I propose, that compels us to engage with landscape as the site of a series of unresolved polarized tensions. In common with Kentridge's charcoal animations, Norfolk's photograph invokes a notion of landscape as forgetfulness at work, and of the earth that it covers as equivalent to the landscape's unconscious. Earth shows through like a subterranean wave of base matter, shattering the manifest pictorial content—the mural, the forests of Jerusalem and Johannesburg, the canvases of the New Horizons school, "[t]he Volschenks and Pierneefs"—by crudely exposing the basis of oblivion upon which the image has been installed.[83] Rather than establishing a binary of representation and reality, it alerts us to the treacherous relationship between image and ground. The meandering pastoral and its cracked earthly support thereby invite us to think about the tear with the territory, the symptom with the scenery. In the same sense, the fault lines and sinkholes struck open in the veld of *Felix in Exile*, first charted through the surveyor lens and then sounded by the seismograph, emit aftershocks of the apartheid system. Along these lines, *Crime Scenery* wants to consider the ability of landscape to pause narration and disrupt the process through which identities are wrought from the land, and to explore the notion that landscape, like the body, "suffers from recollections."[84]

Et in Arcadia Ego

According to a dominant narrative, landscape is the product of a series of historical transitions that gradually have removed mankind from nature. First established in the most densely populated regions of Northern Italy and Holland, then migrating to England and France where it gained wide popularity at the time of the Industrial Revolution, landscape has been understood as a kind of compensatory fantasy, an object of retrospective desire catering to the needs of an urban population. In the words of the art historian Christopher S. Wood, landscape is "a symptom of modern loss," retroactively constructing a state of innocence and unity to which we can't return.[85] The artist Jeff Wall has addressed this expulsion myth in somewhat different terms. "In making a landscape we must withdraw a certain distance—far enough to detach ourselves from the immediate presence of other people," Wall asserts, "it is just at the point where we begin to lose sight of the figures as agents, that landscape crystalizes as a genre."[86] In a series of photographic diptychs and triptychs showcased in the 1996 exhibition *Landscapes and Other Pictures*, Wall meticulously measures out the proper distance between the viewer (the subject who is free to look, who watches from afar, who sees without being seen) and the world on display (held apart, framed, and set in perspective) at which our perceptual field settles into the picture-type called landscape, inferring from this experiment that, "in a landscape, persons are depicted at the point of vanishing."[87] The miniscule staffage-figure—the shepherd in the Roman *Campagna*, or the vanishing American or Arab—is present merely as an indicator of scale and of the passing of an era, serving as a trace of its own imminent disappearance. Landscape effects a moving away; it entails, in Wall's phrase, "a gesture of leave-taking."[88] For this reason, he continues, a graveyard is "the 'perfect' type of landscape." In other words, we wish to leave behind what we cannot project ourselves out of, as the earth, in the end and indiscriminately, claims everybody. Therefore we erroneously refer to a landscape as empty, for it is in fact densely populated, though its population mainly resides underground.

Here, we may recall the cinema of Straub–Huillet that was addressed in the first chapter, and the filmmakers' conception of landscape as tomb, invoking an absent population committed to earth. More directly, Wall's remarks allude to the *memento mori* studied by Poussin's shepherds gathered around the sarcophagus in Arcadia, and it anticipates the artist's own staging of this motif in a composite image called "The Flooded Grave" (1998–2000). Digitally merging two cemeteries in Vancouver with a water tank in his studio, the picture shows a freshly dug grave, a mound of sand and stone piled up on the protective boards, a square cut into the manicured lawn and the opening in the earth at the bottom of which lies an ocean floor filled with sea stars, shells and anemones. Between the still unmarked watery grave and the cultivated hillside, dotted with headstones and pruned trees, the perimeters of recently filled tombs remain visible.

Considered as the prototype landscape—whether made from rocks and trees, paint and canvas, cadmium-coated plates, silver salts or alpha-numeric code—a graveyard bestows an obligation, epitomized by the engraving on the tomb in Arcadia, to commemorate what lies behind or adjacent to it, beyond its surface or framing. But what are we obliged to recall? What is this presence that announces itself in Arcadia? The ambiguous temporal reference of the epitaph ("I too once lived in Arcadia" or "I am also in Arcadia") raises a series of questions pertinent to our present investigation of the relation between trace and landscape. Does the epitaph designate a single event that took place once in the past, or one that is taking place indefinitely? Is it elegiac or anticipatory? Is the crouching shepherd with his index finger fixed on a single glyph yet to decipher the full meaning of the inscription, or is he rather attempting to retrace his own shadow, unsuspectingly foreshadowing his own death in the process?[89] The ambiguity is also spatial, as it remains uncertain whether the message on the tomb refers to its contents or to the environs that envelop it. Developing a notion of the landscape picture as witness, Jonathan Bordo has argued that the first-person epigraphy inscribes a trace of the prehistory of antiquity, and therefore of time, into Arcadia. The tomb "is an outcropping of antiquity" in Arcadia that spatializes time. At its inception, Bordo therefore suggests, "European landscape begins to posit antiquity as a deep history of itself, visually positing two layers."[90] Below, I want to explore this substratum, in light of the questions broached above, by turning to four interlocutors with Poussin's Arcadia.

First by returning once more to Simon Norfolk, for whom the discovery of death in Arcadia has a more specific historical purchase. Presenting his work from Afghanistan, Bosnia, Iraq, Israel-Palestine, Liberia, Libya, Normandy and Yemen as individual chapters in a larger project gathered under the caption *Et in Arcadia Ego*, the artist has explained his long-term engagement with conflicted territories in the following programmatic text:

> What these 'landscapes' have in common—their fundamental basis in war—is always downplayed in our society. I was astounded to discover that the long, straight, bustling, commercial road that runs through my neighborhood of London follows an old Roman road. In places the Roman stones are still buried beneath the modern tarmac. Crucially, it needs to be understood that the road system built by the Romans was their highest military technology, their equivalent of the stealth bomber or the Apache helicopter—a technology that allowed a huge empire to be maintained by a relatively small army, that could move quickly and safely along these paved, all-weather roads. It is extraordinary that London, a city that ought to be shaped by Tudor kings, the British Empire, Victorian engineers and modern international Finance, is a city fundamentally drawn, even to this day, by abandoned Roman military hardware.[91]

Like the military routes radiating from the capital in Rome, subsequently covered with concrete paving to serve as the material substrate for future empires, current battlegrounds are drawn by Norfolk on the templates established by the French painters of the Roman *Campagna*. By the same token, the *Ego* in Norfolk's work, war being the ubiquitous morphological agent of the landscape he photographs, is retroactively acknowledged in the remnants of antiquity (Roman roads and camps, broken arches and fallen columns) that scatter the countryside depicted by Poussin and Lorrain. Resuscitating an obsolete form in order to conjure up its disavowed histories, Norfolk's work may therefore serve to remind us that already, "Arcadia resonated with the black noise of civil war and social tensions."[92]

Our second example prompts another return, this time to the rock-face of Mont Sainte-Victoire. The disclosure of a hidden material order, sunken below the horizon of habitual perception, has often been acknowledged as the unique artistic achievement of Paul Cézanne. In Samuel Beckett's appraisal, the painter conjured a stratum that for centuries had been buried beneath layers of "hyperanthropomorphized" landscapes promulgated from the Flemish Baroque to the French impressionists.[93] Notably, Cézanne maintained a lifelong dialogue with *Shepherds in Arcadia*, copying it in the Louvre in the 1860s and keeping a reproduction of it on the wall of his studio at the time of his death thirty years later. According to Maurice Merleau-Ponty, the painter's stated ambition to "redo Poussin again according to nature"[94] entailed an attack on the efforts of our species to dominate and domesticate the earth. By actively dismantling the historical codes of single-point perspective, and the anthropocentric worldview that they embodied, Cézanne sought to cleanse vision of what Beckett derogatively referred to as "*landscapality*." Merleau-Ponty writes:

> We live in the midst of man-made objects, among tools, in houses, streets, cities, and most of the time we see them only through the human actions which put them to use. We become used to thinking that all of this exists necessarily and unshakably. Cezanne's painting suspends these habits of thought and reveals the base of inhuman nature upon which man has installed himself.[95]

What is striking in the accounts quoted above is that they all conceive of landscape in decidedly dialectical terms, as a form rife with tensions, torn by conflicts, at odds with itself, perched, as Kentridge puts it, between landscape and non-landscape. This is also the central paradox around which our third example pivots, the art historian T.J. Clark's protracted engagement with Poussin's *Landscape with a Man Killed by a Snake* (1648) in *The Sight of Death*. Clark hones in on a more disturbing version of the *vanitas* motif at a site where an atrocity has recently occurred. Unfolding in a series of diary entries written over a period of six months, his "experiment in art writing" gravitates toward the murky and marshy area in the lower left space of the foreground where a boa constrictor coils around a rigidifying corpse in a stream. The enigmatic *Ego* is here viscerally present, voracious, gut-wrenching and "deliberately Virgil in negative."[96]

Slowing down perception in order to gather clues, Clark refers to his diary as "a record of looking taking place and changing through time."[97] Foremost, his ekphrastic meditation delineates a series of tensions, an equilibrium of forces and counterforces, as Poussin pulls the viewer's attention between "the pool of darkness"[98] in the foreground and the crystalline distance, between solidity and putrescence, between the placid horizontal spread and the eruption of mortal danger. The relation between the various elements—the exchange of gestures (outstretched arms and open palms) and gazes (the witness, the fleeing man who sees the snake-entangled corpse, and the witness to the witness, the washerwoman who sees the man in flight, but also the non-witnesses, the oblivious fisherman and the minuscule figures in the forest)—Clark writes, "takes place across such gaps, such emptiness."[99] While we may commit poses and characters to memory, these spaces in-between evade such efforts. The eye is unable to measure or retain the distance between the various planes of action, which "cannot be paraphrased, or held in memory, very efficiently. That is why they ask to be gone back to."[100] In other words, it is the intervals that beckon a return, calling for us to retrace the tenuous relations that they enable.

The tensions that ripple through the limpid daybreak vista exude from the constrictor snake and putrid corpse, oozing out a sickly green pallor that spots the canvas. Plunging us into a non-place within the landscape, the snake is "an abstract track, an empty tube, down which energy flows" Clark writes, "wavelike, limbless, self-generated coiling."[101] Defying geometry, gravity and form, it is also the obverse of all the hallmarks of Poussin's clam, calculated and composed style. "[T]he snake is not just any predator: it is the figure of the opposite of the human," Clark continues, "the chthonic, the lightning-fast, the infinitely adaptable."[102] Yet, in an earlier passage, he suggests that snakes are repulsive, "above all because they figured our intestinal tracts—that whole other, biomechanical system we carry inside us and have no control over." The running man doesn't simply confront death, then, but "an inside coming out."[103]

Grappling with the carnivorous reptile, Clark takes recourse to Warburg's lecture on the snake dance ritual through which the Hopi tribe attempted to control lightning, and thereby rain.[104] At once a demon of the underworld and a deity of healing, the serpent is here presented as an overdetermined trope for the survival of ancient paganism, and Warburg traces its migration from the Old to the New Testament, via the snake-entangled Maenads of the Dionysus cult and the Laocoön, the Roman sculptural group of a Trojan priest and his two sons being strangled by giant serpents. While the mute scream in Poussin's painting—the cavities of gaping mouths and bewildered eyes—is exemplary of the kind of involuntary motor-sensory responses triggered by an alarming stimuli that Warburg understood as engrams, his "nameless science" ultimately sought to grasp something even more elusive.[105] This was the sinuous and self-renewing force of pictorial memory that Warburg likens to the serpent's "ability to cast off its slough," to "slither into the earth and reemerge."[106] Cognate with Clark's observation of how the snake smothers the distinction between interior and exterior, Didi-Huberman writes that in *Laocoön and His Sons*, "the snakes appear to be almost an 'over-arching musculature' of the three personages, or perhaps their innards rendered visible by a kind of phantasmal inversion of the inside and the outside."[107] This entanglement of human and animal discloses the vulnerability of the human form, and of the forms made by human hands, which at any time may be absorbed by its surroundings.

It seems apposite, then, that the reemergence of landscape as a serious endeavor of artistic exploration in the late 1960s found its most iconic manifestation in the coiling figure of a giant snake. It is in Robert Smithson's essay on his earthwork sculpture the *Spiral Jetty* that we find our final iteration of the legacy of Poussin's epitaph. While circling above the red-hued shallows of the Great Salt Lake in a helicopter, Smithson laconically notes: "Et in Utah Ego."[108] The *Spiral Jetty* was inspired by The Great Serpent Mound in Ohio, a prehistoric effigy mound that meanders in the shape of a 1300-foot long snake along the bends of a tributary to the Ohio River. Approximating the length of The Great Serpent, the serpentine form of Smithson's sculpture does not mimic bends in a river, but the swirling countercurrents of a whirlpool.[109] "[T]he entire landscape appear to quake. A dormant earthquake spread into the fluttering stillness," the artist ruminates on his first encounter with the extinct lake.[110] This passage not only brings to mind Warburg's conjunction of seismic and mnestic tremors, which are capable of stirring ancient forms to the surface; it also invokes the double-figure of the snake and the lightning flash explored by Warburg in New Mexico. Smithson again: "I took my chances on a perilous path, along which my steps zigzagged, resembling a spiral lightning bolt."[111] Submerged by rising tides shortly after the untimely death of its maker, the sculpture seemed to confirm Smithson's forecast of energy-drain, decreasing order, and the irreversible process of decay. However, the *Spiral Jetty* would reemerge after nearly three decades under water, encrusted with salt crystals that transformed the counterclockwise spiral of basaltic rock into a sparkling white. Rather than a testament to entropy, Smithson's sedimentary snake thus elicits the convoluted temporality of the moving fossil and its cycles of disappearance and reappearance.

The Dialectical Landscape

"I"—war, paganism, snake-infested swamps, geological deep time—"am also in Arcadia." In the terminology of Smithson, this discord or corrosion is what defines "the dialectical landscape."[112] A decade after the

Spiral Jetty was completed, Rosalind Krauss succinctly paraphrased the project undertaken by the Earth Art movement as an exploration of "the possible combination of *landscape* and *not-landscape*."[113] In the final section of this chapter, I hope to bring together the diverse set of ideas outlined in the montage of artistic and theoretical contributions above through a comparative reading of the friction between landscape and non-landscape in the work of Kentridge and Smithson, and of the connate deterioration of landforms and memories that they respectively trace.

Let us first consider this idea in the terms put forth by the French philosopher Jean-Luc Nancy in a brief essay called *Paysage avec dépaysement*. While the title conflates landscape, *paysage*, with the apparently counterintuitive notion of *dépaysement*, which refers to an experience of exile or dislocation, the preposition *avec* borrows the idiom of the Ideal Landscape painters.[114] For Lorrain and Poussin, a landscape was always a "Landscape with": with calm, with storm, or with tree struck by lightning, with man washing his feet or pursued by snake. The enduring seen together with the ephemeral, the stasis of the setting with the passing of an event, like the shadow cast by the shepherd on the tomb. Gradually emancipated from narrative and mimetic tasks, the event that takes place in the autonomous landscape, following Nancy, is one of voiding and withdrawal: the departure of pagan deities and demons, of nymphs and shepherds, saints and satyrs, even of the peasants, from the scene. Landscape is not the representation of a location, he contends, but the presentation of a dislocation: "*le paysage dépayse*."[115] In other words, for Nancy, landscape is about losing ground, nonbelonging, being out-of-place. Clearing all moral and metaphysical claims staked on the land, it delineates a dehumanized terrain that has devoured and digested its inhabitants, but also, as Nancy adds, where "the humans are always still to come."[116] Notably, the French "paysage" is cognate with the Late Latin *pagensis*, referring to the inhabitant of a district (in Latin, *pagus*) located outside the borders of Rome, the capital of Christianity and the cradle of the Ideal Landscape School.[117] Recalling Bordo's thesis on the prehistory underpinning Poussin's Arcadia, the etymology of *paysage* already posits such a substrate of pagan antiquity.

Thesis with antithesis, scene with obscene, ideal with matter, landscape with non-landscape, *paysage avec depaysement*. But also; remembering with disremembering, renewal with exhaustion. Seeking to reclaim landscape, both as site and concept, Smithson turned to abandoned and disused landforms. To the artist, such "back-waters and fringe areas" were redolent of a new form of monumentality, as they obliquely pointed back toward a former state of activity.[118] In the early autumn of 1967, Smithson embarked on a field trip to the toxic, post-industrial wasteland along the banks of the Passaic River, recording its main attractions—sewer pipes, derricks, and unfinished construction work—in a series of black-and-white Instamatic photographs. "A Tour of the Monuments of Passaic, New Jersey" unfolds as a travesty of the Grand Tour, which had taken leisure travelers of British aristocracy on an educational rite of passage of self-improvement from the Alps to the ruins of Rome, the key destination for the landed gentry in search of inspiration for building the British Empire. Smithson's essay begins with a blurry, low-resolution reproduction of Samuel F.B. Morse's "Allegorical Landscape of New York University" (1836), which is subjected to a brief ekphrastic parody. The painting presents a hyperbolic example of landscape in the servitude of grandiose idealism, transposing the New York University building to a Lorrain-like setting, complete with screening trees, figures in togas, and a gilded lagoon with Mount Helicon towering on its shores. Inverting Morse's notion of New York as the new Athens, and degrading the lustrous oil canvas into a grim "newsprint grey," Smithson proposes that the decaying industrial town of Passaic has now replaced Rome as The Eternal City.[119]

"Actually, the landscape was no landscape," Smithson concludes before leaving the construction sites, which lack any redolence of the past. The monuments recorded on his odyssey do not commemorate any historical events, then, but an oblivious blank. Positing another layer of Greco-Roman antiquity, maybe the Passaic River, as Jennifer L. Roberts has proposed, is a modern-day Lethe.[120] Smithson himself seems rather to suggest that the banks between the two rivers in Hades have eroded, and that the currents of oblivion and memory flow together. In an essay on his mirror installations in the Yucatan, the artist makes a comparison between the sediments of clay shored up by the river and the memories and visions shored up by the mind. Such residues, like those of Imperial Rome and the Mountain of the Muses in Morse's painting, are scattered through Smithson's sightseeing tour. Most persistent of these is the trope of the westward progression of the sun guiding civilization into the New World, prevalent in nineteenth-century American landscape painting. In Passaic, the dead sunlight instead transfixes the sights into what Smithson variously describes as "an over-exposed picture," a "zero panorama" and a "self-destroying postcard world."[121] Like Kentridge's Johannesburg, then, Passaic is not merely ridden with amnesia, but also with "the plague of the picturesque."

While Kentridge regards the picturesque as an adversary to avenge, Smithson acknowledges it as a precursor to his processual notion of the dialectical landscape. His instrument of choice was not the tuning fork but the geologists' hammer: "the mallet instead of the chisel" as William Gilpin, the key theorist of the picturesque, wrote in 1792,[122] or a "bulldozer" instead of a "paintbrush" in Smithson's updated version.[123] Equally hostile to the virginal ideal of natural beauty promulgated in ornamental gardens and national parks as to the highbrow notion of landscape as a gateway for an autonomous art, Smithson's earth projects aimed to reel landscape back to its crude material base, drastically redirecting it from ethereal abstractions to soiling, making a mess.[124] Placing mirrors and broken glass in the environment, pouring asphalt, glue and cement down hillsides, and planting tree trunks upside down, his earthworks also constituted an assault on the Greenbergian doctrine of purity and media-specificity. "My work is impure," Smithson declared, "clogged with matter."[125] If the dominant tradition of landscape art can be described as a technique to evade the disquieting presence of soil and mud, earthworks instead provoked an eruption of "the physical abyss of raw matter."[126]

Despite Kentridge's resentment of the picturesque tradition, his work ultimately perpetuates its penchant for ruins, hollows and gorges. These voids further delineate a common ground between Kentridge and Smithson. Seeking out locations depleted by the mining industry, the work of both artists relentlessly gravitate toward chasms and caverns, to sinkholes, open strip mines and empty plots of land, to fissures and gaps in the topographical fabric. Notably, for a collaborative project called *Memory and Geography* (1995), Kentridge created two earthworks, only fully visible from the air, on vacant fields outside and within the city of Johannesburg.[127] Like Johannesburg and its surroundings, "Passaic seems full of 'holes'" Smithson notes, "and those holes in a sense are the monumental vacancies that define, without trying, the memory-traces of an abandoned set of futures."[128]

Like Smithson, Kentridge is, to quote Susan Stewart's deft characterization, "a messenger of the obscene."[129] Refracting their landscapes through diagrammatic charts, grafts and columns, the rigid geometrical grid of renaissance perspective, usually sublimated beneath gentle curvilinear forms, is bluntly exposed. Their respective medium, earth sculpture and charcoal animation, instigates a principle of accretion and sedimentation that blurs the view by stirring up underlying prehistoric or fossilized forms. "Why not reconstruct one's inability to see?" Smithson ponders in one of his essays, "and develop a kind of 'anti-vision' or negative seeing."[130] The possibility for reconstructing the blind spots of vision, following Kentridge, is conditioned by the impasse or interval between landscape and non-landscape.

From such vacancies and gaps, an alternative mode of seeing and remembering may emerge. Like the earth itself, however, memory is constantly eroding. And in common with Smithson's sculptures, gradually reclaimed by the earth from which they have been wrought, Kentridge's charcoal animated landscape vanishes as it develops, but it does not vanish completely. In their wake remains what Smithson refers to as memory traces, Freud's *Erinnerungsspur*. "Space is the remains, or corpse, of time, it has dimensions," Smithson writes in his mirror-travel essay: "It is the dimension of absence that remains to be found."[131]

* * *

The vertical segregation of the communities of Gilo and Beit Jala, with the Jewish settlement perched on the hilltop above the Palestinian city, is exemplary of a general strategy of environmental and architectural planning implemented on the West Bank. The housing developments quarried into the folded summits that reach from Hebron to Nablus do not merely provide the optical advantage of reconnaissance, they also stake out the spiritual basis of the settlement project. By settling the high places, Eyal Weizman writes, the religious right "sought to re-establish the relation between terrain and sacred text. Topography turned into scenography" in order to yoke together "a physical entity and an imagined, mythical geography."[132]

In 2004, the Israeli artist Yair Barak produced a series of photographs called *Earth Works*.[133] It is not merely the title that Barak borrows from Smithson, but also the favorite topoi explored by his American predecessor: the quarry or strip mine. Traditionally, the limestone quarry has served as a heroic motif in Zionist iconography, providing the raw materials from which the homeland in Eretz-Israel is wrought. In the series, Barak contrasts two oblique viewpoints of the quarries. At a cursory glance, some of the images may be taken for vast panoramas of Alpine

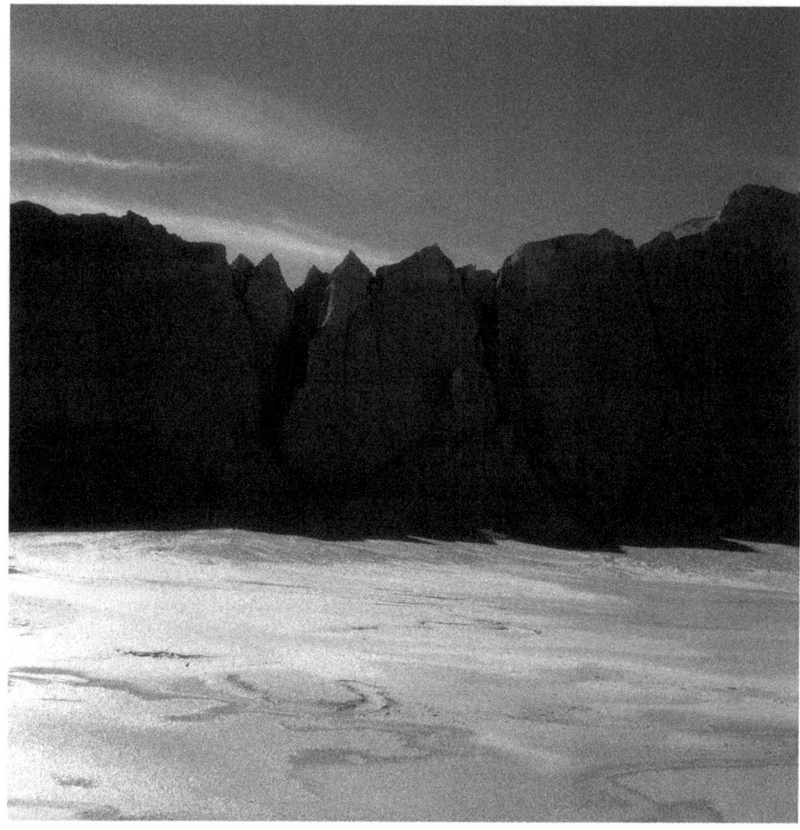

Fig. 2.2 Yair Barak *Earth Works #6* (The dark cliff). Archival pigment print, 105/105 cm, 2004. Courtesy of the artist

ridges beneath blue skies (Fig. 2.2). In common with Smithson, however, Barak is playing tricks with scale and orientation. What first appear to be natural features sculptured over eons of tectonic activity and glacial uplift are in fact merely the collateral damage of modern housing projects: steep mounds of limestone, used for producing cement, scooped into high banks. Other images reverse the perspective by tilting the lens downwards into the craters left at the bottom of the deep pits (Fig. 2.3). Like Gilo and Beit Jala, separating the sacred summits from the secular

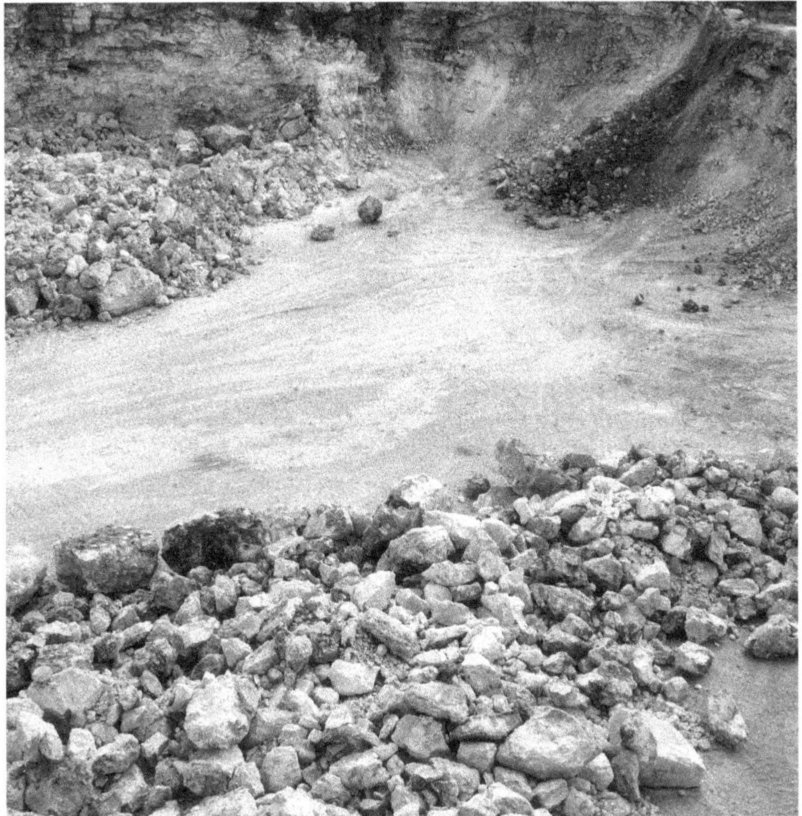

Fig. 2.3 Yair Barak *Earth Works #4* (The stones valley). Archival pigment print, 105/105 cm, 2004. Courtesy of the artist

plains, the above/below, upward/downward axiality of Barak's *Earth Works*, oscillating between ascending masses of scree and gaping cuts in the ground, reflects two irreconcilable notions of the land.

The images of the earth broken up and caving in considered above bring us back to Warburg's intuition of being a seismograph, and the concomitant idea that the surface of the image is in some ways similar to the surface of the earth. Unremittingly besieged, broken up, moved around and remapped, it is "traversed by the discontinuity of fractures, earthquakes, and the movements of tectonic plates."[134] The drive to peel back the skin of landscape, to unearth, undermine and quarry, is expressive of an urge to replace representation—whether the grand narratives of a nation and its people, or the master narrative of modernist abstraction—with something obtrusively, and obscenely, present. Herein lies the paradox of the landscape as deep surface: both present and ancient, semiotic system and material substrate, scene and obscene. At once a screen for the projection of common pasts and shared futures, and a disposable crust that at any moment may be raked off the surface of the earth.

Notes

1. "The long and winding *trompe l'oeil* slab is devoid of Arab inhabitants, and none of the buildings in the distance appears to have been shelled by Israeli tanks. The blurry, distant villages have been settlerized; a disproportionate number of buildings are painted with salmon-tiled gabled roofs, an architectural conceit unknown to the Palestinians, whose villages typically have flat white roofs." Richard Fleming "Paint Your Troubles Away" *Cabinet* issue 9 (Winter 2002/2003) http://cabinet-magazine.org/issues/9/fleming.php (accessed 4 May 2018).
2. On all three occasions that I've had the privilege to hear Mitchell give a lecture, he has shown Miki Kratsman's photograph of Gilo Wall. It also decorates Mitchell's homepage "Welcome to the Jungle of the Imaginary" https://lucian.uchicago.edu/blogs/wjtmitchell/ (accessed 4 May 2018).
3. For an additional example, see Gaston Zvi Ickowicz's photographic triptych "Monument" (2004). The first picture frames Gilo Wall frontally and from below, emphasizing the lateral extension of ground and sky; the second, from across the road with a vast stretch of tarmac dominating the foreground; the third is taken from a further remove at the wall's end, revealing the unpainted side on the last concrete unit straddling the drab hillside above Beit Jala.
4. In a follow-up project to *Infected Landscape* called *Fallen Empires*, Shai Kremer extends the scope of his geographical investigation to explore the strata of succeeding empires (Persian, Roman-Byzantine, Christian, Mameluke, Ottoman, and British). Like its predecessor, *Fallen Empires* raises the question: what is the relation between the ruins disclosed *in* the landscape and the form *through* which they are depicted? These companion volumes are both steeped in *vanitas* philosophy, picturesque decay, and biblical imagery, as when the urban warfare training zone Chicago appears in the midst of a vast, swirling sandstorm in *Infected*

Landscape. Fallen Empires belongs to a prolific vogue of lavishly produced books that develop a postmodern picturesque of collateral damage. Exhibiting landscapes wrought by resource extractions, nuclear testing and oil wars, or roaming the remnants of Post-Fordist or Post-Stalinist architecture, the romantic infatuation with ruins has degraded from "ruin lust" to "ruin porn," and the Grand Tour of moral self-improvement into a thanatourism of the disaster zones of modernity. From the muted earth-tones and auratic textures of the ancient building materials of crusader castles and Bedouin villages, to the more recent remnants of crushed bricks, reinforcing rods, lumps of concrete and garish synthetics, the accelerating process of demolition and reconstruction chronicled in *Fallen Empires* appears gradually less appealing the closer we get to the present. Occasionally, long exposures blur out the movements of patrolling soldiers or Israeli flags fluttering in the wind to mark their transience within this cycle of conquest and decay. These compositional strategies reflect Kremer's stated intention to interrogate Israel as "a case study about the phenomena of empires." In the words of the artist, "[s]uch cases open a window through time." Kremer also regularly uses windows, or window-like apertures, as framing devices. Edged by gaping doorways, blasted windows and damaged walls, the desecrated interiors set up sequential effects of spatial recession through which one historical moment of ruination opens to another, stratifying both the photographic depth field and the depth of historical time. In his introductory statement, Kremer writes that the camera can be used as a tool that "reveals inconvenient truths and explores the landscape as a place of amnesia and erasure." Therefore, it may also serve to remedy this oblivion: "I am pointing my camera at the landscape in order to dig." If the windows through time opened up by Kremer's apparatus allow us to peer back through the ages, the metaphor is given a different twist in the final image of *Fallen Empire*: a frontal close-up of a bricked-up window. Shai Kremer *Fallen Empires* (Stockport, UK: Dewi Lewis 2011) n.p.

5. René Magritte made two versions of this motif, in 1933 and 1935, both bearing the title *La condition humaine*. Stephen Shore's photograph of the snowcapped mountain billboard is titled *U.S. 97, South of Klamath Falls, Oregon, July 21, 1973* and appears in his photo-diary roadbook *American Surfaces*.
6. Susan Meiselas *Reframing History: Nicaragua 25th Anniversary Mural Project* (2004).
7. W.J.T. Mitchell "Imperial Landscape" *Landscape and Power* ed. W.J.T. Mitchell (Chicago: The University of Chicago Press 1994) 10.
8. Ibid. 29.

9. While commonly associated with the Zionist movement, the slogan "A Land without a People for a People without a Land" was first coined by the Christian Restorationist clergyman Alexander Keith in his 1843 book *The Land of Israel*.
10. W.J.T. Mitchell "Holy Landscape: Israel, Palestine, and the American Wilderness" *Landscape and Power* 261–290, 263.
11. Mitchell "Imperial Landscape" 13.
12. Ibid. 15.
13. Elaine de Kooning as quoted in James E.B. Breslin *Mark Rothko: A Biography* (Chicago and London: The University of Chicago Press 1993) 388.
14. Robert Rosenblum "The Abstract Sublime" [1961] *New York Painting and Sculpture: 1940–1970* ed. Henry Geldzahler (New York: Pall Mall Press 1969) 350–359, 358. See also Rosenblum's *Modern Painting and the Northern Romantic Tradition: Friedrich to Rothko* (New York, Evanston, San Francisco, and London: Harper & Row 1975).
15. Larry Abramson "What Does Landscape Want? A Walk in W.J.T. Mitchell's Holy Landscape" *The Pictorial Turn* ed. Neal Curtis (New York: Routledge 2010) 178–191, 184.
16. "Landscape is a way of seeing the world" is cultural geographer Denis E. Cosgrove's riff on John Berger in *Social Formation and Symbolic Landscape* (Madison: The University of Wisconsin Press 1984) 13.
17. W.J.T. Mitchell "Landscape and Invisibility: Gilo's Wall and Christo's *Gates*" *Sites Unseen: Landscape and Vision* eds. Dianne Harris and D. Fairchild Ruggles (Pittsburg: University of Pittsburg Press 2007) 35.
18. W.J.T. Mitchell "Showing Seeing: A Critique of Visual Culture" *Journal of Visual Culture* Vol. 1 No. 2 (2002) 165–181.
19. James Elkins *The Object Stares Back: On the Nature of Seeing* (San Diego, New York, and London: Harcourt Brace 1996) 23.
20. Mitchell "Landscape and Invisibility" 35.
21. "The paradoxical character of seeing landscape, 'looking at the view,' is materialized for us most vividly in the phenomena of walls and gates, the things we build around ourselves to obstruct the view, and the holes we punch in those obstructions to allow ourselves to pass through, visually and bodily, what we have erected precisely to prevent such a passage." Mitchell "Landscape and Invisibility" 35.
22. "The analyst has neither experienced nor repressed any of the material under consideration; his task cannot be to remember anything. What then is the task? His task is to make out what has been forgotten from the traces which it has left behind or, more correctly, to *construct* it. … His work of construction, or, if it is preferred, of reconstruction, resembles to a great extent an archaeologist's excavation of some

dwelling-place that has been destroyed and buried by some ancient edifice. The two processes are in fact identical ... since what he is dealing with is not something destroyed but something that is still alive ... Both of them have an undisputable right to reconstruct by means of supplementing and combining the surviving remains." Sigmund Freud "Constructions in Analysis" [1937] *Collected Papers: Authorized Translation Under the Supervision of Joan Riviere* Vol. 5 (New York: Basic Books 1959) 358–371, 360.

23. Adam Broomberg and Oliver Chanarin *Chicago* (Göttingen: Steidl 2006).
24. "Desert Bloom" is also the title of the middle part of Fazal Sheikh's *The Erasure Trilogy* (2015). Documenting traces of displacement, demolition, settlement and forestation the Negev desert in sepia-toned aerial photographs, *Desert Bloom* explores the desert floor as a site of memory loss and repression.
25. Simon Schama *Landscape and Memory* (New York: Random House 1995). This prologue serves as a counterpoint to Schama's subsequent discussion of the ancestral woodland of Taciticus' *Germania* as the foundation of the Nazi myth of *Blut und Boden.*
26. Ibid. 16–17.
27. Broomberg and Chanarin *Chicago* n.p.
28. Schama 6.
29. Irus Braverman "Planting the Promised Landscape: Zionism, Nature, and Resistance in Israel/Palestine" *Natural Resource Journal* Vol. 49 (Spring 2009) 317–365, 343. See also Carol B. Bardenstein "Trees, Forests and the Shaping of Palestinian and Israeli Collective Memory" *Acts of Memory: Cultural Recall in the Present* eds. Mieke Bal, Jonathan Crewe, and Leo Spitzer (Hanover and London: University Press of New England 1999) 148–168.
30. Mitchell "Holy Landscape" 262.
31. Ibid. 263.
32. Ibid. 262–264.
33. Eyal Weizman *Hollow Land: Israel's Architecture of Occupation* (London and New York: Verso 2007) 39.
34. William Kentridge *Six Drawing Lessons: The Charles Eliot Norton Lectures* (Cambridge, MA and London, UK: Harvard University Press 2014) 79.
35. Kentridge *Six Drawing Lessons* 80.
36. William Kentridge "Felix in Exile: Geography of Memory"; Carolyn Christov-Bakargiev *William Kentridge* (Brussels: Palais des Beaux-Art 1998) 93–97, 95
37. Kentridge *Six Drawing Lessons* 82.
38. Ibid. 81.

39. William Kentridge "Landscape in a Stage Siege" *October Files: William Kentridge* ed. Rosalind Krauss (Cambridge and London: MIT Press 2017) 107–112.
40. Ibid. 109. As Rosalind C. Morris has observed, many of Kentridge's landscapes themselves appear depopulated: "The desiccation and evacuation of the landscape is, of course, one of the 'signifieds' of these complexly referential drawings, and in this sense, the absence of human beings is akin to the vacuity of Atget's photographs, as described by Walter Benjamin. It implies the scene of a crime, a socioeconomic crime orchestrated through legislative processes and authorized under the name of law's rule." Rosalind C. Morris "Drawing the Line at a Tree-Search: The New Landscapes of William Kentridge" *October Files: William Kentridge* 113–146, 118.
41. Mitchell "Holy Landscape" 262–263.
42. Kentridge *Six Drawing Lessons* 82.
43. Ibid. 83–84.
44. Ibid. 84.
45. Kentridge himself describes the relation between the forensic photographs found in his father's office and the creation of *Felix in Exile* as an instant of *Nachträglichkeit*: "when I was drawing the bodies for *Felix in Exile* I did not have the Sharpeville massacre in mind—this was only a connection I made some months or years later." Kentridge cited by Neal Benezra in "William Kentridge: Drawings for Projection" *William Kentridge* ed. Michael Sittenfeld (Chicago: Museum of Contemporary Art and New York: New Museum of Contemporary Art in association with Harry N. Abrams 2001) 11–27, 22.
46. The imagery of the slain bodies wrapped in paper and absorbed by the ground anticipates the artist's commentary on the historical moment of the Truth and Reconciliation Commission as "a battle between the paper shredders and the Photostat machines." William Kentridge "Director's Note: The Crocodile's Mouth" *Ubu and the Truth Commission* ed. Jane Taylor (Cape Town: University of Cape Town Press 1998) viii–xv, viii.
47. Kentridge "'Fortuna': Neither Program Nor Chance in the Making of Images" Christov-Bakargiev 61–69, 61.
48. Joseph Koerner's Lecture "The Evidence of Images: William Kentridge" at the Warburg Institute in London, 16 March 2016 https://www.youtube.com/watch?v=FQohMdCcmxg (accessed 4 May 2018).
49. Mitchell "Imperial Landscape" 5.
50. Kentridge as cited in Christov-Bakargiev 93.
51. Kentridge "Fortuna" Christov-Bakargiev 64.
52. Kentridge "Landscape in a Stage Siege" 107.

53. Kentridge *Six Drawing Lessons* 95.
54. "There is a sense of drawing a social or historical landscape. The process of actually making the drawing finds that history because the landscape itself hides it." Kentridge Statement on *Colonial Landscapes* (1996) cited in Christov-Bakargiev 23.
55. Kentridge "Landscape in a Stage Siege" 110.
56. J.M. Coetzee *White Writing: On the Culture of Letters in South Africa* (New Haven and London: Yale University Press 1988) 167–168.
57. Kentridge *Six Drawing Lessons* 78.
58. Ibid. 78–79.
59. In Gertrud Bing's phrase, *Pathosformeln* are "visible expressions of psychic states that had become fossilized, so to speak, in the images." Gertrud Bing quoted in Georges Didi-Huberman "Knowledge: Movement (The Man Who Spoke to Butterflies)" foreword to Philippe-Alain Michaud's *Aby Warburg and the Image in Motion* (New York: Zone Books 2004) 7–19, 16.
60. In his biography on Warburg, Ernst Gombrich explains: "Any event affecting living matter leaves a trace which Semon calls an '*engram*'. The potential energy conserved in this 'engram' may, under suitable conditions, be reactivated and discharged … In the life of civilizations it is the *symbol* which corresponds to Semon's 'engram'. In the symbol—in the widest sense of the term—we find preserved those energies of which it is, itself, the result." Ernst Gombrich *Aby Warburg: An Intellectual Biography* [1970] (Chicago: University of Chicago Press 1986) 242–243.
61. Georges Didi-Huberman "Warburg's Haunted House" *Common Knowledge* Vol. 18 No. 1 (Winter 2012) 50–78, 50.
62. Aby Warburg *Images from the Region of the Pueblo Indians of North America* [1923] trans. Michael P. Steinberg (Ithaca and London: Cornell University Press 1995) 2.
63. Notably, Warburg begins his lecture on the snake dance rituals performed by the Pueblo Indians in New Mexico with a geological survey of the eroded canyons, gorges and plateaus formed by volcanism and erosions, a location where "the ruined sites of prehistoric communities survive alongside the currently inhabited Indian villages." Ibid. 5.
64. I am quoting this phrase from Coetzee, used in relation to "the geological turn" of South African landscape poetry discussed in *White Writing* 168.
65. Martin Warnke *Political Landscape—The Art History of Nature* [1992] (Cambridge: Harvard University Press 1995).
66. Aby Warburg "Italian Art and International Astrology in the Palazzo Schifanoia, Ferrara" [1912] *The Renewal of Pagan Antiquity:*

Contributions to the Cultural History of the European Renaissance (Los Angeles: Getty Research Institute for the History of Art and the Humanities 1999) 563–591, 585.

67. Maurice Halbwachs "The Legendary Topography of the Gospel in the Holy Land" [*Topographie légendaire des évanglis en Terre Sainte*, 1941] *On Collective Memory* [1925] ed. and trans. Lewis A. Coser (Chicago and London: The University of Chicago Press 1992).
68. Ibid. 224.
69. Halbwachs *On Collective Memory* 86.
70. Ibid. 60.
71. Georges Didi-Huberman *Confronting Images: Questioning the Ends of a Certain History of Art* [1990] trans. John Goodman (University Park: The Pennsylvania State University Press 2005) 158.
72. Ibid. 146.
73. Georges Didi-Huberman *The Surviving Image: Phantoms of Time and Time of Phantoms* [2002] trans. Harvey L. Mendelsohn (University Park: The Pennsylvania State University Press 2017) 151.
74. Georges Didi-Huberman "Of Images and Ills" *Critical Inquiry* Vol. 42 (Spring 2016) 439–472, 441.
75. Didi-Huberman *The Surviving Image* 206.
76. Ibid. 235. In a lecture titled "Shatter zone memory: Croatia, Yugoslavia and the First World War," cultural historian Tea Sindbaek Andersen offers an intriguing conceptualization of the dynamics of memories as perceived through the metaphor of tectonic relationships. As nation states fall apart and new ones declare their independence, frictions and sudden erosions of memories occur. A memorial shatter zone, following Andersen, is a region where Grand Memory Narratives collide and divide to create unstable zones where old narratives of the past are disputed or abandoned, and where previously submerged narratives may resurface. The lecture was given at "After the War: Commemorating the Great War in Ireland" symposium at the Humanities Institute, University College Dublin and is available at https://soundcloud.com/ucd-humanities/tea-sindbaek-andersen-shatter-zone-memory-croatia-yugoslavia-and-the-first-world-war (accessed 1 August 2018).
77. Didi-Huberman *The Surviving Image* 326. These obscure undercurrents, Didi-Huberman writes, are filled with "chunks which have broken off from the mountain, broken stones, sediments, geological impressions, and sands moved by a rhythm completely different from the one above." The black canvas of the atlas is "like an ocean in which flotsam and jetsam, originating at many different times, have become amassed at the bottom of the dark water." *The Surviving Image* 206, 326–327.
78. Ibid. 329, 332.

79. Didi-Huberman “Knowledge: Movement (The Man Who Spoke to Butterflies)” 16.
80. Didi-Huberman *Confronting Images* 210.
81. While the Italian artist and critic Giorgio Vasari retrospectively had designated the transition from Gothicism to the Italian revival of antique art as a *rinascita*, the French term *Renaissance* first gained currency as the name for a historical period with the publication of *Histoire de France* written by the French historian Jules Michelet in 1855.
82. Jacob Wamberg quoted from the “Art Seminar” section in *Landscape Theory* eds. Rachael Ziady and James Elkins (New York and London: Routledge 2008) 103.
83. Kentridge “Landscape in a Stage Siege” 109.
84. Didi-Huberman *The Surviving Image* 277.
85. Christopher S. Wood *Albrecht Altdorfer and the Origins of Landscape*. Revised and Expanded Second Edition (London: Reaktion Books 2014) 26.
86. Jeff Wall “About Making Landscapes” *Jeff Wall: Landscapes and Other Pictures* (Wolfsburg: Cantz Verlag 1996) 8–12, 11.
87. Ibid. 12.
88. Ibid. 11.
89. See Lawrence D. Steefel Jr. “A Neglected Shadow in Poussin’s *Et in Arcadia Ego*” *The Art Bulletin* Vol. 57 No. 1 (March 1975) 99–101. Following this interpretation, the shepherd’s gesture recaps the natal moment of the pictorial arts. In the legend of Dibutade, as told by Pliny the Elder, a Corinthian girl retraced the outline of her lover’s shadow cast on a wall in order to inscribe and store the transient body, soon to go missing in war, in a material support.
90. Jonathan Bordo “Picture and Witness at the Site of the Wilderness” *Landscape and Power* 291–315, 303.
91. Artist homepage https://www.simonnorfolk.com/simon.swf (accessed 1 August 2018).
92. Nina M. Athanassoglou-Kallmyer *Cézanne and Provence: The Painter in His Culture* (Chicago and London: The University of Chicago Press 2003) 189.
93. Beckett expressed his admiration for Cézanne’s “atomistic landscape,” which he described as “unapproachably alien, unintelligible” and “incommensurable with all human expressions all together,” in two letters to the Irish poet Thomas McGreevy in September 1934 after seeing Mont Sainte-Victoire in the Tate gallery in 1934. *The Letters of Samuel Beckett. Volume One, 1929–1940* eds. Martha Dow Fehsenfeld and Lois More Overbrook (Cambridge: Cambridge University Press 2009) 222.

94. As quoted by Keith Christiansen "The Critical Fortunes of Poussin's Landscapes" *Poussin and Nature: Arcadian Visions* eds. Pierre Rosenberg and Keith Christiansen (New Haven and London: Yale University Press 2008) 9–37, 18.
95. Maurice Merleau-Ponty "Cézanne's Doubt" [1945] *The Merleau-Ponty Reader* eds. Ted Toadvine and Leonard Lawlor (Evanston: Northwestern University Press 2007) 76.
96. T.J. Clark *The Sight of Death: An Experiment in Art Writing* (New Haven and London: Yale University Press 2006) 94.
97. Ibid. 5.
98. Ibid. 105.
99. Ibid. 118.
100. Ibid. 184.
101. Ibid. 172, 177.
102. Ibid. 228.
103. Ibid. 82.
104. Ibid. 172–173.
105. Giorgio Agamben "Aby Warburg and the Nameless Science" [1975] *Potentialities: Collected Essays in Philosophy* eds. and trans. Werner Hamacher and David E. Wellbery (Stanford: Stanford University Press 1999).
106. Warburg *Images from the Region of the Pueblo Indians of North America* 42.
107. Didi-Huberman *The Surviving Image* 140.
108. Robert Smithson "A Sedimentation of the Mind: Earth Projects" [1968] *Robert Smithson: The Collected Writings* ed. Jack Flam (Berkeley, Los Angeles, and London: University of California Press 1996) 100–113, 113.
109. One of the items in Smithson's imaginary exposé of the Hayden Planetarium at the American Museum of Natural History in "The Domain of the Great Bear" (1966, co-authored with Mel Bochner) is "World Serpent Twined about Earth Egg," a reference to the Serpent Mound in Ohio, which holds an egg in its open mouth. Furthermore, in "Incidents of Mirror Travel in the Yucatan" Smithson aligns his mirror installations with "the networks of Coatlicue, known to the Mayans as the Serpent Lady; Mother Earth." *Robert Smithson: The Collected Writings* 119–133, 126.
110. Robert Smithson "The Spiral Jetty" [1972] *Robert Smithson: The Collected Writings* 143–153, 146.
111. Ibid. 147–148.
112. Robert Smithson "Frederick Law Olmsted and the Dialectical Landscape" [1973] *Robert Smithson: The Collected Writings* 157–171.

113. Rosalind Krauss "Sculpture in the Expanded Field" *October* Vol. 8 (Spring 1979) 30–44, 41.
114. Colloquially referring to a condition of exile or dislocation, the concept of *dépaysement* pertains more specifically to artistic strategies that aim to disorient the senses by uprooting prosaic objects from their familiar habitats, as first developed by the Surrealists after the First World War and later resumed in the new, objective literature pioneered by Alain Robbe-Grillet in the late 1950s. For Nancy, it is rather the habitat itself that becomes "estranged and unsettled." Jean-Luc Nancy "Uncanny Landscape" *The Ground of the Image* (New York: Fordham University Press 2005) 51–62, 62.
115. Ibid. 61.
116. Ibid. 62.
117. Ibid. 56.
118. "Interview with Robert Smithson for the Archives of American Art/ Smithsonian Institution" (1972) *Robert Smithson: The Collected Writings* 270–296, 295.
119. Robert Smithson "A Tour of the Monuments of Passaic, New Jersey" [1967] *Robert Smithson: The Collected Writings* 68–74, 69, 74.
120. Jennifer L. Roberts *Mirror-Travels: Robert Smithson and History* (New Haven and London: Yale University Press 2004) 62.
121. Smithson "A Tour of the Monuments of Passaic, New Jersey" 70, 72.
122. William Gilpin *Essay on Picturesque Beauty* [1792] *Nineteenth-Century Theories of Art* ed. Joshua C. Taylor (Berkeley, Los Angeles, and London: University of California Press 1987) 47–61, 51.
123. Robert Smithson "A Thing Is a Hole in a Thing It Is Not" [1968] *Robert Smithson: The Collected Writings* 95–96, 95.
124. I'm paraphrasing two quotations from Smithson: "a kind of 'virgin' beauty was established in the early days of this country and most people who don't look too hard tend to see the world through postcards and calendars, so that affects their idea of what they think nature should be rather than what it is." ("Conversation in Salt Lake City" [1972] 298). "We live in frameworks, and are surrounded by frames of references, yet nature dismantles them and returns them to a state where they no longer have integrity." ("Art Through the Camera's Eye" [c. 1971] 375). Both in *Robert Smithson: The Collected Writings.*
125. Smithson quoted by Jack Flam in "Introduction: Reading Robert Smithson" *Robert Smithson: The Collected Writings* xiii–xxv, xvii.
126. Smithson "A Sedimentation of the Mind: Earth Projects" 102.
127. The two earthworks evolved from a collaboration between Kentridge and Doris Bloom for the Johannesburg biennale in 1994. The first outdoor installation, "Heart," is an anatomical white chalk drawing of

a heart made on a barren field south of the city. The second, "Fire/Gate" (1995), depicts an ornamental gate, which also contains the figure of a heart, on an empty plot of land adjacent to a power plant in Newtown Johannesburg. The latter was made from sand embankments soaked with gasoline and set on fire. We may recall the phrase "The Heart has its own Memory" which appears in Albert Camus' novel *The Fall.* This quotation was later used for the title for an exhibition of two of Kentridge's films, *Felix in Exile* and *History of the Main Complaint* (1996), at the Madison Museum of Contemporary Art in 2016.

128. Robert Smithson "A Tour of the Monuments of Passaic, New Jersey" 68–74, 72.
129. Susan Stewart "A Messenger" *Parkett* 63 (2001) 82–87, 82.
130. Robert Smithson "Incidents of Mirror Travel in the Yucatan" 130.
131. Ibid. 122, 133.
132. Weizman *Hollow Land* 135.
133. Barak was trained at the Camera Obscura School of Art in Tel Aviv, in common with fellow artists like Miki Kratsman and Shai Kremer whose portrayals of Gilo Wall provided the entry point for this chapter.
134. Didi-Huberman *The Surviving Image* 216.

CHAPTER 3

Intruders in the Dust

In the fall of 2003, the French artist and photographer Sophie Ristelhueber traveled on the West Bank, inspired by a newspaper clipping showing a newly constructed Israeli settlement photographed from the air. To the artist, the colony's neat rows of identical, white houses resembled "a décor" or "Lego toys."[1] At the time, the Separation Wall was beginning to carve its route around the landlocked area between Jordan and the State of Israel. For its sheer material monstrosity it has remained, in Simon Faulkner's estimation, "the most photographed wall in the world."[2] The early stages of construction along the seam-zone, with its intricate infrastructure of fences, trenches and surveillance areas, were captured in Simone Bitton's film *Wall* (*Mur*, 2004). Following the opening traveling shot propelling sideways along Gilo Wall for several minutes, Bitton cuts to a static frame of a construction crew at work on its successor, adding one vertical slab of concrete after another until the sky is blocked out by a uniformly gray surface. Ristelhueber, however, had something else in mind: "I saw it being built, but formally it was an object that did not interest me at all," she admits, "it was like a screen standing between two landscapes."[3] Instead, she started to pursue country roads meandering through the hills and groves on the West Bank, tilting her camera downward to depict the conflict at close range from above. Prompted by the aerial press photograph of the toy-sized settler colony, Ristelhueber worked out an alternative form of miniaturization, photographing mounds of stones from a ladder a few meters above the ground (Fig. 3.1).

H. Gustafsson, *Crime Scenery in Postwar Film and Photography*,
https://doi.org/10.1007/978-3-030-04867-9_3

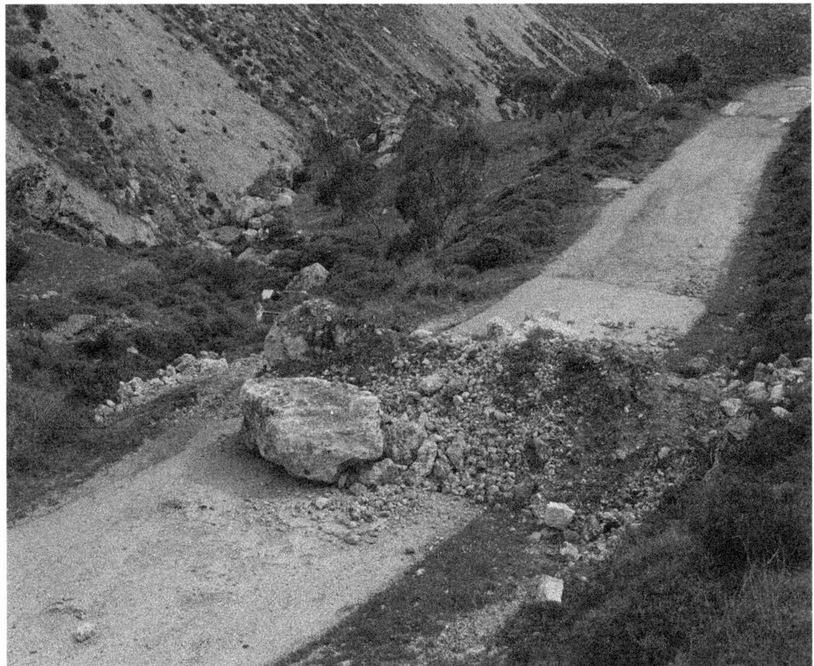

Fig. 3.1 Sophie Ristelhueber, *WB #7* (2005) © Sophie Ristelhueber / BONO, Oslo 2018. Color photograph, silver print mounted on aluminum

The resulting work, *WB* (2005), consists of fifty-four color photographs. Each image is a variation of the same motif: a road deprived of its destination, cut off by a trench or some physical obstacle—a pile of gravel or concrete blocks—with occasional close-ups of torn-up tarmac or twisted iron railings. On the rare occasions when a skyline appears, it is usually reduced to a thin streak in the upper margin of the picture. Retaining the same line of sight throughout the series, repeating the motif over and over with minor variations, this taxonomy of roads cut in two brings the conflict down to its mineral nucleus as "a war of stones," with a phrase borrowed from Elias Sanbar.[4] Set in the pastoral confines of olive orchards and terraced valleys, *WB* at once invokes and refutes the most cherished compositional cue of the landscape genre: the country lane or footpath that entices our gaze through the receding planes of the picture. By way of this absorptive design, usually augmented by a slight elevation, the natural, physical world is transfigured into an artfully produced stage-set for human affairs to unfold. In *WB*, conversely, the blocked roads and broken railings palpably arrest any flight into space, offering neither foreground (a ground for perception) nor distance (a destination for the gaze). As the artist explains: "I do not pay attention to perspective. I avoid the sky and focal points. I privilege saturated, compartmentalised spaces. The eye cannot fix itself to any path or cloud. There is no escape."[5] In Ristelhueber's work, the spectator does not flee into the scene, but runs aground.

Another road cut in two, split apart by a raging flood, appears in an earlier project made in Bosnia between 1991 and 1996. *La Campagne* (1996) is by far Ristelhueber's most rustic work, lush and leafy, full of deep gorges, forested hillsides and meadows sprinkled with dandelions. Like the sites depicted, however, the title has a duplicitous designation. *La Campagne*, French for "the countryside," derives from the Roman *Campagna*, the rural plains outside the city walls and the germinal site of Virgil's *Bucolics* and the Ideal Landscape tradition. The second connotation is that of military campaigns. Thus, the word itself appears as a strategic hiding place, intimating that landscape from its inception has been embroiled in military imaginations and activities. Ristelhueber explains that, "in order to evoke the genocide in Bosnia, I have used images of lush plants, bucolic landscapes that, if you moved close to them, contained demolished houses, trees strafed by machine-gun fire, muddy earth plowed over mass graves."[6] Beckoning a closer look, *La Campagne* facilitates a passage from a unifying landscape gaze to a discrete forensic scrutiny. The flood that has left the raw gash in the dirt road was in fact caused by the excavation of a mass grave, and in the distance derelict farmhouses with broken windows can be discerned.[7]

When exhibiting *La Campagne*, Ristelhueber has stacked the photographic prints, some in black and white and others in color, against the gallery wall in an apparently disassembled manner, so that they lean over and partly cover one another. The images are not merely cut out of context but are also cut into one another, as each screen partly screens out the view behind. Shown together with a small list of seventeen place names, some anonymous, others familiar (Mostar, Sarajevo, Srebrenica), *La Campagne* is displayed as an atlas in reverse, scattered in three-dimensional space rather than projected on a two-dimensional page. This appearance that the photographs have been grasped or cut from context is amplified by Ristelhueber's habit to exhibit her work unframed, affixing the prints to the edges of thin cardboard or aluminum trestles placed upright as vertical boards directly on the floor. Or, as a variation of this, by applying large-scale prints like wallpaper in the gallery rooms so that the images become fractured by the nooks and corners of the walls.

Our third example, an untitled piece from 2011, offers a sort of counter-shot to *La Campagne*. Evocative of an endoscopy, the four photographs show the drainage system below the Latona Fountain in the gardens of Versailles. Illuminated with a flashbulb, the murky ochre imagery of the lead hoses and copper pipes resemble bloated entrails with swollen veins, or a pile of monstrous serpents in the underworld. In the medical vocabulary typical of the artist, she has referred to these rusty entrails as a *plexus*, a branching network of nerves or vessels.[8] As Chandra Mukerji has shown in her study *Territorial Ambitions and the Gardens of Versailles*, the massive earthworks and waterworks, monitored by the vast hydraulic system exposed by Ristelhueber's flashbulb, presented a dazzling display of martial engineering and survey techniques.[9] Cognate with the duplicitous etymology of *La Campagne*, the grand perspectival layout of the Baroque gardens was not primarily intended for recreation, but for exercising a military vision. The view from the barricade wall above the Latona fountain offered the most comprehensive view of the estate, managed by prospectively cut hedges and balustrades. From his seat of power, the omnipotent gaze of the Sun King radiated along rigid orthogonal vectors of sight with "the great avenues of Versailles as potential lines of fire against a subversive mob."[10] The long rows of trees planted along the walkways, a symbolic army standing on guard, reproduced the design of the nation's fortified towns, and warrior statuary were continually added to commemorate military victories.

From these three projects, spread across as many decades, we may deduce a set of pervasive themes and strategies that informs Ristelhueber's work. The blocked roads on the West Bank, the flooded lane in the Balkans, and the mesh of nerves exposed below the royal avenue in Versailles, are all emblematic of the manner in which Ristelhueber's images obstruct straight signification. Undercutting the conventions of war reportage, our response is not directed along a "familiar emotional pathway," as Debbie Lisle puts it, that canalizes empathy into political action.[11] Equally disruptive in relation to the conventions of landscape art, space does not recede along perspectival sightlines, but appears abruptly stalled and stacked in broken masses.

Pictorial devices used for modulating depth (vanishing points, *repoussoirs*, dark coulisses, chiaroscuro) are conspicuously lacking. The frame does not act to resolve pictorial composition by eliciting a temporal succession from the foreground into the future; instead it makes a scission, cropping out everything but a patch of damaged ground. Ristelhueber not merely abstains from the decisive moment of photojournalism, then, but also from the events and contingencies of landscape photography: an expressive cloud-formation pierced by shafts of light, foliage or water stirred by a gust of wind, sunrises and sunsets. Matter is not transformed by luminance, taking on the unique characteristics of a particular time of day or season. Rather than an attack on photographic conventions, the double negation outlined above is indicative of a creative process that un-works landscape, not through the strategic reversals, or *détournements*, that we may find, for example, in the photography of Simon Norfolk, but by wrestling it out of its perspectival schema, and the viewer out of a scenic relation to the land. Like Norfolk, however, it solicits attention to the multifarious ways in which the land—whether the quaint countryside of *La Campagne* or the manicured gardens of Versailles—is formed by the demands of war.

While Ristelhueber's extensive corpus of photographic projects, artist books, installations and films is the key focus of this chapter, it will be set in dialogue with works by two other artists who, in common with Ristelhueber, pay close attention to the expressive agency of forms. First, Jananne Al-Ani's airborne archaeology of the Jordanian desert in her two *Shadow Sites* films (2011). Second, as the coda for the chapter, two films by the Belgian filmmaker Sarah Vanagt called *The Wave* (made together with Katrien Vermeire, 2012) and *Dust Breeding* (2013), which meditate on the forensic exhumation of mass graves in Post-Franco Spain and former Yugoslavia. My intention is not to establish a genealogy between these three artists, however, but to circumscribe a set of interrelated themes that ramify from their rigorous examination of terrestrial marks and patterns of disturbed earth. More specifically, they all enact the transfigurative effects of the airborne gaze and its capacity to turn the territory surveyed into a set of clues to be deciphered.

As a method for trace detection, the aerial vantage point disperses the volumetric space of the classical landscape to afford instead an abstract and anatomized view of the surface of the earth; a surface, as we shall see, that in certain regards is analogous to the sensitized support of photography. The airborne gaze furthermore provides an intersection where different specular regimes—military, medical, archaeological, forensic—converge with the gridded picture plane of Modernist art. Finally, its ambiguity of scale also facilitates a heuristic prism for exploring the key questions around which the following analysis revolves: how traces relate to time, aftermaths to events, and bodies to terrains. As a matrix for the arcane semiotics of the trace explored in this constellation of artworks, the analysis will draw on two seminal sources: the atlas of engrammatic signatures assembled by Aby Warburg and a fabled image of the avant-garde, Man Ray's photograph of a work-in-progress by Marcel Duchamp known as *Dust Breeding* (*Elevage de poussière*, 1920).

Anatomy Lessons

In her 1998 monograph on Ristelhueber, Ann Hindry quotes the artist as saying: "The landscape that we are used to is a parenthesis."[12] This aphorism has at least two implications. From a geological perspective, the landscape is merely an interlude bracketed by glacial drift and plate tectonics. As "a way of seeing," its time span is even briefer, germinating out of renaissance perspectivalism and chiaroscuro. Cropping out this parenthesis is therefore as much a result of the surgical incisions performed by Ristelhueber's camera as of the topoi that she seeks out: sites shattered by a sudden burst of energy, caught in the interim between the event and the effacement of its traces, before the earth regains its balance and covers the tracks.

The landscape may also be omitted by invoking prehistoric strata, or by recourse to allegory, as in *Sodom* (1996) or *Babylone* (2016). "[O]n the banks of the river Lot," a short poem penned by the artist declares, "the world was not a landscape."[13] These lines appear on the first page of the tiny "prayer book" that Ristelhueber made for her exhibition *Mémoires du Lot* (1990).[14] While the project was commissioned by the department of Lot, a region near the Lascaux caves in the southwest of France, none of its picturesque river gorges, vineyards or medieval villages were to be found in the black-and-white photographs on display in the tiny Romanesque chapel that housed the exhibition. Instead, these images were made in the Negev desert, the *Jardin des Plantes*, and the artist's studio, and framed either vertically (a city plaza and desert), or as close-ups of anonymous *rückenfiguren* (a man and a rhinoceros). As so often in Ristelhueber's oeuvre the title suggests a *double entendre*, since Lot may refer both to a place and to a biblical story. Lot's wife, the Book of Genesis tells us, disobeys the angels, looks back at the destruction of Sodom and Gomorrah and turns into a pillar of Salt. Looking back and turning into salt is also an elementary definition of photography. Following this allegorical interpretation, the petrification of silver salts crystalizes, on a monocular level, the embalmed and irrevocable time of the photographic image, and, more specifically, the late photographer's numb gaze at a scene of devastation after the dust has settled. In Ristelhueber's photographs and videos, the sense of arrest and stasis is further augmented because the subjects framed by her camera are already still, unless we expand the notion of movement, as this chapter will attempt, to encompass a slower, recursive time of material duration.

The process of encrustation that *takes place* as nitrate dust interacts with rays of light on the emulsive ground furthermore invites an analogy between photography and topography. This is not to say that Ristelhueber is particularly concerned with the question of medium specificity as such. Rather, her interest lies with the manner in which an external force solidifies into a form: "I have these obsessions that I do not completely understand, with the deep mark, with the ruptured surface, with scars and traces, traces that human beings are leaving on the earth," the artist attests.[15] Calling attention to the at once disruptive and connective nature of such scars and traces, she refers to them both as "fractures, and disappearances"[16] and as "threads of reality."[17] The impulse to unsettle and estrange manmade geographies and ways of seeing spurred by Ristelhueber's obsessions thus ultimately aims to map a deeper, connective tissue.

In Ristelhueber's own metaphor, her work has been intent to maintain, "the analytical distance of an anatomy lesson."[18] We recognize this trope from Walter Benjamin, who compared the optical instruments of the photographer with the hands of the surgeon cutting into the patient's body.[19] The particular facets of this analogy, which implies both a deliberate staging of the gaze and a theatricalization of space, have a more specific purchase on the vantage point calibrated by Ristelhueber. In his study of the renaissance anatomy theater, Jonathan Sawday notes that the cadaver on the dissecting table was charted as "a geophysical entity. The body was a territory, a (yet) undiscovered country," a terra incognita that required the skill of a new kind of cartographer.[20] The metaphor was implemented in the genre of the anatomical atlas, where the shapeless and opaque masses of the body were folded out onto a planar surface. Anatomy, from the Greek *anatémnō*, to "cut up" or "cut open," pertains to the manifold connotations of cutting integral to Ristelhueber's work: cutting out characters and contexts; to intervene or interrupt by cutting off habitual routes of interpretation; but also, to cut together and join something across a gap. A cut—a cross-section, sample or segment—is defined by its axis; in this case, by the angle of vision that, like the click of the camera shutter, slices up the world into discrete objects, Below, I will attempt to unpack the ethical and epistemological implications of cutting with equal regard to the cuts figured *in* Ristelhueber's work (the various wounds it displays) and the cuts figured *through* her work (the particular forms it carves out).

The analogy between photography and anatomy has been firmly in place ever since Ristelhueber's first solo project in 1982, set in the operating theater of a Paris hospital. It is a claire-obscure study of surgical sites on anesthetized bodies illuminated by spotlights, showing cataract needles, scalpels and forceps, masked faces and gloved hands. Two years later, this close-up study of the process of repairing the body was followed by *Beirut* (Beyrouth, photographies, 1984), a study of a contemporary city in ruins. Made in the immediate aftermath of the first Lebanon War, *Beirut* showed modern edifices—a sport stadium, a movie theater, the bank quarters—reduced to crushed concrete, twisted metal, and mangle of wire, with the impact of artillery fire on pockmarked buildings evoking, in Ristelhueber's medical terminology, "a skin disease."[21] In retrospect, these two works established a bipolar pattern that can be traced across the artist's creative output in its entirety. Often, her projects come in pairs, with one series of images germinating from the one preceding it in order to set up its reverse shot. This effect was most strikingly accomplished in two companion pieces from the early 1990s, both made in response to a current atrocity: *Fait* (1992) to the First Gulf War, and *Every One* (1994) to the Civil War in the Balkans.

Ristelhueber arrived in Kuwait in October 1991, six months after the military operation in the Persian Gulf had ended, to photograph aerial views and ground level shots of the deserted battlefield along its border with Iraq. The resulting series of seventy-one photographs are uniformly monochrome, altering between drab sandy hues and shiny blacks and whites. Occasionally, an opaque, dust-filled sky is visible. With the close-ups and long-distance shots all printed in the same size and installed in uniform rows on the gallery wall, *Fait* both emulates and undermines the gridded visual field of aerial reconnaissance. Instead of suturing together a coherent photomosaic atlas of successive shots, it prompts the viewer continually to adjust perception while moving from one scale to another. Fitted into wooden boxes waxed with golden polish, the large-format prints were crafted "into objects that were at once precious and much like camouflage," the artist explains, "linked together by a sort of glowing halo."[22] Additional cuts are made in the artist's book by printing the images across the fold between the pages so that the stitches of the binding create a scission in each photograph. Furthermore, the series is framed by two extracts, abruptly cut in the middle of a sentence, from the Prussian military strategist Carl von Clausewitz's philosophical treatise *On War* (*Vom Kriege*, 1832), in a manner that recalls the Dadaist praxis of *découpé* (cut-up writing).

Fait translates both as "fact" and "what has been done"—that is, what the documentary image allegedly contains and conveys. Edward Steichen, the fine art photographer who commanded the military reconnaissance unit of the American Air Force during the First World War, referred to the airborne prints of the Western Front as "an unequalled historical document of the great war. They represent neither opinions nor prejudice, but indisputable facts."[23] However, as Allan Sekula argued in his essay "The Instrumental Image: Steichen at War," to label these images as historical documents, as archival artifacts to be scrutinized after the fact, is also to obscure their instrumental function as "cues for military action."[24] Gathering evidence to track and target the enemy, the instrumental image serves as a crucial means, an agent or tool, causing something to be done. The laconic title, *Fait* or "Done," thus invokes at once the facticity of the photographic image and the instrumentality of the aerial view.

Fait also taps into a more contemporaneous discourse, bearing a marked resonance with two prophetic essays published in 1991. According to Paul Virilio's *Desert Screen*, the Persian Gulf set the stage for a new kind of warfare where, "the first of the 'ruses de guerre' is no longer a more or less ingenious stratagem, but an abolition of the appearance of facts. From now on the defeat of facts [*la défaite des faits*] precedes those of arms."[25] Extending Virilio's claim, a second essay by Jean Baudrillard notoriously claimed that *The Gulf War Did Not Take Place*.[26] For the two philosophers the unilateral military operation was a war only by name, as the media event of the Gulf War, disseminated across the Desert Screen, displaced what in reality were a few weeks of atrocious bombing raids. What took place in the Persian Gulf was, in Virilio's formulation, "the disappearance of the event."[27]

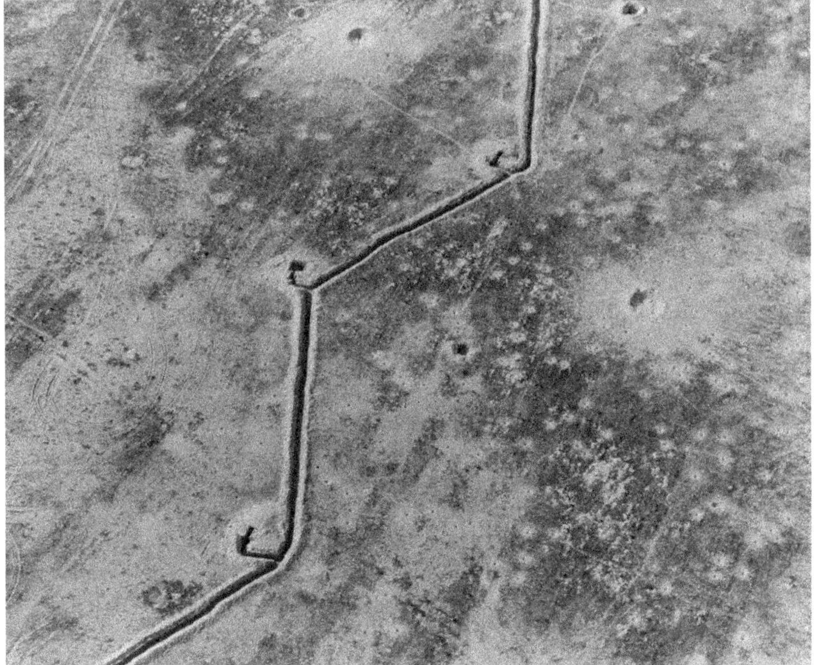

Fig. 3.2 Sophie Ristelhueber, *Fait #20* (*Aftermath*, 1992) © Sophie Ristelhueber / BONO, Oslo 2018. Color photograph, aluminum silver print on laminated paper with golden polished frame

While returning us to the real of the location, to the place of the event, Ristelhueber does not present an account of these events, but a record of their material impact. The effects are evident—the patterns of tank tracks, trench lines, bomb craters and spent ammunition—but their causes remain enigmatic (Fig. 3.2). "It was as if I were fifty centimeters from my subject, like in an operating theatre," Ristelhueber recalls from her flights above the desert floor.[28] Displaced from the geophysical terrain of battle to the operating table, *Fait* replays the medical euphemisms through which the bombing raids were narrated: the sanitized discourse of the "clinical precision" of "surgical strikes" that conjured a clean war executed by expert technicians and intelligent weapons—a war primarily waged, in Virilio's phrase, "inside the organs of the missile."[29]

The physical scars in the earth exposed, but not explained, in *Fait*, are echoed in the scarred bodies in Paris hospitals that Ristelhueber photographed for her next project, *Every One* (1994). The series, which was inspired by the aerial view of a zigzag trench formation in Kuwait, consists of magnified close-ups of fresh surgical stitches.[30] At once maintaining and reversing the optics of *Fait*, the framed sections of human flesh remain oddly disorienting as the sheer size of the prints makes the wounded tissue on a chin or torso assume territorial dimensions. As the interstice between *Every* and *One* implies, cutting entails both separation (to splice apart, to disassemble) and relationality (to splice together, to reassemble), or, in Ristelhueber's words, both "fractures" and "threads." The intersection of the plural in the singular, and of the common in the particular, conveyed by *Every One* is poignantly expressed in a passage from Gilles Deleuze's 1969 treatise *The Logic of Sense*. Developing his philosophy of the event, Deleuze writes:

> there are no private or collective events, no more than there are individuals and universals, particularities and generalities. Everything is singular, and thus both collective and private, particular and general, neither individual nor universal. Which war, for example, is not a private affair? Conversely, which wound is not inflicted by war and derived from society as a whole?[31]

The event, as understood by Deleuze, folds interiority and exteriority together. Ristelhueber's projects tend to revolve around such pivot points (roadblocks, craters, stitches, trenches) pierced by an anonymous force. In a key formulation that underpins the argument of this chapter, the artist refers to them as "details of the world," as isolated specimens dispersed and linked across "the terrain of the real and of collective emotions."[32] The latter statement may seem surprising in light of the formal detachment that governs her work, refuting the humanitarian stance of photojournalism along with its messages about victims and aggressors and allocations of innocence and guilt. Taking my cue from the metaphor of an anatomical atlas, the next section will consider the relationship between the detail and the terrain in Ristelhueber's work through the lens of Aby Warburg's atlas of emotive formulas.

Geography Lessons

In 2010, Georges Didi-Huberman curated the first in a series of shows inspired by Warburg's *Bilderatlas*. On the very last page of the introductory text for the exhibition catalogue, Didi-Huberman cites *Fait* as an exemplary successor to the novel form of mapmaking envisioned by Warburg.[33] The conceptual framework of an atlas that aims to "gather the scattered pieces of the world" in order to invent "alternative geographies,"[34] pertains to the nomadic and "scattered" nature of Ristelhueber's work as a whole, to the sheer territorial range that it covers, as well as its abiding concern with maps, territories and borders. Consider, for instance, *The Air Belongs to Everybody* (L'Air est à tout le monde, 1997–2002) which charts a series of borders in Central Asia; *Fait divers* (2005) which follows the reaches of the Danube, a former political border during the communist era, from the mouth of the delta till it merges with the Black Sea; or *The Equator Line* (La Ligne de l'équateur—1988, 1996), a photograph of latitude zero taken from a deserted terrace on an island in the Gulf of Guinea. This subtle yet stubborn defiance of geography's disciplinary effects of inclusion and exclusion marks a shared impetus for the alternative geographies constructed by Ristelhueber and Warburg.

The principle purpose of the *Mnemosyne* atlas was not to chart a given territory, but to trace its latent fluxes and fault lines. Situating Warburg, the self-declared "psycho-historian,"[35] in a medical context, Didi-Huberman understands the *Mnemosyne* as a diagnostic instrument, or what he coins as "*an atlas of the symptom*."[36] Rather than an encyclopedia of images, the photographic reproductions disseminated across the panels in the oval reading room of Warburg's library, which was designed like a renaissance anatomy theater,[37] facilitate a startling montage of jump-cuts that, much like *Fait*, engender, "violent shifts in scale … and reversals of spatial orientation (an aerial view right next to a subterranean view)."[38] At the outset, the *Mnemosyne* literalizes the notion of an anatomical atlas as the celestial and terrestrial maps displayed on the triad of introductory panels (A, B and C) are followed on the first numbered panel by four anatomical clay models of sheep's livers used for divinatory purposes in ancient Babylon. These abrupt shifts between the visceral and telluric demonstrate that a process of cutting is intrinsic to the model of historical memory implemented by Warburg, seeking to create "cross-sections of chaos" and "traversal sections in the *longue durée*."[39] For Warburg, then, and in marked contrast to Cartier-Bresson's idiom of the decisive moment, the time of the historical event (the click of the shutter) and the time of the image do not coincide. Conversely, it was the task of the atlas to pierce open this relation through a series of anachronistic breaks and ruptures. In analogy, the repeated forms of gaping holes and closing wounds, of eruptions of earth, tears in the flesh, and weird patterns in the sand that spread across Ristelhueber's body of work are not records of discrete and punctual events, with beginnings and aftermaths. Instead, they comprise a collection of symptoms that unfolds as a morphological map of the recurring shapes of violent upheaval.

Unlike the *Mnemosyne*, Ristelhueber's atlas is not one of agitated or ecstatic gestures, but of physical blows, heavy indentions and touch points. Indeed, the inaugural gesture of her work, established with *Beirut*, constitutes an inversion of the *Pathosformel*. In common with several of her most ambitious projects, *Beirut* evolved from a chance encounter with a news item; in this case, a newspaper clipping from the besieged city that showed a woman mourning her dead. What attracted the artist's attention, however, was not the posture of the grieving mother, but the damaged architecture glimpsed in the background of events. Rather than charting life in motion (*bewegtes Leben*), Ristelhueber is concerned with life injured or interrupted. And instead of the vivid corporeal expression, the presence of the human is discreetly marked in her work by the traces left behind. Most importantly, her work patently refutes pathos and tragedy. Nonetheless, it confronts us with expressions of suffering. For Ristelhueber and Warburg alike, to borrow a line from T.S. Eliot, "[t]he whole earth is our hospital."[40]

This brings us to a final context for considering the juncture between Ristelhueber's work and the terrain of collective emotions mapped in the *Mnemosyne* atlas. At the time of the defeat of the German army and the November Revolution in 1918, Warburg suffered a mental breakdown. Diagnosed with schizophrenia, manic depression and paranoid psychosis, he was committed to various mental asylums for the next five years. During the five years leading up to his confinement, however, Warburg had assembled a vast archive of the Great War, consisting of press clippings, pamphlets, postcards and propaganda material. Stored in 72 file boxes, of which only three have survived, the task of the *Kriegskartothek* was to index what Peter J. Schwartz sums up as, "the political instrumentalization of human irrationality in wartime."[41] In this sense, Warburg's *Kriegskartothek* also planted the seeds of his *Bilderatlas* project. Whether culled from news bulletins or art history, Warburg conceived of these diverse samples as repositories of "unchained, elemental man."[42] Furthermore, his intuition of the Renaissance as haunted by demonic antiquity was galvanized by an unexpected turn of events in 1915, when the Italian government signed a treatise to form an alliance with Anglo-French forces against his native Germany.

The *Kriegskartothek* comprised ninety thousand files of iconographic material, including a collection of around five thousand photographs. Some of them evince a surreal constellation of the topical and archaic, like a soldier on horseback armed with a lance and gas mask, or a submarine steering toward a three-masted barque.[43] Others, like the following samples identified by Didi-Huberman, more directly resonate with Ristelhueber's "details" and "obsessions":

> villages in ruins [...] carcasses of tanks [...] bombs left on a beach, houses destroyed from the inside, bridges broken in two [...] Doric columns speckled with the impact of machine-gun bullets ... aerial perspectives, most of a lunar or prehistoric appearance, suggesting that destruction leads to archaeology ... Everywhere is the stigmata of the *Urkatastrophe*.[44]

The interrupted genealogy between the *Kriegskartothek*, amassed from the battlegrounds of the world's first industrially scaled war, and the *Bilderatlas*, charting the archaic language of bodily expressions, intimates a proximity between the terrestrial and the corporeal that is also at the core of Ristelhueber's work. "For me, the bodies and the territories are the same thing," the artist has remarked.[45] Paying equal attention to their injuries as to the bandages and stitches that pull and piece them together, bodies and territories are the same *thing* in that their material presence marks sites where events take place. They converge as physical objects cut from the same cloth and caught in a cycle of tear and repair, both in regard to the damage wreaked upon them and to the formal rigor through which they are grasped by the artist. "In Kuwait I wanted to become one with the territory, even though it was bristling with mines. It was also a way of formulating the problem of representation, and, in the end, the problem of art," Ristelhueber states.[46]

The metaphor of an anatomy lesson is Ristelhueber's concise response to "the problem of art." The surgical cuts that she performs, and her desire to split herself and become one with the mine-infested desert, posit an innate relation between the violent act and the making of an image, converging in the moment when the skin breaks and a scar grows. With a more general implication, Jean-Luc Nancy has extrapolated this relation in his essay "Image and Violence," which, in common with his essay on landscape that was addressed in the previous chapter, appears in the collection *Au fond des images* (The Ground of the Image).[47] Violence imprints its image by force, Nancy contends, it leaves a mark in order to expose and make evident its effect. For Nancy, this is also a definition of the image, which "makes its mark," "its *stigma*" or "its scar" as it grasps itself, "as if with claws or pincers, out of nothing."[48] Setting itself apart from the invisible ground that surrounds it, the image is at once "cut out within a ground" and "detached from a ground."[49] Pulled into relief against the ground, it bears within itself the volatile energy of this tearing away. For Nancy, in other words, the image follows the exact opposite principle to that of camouflage, which aims to level the figure with the ground in order to render forms indifferent from their surroundings.

In Ristelhueber's work, however, camouflage cuts two ways, as the cuts she inflicts have a propensity both to reveal and conceal. On the one hand, we may say that she inverts its logic by facilitating attention to the unnoticed and undistinguished ground. On the other, camouflage can be identified as a shorthand for a range of iconoclastic strategies advanced by the artist in order to break our habits of perception: to delay recognition, to defer knowledge, to divorce from agency, to disorient and dissimulate.[50] Despite, or rather because of, its ubiquitous visibility, saturating every media, war remains hidden. The task to perceive war, or to perceive it differently, therefore entails, in the words of media theorists Sarah Kember and Joanna Zylinska, "an active process of cutting through the flow of mediation."[51] In Ristelhueber's case, these cuts mark the ground into which events are liable to disappear without a trace. It is with recourse to camouflage that the next section tries to grasp the ambiguous relation between event and aftermath, body and environment, interior and exterior, that informs her artistic practice.

Butterfly Hunters

In an interview published in the *Independent* in 2004, the forensic anthropologist Margaret Cox talks about her work of uncovering mass graves and identifying the skeletonized remains of Kurds in Iraq following the Second Gulf War.[52] The article was called "The Butterfly Hunter," referring to an anecdote related by Cox concerning an earlier excavation in Kosovo. In search of mass-burial sites of Albanian victims of Serbian genocide, Cox's forensic team was looking for a particular species of blue butterflies that only feed on a certain species of wildflower, *Artemisia vulgaris*, mugwort or wormwood, an invasive weed growing in nitrogenous soil where the seedbed has been disturbed.

Indexing "a geophysical anomaly," blue butterflies and wildflowers thus provided the visible symptoms of disappeared and decomposing bodies. The story has been cited by Iraqi-born artist Jananne Al-Ani as the initial inspiration for an aerial photography project undertaken in the Jordanian desert. Before discussing Al-Ani's *Shadow Sites* films in more detail in the next two sections, however, I want to reflect for a moment on butterflies as a key trope for figure and ground relations in the discourse on Warburg's science of images. This reflection will also provide our point of entry for considering the conundrum of camouflage in Ristelhueber's work, and the capacity of the aerial view not only to isolate and itemize disturbances in the ground, but also to conjure relations between remote times and spaces.

Mnemosyne may have appealed to Warburg not only for being the goddess of memory in Greek mythology, but also the Latin name for the clouded Apollo butterfly (*Parnassius mnemosyne*). During Warburg's three-year confinement at the Kreuzlingen sanatorium, Doctor Ludwig Binswanger made a journal entry noting that his patient "practices a cult with the moths and butterflies that fly into his room at night. He speaks to them for hours. He calls them his little soul animals [*Seelentierchen*] and tells them about his suffering."[53] Much has subsequently been made of Binswanger's entry, read together with a passing reference in a letter where Warburg compares the aerobatics of the *Pathosformel* to a butterfly. In his foreword for Philippe-Alain Michaud's *Aby Warburg and the Image in Motion*, the purple covers of which are decorated with a swarm of luminous butterflies, Georges Didi-Huberman speculates: "One might say that Warburg never managed—or wanted—to cure himself of his images. Was not speaking to butterflies for hours on end the definitive way of questioning the image as such, the living image, the *image-fluttering* that a naturalist's pin would only kill?"[54] As a paradigm for the latency of the image that suddenly "flits by," as well as for Warburg's own erratic and cross-disciplinary itineraries, butterflies have to be observed in their vibrant and unpredictable flight.[55] Pinned to a board and put under glass, we can no longer grasp the phantasmatic transformations of opening and closing. Able to disappear into its surroundings merely by folding its wings and turning into a gray branch, or by unfolding them to simulate the head of a predator, hunting for butterflies requires a gaze sensitized to the slightest disturbance in which a figure distinguishes itself from the ground.

It is in this undulation of figure and ground, species and habitat, that the delicate metaphor of the image-as-butterfly intersects with the more crude metaphor that was established in the previous chapter: that of the image as akin to the surface of the earth, and of the *Mnemosyne* atlas as a seismic instrument for eliciting the unseen energies that cause the earth to tremor. Notably, the first prototype of military camouflage was developed in the early twentieth century by the New England naturalist Abbott H. Thayer in a series of landscapes made out of butterfly wings and bird skin. Spurred by the Spanish-American War, Thayer experimented with chromatic variations, disruptive patterning and cut-up animal forms in order to demonstrate the defensive principles of mimicry and crypsis, and to promote its application in battle to deflect the enemy's attention. "Thayer's Law," coined in his neologism "countershading," refers to the effacement of contrasts between an organism and its milieu common to the species that he sought to emulate. The biotechnics of countershading therefore invert the techniques of landscape art, which conjures its illusion of solids, voids and volumetric depths by highlighting tonal and topographical contrasts and relief effects. Maggie M. Cao has interpreted "the squashed, mangled, and dispersed bodies that Thayer turned into brilliantly hued backgrounds" as prophetic of the dismemberment and dispersion soon to take place on the killing fields of the Great War.[56] Only in the hindsight of global warfare, Cao proposes, "could camouflage's implications of death-by-becoming-space" fully emerge from Thayer's disorienting picture puzzles.[57]

Thayer also conducted his investigations of background picturing and concealing coloration by means of ornamental materials used for interior decoration. Transposing the color patterns of birds and butterflies onto strips of wallpaper, flora and fauna were leveled into evenly speckled surfaces. In common with Thayer, Ristelhueber deliberately confounds the relation between domestic and geopolitical spaces by blurring the distinction between manmade and natural design. In *Vulaines* (1989), the artist makes the first of a series of revisits to the country estate in the village of Vulaines near the Fontainebleau forest where she spent her childhood summers. Framed low and positioned at floor level in the gallery, the large-format color photographs emulate a childlike engulfment into a world of mundane objects, which assume the dimensions of an unknown territory (Fig. 3.3). Moreover, the summerhouse is profuse with botanic forms: faded floral patterns squiggle on shower curtains, on brocades stained with mildew, and on the paper peeling off the walls, conveying the impression of an opulent but moldy orchard. Ristelhueber has subsequently reframed and re-photographed her inventory of the family house in different contexts and media projects, including *The Mysterious Barricades* (Les Barricades Mystérieuses, 1995) and *Fatigues* (2008–2009). “Why did I want to go back,” Ristelhueber ponders, followed by a characteristically disorienting turn of phrase, “to lean over the materials of this house as if I was working on an operative field?”[58] For the anatomist-artist, the materials of this house, with its fabrics and folds, facilitate topological nodes of contact between bourgeois interiors and military theaters of operation. This reciprocity was explicitly staged in the video installation *Fatigues*. Mounted on a dolly, the camera scans two magnified prints that have been applied like wallpaper in the studio to “act as a ‘natural setting’.”[59] The first setting is a bedroom in Vulaines: accompanied by chirping birds, the camera tracks back from a bedspread garnished with exotic plants to reveal a deep depression in the mattress and then the flat print itself, pasted onto the studio wall. The second setting was shot outside Basra in southern Iraq, showing a grove of charred palm trees cut in half by artillery fire. The voluptuous plants on the bedcover cut together with the decapitated trees not only suggest a failed garden, but a sudden loss of breath, which is one of the symptoms of fatigue. Along these lines, Ristelhueber speaks of how the low vantage point assumed in *Vulaines*, approximating the height of a five-year-old, was intended to convey at once enthrallment and oppression, a lost paradise and a nightmare, and a sensation that the heavy fabrics, furniture and narrow passages may, “prevent you from breathing.”[60] Ristelhueber adds: “I was an asthmatic child since the age of five, and asthmatics all have the same experience, they always wonder if there will be a next breath.”[61] Breathing is also alluded to in *Les barricades mystérieuses*, originally the title of a baroque harpsichord piece by François Couperin, whose rising and falling structure emulates the undulating wave of inhaling and exhaling.

Most recently, Ristelhueber returned to the summerhouse for her film *Pères* (Fathers, 2014), which was commissioned for the centennial commemoration of the First World War. This time, the inventory is accompanied by Franz Schubert’s arrangement of Goethe’s *Der Erlkönig (Mein Vater)*, where a young boy is assailed by supernatural visions that his father tries to rationalize as rising mist, rustling leafs and flickering willows. The treacherous setting of the nocturnal ride in Goethe’s ballad is transposed to the interior domains in Vulaines by the tracking camera,

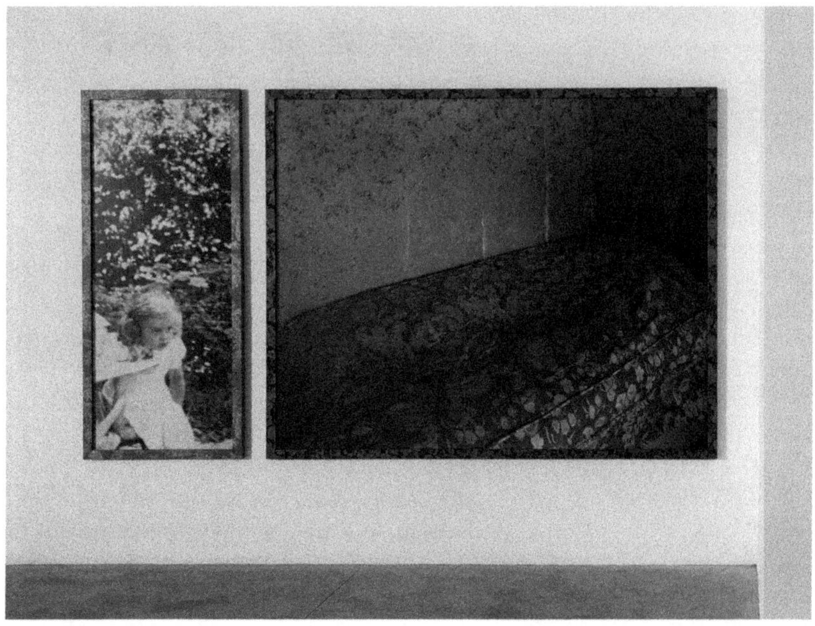

Fig. 3.3 Sophie Ristelhueber, *Vulaines III* (1989) © Sophie Ristelhueber / BONO, Oslo 2018. Diptych, color and black-and-white silver print, laminated on aluminum, with wallpaper-covered frame. Installation view at Galerie Joost Declercq, Ghent, 1989

as it scans the pipes and plumbing, and hovers above the padded armchairs and frayed carpets trodden for more than a century by members of the artist's family. Among them was her great-uncle, who was enlisted in the war in 1914 and perished two years later. When seen from a great height, as Félix Nadar mused on the very first aerial photograph that he made from a tethered balloon above Paris in 1858, "[t]he earth unfolds into an immense carpet."[62] Conversely, in the high-angle shots of *Pères*, the worn and muted textiles and scratches on wooden floors and tiles conjure the outlines of the equally enigmatic patterns recorded on the military surveillance missions above the trench-crossed frontlines of the Great War.

Whether made from a ladder or an airplane, in a desert or dining room, the vertical shot elicits an indeterminacy of scale: between interior and exterior realities, between prosaic and foreign, near and distant, carpet and earth. Counterpointing the defamiliarizing optics of the aerial gaze, intimate household objects frequently appear in the post-operational terrains framed by Ristelhueber's camera: a carpet that dangles out of a crushed apartment block in Beirut; a mattress that stuffs a wall blasted by a bazooka in Sarajevo; Scottish blankets and a chest of drawers washed over with sand in Kuwait. As the artist notes, "[s]uch 'still lifes' highlight the prosaic side of warfare. At the same time, once divorced from their purposes, objects too become abstractions."[63] By the same token, once divorced from their operative function, like the facts in Kuwait cut loose from scale and enveloped by a golden halo, instrumental images turn into objects. The same principle can be applied to operational language, as in the political slogans that Ristelhueber embroidered in red cross-stitch for *Stitches* (2005), or the military codenames that she assembled for the slideshow projection *Operations* (2007).

Ristelhueber's apprehension of the detritus of warfare as still lifes, ready-mades and concrete poems has inevitably raised the critique of aestheticization. This is a charge that frequently has been leveled against the genre of late photography more generally, reproaching the contemplative stillness of the aftermath aesthetics for numbing affect and obfuscating political stakes and agencies.[64] Much to the artist's dismay, *Fait* was translated into English as "Aftermath," and construed as a progenitor to what David Campany, in the wake of the attacks on the World Trade Center, detected as "a highly visible turn toward photographing the aftermath of events."[65] While an aftermath implies an anteceding event, however, the time-trace relationships constructed by Ristelhueber seem to evade such causal determinations. The temporal discord between the state-of-the-art technology of the coalition forces and the trenches dug by Iraqi troops in *Fait*, for instance, implies that there is more than one aftermath to account for. As Marc Mayer points out, the trench systems appear as a "futile and antiquarian" defensive strategy derived from the First World War.[66] This anachronistic element opens up an oblique terrain between two apparently remote conflicts, as the arbitrarily marked-up swaths of desert displayed in *Fait* invite us to ponder how the borders of the modern Middle East once were drawn, like lines in the sand, in the wake of the Great War. Constituted as a League of Nations mandate, the newly founded state of Iraq was placed under the vigilant eye of the British Air Force by colonial secretary Winston Churchill, who estimated that aerial bombardment was the most cost-effective means for policing the empire. We may also be reminded of this legacy by the single image included in *Fait* that Ristelhueber shot above Iraqi territory. It shows a lunar tract of heavily cratered ground, riddled by years of intense shelling during the Iran-Iraq war. Contrary to the "trashcan"[67] left in Kuwait by the Desert Storm campaign, this image more closely resembles the pockmarked fields recorded by Steichen's unit above the Western Front.[68] From yet another perspective, the aftermath is only the beginning. Submitted to the shock therapy of disaster capitalism, the Gulf Wars blasted open the free market for private contractors and postwar reconstruction.[69] Perceived in this light, *Fait* instead presents a site of anticipation: a prospect, in the double sense of the word. Hence, we may ask if Ristelhueber has arrived in the wake of a past event, or in the shadow of a future one. Indeed, where do we draw the line between the two?

As Frank Möller has pointed out, the aftermath remains a curiously unexamined concept in photographic theory. In light of the Tate Modern exhibition *Conflict, Time, Photography* in 2014, which included *Fait* in its entirety, Möller raises a series of salient questions about the temporal and causal relationships implied by the structural arc of the show, which was organized around aftermaths of various durations (hours, months, years). When does the aftermath begin, and when, if ever, does it end? Furthermore, he asks, "[w]hat comes after the aftermath?"[70] Maybe, then, we should rather take the aftermath as an incentive to question the assumptions that underlie the production of historical events, which appear to accelerate with each passing day? In her recent study *Aerial Aftermaths*, Caren Kaplan makes a similar case. Taking note of the Old English etymology of "aftermath," which originally referred to a second crop after a field had been harvested, she argues that the aftermath not only urges us to contemplate what has been lost, but, more importantly, what endures in the wake of conflicts and hostilities. The asymmetrical modes of power and governmentality instigated by the British aerial campaigns over Mesopotamia opened up a new field of uncontained and unaccountable violence that has muddled the border between war and peace, beginnings and endings, Kaplan writes, by "folding the past into the fluidly expansive 'colonial present'."[71] From the vantage point of airborne reconnaissance and retribution, the aftermath constitutes a political technology that operates in "a period of undeclared war."[72] In Iraq, this interlude extends from the Treaty of Versailles to the declaration of a War on Terror. A final iteration on the aftermath, one that literalizes the notion of a delayed and "deathly crop," is offered in Rob Nixon's account of the long-term effects of the depleted-uranium shells and undetonated munitions left in the wake of the First Gulf War.[73] As Nixon points out, it is not merely the boundaries between war and peace that are redrawn, but also between survivors and casualties, as the "slow violence" of toxins and land mines remains indefinitely active in cellular tissue and "inches beneath our planet's skin" after the operation was completed.[74] The queries raised by Möller, Kaplan and Nixon thus call for a closer scrutiny of the penumbral edge between the illuminated event and its eclipsed aftermaths. For the purpose of our present discussion, this prompts a consideration of the capacity of the aerial view to expose and estrange the face of the earth and the traces of time impressed upon it.

Evolving in tandem with the concealed nature of trench warfare, high-altitude reconnaissance depicts the surface of the earth, Jacques Derrida tells us, "devoid of any shadow, beneath the gaze, exposed to an all-powerful photographic apparatus."[75] It was the rapidly expanding domain of this omniscient surveillance machine that camouflage sought to escape. Implementing Thayer's experiments on the ground, a new form of landscape design emerged, planting ocular decoys and *tromp l'oeils* in the terrain in order to deflect enemy attention. Crafted from paint, canvas and cardboard, the surface of the earth was transformed, as Harun Farocki says, into "a world of pure military fiction."[76] Ironically, the disappearance of shadows, and therefore of forms, enacted by Thayer in his studio would become a decisive factor in the decryption of enemy terrain. On the large photographic prints, skewed or absent shadows served as a telltale sign that reality had been tampered with. Moreover, aviation held an unforeseen facility to disclose a new species of shadows, shadows that delineated the contours of a buried past. Hence, while the technical advancement of aerial reconnaissance was impelled by a causal logic—flying over the same sites, comparing before-and-after images, evaluating targets and assessing damage—the tilting of the earth also opened up a hitherto unrecognized temporal horizon. This returns us to the proposition that was advanced in the previous chapter: that the terrain, in common with the body, may suffer from recollections.

Chasing Shadows

In 2010, the story about the forensic team in search of butterflies in Kosovo spurred Jananne Al-Ani to embark on an aerial photography project, shooting two short films over southern Jordan with a camera mounted on a light aircraft. Al-Ani set out in pursuit of traces that, in common with the flickering rhythm of butterfly wings, can only be perceived in flight, and during the transient conditions when they open up and distinguish themselves from their surroundings. Instead of hunting butterflies, however, Al-Ani was chasing shadows.

The *Shadow Sites* films follow two distinct vectors. The first film soars above the desert floor, scanning the patterns left from Neolithic settlements and Roman forts to Ottoman trench systems and British mandate runways. The artist explains: "I wanted each shot that appeared in the films to include evidence of human occupation, reinforcing the basic principle in forensics that every single action, however discreet, leaves a mark."[77] These marks are organized chronologically as the glacially paced footage moves from the prehistoric to the present. The second film instead unfolds as an uninterrupted succession of zoom-ins. Plunging through a series of high-resolution photographs taken by a large-format camera, each zoom-in is followed by a dissolve into a new print. This device conveys the impression of a relentless decent, or, as glossed in the artist statement, "like a mineshaft tunneling deep into a substrate of memories preserved over time."[78] The submerged footprint of the past—burial mounds, plow lines, copper mines, Roman limes, irrigation systems—is graphically rendered as pale lines, murky stains, concentric circles and dark striations indelibly etched on the earth.

A shadow site is a technical term in the discourse of aerial archaeology. Seen from the air in the raking light at dawn or dusk, even low-lying features at ground level will cast long shadows. Aerial archaeology uncovered, by optical means, the land below as a palimpsest formed over millennia. Gradually illuminated in the first hour after sunrise, Al-Ani explains, the desert floor "acts as a photographic plate" summoning "the possibility of the landscape itself becoming a bearer of particularly resilient and recurring memories by exposing signs on the surface, not only of loss but also of survival."[79] Periodically revealed in the low sun, these mnestic inscriptions are analogous to a latent image, which remains invisible during the lag-time between exposure and development.

The method of aerial archaeology evolved out of the discoveries of ancient earthworks that appeared, so to speak, out of the blue on the photographic prints made on routine reconnaissance missions during the First World War. Hence, a technology utilized to monitor ballistic paths and troop movements opened up a lens toward the past. To paraphrase Sekula, instrumental images retroactively gained the status of archaeological artifacts. A similar chance discovery made from an aircraft during the Great War has been credited to Marc Bloch. Transferred to serve as an intelligence officer to supervise reconnaissance reports, it was while observing the crisscrossing patterns of the trenches, dugouts and shell craters that Bloch first conceived of the notion of a *longue durée*.[80] Flattening topography into a geometrical grid, the steep angulation and inhuman scale of aerovison conjured the unconscious and invisible dimensions of a long-term history. It was precisely such an anatomized view of slowly evolving structures that the *Annales* School of French social historiography that Bloch founded together with Lucien Febvre in the following decade sought to discern. Fernand Braudel, who led the second era of the *Annales* School, referred to this previously unexplored dimension as a "geo-history," described by him as, "that other, submerged history, almost silent and always discreet."[81] From a great height, the past, which we associate with depth and distance, is transformed into a spatial plane where events (and figures) diminish, while the aftermath (and ground) is endowed with an agency and afterlife of its own.

Al-Ani borrows the metaphoric notion of the earth as a latent image from Kitty Hauser's book-length study of the phenomenon of shadow sites photography.[82] Elaborating on the revelatory capacity of aerial archaeology, Hauser takes recourse to three exemplary cases of the indexical image. First, by characterizing the miraculous apparition of the past in the low sun as a form of *acheiropoietos*.[83] Advanced during the Byzantine era as an argument against iconoclasm, an acheiropoieta is an image made without the intervention of human hands, like the Shroud of Turin or The Veil of Veronica. These Christian relics are also crucial for Didi-Huberman's conceptualization of the "contact image." Second, the author compares the shadow site to a photogram, where a negative shadow image is created by placing an object on a sheet of photosensitized paper and exposing it to light. Man Ray pioneered this technique of cameraless photography in his *rayographs* from the early 1920s. Third, Hauser relates the notion of the latent image to Freud's archaeology of the human psyche. Like an exposed but yet undeveloped film, the unconscious preserves mnestic traces that, under the right conditions, may once again come to light. Indeed, in *Moses and Monotheism*, Freud likens the resurfacing of latent memories from oblivion "with a photographic exposure which can be developed after any interval of time and transformed into a picture."[84] According to Freud, memory therefore not only entails a process of inscription and storage, but also of exposure and development.

We will return to Bloch's notion of the *longue durée*, to Man Ray's photographic experiments, and to Didi-Huberman's contact image in due time. Notably, each of these paradigms poses anew the question of figure (trace) and ground (earth, paper, unconscious). To this triad of indexes, I want to add Warburg's conception of the engram, a term that he appropriated from Richard Semon's 1906 study *Die Mneme*. In neuropsychology, the engram refers to a physical alteration in the neural tissue resulting from an external impact or stimulus stored as a memory trace. For Warburg, however, and in contrast to the various manifestations of the trace in the examples given by Hauser, the ground where mnestic impressions are buried evades locatability. Rather, it designates a non-place, as the spark that reactivates the past is ignited in the intermediary space of a *Zwischenraum*. According to Warburg's biographer Ernst Gombrich, Semon's notion of the engram is predicated on the assumption that, "memory is not a property of consciousness but the one quality which distinguishes living from dead matter. It is the capacity to react to an event over a period of time; that is, a form of preserving and transmitting energy not known to the physical world."[85] This distinction raises the question of the relation between memory and matter in Ristelhueber's work. Her interest is primarily in the form, the residual mark, regardless of the material where it appears. Yet, these materials—mineral, tarmac, concrete, textile—are relentlessly apprehended by the artist as corporeal entities: the entrails spilling out of the gutted buildings in Beirut; the mesh of nerves in the underbelly of Versailles; the "blackened palm trees, charred and strewn like a routed army" in Iraq[86]; or the off-kilter buildings in Armenia shattered by an earthquake that appear "like destabilized bodies, leaning forward, backward."[87] In light of Ristelhueber's trope of an anatomy lesson, it is noteworthy that prior to entering the discourse of psychoanalysis, trauma was a surgeons' term that referred to a physical, rather than a mental, injury inflicted in battle.[88] Cognate with trauma, which confounds the distinction between interior and exterior wounds, the engrams focalized by Ristelhueber thus invalidate the basis of Gombrich's anthropocentric definition of the engram. Instead of separating living and dead matter, it stitches them together.

Open Tombs

The *Shadow Sites* films belong to a larger project called "The Aesthetics of Disappearance: A Land Without People" (2007–ongoing). It investigates the capacity of photography not only to retain but also to remove from view, and to eradicate physical as well as virtual bodies from its field of vision. The first part of the title is an expression first coined by Paul Virilio in his 1975 investigation of the remnants of the Atlantikwall in *Bunker Archaeology*, and a concept that he continued to develop throughout his subsequent writings. The advent of the aesthetics of disappearance is traced by Virilio to the use of concealing colorations during the First World War, where camouflage simultaneously instigated a disembodiment of combatants and a deterritorialization of the battlefield.[89] As the second half of the title ("A Land Without People") signals, the particular aesthetics of disappearance that Al-Ani is concerned with, the disembodied and disembodying perspective of aerial surveillance, is historicized with regard to the orientalist imaginary of the Middle East as a depopulated and immemorial desert.

Before returning to Ristelhueber, let us briefly consider two such vanishing acts, both cited by Al-Ani as key sources for the conceptualization of the *Shadow Sites* project.[90] The first was performed by Antoine Poidebard, an air force officer and archaeologist working in the French Mandate zone of the so-called *Levant* states (literally, the *rising*, i.e. the land where the sun rises in the East). In his 1933 picture atlas *La Trace de Rome* (The Trace of Rome), Poidebard exploited the novel method for photographical detection of archaeological sites from oblique angles with illuminating backlight. As Daniel K. Helbig has pointed out, however, Poidebard utilized the technology of shadow sites photography to facilitate a highly selective map, not only of the past but also in terms of its bearings on the present, with the explicit purpose to align the French Mandate with the ancient Roman frontier toward the East.[91] From the right angle and altitude, the traces of Arab occupation could be brushed aside and an imperial legacy recovered from the desert sand.

The second vanishing act appears between two photographic prints made by the German archaeologist Ernst Herzfeld during his campaigns to Iran and Iraq in the first decades of the twentieth century. Notably, Herzfeld did not merely photograph artifacts and architecture but also the vast desert expanses surrounding the archaeological sites, which he framed in elongated, sepia-toned panoramas. In particular, it was a pair of photographs printed from the same negative, depicting the great archway of the ancient city of Ctesiphon on the banks of Tigris, which attracted Al-Ani's attention. In the first test print, the photographer casts his shadow in the foreground. For the second version, Herzfeld has retouched the image in order to efface his presence from the scene.

While the *Shadow Sites* films invite a number of comparisons to Ristelhueber's work, in particular to the airborne frames of *Fait*, the traces that they respectively chart adhere to two markedly distinct temporal logics. Countering the myth of the desert as devoid of civilization, the relic traces revealed by Al-Ani perform a sort of redemption of the disavowed histories of the Middle East. Strung together into a chronological chain from the prehistoric to the present, the dissolves convey the impression of a single take fluidly traversing time. Ristelhueber, as we have seen, prefers the broken itinerary. Contrary to the immersive logic of Al-Ani's desert epic, cuts are not soothed over but brought into stark juxtapositions. The prevalence of wounded and disfigured bodies, animate or inanimate, attests to this need to break things open. As simply stated by the artist: "When an object is broken, it is seen better. It seems undressed."[92] In similar terms, Maurice Blanchot has remarked, "that a tool, when damaged, becomes its *image*." That is to say, when rendered inoperative, "the tool, no longer disappearing into its use, *appears*."[93] Denuded, robbed of utility, divorced from their operative dimension, things appear: like Beirut after the withdrawal of the Israeli army, described by the artist as, "a city undressed."[94]

The archway of Ctesiphon also features in a retouched image made by Ristelhueber. It is one of the *Eleven Blowups* that she created in 2006 in response to the recent newsreel footage of a crater left in a street in Beirut after the bombing of Lebanon's former Prime Minister Rafic Hariri's motorcade. The series was based on digitally manipulated stills drawn from video rushes retrieved from the Reuters agency in London: "I was looking for pictures of the craters—the 'tombs'—that open up in the ground in Iraq several times a week, or even a day."[95] Probing the news archive, she waited for the moment when the camera lens offered a glimpse of the shell-shocked ground after a suicide attack. From these poor-resolution images, transmitted via satellite, Ristelhueber then fabricated a series of eleven craters by digitally amalgamating the found footage with raw materials drawn from her previous work. Cut together from twenty-five years of debris collected from the Middle East to Central Asia, the ancient ruins of Ctesiphon outside Baghdad could then serve as the backdrop for a crater from the 1988 earthquake in Armenia.

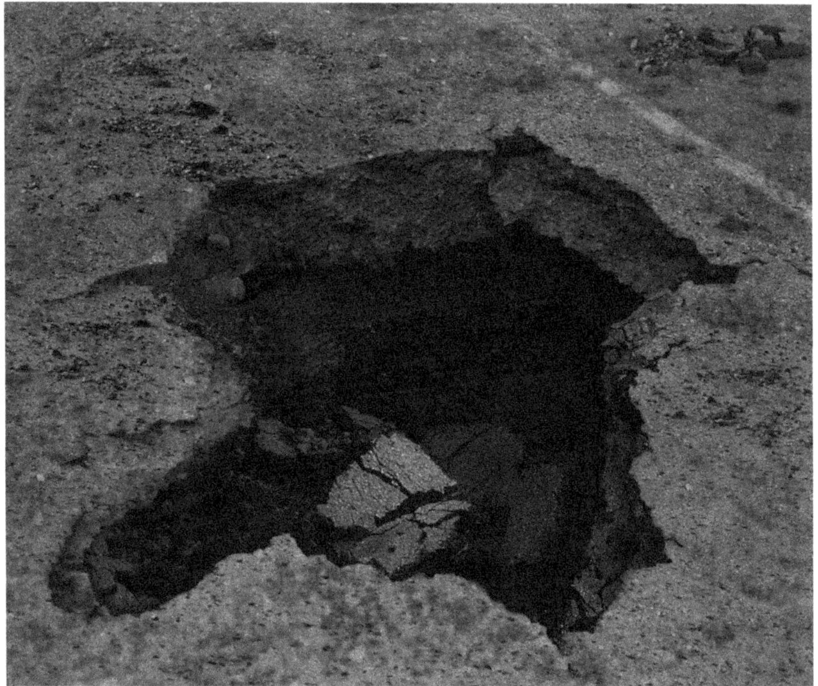

Fig. 3.4 Sophie Ristelhueber, *Eleven Blowups #11* (2006) © Sophie Ristelhueber / BONO, Oslo 2018. Color silver print mounted on aluminum and framed

"What prompted me to make these pictures was the impression that the ground was ripped by the shock," Ristelhueber explains, "as if the earth was sucked out from its own centre. I was inspired by the idea of earth charged with history swallowing itself up."[96] Augmenting the analogy between the photographic *prints*, affixed onto a wall or a piece of cardboard, and the material *imprints* they depict, *Eleven Blowups* blatantly conflates the violence of the photographic act (the blow-up) and of the subject matter (the crater), one that was of little interest to the local correspondents who shot the footage (Fig. 3.4). In common with Al-Ani, then, Ristelhueber is engaged with an aesthetics of disappearance. The torn-up ground also figures two additional forms of disappearances: first, the split second in which a body detonates and disappears; second, the event of a place suddenly deprived of its former identity, when it ceases to be a road, a city or a desert.

An analogous practice of cross-cutting informs Ristelhueber's use of literary sources and quotations. For *Beirut*, she selected a passage from Lucretius' two-thousand-year-old poem *On the Nature of Things*; for *Mémoires du Lot*, the prologue from *The Book of Ecclesiastes*; for *Fait*, two excerpts from Clausewitz's *On War* written during the Napoleonic era; and for *Every One*, Thucydides' *The History of the Peloponnesian War* from the fifth century BC. Similar stratifications of the ancient and recent past are highlighted in *Beirut*, which concludes with an image of the temple columns at Baalbek, and in *Dead Set* (2001), where deserted housing projects in Syria are shown next to rows of antique colonnades.

Illuminating in this regard is an episode recalled by Ristelhueber in her conversation with Catherine Grenier. It concerns a visit to Iraq three years before the invasion of the US-led coalition when an archaeologist showed her the excavation site of Babylon. She describes this experience "[a]s a moment of reconciliation with myself, as if I were at the junction point between −2000 and +2000," at once "in the midst of all these strata accumulated over millennia" but also "in the heart of Iraqi news—above my head passed the famous British and American reconnaissance mission—and at the same time I returned thousands year back."[97] In recent years, this allusive anecdote has accrued an additional layer of irony. From Sabratha to Palmyra, Roman amphitheaters and victory arches have set the stage for a current theater of war, with frontlines strategically drawn on ancient military strongholds. A war waged on archaeology and funded by looted antiquities, the Islamic State did not merely demolish the heritage sites; it also buried the dust to prevent their future reconstruction. Dust, which is the tiniest material manifestation of traces and photographic emulsions alike, as well as the lowest common denominator of figure and ground, body and earth, will be our principle concern for the remainder of this chapter.

An Atlas of Dust

Let us return here for a moment to James Elkins' claim, cited at the beginning of Chapter 2, that looking at the view is like looking at the gaps between looking. It is precisely such gaps, or what Elkins terms "the surround," that is at the center of attention of his book *What Photography Is*. The surround is the seemingly irrelevant, blurred or nondescript areas indiscriminately recorded by the camera, like the swaths of cratered ground accidently caught on film by local correspondents in Iraq, or the pockmarked concrete behind a grieving mother in Beirut. The surround challenges the viewer's attention by revealing so little, Elkins suggests; or rather, what it reveals is "something about the world's own deadness, its inert resistance to whatever it is we may hope or want."[98] In certain specialized fields of photography, the surround is advanced as the primary object of interest, as is the case in re-photography projects of geological surveys, or photographs scrutinized by forensic analysts in order to track down the location of a crime. A particularly pertinent case for our current discussion is *The Particle Atlas* (1967), which was assembled by the McCrone Research Institute in Chicago for the purpose of identifying various specimens of dust. Elkins' preference is not only for "faceless pictures," then, but for ostensibly pointless ones, as in the various distractions that he itemizes as "rocks… splotches and stains, cracks … errant dust, blooms of mould."[99] Denied of a subject or story to identify with, a scene to attach one's memories to, or even the reward of recognition, the surround, Elkins writes, refuses to "help my eye escape."[100] Unable to escape, however, "I recognize myself seeing—and that is exactly because I do not register what I am seeing."[101]

From the perspective of Elkins' ontological inquiry, we may say that the art of Ristelhueber is devoted to the surround, to the anonymous background that we fail to register. Along these lines, she has referred to *Fait* as "a statement on how little we see."[102] The comment paraphrases the puzzled reactions of the international forces pilots she persuaded to take her onboard their aircraft ("Why are you going into the desert? … There's absolutely nothing to see").[103] It also anticipates the artist's own belated discovery, when she recognized in one of her prints what she almost two decades later came to acknowledge as "a foundational image" for her work (Fig. 3.5).[104] Ristelhueber explains:

> I was flying over the desert and knew exactly what I was looking for: all those traces, the lines of the trenches. I was so excited I didn't realise that what I was looking at echoed *Dust Breeding*, a famous photograph by Man Ray. It wasn't until I got home and saw the contact sheet that I spotted the connection. … If you compare it with my shot, you'd think it was ingrained in my head. At the time, I was embarrassed. I put it away: I thought it looked too obvious, like I'd copied Man Ray. But I eventually showed it. I call it *Because of Dust Breeding*.[105]

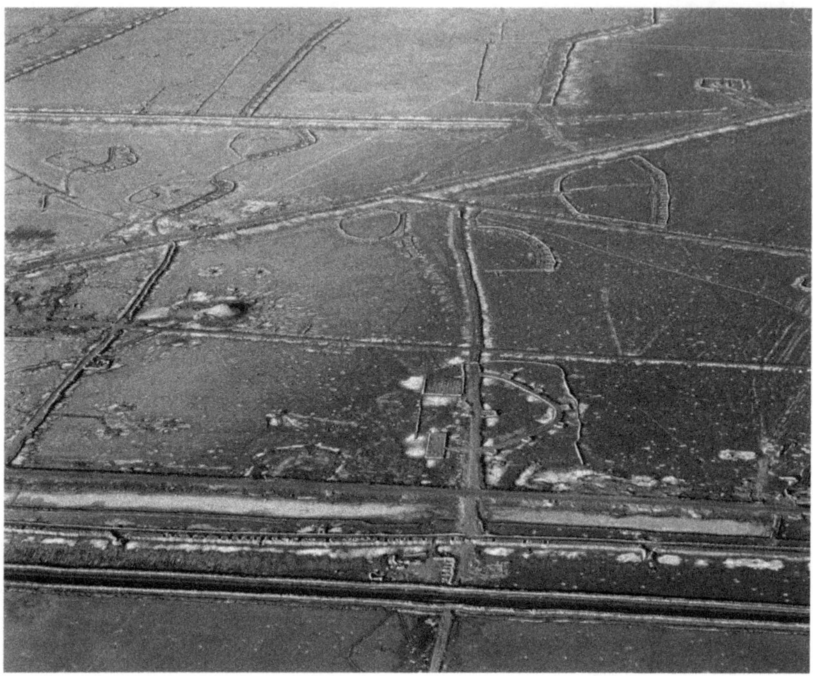

Fig. 3.5 Sophie Ristelhueber, *A cause de l'Elevage de poussière* (*Because of the Dust Breeding*, 1991–2007) © Sophie Ristelhueber / BONO, Oslo 2018. Black-and-white photograph, pigment print on paper mounted on aluminum and framed under Plexiglas

At once transient (an echo) and tenacious (ingrained), both hidden and obvious, the image belatedly recognized by Ristelhueber resurfaces as a *Pathosformel*. With a more general implication, I propose that we may understand this foundational image as a formula for the construction of alternative, and relational, geographies. Pursuing this expressive form as it extends in numerous directions across Ristelhueber's work will also provide an opportunity to reassess the category of late photography, not as the record of an aftermath, but in terms of delay and duration, repercussions and premonitions, or what Warburg called *Nachleben*, afterlife.

Man Ray's *Dust Breeding* depicts the backside of the lower section of Marcel Duchamp's sculpture *The Bride Stripped Bare by Her Bachelors, Even* (La Mariée mise à nu par ses célibataires, même, 1915–1923), also known as *The Large Glass* (Le Grand Verre). Duchamp had mounted one of the glass panes face down on sawhorses near an open window in his New York studio, allowing dust to gather over a period of six months. Originally intended as a document of a work-in-progress, Man Ray later cropped the photograph on all sides in order to simulate a bird's-eye view. Through this simple intervention, the dust-strewn glass was transfigured into arid reaches of land with low ranges or sand dunes and marks of human habitation spreading across its surface. In support of this reading, the picture was captioned *View from an Airplane* (Vue prise en aeroplane par Man Ray—1921) upon its first public appearance in the Dadaist journal *Littérature* in October 1922. Furthermore, the oblique angle of Man Ray's camera portended the method of shadow sites photography. Cast in relief by the slanting light, the branching network of lead foil and fuse wire became redolent of an archaeological site, suggestive of geoglyphs of a long-lost civilization, or "an excavation of some Roman imperial building complex."[106]

Ristelhueber's *Because of the Dust Breeding* (A cause de l'Elevage de poussière) is dated 1991–2007, spanning sixteen years from the first Gulf War, which was glossed by Baudrillard as a "war stripped bare by its technicians even."[107] Transposing Duchamp's land of dust to the desert battlefield in the Persian Gulf, Ristelhueber replays in reverse Man Ray's counterfeit aerial photograph, thereby opening up a series of relations that allow the facts of the Gulf War to be discerned through the fiction of Man Ray's aerial view. In this context, it is noteworthy that Duchamp began working on *The Large Glass* in 1915 during his first year of exile in the USA to escape the First World War. This was also the year when the first British aerial patrol arrived in Mesopotamia, never to be dismantled.[108] From this perspective, *Because of the Dust Breeding* abbreviates a legacy of desert wars from 1915 to 1991.

While early interpreters of Man Ray's photograph tended to note its resemblance to an archaic or extraterrestrial site, later readings, inflected by Sekula's and Virilio's research into the synergies of aviation and warfare, have instead associated it with the blasted no man's land of the Western Front as recorded by Steichen's reconnaissance corps. Defoliated and devoid of recognizable landmarks, the territory displayed on these prints appeared doubly transformed: first by the high-powered artillery fire, and then by the high-altitude vantage point. Revealing the inhuman scale of destruction along the trench lines, the airborne imagery formalized an abstract optics of modern warfare that evacuated human agents from the scene but maintained the traces of their actions. "The landscape had the transparency of glass," as Ernst Jünger reflected in his Western Front memoir *Storms of Steel* (In Stahlgewittern, 1920).[109] Toppled over from a natural space of immersion to a table of operation, like a body turned into glass under the anatomist's eye, the countryside was exposed to the onslaughts of air raids and dive-bombers. Moreover, the terrain was stripped bare of the familiar array of spatial cues that undergirded the formula of landscape art. Pushing the ground upwards and pressing figures downwards, perspectival space was crushed into a flat all-over picture plane, or what a British Royal Air Force atlas referred to as "futurist" or "cubist" country.[110] Toward the end of the war, however, as Steichen's records demonstrate, this futuristic domain appeared more like a formless, prehistoric muck. As summed up by Paul K. Saint-Amour in his analysis of the corollary discourses of wartime reconnaissance and avant-garde formalism:

> Aerial photographs possessed the conceit of laying reality bare by their deadly accuracy, their vertical penetration, their plenitude or even excess of detail, and their ability to reveal facts, objects, and strategic intentions not otherwise accessible. But this realist conceit was mitigated by an accompanying insistence on the defamiliarizing power of the vertical view, on the sense that even the reality beneath the enemy's camouflage was self-camouflaging, and on the need for new codes by which a highly trained interpretive elite could decipher the camouflage of the real.[111]

Doubling this conceit, *Dust Breeding* suggested that new interpretive protocols were in demand not only in order to decrypt the modern battlefield, but also the modern work of art. This idea has been elaborated at length by David Campany, who in 2015 curated an entire exhibition around Man Ray's photograph.[112] In his catalogue essay, *A Handful of Dust*, Campany argues that *Dust Breeding* heralded a profound change for the interpretation of artwork in the twentieth century: "Making sense of it would not be a matter of subjective response so much as puzzling it out, like a forensic detective sifting clues at a crime scene."[113] While it may be argued that all photographs are forensic in the sense that they record details that escape the human eye in order to preserve them for later scrutiny, this notion attains a particular poignancy when applied to the dust-covered "bachelor machine"[114] framed by Man Ray.

First, we may note that the burgeoning discourse of forensic science was founded on dust. In its inaugural treatise, "The Analysis of Dust Traces" from 1929, the French criminologist Edmond Locard meticulously describes various methods for collecting, categorizing and examining dust, a substance that he defines as, "the mute evidence, sure and faithful, of all our movements and all our encounters."[115] In *Dust Breeding*, this mute evidence, to borrow a phrase from Locard, "completely covers the surface of the earth."[116] Pondering the paradoxical notion of breeding dust, David Hopkins takes note of how T.S. Eliot's *The Wasteland*, whose first publication coincided with that of *Dust Breeding*, conjured "a similarly weird mix of bareness and the stirrings of new life."[117] The crime scene obliquely reflected in Duchamp's dust-laden glass, he further conjectures, is the killing fields of the Great War. Framing the lower half of the Bachelors' domain on Duchamp's sculpture, Hopkins contends that *Dust Breeding* conveys "a paradoxical male fertility, in an age that had seen the men of his native France slaughtered in their thousands."[118] Three years after *The Wasteland* and *Dust Breeding*, we may add, F. Scott Fitzgerald similarly envisioned, "the valley of ashes, a fantastic farm where ashes grow like wheat into ridges and hills and grotesque gardens."[119] Considering the long-term vantage point that Ristelhueber frequently adopts on her subject matters, however, a more ancient source, which the artist quoted as the epigraph for *Beirut*, may provide us with the most apt reflection on such terraforming energies. In a passage from *On the Nature of Things*, the Roman philosopher and poet Lucretius meditates on how the activities of dust particles become visible in the rays of daylight that break into a darkened room: "you will see many minute bodies in many ways through the apparent void mingle in the midst of the light of the rays, and as in never ending conflict, skirmish and give battle, combating in troops and never halting." From this observation, Lucretius infers that "a small thing may give an illustration of great things and put you on the track of knowledge."[120]

These observations prompt a brief return to the provincial summerhouse in Vulaines. While apparently remote from the operational fields of geopolitics, this stuffy and confined world, abandoned except for the summer, yields signatures that spread from the desert storms of the Far East to the storms of steel on the Western Front. In *Pères*, "Fathers," Hopkins' notion of an ominous paternal fertility looms large as the vertical imagery of the ornate botanic forms on threadbare carpets analogically figures the bizarrely patterned theater of the Great War as surveyed by an airborne camera. The founding experience conveyed by Ristelhueber in these domestic inventories, that of being devoured by space and deprived of breath, has its formal correlate in the vertical view, which cuts out breathing space and levels bodies and terrains onto a single plane. The interiors miniaturized and magnified into remote terrains through the lens of Ristelhueber and Man Ray further instantiate a reversibility between inside and outside, the intimate and remote. *Dust Breeding* precipitates such a suspension of binary terms, straddling the border between interior and exterior (the studio loft and the aerial view), archaic and current (archaeological site and modern battlefield), visibility and invisibility (territorial expanses and specks of dust), transparency and opacity (the dust-coated glass), transience and permanence (a small section of the dust was coated with clear varnish while the rest of the glass was wiped clean). Dust, furthermore, defies territorial boundaries as well as temporal containment. As Carolyn Steedman notes, dust "is about circularity, the impossibility of things disappearing, or going away, or being gone."[121] This warrants a concluding remark on the time-trace relationships opened up by Ristelhueber between *The Large Glass* and the post-operational field in Kuwait.

Duchamp subtitled his sculpture "a delay in glass."[122] Exposed over the course of an hour, Man Ray's *Dust Breeding* augments this delay through its doubled indexicality (the particles of the pulverized matter and particles of light crystalized as silver salts). *Because of the Dust Breeding* extends the Duchampian delay further. First, there is the protracted duration of the artworks themselves: the six months of accumulating dust and the hour-long exposure of Man Ray's photograph; the six months that passed between the Gulf War and *Fait*; and the arc of seventeen years comprised in the title of Ristelhueber's late homage. Then, there is the long duration of the work that it depicts: the slow violence of dust as it moves across numerous scales. Dust is a by-product of the human body, compounded of skin flakes, hair and secretions, pulverized and airborne. Mountains erode into dust over eons, and cities attacked from above are ground to dust within a matter of hours. Dust accumulates and is swept away, just like the marks recorded in *Fait* were first inflicted, and then erased, by Desert Storm, by a power foreign to the land that it marks and sweeps.

Itself a cluster of traces, the terrain of *Dust Breeding* is entirely made of aftermath, a deposit of spent energies, literalizing Irit Rogoff's notion of an "exhausted geography." The gathering of marks and traces, on Duchamp's *Large Glass* as well as on the glass-plate in Man Ray's camera, has made *Dust Breeding* a seminal reference point in photographic theory. Indeed, Rosalind Krauss has argued that Duchamp was the first to connect photography with the semiotic category of the index, speculating that *The Large Glass* was, in fact, conceived by the artist "as a kind of photograph."[123] Krauss' reading of Duchamp's *Large Glass* further endows it with the characteristics of a crime scene, as she notes that "the signs it bears are organized as traces, deposited there like footprints left in sand, or the rings that icy glasses leave on tables. They are imprints rather than images, striking a receptive surface—like that of nervous tissue."[124] This associative leap from inert matter to neural tissue precisely recaps the bifurcated nature of the trace in Ristelhueber's work.

Our question is therefore how "the problem of art," as Ristelhueber put it, relates to the problem of time and historical discourse. This was also the problem that spurred Warburg in his construction of the *Mnemosyne* atlas. Furthermore, as we saw above, it underlines Frank Möller's problematization of the categories of "late" or "aftermath" photography, terms that inevitably seem predicated on a history of happenings, of events taking place one after the other. In each case, it is the event of war that triggers this inquiry. Along these lines, Didi-Huberman has argued that the *Mnemosyne* primarily should be understood as a tool for rethinking historical relations in the wake of the disasters of the First World War. Seeking to grasp the knowledge pursued through the atlas's spatial and temporal dislocations and disorienting reversals of scale, Didi-Huberman identifies an elective affinity between the critiques of positivist historicity that was formulated by the *Annales* School, founded in 1929, and the *Bilderatlas*, left unfinished at Warburg's death the same year. This criticism respectively hinged on the concepts of *longue durée* and *Nachleben*, both terms which denote a long-term survival, cautioning the researcher not to dramatize history as a linear succession of causally driven events.

For the new school of historiography in France, the notion of a *longue durée* implemented a geological sensibility of deep time, strata and morphology into the social sciences, facilitating a shift from an event-based history, focused on individual biographies and decisive battles, toward slowly evolving structures. In analogy to Ferdinand Braudel, the geographer turned historian, Warburg, the art historian turned cartographer, espoused a turn away from individual artists and aesthetic canons toward the long-term migration of expressive forms. And just as *longue durée* "approximates physical geography,"[125] Warburg's cartographic metaphor implements a spatial stratification of time. Addressing these parallel projects within the context of the upheavals of the First World War, Didi-Huberman further compares the visual material that was gathered by Marc Bloch and Lucien Febvre while they served on the front line, including photographs, maps and drawings that documented the devastation of the war, and the documents assembled by Warburg in his *Kriegskartothek*, by which he sought to keep "track of the *trench lines*, those 'schisms' produced in Europe's soil which engulfed men by the millions."[126] Warburg thus conceived of the war as another instance of the "reawakening of antiquity,"[127] whose demons erupted in the zigzagging patterns of the fortified entrenchments, retraced by Warburg's pen like errant stitches on the map. In *The Surviving Image*, Didi-Huberman calls attention to the graphic similarity between these ink drawings and the erratic scribbles, "contorted, multidirectional and contradictory,"[128] which fill Warburg's notebooks during his descent into psychosis. Didi-Huberman reads these jagged lines as the inscriptions of a broken seismograph. This invites us to understand the *Mnemosyne* atlas as a critical response to the problem posed by the *Kriegskartothek*, a problem that required "a new form of visual knowledge"[129] able to restore the distance from where these unruly energies may again become legible, implementing a long-term historical view that doesn't succumb to a history of events (glossed by the *Annales* scholars as a *histoire événementielle*).[130] Didi-Huberman defines this new epistemic mode as "analytical knowledge, knowledge through cuts, re-framings or 'dissections'."[131]

Ristelhueber instills this analytical distance by other means. Instead of the "emotive intensity" and "agitated mobility"[132] fossilized in the *Pathosformeln* as conceived by Warburg, "the terrain of the real and of collective emotion" is mapped through details and facts that are overtly static and inert, cut from a cause. Their impression as "mute evidence," to borrow Locard's phrase, is further enhanced by the palpable stillness that a recently deserted place exudes. Like Warburg, Ristelhueber highlights the at once formalized and hidden aspects of the trace, but instead of windblown hair and garments, she attends to the discarded objects left after a great wind has swept the land. In their own distinct way, however, both facilitate a migration—between East and West, prosaic and foreign, near and distant—*through* the agency of forms. "The dumb fact of the willful mark, the elusive *ur*-sign of art and language, is the point of departure for most of her work" Marc Mayer reflects, "as if attempting to outline the ultimate boundaries of signification."[133] In similar terms, Didi-Huberman notes that Ristelhueber's work "carries the use value of the document to a point of intensity where each photograph seems to demonstrate both the silence of the event and the cry left by its trace."[134] This point of intensity is also a "quilting point" or "time knot," a point of jointure around which various times and places gather and scatter.[135] Ann Hindry refers to it as "a crisis point."[136] Moreover, Hindry succinctly notes that it is precisely the semantically voided character of Ristelhueber's images, drained of narrative context, which allows for the "semantic leap from human body to landscape."[137] Through this procedure, mute traces can become "conveyors of crosswise, universal, and possibly renewable signs."[138] Cut from topicality and stripped of contextualizing information and discursive frameworks, traces are endowed with the ability to migrate across the post-operative planes mapped by the artist, whether mineral, carnal or architectonic. Paradoxically, then, it is their inanimate nature (from the Latin *anima*, meaning a current of air or breath) that enables their survival.

Rubbing History the Wrong Way

The gestures of retracing considered above, and the set of analogical relationships that they engender—between figure and ground, body and earth, photography and topography, forensic analysis and formal abstraction—converge in a remarkably condensed form in the two works to which I want to devote the final pages of this chapter. In common with Ristelhueber and Al-Ani, the artistic practice of Belgian filmmaker Sarah Vanagt relies on extensive fieldwork. A number of her short films pivot on the construction of relational geographies, vacillating between carefully choreographed explorations of the monumental architecture and statuary of Brussels and projects that adopt a direct cinema approach, shot on location in the nation's former colonies in Congo and Rwanda. The two films that concern us here both deal with the exhumation of mass-burial sites in the aftermath of civil war.

Shot in the winter of 2010, *Dust Breeding* follows the trial of Radovan Karadžić at the International Criminal Tribunal of the Former Yugoslavia (ICTY) in the Hague. More specifically, it engages with the forensic

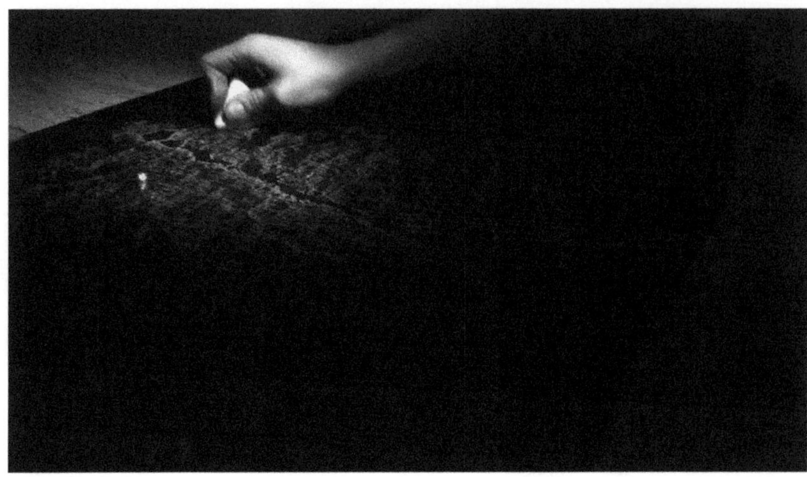

Fig. 3.6 Sarah Vanagt *Dust Breeding* (2013). Lobby Floor. Courtesy of the artist

imagery of atrocity sites in Bosnia and Herzegovina, retrieved from the online ICTY Court Records Database by means of search terms such as "*crater*, *surface*, *residue*, *exhumation*. Everything to do with surface," as Vanagt explains.[139] During the proceedings, these satellite images are arranged as diptychs for comparative analysis. On the screen, the murky footage of areas of disturbed earth are inscribed with colorful lines, dots, circles and arrows, made with marker pens by invisible hands. The task of the prosecution is to translate these abstract signs into events, into palpable trajectories of bodies being dragged and soil broken. As the analysis proceeds, relayed by monitors, earphones and expert witnesses, a scratching sound intrudes on the soundtrack, emerging from a different kind of interface between a moving hand and a static surface (Fig. 3.6).

Vanagt responds to the hearings by making a series of rubbings on a thin fabric material, either by rubbing a granite pencil on a long roll of white silk paper, or by rubbing a white wax crayon over black silk paper. The rubbings cover the floor of the tribunal's entrance hall, the glass panel between the courtroom and the public gallery, the desk of the judges, the seat of the defendant, the microphone of the witness, the control panel of the TV booth, and the exterior balustrade of the ICTY building. The project was inspired by Didi-Huberman's concept of the contact image, variously defined by him as "(i)mage obstacles ... images that surface and skim ... modeled by shadow ... carved by exposure time," and, most pertinently in the context of Vanagt's film, as "[i]mages that move our hand."[140] In *Dust Breeding*, the indiscriminate rubbings generate a topographical record, a relief image that deposits marks of elevations and depressions in a textured surface. Rubbing, or *frottage*, was introduced as a technique of surrealist automatism by Max Ernst in the 1920s, and later resumed by Henri Michaux who referred to them as "apparitions." As the image obtained by this procedure is transmitted from below, as opposed to attacking the canvas as a "field of operation" from above in Abstract Expressionist drip or action painting,[141] frottage goes against the high modernist tenet of the gestural trace as the true mark of spontaneity, expressivity and artistic temperament. In common with the surrealist draftsman, Vanagt's compulsive gesture constitutes a form of automatic writing, as the latent marks that are rubbed into visibility preexist her intervention. Recalling the surreal landscapes that Ernst collected in the volume *Histoire Naturelle* (1926), rubbed forth from floorboards, bread crumbs and wire mesh, Vanagt's rubbings not merely index the traces of the Tribunal, they also serve as analogical representations of the remote sites investigated during the courtroom proceedings.

In contrast to the pixelated satellite images screened at the ICTY, the specks of carbonaceous dust or wax particles more closely resemble photographic grains. Facilitating an analogue transfer from one surface to another, Vanagt's rubbings precisely corroborate Susan Sontag's definition of photography as, "something directly stenciled off the real."[142] The procedure is also overtly forensic, not merely by being performed within the space of the forum, from which the term forensics derives, but also in its blunt application of Locard's Exchange Principle, which stipulates that, "every contact leaves a trace." Furthermore, as Berber Bevernage notes, the rubbings are "reminiscent of the forensic technique of dactyloscopy whereby, using brushed powder, latent fingerprints are made visible."[143] Ultimately, however, the dust raised through Vanagt's monotone gesture, filmed in extreme close-up, invokes the content of the unmarked graves themselves, photographed from a satellite and "put under microscope"[144] in the sanitized and dust-free environment of the Tribunal.

Vanagt has described her rubbings as, "attempts to decipher the secret language formed by traces of war."[145] After a rubbing is completed the camera briefly inspects its surface, as if it was a satellite photograph scrutinized for incriminating details, before it is rolled up into a scroll. Together, these topographical reliefs constitute an atlas of shadow sites charting the intermediary zone between the killing grounds in Bosnia and the placeless space of international justice. Conceptually, they also invite a comparison to the charcoal animations of William Kentridge that was addressed in the previous chapter. In common with Kentridge's manually laborious technique of stone-age filmmaking, which evolved as a response to the reconciliation efforts of the publicly aired proceedings of the Truth and Reconciliation Commission, Vanagt invents a crude, lowbrow medium as a means to intercept the ordered and systematic hearings in the Hague, which were transcribed simultaneously in four languages, filmed by six cameras, and streamed online with a thirty-minute delay. Vanagt's rubbings also mark out another kind of interstice, poised between the activities of decrypting and encrypting the documents (satellite footage, propaganda videos, forensic photographs, soil samples and ballistic reports) and the attempts of the defense to obscure their denotations. "I wanted to film the movement of the hand trying to rub *something* away, while the same gesture actually makes something appear" Vanagt explains.[146] In another unexpected spatial turn taking place on November 29, 2017, less than a month before its mandate was terminated, the Tribunal was itself declared a crime scene after a former commander of Bosnia Croat forces, Slobodan Praljak, emptied a bottle of poison while his verdict was being read.

Other invisible hands are at work in *Dust Breeding*'s dialectical partner, *The Wave*, which follows a three-week long forensic exhumation conducted in October 2011. In 1939, nine men were executed by the Franco regime and buried in a former bomb crater in Castilla-La Mancha, one of thousands of mass-burial sites dating from the summary executions carried out by extra-judicial death squads during the Spanish Civil War. The excavation site is introduced by a high-angle shot overlooking the windswept plateau as the mist clears over the vineyards to reveal a stream that meanders in a mercury ribbon toward distant foothills. No witness accounts are heard, except for the voiceover of a granddaughter to one of the victims who expresses her anxiety that nothing will be found. Following the panorama, another scale and rhythm is introduced in the form of a time-lapse montage of the exhumation process shot in close-up, subtly counterpointed by the ambient sound of cicadas, wind and cowbells. Through a simple device—slowing down the frame rate frequency and editing out the presence of the forensic archaeologists—the earth appears to be moving on its own accord, undergoing a constant metamorphosis. Shadows flicker, sand and clay are shifted, pebbles pour, and muddy water springs forth, while the skeletonized remains resurface as if from an erosion or landslide. The time-lapse photography also elicits a corollary between the opening and closing of the shutter and the opening and closing of the earth, as well as of the wounds of the relatives.

At dusk, relatives to the disappeared gather at the site to photograph the remains. A nocturnal shot shows the excavation site demarcated with red-and-white ribbons of polyethylene tape. The silent flashes of the cameras appear like sparks of subterranean lightning flaring up from the bowels of the earth. When the excavation is finished, the mesh of bones is marked with yellow number tags, as bodies are identified and assimilated back into history. Photographs of the reappeared are placed on the mound of earth before an excavator covers the crater, burying the flowers with the remains. This wave of unburying and reburying is bookended by the high panorama, which is shown once more as the film draws to a close, just as the clouds break to light up the arid plateau.

* * *

Among the scattered bones recovered from the crater in *The Wave*, a pair of boots appears. An empty boot is a particular trace, both a mold of an absent body and a reminder of its former presence on the earth. This finding thereby yields a connection between the static remains, the photographic portraits, and the resistance against the Franco regime. Another pair of boots is displayed in *Fait*. This is also the single item of human clothing to appear in the series, serving as a subtle intimation of the bodies gone missing in the desert. It is a monochrome close-up that at a casual glance merely shows some encrustations in the desert grit. In the granular texture, however, a dark opening and a curvilinear shadow can, on closer scrutiny, be identified as the shape of a pair of military boots; one standing, the other tossed to the side. Whether the graininess is due to the photographic emulsion or the photographed object remains uncertain; nor can we determine where the boots end and the ground begins. These two pairs of boots recovered from the earth call to mind Martin Heidegger's discussion of a pair of peasant shoes painted by Vincent van Gogh. "From the dark opening of the worn inside of the shoes the toilsome tread of the worker stares forth," Heidegger muses in his essay on *The Origin of the Work of Art*. "In the shoes vibrates the silent call of the earth," and in their worn leather "the field swept by a raw wind" continues to resound.[147] Another workforce stares back at us from the dark opening of the sand-caked boot in Kuwait, and a different wind rumbles: the manmade cataclysm of Desert Storm, followed by the motions of wind and sand covering the toil on the battlefield beneath a cloak of dust.

Like the aerial reconnaissance photographs of the battleground of the Great War, the arcane patterns that arise from Vanagt's gestures of rubbing in *Dust Breeding* seem to elicit a secret code decipherable only by the specialists' eyes. At one occasion, however, we may notice a few legible figures that distinguish themselves from the uniform ground of coarse and crumpled paper. This rubbing is made in response to the investigation of a high-angle photograph of the site of an alleged mass execution. The image displayed on the monitor is untypically postcard-like: a rustic, brightly colored vista of low hills and farmland. Like the grimmer, gray scale satellite photographs, however, it is swiftly marked up with red lines, dates and numbers as the testimony ensues. The electronically distorted voice of a survivor, whose face appears on the screen as a swarm of pixels, recounts the massacre that took place in the wheatfields

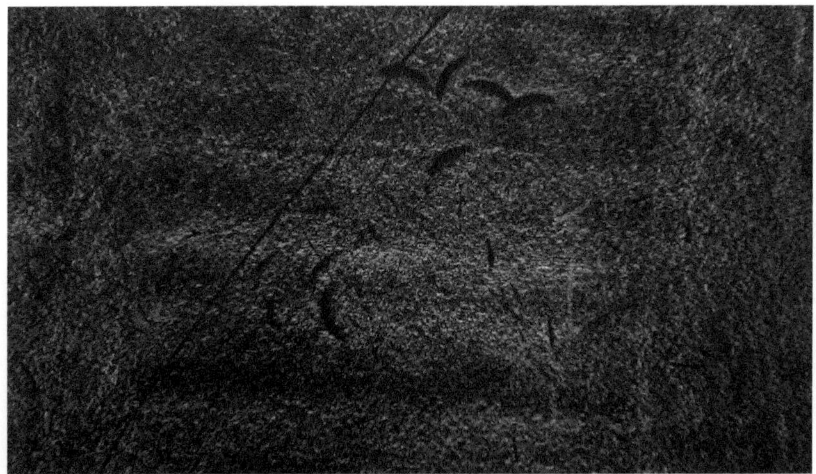

Fig. 3.7 Sarah Vanagt *Dust Breeding* (2013). Desk of the Judges. Courtesy of the artist

surrounding the farm. Karadžić's cross-examination concerns the identity of the site: Was it in fact a wheatfield? Were there haystacks to hide in? If not, how was it possible to take cover in the stumpy grass? Vanagt unrolls a long scroll of black silk paper across the desk of the judges and begins to rub it with a white crayon. A few dark dents, redolent of animate beings, emerge on the panoramic rubbing (Fig. 3.7). More precisely, these scattered, V-shaped marks resemble a skein of birds, obliquely reminiscent of the last dashes of black paint that van Gogh added above a wheatfield in Arles, in what was long believed to have been his final painting. The next chapter will continue to explore the nexus of trace and territory, event and aftermath, body and earth, through the prism of Warburg's *Pathosformel*; not in pursuit of butterflies, but in order to track the equally errant flight of van Gogh's carrion crows.

Notes

1. Catherine Grenier *Sophie Ristelhueber: La guerre intérieure* (Dijon: Les Presses du reel 2010) 77. All translations from this volume are my own.
2. Simon Faulkner "The Most Photographed Wall in the World" *Photographies* Vol. 5 No. 2 (September 2012) 223–242.
3. Grenier 77–78.
4. Elias Sanbar "Une guerre de pierres" *Les Inrockuptibles* 484 (9–15 March) 66–70.
5. Cheryl Brutvan *Details of the World* (Boston: MFA Publications 2001) 83.
6. Artist statement http://www.worldpress.org/Europe/279.cfm (accessed 1 August 2018).
7. Ann Hindry *Sophie Ristelhueber* (Paris: Éditions Hazan 1998) 68.
8. See booklet for a 2011 exhibition at Galerie Blancpain—Art Contemporain http://www.blancpain-artcontemporain.ch/artistes/sophie_ristelhueber/CP_sophie_ristelhueber.pdf (accessed 1 August 2018).
9. Chandra Mukerji *Territorial Ambitions and the Gardens of Versailles* (Cambridge: Cambridge University Press 1997).
10. Denis E. Cosgrove *Social Formation and Symbolic Landscape* (Madison: The University of Wisconsin Press 1984) 189.
11. Debbie Lisle "The Surprising Detritus of Leisure: Encountering the Late Photography of War" *Environment and Planning D: Society and Space* Vol. 29 No. 5 (October 2011) 873–890, 874.
12. Hindry 69.
13. The artist book *Mémoires du Lot* is reproduced in *Sophie Ristelhueber: Operations*, exhibition catalogue for Jeu De Paume, 20 January–22 March 2009, curated by Marta Gili. Texts by Bruno Latour, David

Mellor, and Thomas Schlesser, trans. Olga Grlic (London: Thames & Hudson 2009) 274. My translation.
14. Ristelhueber quoted in Brutvan 286.
15. Ibid. 11.
16. *Sophie Ristelhueber: Operations* 290.
17. As quoted in Brutvan, 14.
18. *Sophie Ristelhueber: Operations* 260.
19. Walter Benjamin "The Work of Art in the Age of Mechanical Reproduction" [1936] *Illuminations* ed. Hannah Arendt, trans. Harry Zone (London: Pimlico 1999) 226–227.
20. Jonathan Sawday *The Body Emblazoned: Dissection and the Human Body in Renaissance Culture* (London and New York: Routledge 1995) 23.
21. Grenier 37.
22. Ristelhueber quoted in *Sophie Ristelhueber: Operations* 282.
23. As quoted by Paul K. Saint-Amour "Modernist Reconnaissance" *Modernism/Modernity* Vol. 10 No. 2 (2003) 349–380, 355.
24. Allan Sekula "The Instrumental Image: Steichen at War" [1975] *Photography Against the Grain: Essays and Photo Works 1973–1983* (Halifax: The Press of the Nova Scotia College of Art and Design 1984) 32–51, 34.
25. Paul Virilio "Desert Screen" [1991] *The Virilio Reader* ed. James Der Derian, trans. Michael Degener and Lauren Osepchuk (Oxford: Blackwell 1998) 176.
26. Jean Baudrillard *The Gulf War Did Not Take Place* [1991] trans. Paul Patton (Bloomington: Indiana University Press 1995).
27. Paul Virilio *A Landscape of Events* [1995] trans. Julie Rose (Cambridge: MIT Press 2000) 24.
28. Brutvan 136–137.
29. Virilio *A Landscape of Events* 27.
30. Grenier 53.
31. Gilles Deleuze *The Logic of Sense* [1969] ed. Constantin V. Boundas, trans. Mark Lester and Charles Stivale (New York: Columbia University Press 1990) 152.
32. Ristelhueber quoted in Brutvan 18.
33. Georges Didi-Huberman *Atlas, or the Anxious Gay Science* [2011] trans. Shane Lillis (Chicago and London: Chicago University Press 2018) 254. This book was originally published as the introductory text to the catalogue for the exhibition *Atlas: How to Carry the World on One's Back?* that Didi-Huberman organized at the Museo Nacional Centro de Arte Reina Sofía in Madrid in 2010. Two sequels have since been curated by Didi-Huberman together with the photographer Arno

Gisinger: *Afteratlas* in 2012 and *Nouvelles histoires de fantômes (New Ghost Stories)* in 2014.

34. Quoted from Didi-Huberman's short introductory text to the exhibition *Atlas: How to Carry the World on One's Back?* http://www.museoreinasofia.es/sites/default/files/notas-de-prensa/2010-004-dossier-en.pdf (accessed 1 August 2018).
35. Warburg quoted by Giorgio Agamben "Aby Warburg and the Nameless Science" [1975] *Potentialities: Collected Essays in Philosophy* eds. and trans. Werner Hamacher and David E. Wellbery (Stanford: Stanford University Press 1999) 97.
36. Georges Didi-Huberman *The Surviving Image: Phantoms of Time and Time of Phantoms* [2002] trans. Harvey L. Mendelsohn (University Park: The Pennsylvania State University Press 2017) 302.
37. Kurt W. Forster "Introduction" Aby Warburg *The Renewal of Pagan Antiquity* (Los Angeles: Getty Publications 1999) 1–75, 28, 52.
38. Didi-Huberman *The Surviving Image* 298.
39. Georges Didi-Huberman "Warburg's Haunted House" *Common Knowledge* Vol. 18 No. 1 (Winter 2012) 50–78, 50, 52. This text first appeared as part of Didi-Huberman's catalogue essay for the first *Atlas* exhibition.
40. T.S. Eliot *The Complete Poems and Plays, 1909–1950* (New York, San Diego, and London: Harcourt Brace & Company 1952) 128.
41. Peter J. Schwartz "Aby Warburgs Kriegskartothek. Vorbericht einer Rekonstruktion" *Kasten 117: Aby Warburg und der Aberglaube im Ersten Weltkrieg* eds. Gottfried Korff (Tübingen: Tübinger Vereinigung für Volkskunde e. V. 2007) 39–69, 66. My translation.
42. Letter from Warburg, 26 December 1923. Quoted by Forster 25.
43. Schwartz 56.
44. Didi-Huberman "Warburg's Haunted House" 67, 70.
45. Grenier 58.
46. Michel Guerrin "Scars Across the Face of the Earth" *Guardian Weekly* (1 November 1992) 15. Quoted in David Mellor "Rents in the Fabric of Reality: Contexts for Sophie Ristelhueber" *Sophie Ristelhueber: Operations* 228.
47. Jean-Luc Nancy "Image and Violence" *The Ground of the Image* (New York: Fordham University Press 2005) 16.
48. Ibid. 23.
49. Jean-Luc Nancy "The Image—The Distinct" *The Ground of the Image* 7.
50. See Dario Gamboni's history of modern iconoclasm in *The Destruction of Art: Iconoclasm and Vandalism Since the French Revolution* (London: Reaktion Books 1997).

51. Sarah Kember and Joanna Zylinska *Life After New Media: Mediation as a Vital Process* (Cambridge: MIT Press 2012) 71.
52. "The Butterfly Hunter" Margaret Cox interviewed by Harriet Warner in *The Independent*, Saturday 17 July 2004 http://www.independent.co.uk/news/world/africa/the-butterfly-hunter-553266.html (accessed 1 August 2018).
53. Binswanger quoted by Philippe-Alain Michaud *Aby Warburg and the Image in Motion* [1998] trans. Sophie Hawkes (New York: Zone Books 2004) 171–173. See also Vlad Ionescu "On Moths and Butterflies, or How to Orient Oneself Through Images. Georges Didi-Huberman's Art Criticism in Context" *Journal of Art Historiography* No. 16 (June 2017) 1–16.
54. Georges Didi-Huberman "Knowledge: Movement (The Man Who Spoke to Butterflies)" foreword to Philippe-Alain Michaud's *Aby Warburg and the Image in Motion* (New York: Zone Books 2004) 7–19, 14.
55. "The true picture of the past flits by." Walter Benjamin "Theses on the Philosophy of History" [1940] *Illuminations: Essays and Reflections* trans. Harry Zohn (New York: Schocken Books 1968) 253–264, 255.
56. Maggie M. Cao "Abbott Thayer and the Invention of Camouflage" *Art History* Vol. 39 No. 3 (June 2016) 486–511, 510.
57. Ibid. 508.
58. Grenier 89.
59. Ristelhueber quoted in *Sophie Ristelhueber: Operations* 400.
60. Grenier 44.
61. Ibid. 39.
62. Félix Nadar (Gaspard Felix Tournachon) *When I Was a Photographer* [1900] (Cambridge: MIT Press 2015).
63. Brutvan 147.
64. See for example Campany's "Safety in Numbness" essay, and Sarah James "Making an Ugly World Beautiful? Morality and Ethics in the Aftermath" *Memory of a Fire: The War of Images and Images of War* (Brighton: Photoworks and Brighton Photo Biennial 2008) 12–15.
65. David Campany "Safety in Numbness: Some Remarks on Problems of 'Late Photography'" *Where Is the Photograph?* ed. David Green (Brighton and Kent: Photoforum and Photoworks 2003) 123–132, 124.
66. Marc Mayer "Fait" *Sophie Ristelhueber: Fait* (New York: Errata Editions 2009) n.p.
67. Grenier 46.
68. Ristelhueber discusses this photograph in her conversation with Grenier 72

69. Naomi Klein *The Shock Doctrine: The Rise of Disaster Capitalism* (New York: Metropolitan Books 2008). For a comparative analysis of *Fait* and Werner Herzog's *Lessons of Darkness* (1991) in light of neoliberal capitalism, see Krzysztof Pijarski's "A Model Desert: The Gulf War, Landscape and the Pensive Image" in the online journal *View. Theories and Practices of Visual Culture* No. 8 (2014) http://pismowidok.org/index.php/one/article/view/254/467 (accessed 1 August 2018).
70. Frank Möller "From Aftermath to Peace: Reflections on a Photography of Peace" *Global Society* (published online 3 November 2016) 1–21, 3 http://www.tandfonline.com/doi/abs/10.1080/13600826.2016.1220926 (accessed 1 August 2018).
71. Caren Kaplan *Aerial Aftermaths: Wartime from Above* (Durham and London: Duke University Press 2018) 144. The last chapter of Kaplan's study, which I received merely a couple of weeks before the deadline of my manuscript for *Crime Scenery*, analyzes airborne artworks including Ristelhueber's *Fait*, Al-Ani's *Shadow Sites* films, and Fazal Sheikh and Eyal Weizman's collaborative project *The Conflict Shoreline* (2015), which retraces the dispossession of Bedouin land in the Negev Desert.
72. Ibid. 175.
73. Rob Nixon *Slow Violence and the Environmentalism of the Poor* (Cambridge and London: Harvard University Press 2011) 225.
74. Ibid. 222.
75. Jacques Derrida *Copy, Archive, Signature* ed. Gerhard Richter (Stanford: Stanford University Press 2010) 47.
76. Quoted from the voiceover narration of Harun Farocki's film *Bilder der Welt und Inschrift des Krieges* (*Images of the World and the Inscription of War*, 1989).
77. "Interview Jananne Al-Ani" by Julian Ross at *Sonic Acts Festival* 26 May 2015 n.p. http://www.sonicacts.com/portal/interview-jananne-al-ani (accessed 1 August 2018).
78. Statement by Sharmini Pereira in collaboration with the artist http://edgeofarabia.com/artists/jananne-al-ani (accessed 1 August 2018).
79. "Jananne Al-Ani in conversation with Nat Muller" online forum *Ibraz: Contemporary Visual Culture in North Africa and the Middle-East* http://www.ibraaz.org/interviews/137 (accessed 1 August 2018).
80. See Jeanne Haffner *The View from Above: The Science of Social Space* (Cambridge: MIT Press 2013) 30; Paula Amad "From God's-Eye to Camera-Eye: Aerial Photography's Post-humanist and Neo-humanist Visions of the World" *History of Photography* Vol. 36 No. 1 (February 2012) 66–86, 85.
81. Braudel quoted by Richard E. Lee "Fernand Braudel, the *Longue Durée*, and World-Systems Analysis" *The Longue Durée and World-Systems*

Analysis ed. Richard E. Lee (Albany: State University of New York Press 2012) 1.

82. "For the purposes of aerial archaeology, the landscape itself acts like a photographic plate, where a latent image (the foundations of a Roman villa, for example) is periodically if unpredictably developed." Kitty Hauser *Shadow Sites: Photography, Archaeology & the British Landscape 1927–1955* (Oxford: Oxford University Press 2007) 172.
83. Ibid. 172.
84. Sigmund Freud *Moses and Monotheism* as quoted by Hauser 176 n. 86. To Hauser's triad we may add another form of skiagraphy (i.e. "shadow writing") inaugurated by the atomic age. As Paul Virilio has pointed out, the metaphoric conflation of photography and topography was literalized on August 6, 1945 when the searing nuclear flash above Hiroshima "photographed the shadow cast by beings and things so that every surface immediately became war's *recording* surface, its *film*." Paul Virilio *War and Cinema: The Logistics of Perception* [1984] (London and New York: Verso 1989) 85.
85. E.H. Gombrich *Aby Warburg: An Intellectual Biography* [1970] (Oxford: Phaidon 1986) 242.
86. Ristelhueber quoted in *Sophie Ristelhueber: Operations* 334
87. Grenier 43
88. "Trauma took the leap from body to mind just over a century ago," Ian Hacking writes, "and during the time when the sciences of memory were coming into being." *Rewriting the Soul: Multiple Personality and the Sciences of Memory* (Princeton: Princeton University Press 1995) 183.
89. Paul Virilio *Negative Horizon: An Essay in Dromoscopy* (London: Continuum 2006) 79–91. While the aesthetics of disappearance is elaborated here in relation to camouflage tactics, it pertains to a vast set of issues—the logistics of perception, dromology and telepresence—developed across Virilio's writing as a whole.
90. Jananne Al-Ani has discussed the influence of the photographs of Poidebard, Herzfeld and Steichen, as well as Ristelhueber's *Fait*, in her "Shadow Sites" lecture given at the *Sonic Acts Festival—The Geological Imagination* in Amsterdam on 28 February 2015. The lecture, which includes full screenings of the two *Shadow Sites* films, is available at https://vimeo.com/124240024 (accessed 1 August 2018).
91. Daniela K. Helbig "*La Trace de Rome*? Aerial Photography and Archaeology in Mandate Syria and Lebanon" *History of Photography* Vol. 40 No. 3 (August 2016) 283–300.
92. Artist quoted in *Sophie Ristelhueber: Operations* 400.

93. Maurice Blanchot "The Two Versions of the Imaginary" [1955] *The Space of Literature* trans. Ann Smock (Lincoln and London: University of Nebraska Press 1989) 258.
94. Grenier 43.
95. Ristelhueber cited in *Sophie Ristelhueber: Operations* 382.
96. Like *Eleven Blowups*, this quotation is a composite: the first clause is drawn from Ristelhueber's guided tour of the exhibition in the Gallery video from the Jeu de Paume exhibition, 20 January–22 March 2009 http://www.jeudepaume.org/?page=article&idArt=814&lieu=1 (accessed 1 August 2018). The second two clauses are quoted from *Sophie Ristelhueber: Operations* 380.
97. Grenier 40.
98. James Elkins *What Photography Is* (New York: Routledge 2011) xii.
99. Ibid. 158, 174.
100. Ibid. 87.
101. Ibid. 56.
102. "Conflict, Time, Photography" artist interview https://www.tate.org.uk/context-comment/audio/sophie-ristelheuber-on-fait (accessed 1 August 2018).
103. Amy Serafin "A Specialist in Ravaged Leftovers of Humanity" *The New York Times* (28 October 2001) 32.
104. Michel Guerrin "The Arts in a Time of Crisis: Reacting to a Situation Beyond Imagination" *World Press Review* Vol. 48 No. 12 (December 2001) http://www.worldpress.org/Europe/279.cfm (accessed 1 August 2018).
105. "Artist and Photographer Sophie Ristelhueber's Best Shot" interview by Sarah Phillips in *The Guardian*, 28 April 2010. Italicizations are mine https://www.theguardian.com/artanddesign/2010/apr/28/photography-sophie-ristelhueber-best-shot (accessed 1 August 2018).
106. Joseph Masheck *Marcel Duchamp in Perspective* (Cambridge: Da Capo Press 2002) 18.
107. Baudrillard *The Gulf War Did Not Take Place* 64.
108. For an account of the *longue durée* of airborne British military presence in the Persian Gulf, see Caren Kaplan "Desert Wars: Virilio and the Limits of 'Genuine Knowledge'" *Virilio and Visual Culture* ed. Ryan Bishop (Edinburgh: Edinburgh University Press 2013) 69–85; Priya Satia "Drones: A History from the British Middle East" *Humanity: An International Journal of Human Rights, Humanitarianism, and Development* Vol. 5 No. 1 (Spring 2014) 1–31.
109. Virilio *War and Cinema* 90.

110. Paul K. Saint-Amour "'Applied Modernism': Military and Civilian Uses of the Aerial Photomosaic" *Theory, Culture, and Society* Vol. 28 No. 7–8 (December 2011) 241–269, 252.
111. Saint-Amour "Modernist Reconnaissance" 356.
112. The 1922 publications of *Dust Breeding* and *The Wasteland* also provide the starting point for the exhibition *A Handful of Dust*, curated by David Campany at Le Bal in Paris (16 October 2015–17 January 2016).
113. David Campany *A Handful of Dust: From the Cosmic to the Domestic* (Paris: Le Bal and Mack 2015) 18.
114. Duchamp used the term "bachelor machine" for the various objects, like the chocolate grinder, assembled in the lower portion of the glass. The conflation of forensics and landscape is in fact an enduring theme in Duchamp's work, where landscapes tend to be encrypted as sites of intricate mysteries, often with overtly morbid overtones and illicit associations. His *Paysage fautif* (*Faulty Landscape*), made in 1946, itself became an object of forensic investigation by the FBI whose laboratory report identified the abstract configuration as stains of seminal fluid on a sheet of black satin. The same year, Duchamp made a series of photographs of a waterfall in Switzerland that provided the basis for the plywood collage of his final, secret project. Unveiled after his death in 1968 at the Philadelphia Museum of Art, *Etant donnés* (1946–1966) consists of two peepholes in a wooden door through which the spectator peers into an autumnal diorama of forested hills and a sparkling waterfall. In the foreground of this hyper-realistic pastoral setting, a naked and headless female figure reclines in the dry grass. In this light, we may read Ristelhueber's inversion Latona Fountain in Versailles as part of an ongoing dialogue with Duchamp, evoking the urinal that he tilted upside down in 1917 and titled "Fountain."
115. Edmond Locard "The Analysis of Dust Traces. Part I" [1929] *The American Journal of Police Science* Vol. 1 No. 3 (May–June 1930) 276–298, 276.
116. Ibid. 278
117. David Hopkins '"The Domain of Rrose Sélavy": *Dust Breeding* and Aerial Photography" *Seeing from Above: The Aerial View in Visual Culture* eds. Mark Dorrian and Frédéric Poussin (London and New York: I.B. Tauris 2013) 134–146, 143.
118. Ibid. 145.
119. F. Scott Fitzgerald *The Great Gatsby* [1925] (New York: Charles Scribner's Sons 1953) 23.
120. Lucretius *On the Nature of Things*: De Rerum Natura ed. and trans. Anthony M. Eselen (Baltimore: Johns Hopkins University 1995) 60.

121. Carolyn Steedman *Dust* (Manchester: Manchester University Press 2001) 164.
122. Marcel Duchamp "The Green Box" [1934] *Salt Seller: The Writings of Marcel Duchamp* eds. Michel Sanouillet and Elmer Petersen (New York: Oxford University Press 1973) 26–71, 26.
123. Rosalind Krauss "Notes on the Index: Seventies Art in America" *October* Vol. 3 (Spring 1977) 77.
124. Rosalind Krauss *The Optical Unconscious* (Cambridge and London: The MIT Press 1993) 119.
125. Dale Tomich "The Order of Historical Time: The *Longue Durée* and Micro-History" Lee *The Longue Durée and World-Systems Analysis* 11.
126. Didi-Huberman *The Surviving Image* 239.
127. Aby Warburg "Dürer and Italian Antiquity" *The Renewal of Pagan Antiquity* 553–558, 553.
128. Didi-Huberman *The Surviving Image* 244.
129. Didi-Huberman *Atlas, or the Anxious Gay Science* 227.
130. "Events are dust" Ferdinand Braudel asserted, transient facts scattered on the soil of history. While "[a]n event is explosive," he continues, "[i]ts delusive smoke fills the minds of its contemporaries, but it does not last, and its flame can scarcely ever be discerned." For Braudel, then, events are camouflage—from the French *camouflet*, literally meaning to blow a puff of smoke in someone's eyes. Fernand Braudel "History and the Social Sciences: The Longue Durée" *The Mediterranean in Histories: French Constructions of the Past* ed. Jacques Revel and Lynn Hunt (New York: New Press 1995) 118.
130. Didi-Huberman *Atlas, or the Anxious Gay Science* 9.
132. Aby Warburg "Dürer and Italian Antiquity" 555, 556.
133. Mayer "Fait" n.p.
134. Georges Didi-Huberman "Emotion Does Not Say 'I'" *Alfredo Jaar: la politique des images* ed. Nicole Schweizer (Lausanne: JRP and Ringier 2007) 67.
135. Didi-Huberman *The Surviving Image* 210 and "The Surviving Image: Aby Warburg and Taylorian Anthropology" *Oxford Art Journal* Vol. 25 No. 1 (2002) 59–70, 62.
136. Hindry 65.
137. Ibid. 62.
138. Ibid. 63.
139. Sarah Vanagt "'Disturbed Earth', A Conversation Between Sarah Vanagt and Tobias Hering" [2012] *Elevage de poussière/Dust Breeding/The Wave* (Brussels: Balthasar 2014) 15–71, 32.
140. Georges Didi-Huberman "Contact Images" [1997] trans. Alisa Hartz, as quoted in Vanagt *Elevage de poussière/Dust Breeding/The Wave* 12.

141. Meyer Shapiro "The Liberation Quality of the Avant-Garde" *Art News* Vol. 56 No. 4 (Summer 1957) 36–42, 38.
142. Susan Sontag *On Photography* (New York: Penguin Books 1977) 154.
143. Berber Bevernage "Bringing War Criminals to Justice Was Our Mandate, the Triumph of Justice Is Our Legacy" [2013] trans. Jodie Hruby. Available at http://www.kfda.be/en/program/elevage-de-poussiere--dust-breeding (accessed 1 August 2018).
144. "'Disturbed Earth', A Conversation Between Sarah Vanagt and Tobias Hering" 41.
145. Quoted from the synopsis of *Dust Breeding* http://www.kfda.be/en/program/elevage-de-poussiere--dust-breeding (accessed 1 August 2018).
146. "'Disturbed Earth', A Conversation Between Sarah Vanagt and Tobias Hering" 16.
147. Martin Heidegger "The Origin of the Work of Art" [1935–1937] *Basic Writings: From Being and Time (1927) to The Task of Thinking (1964)* ed. David Farrell Krell (London and Henley: Routledge & Kegan Paul 1978) 149–187, 163. In his phenomenological analysis, Heidegger posits that World and Earth are bound together in permanent strife. The former represents the familiar horizon along which we orient our everyday life: the equipment we rely upon, the web of social signification, logic and convention. Earth, conversely, is the ground upon which our human projects have been installed: the density of obtuse and mindless matter that refuses to be translated into legible meaning. Heidegger thus understands the work of art in terms of an unresolved tension between the crossing axis of Earth and World; the latter bringing forth what the former obdurately withholds and withdraws into itself. The artwork does not reconcile World and Earth, then, but allows us to glimpse how they coexist in conflict.

CHAPTER 4

A Murder of Crows

At the end of his 1971 essay "Art through the camera's eye," Robert Smithson reflects on a recent news item that has attracted his attention:

> A few weeks ago I read in *New York Times* that Alain Resnais is working on a film that deals with a frustrated movie producer, who turns to fighting pollution. The relationship between pollution and filmmaking strikes me as a worthwhile area of investigation. Resnais's landscapes and sites have always revealed a degree of horror and entrapment. In *Night and Fog*, Resnais contrasts a pastoral site (shot in Technicolor) of a concentration camp overgrown with grass and flowers, with black and white photographs of horrors from its past. This suggests that each landscape, no matter how calm and lovely, conceals a substrata of disaster—a story that discloses 'no story, no buoyancy, no plot' (Jean Cayrol: *Lazare parmi nous*). If art history is a nightmare, then what is natural history?[1]

Several interrelated themes, which will inform the following analysis, can be extrapolated from these paragraphs. Let us begin with pollution, the topic of Alain Resnais' new film. In the early 1970s, the French director worked together with Stan Lee, the creator of Marvel comics, on two scripts, both set in New York City. The first, a romantic comedy titled *The Inmates*, was based on the premise that "the human race was so badly conceived ... that it had to be quarantined on earth."[2] The second was called *The Monster Maker*, a pop-art parody about the misfortunes of a third-rate horror movie producer who is blackmailed

H. Gustafsson, *Crime Scenery in Postwar Film and Photography*,
https://doi.org/10.1007/978-3-030-04867-9_4

into making a film about pollution. In the climactic sequence of the film, the entire city is engulfed by sewage; the bay is clogged with dreck, the sky choked with smog, and the streets overflow with garbage.[3]

Neither of these films were made, and the concluding montage of *The Monster Maker* only survives as the coda for another project, *Repérages*, a photographic album of location studies in black and white taken between 1949, the year after Resnais completed his first major film, a two-reel experimental documentary on Vincent van Gogh, and 1974. Together with the two Stan Lee projects, it includes locations for a documentary on H.P. Lovecraft, an essay on marquis de Sade, and an adaptation of the adventures of the pulp magazine detective Harry Dickson. The term *Repérages* translates as reconnaissance or location scouting, but is also used, as James Monaco has noted, "to refer to the synchronization of sound and image in film."[4] Shunning recognizable landmarks, the prospective settings in *Repérages*, which extend from Paris and London to New York and Hiroshima, call to mind the deserted urban scenes captured by Eugène Atget. Bereft of actors and abandoned by the filmmaker, as if a plague had swept through the streets of this composite city, many of Resnais' photographs further reiterate Atget's topoi of bare trees, brick walls, lampposts, trashcans, and mannequins in store windows.

It is fitting, then, that this inventory of unrealized and abandoned projects should end with a photomontage of accumulating waste. As portended by Smithson, the last pages of *Repérages* also render the link between *Night and Fog* (Nuit et brouillard, 1956) and *The Monster Maker* explicit. The picture of a smoldering landfill fenced off from the surrounding city, or the close-up of barbwire strings framed against a blank sky, echo similar frames from the posthumous inventory of Majdanek and Auschwitz-Birkenau, cities designed to turn their inhabitants into waste, conducted in *Night and Fog*. Notably, Smithson furthermore quotes Jean Cayrol's *Lazare parmi nous* (Lazarus Among Us, 1950) as the intertext for the horrors dug out by Resnais' camera. In this brief volume, the surrealist poet and former inmate of the Mauthausen-Gusen concentration camp developed the notion of a Lazarean art, invoking Lazarus' return from the dead in the New Testament as a parable for the experience of having physically survived the Nazi extermination machine. Himself a subject of the *Nacht und Nebel* decree, which stipulated the clandestine arrests and deportations of resisters in the occupied territories, Cayrol authored the commentary to

Night and Fog a decade after his collection *Poems of the Night and of the Fog* (Poèmes de la nuit et du brouillard, 1946) had been published.

The collaboration between Cayrol and Resnais, and "[t]he relationship between pollution and filmmaking" identified by Smithson, has more recently been the subject of a wide-ranging investigation under the aegis of the research project *Concentrationary Memories.*[5] In their co-authored introduction to the first in a series of anthologies to germinate out of this project, Griselda Pollock and Max Silverman define Cayrol's Lazarean art as one determined to "expose us to contamination."[6] The inaugural moment for a Lazarean cinema is announced, Silverman writes, in the opening sequence of *Night and Fog* when the camera cranes down from a spacious, high-angle view of a sky and field to frame the rural scene through the barbed wired fence poles.[7] The descending gaze places us inside, looking out, thereby establishing a key theme of the narration: that what is inside and outside cannot possibly be conceived as part of the same world. One reality revokes the other; or rather, one reality transforms the other into an illusion. As the voiceover relentlessly reminds us, the image of the past is weak and unreliable, susceptible to fade and vanish. Hence, "we can only show you the shell, the shadow," the "façade," "surface" or "décor." Whereas the external world loomed like "peaceful landscapes" on the far side of the fence for the inmates, for the present-day visitor, the crematorium appears as a "picture postcard." The everyday inside the camp turned the everyday outside its enclosures into a mirage. However, what first appears to be mired in a real-image binary is, on closer inspection, a zone of contiguity and contamination between them.

This experience is recounted in the first part of *Lazarus Among Us*, called *Les Rêves lazaréens*, which is devoted to the dream life of the deportees. "Landscape-dreams were the most frequent," Cayrol recalls, "mostly of immense panoramas," or of idyllic camps with grassland, flowers and trees where the inmates were reunited with their unaware families.[8] Another former inmate, Primo Levi, reports this scenario in reverse when he describes the recurring dream of the outsider, the survivor who cannot prevent the experience of the camps from incessantly returning. At the beginning of the dream, Levi writes, he is with family and friends, "in the countryside—in a surrounding that is, in other words, peaceful and relaxed." Then, suddenly, "everything falls apart around me … I'm alone at the center of a gray, cloudy emptiness … I am once again in the camp, and nothing outside the camp was true.

The rest—family, flowering, nature, home—was a brief respite, a trick of the senses."[9] Whether the dreamer is inside or outside its confines, the camp is everywhere, at any time.

In *Night and Fog*, this threshold is crossed when the camera retreats from the fence to track a flock of low-flying crows across fields dotted with haystacks (Fig. 4.1). "Even a peaceful landscape, even a meadow in harvest with crows circling overhead," the voiceover cautions us, "can lead to a concentration camp." On a factual level, the viewer is here reminded of the vast infrastructure of the concentrationary universe, which comprised more than ten thousand camps spread across Greater Germany, with Auschwitz alone consisting of a network of forty-eight camps.[10] But the opening lines also hold another implication: not only that any landscape can lead us into the camps, but also any image. In 1947, preceding Theodor Adorno's famous aphorism about the impossibility of writing poetry after Auschwitz by two years, Georges Bataille asserted that "[t]he image of man is henceforth inseparable from a gas chamber."[11] Half a century later, Gérard Wajcman reiterates Bataille's verdict, declaring that "[t]oday it is impossible to eliminate from the image of a body the resonance of the attack on the human image perpetrated in the gas chambers."[12] Along these lines, the human body, disfigured and defaced, has remained the key topos in debates on the politics and ethics of representation, and the Nazi camps its primary historical reference point.[13] As I will show below, however, the opening shots in *Night and Fog* ask us to consider the fraught relation between the image and the gas chamber from the reverse angle, suggesting that landscapes,

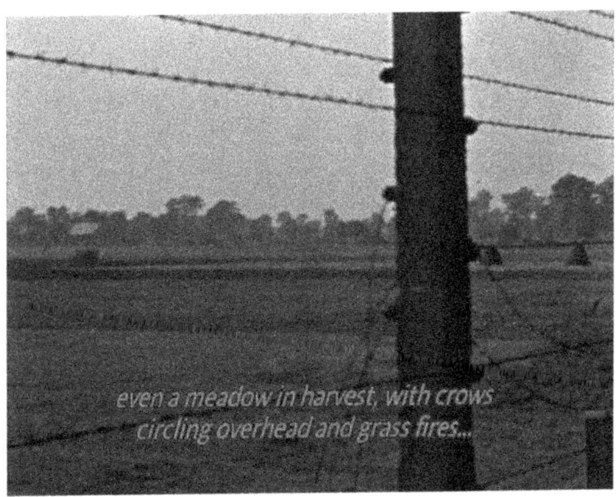

Fig. 4.1 *Night and Fog* (Alain Resnais, 1956)

especially those where no human figures are to be seen, remain haunted by this legacy as well: not only the actual sites where the atrocities took place, but the pictorial genre of landscape as such. Choreographed by the vertical and lateral movements of the camera, the film's overture stages a transition from one image into another, from the rustic tableau outside the fence to the mortified landscape within its enclosures. More precisely, the three opening shots and their accompanying narration perform an ekphrasis of *Wheatfield with Crows* (1890), the painting with which Resnais had concluded his film on van Gogh a few years earlier. Hence, as Eric Klingerman points out, "[d]espite its mistrust in images, *Night and Fog* begins like a painting."[14] Not just any painting, but one with a unique standing in the oeuvre of van Gogh, in the legacy of landscape painting more generally.

Resnais' *Van Gogh* (1948) is made up entirely of a montage of paintings filmed at the Vincent van Gogh retrospective held at the Musée de l'Orangerie in 1947. Famous for their blazing colors, the canvases are shot in black and white, evoking the rough grains of charcoal or newsreels rather than the glazed hues of oil painting. Van Gogh's canvases are not merely "stripped of his yellows," as André Bazin puts it, but also of their framings.[15] Panning, zooming, tilting, and going in and out of focus, Dutch countryside, Paris rooftops, and Provençal pastures merge, like the location studies in *Repérages*, into what Lev Kulshov once termed a creative geography. The meandering path across the vast canvas space comes to an end in the wheatfields of Auvers-sur-Oise in July 1890. The fields are introduced by details of raised hands with sickles cutting stalks and wood cited from *The Reaper* and *The Woodcutter*, both from 1890 and both with the additional title *After Millet*, the painter whom van Gogh referred to as the "voice of the wheat."[16] After this, we are shown samples from the dozen paintings made by van Gogh from his cell at the Saint-Paul Hospital in Provence, which overlooked a square field of wheat on the asylum grounds. Executed from May 1889 to May 1890, the series follows the yearly cycle of furrowing, sowing and reaping, though in most of them, the field remains desolate.[17] As the last point of transit, Resnais cuts to a close-up of the crows in *Landscape at Auvers in the Rain* (July 1890),[18] before the film's final panning shot, sweeping from right to left across the elongated, double-square canvases of *Wheatfield with Crows* and into *Wheatfield under Thunderclouds* where the pan is interrupted halfway and the screen abruptly fades to black.

Long believed to be his last work, *Wheatfield with Crows* is sometimes referred to as the artist's "suicide note," based on the fanciful notion that it was finished in the two-day interim between van Gogh allegedly shooting himself and the time he died from the injuries, and that the crows that swarmed in the sky had in fact been startled by the blast of the lethal gunshot. Most famously, Antonin Artaud promulgated this reading after visiting the same Paris retrospective where Resnais filmed the footage for his film on the Dutch artist. "[W]ith the shot that killed him already in his belly, crowding black crows onto a canvas," Artaud conjectures in "Van Gogh, the Man Suicided by Society" (Van Gogh, Le Suicidé de la société, 1947), the painter "had no choice but to flood a landscape with blood and wine, to drench the earth with a final emulsion."[19] Unfolding as an extended ekphrasis of *Wheatfield with Crows*, Artaud's essayistic poem demands closer attention as it provides us with a series of entry points for pursuing the painting's afterlife within the concentrationary universe staked out by Cayrol and Resnais:

> Van Gogh loosened his crows like the black microbes of his suicide's spleen a few centimeters from the top *and as if from the bottom of the canvas*, following the black slash of that line where the beating of their rich plumage adds to the swirling of the terrestrial storm the heavy menace of a suffocation from above.[20]

Death comes from below and above, but also from within and without. Artaud continues:

> Landscapes undergoing strong convulsions, of frenzied traumatisms, as of a body that fever torments to restore to its perfect health. The body under the skin is an overheated factory, and, outside, the patient glistens, he shines, from all his pores, burst open. Like a landscape by van Gogh at noon. Only perpetual war explains a peace which is only a passing phase, just as milk that is ready to be poured explains the pan in which it was boiling. Beware of the beautiful landscapes of van Gogh, tempestuous and peaceful, convulsed and pacified.[21]

In his second book on cinema, *The Time Image*, Gilles Deleuze closely follows this passage when he commends the final panning shot of Resnais' *Van Gogh* for demonstrating "that, between the apparent death from inside, the attack of madness, and the definitive death from outside as suicide, the sheets of internal life and the layers of external world plunge, extend and intersect with increasing speed up to the final black screen."[22] Artaud expresses this blurring of boundaries through a series of drastic transpositions: from portrait to landscape ("I saw the face of van Gogh, red with blood in the explosion of his landscapes"); from body to soil ("having been bodily the battlefield"); from earth to flesh ("Carded by van Gogh's nail, the landscapes show their hostile flesh"); and from solid to liquid ("the earth become equivalent to the sea").[23] At once nurturing and devouring, the hitherto "unpainted nature" envisioned by van Gogh is consistently grasped by Artaud's hyperbolic prose in visceral and abdominal terms, referring to the crows as "excremental," "microbes," "musk," and "truffles," and to the field as "wine," "vinegar" and "wet blood."[24] Anticipating Cayrol's elliptical account of the Lazarean novel ("no story, no buoyancy, no plot"), Artaud further extolls *Wheatfield with Crows* for its blunt disregard of perspectival conventions as well as storytelling, proffering "no drama, no subject, and I would even say no object, for what is the motif?"[25] Still, Artaud suggests that the oncoming crows carry some sort of oblique message when he asks: "what does the earth complain of down there under the wings of those *auspicious* crows, auspicious, no doubt, for van Gogh alone, and on the other hand, sumptuous augury of an evil which can no longer touch him?"[26] This calls for a brief etymological reflection, as an auspice originally referred to an observation made by an augur, an official diviner in ancient Rome whose task it was to interpret the flight of birds in order to foretell future events. In Latin, crowing is rendered as "cras, cras," meaning "tomorrow, tomorrow," which was considered a cry of warning. Due to their ability to apprehend a hurt or sick animal, thereby showing the way for wolves and other predators, crows have been regarded as bearers of ill omens and harbingers of death. Furthermore, carrion crows are scavengers, birds of the battleground feeding on slain combatants (hence sometimes referred to as "crowfood"), earning the species epithets such as *galgenfugl* or *todenfugl*.[27] In medieval English, we may further note, a flock of crows was known as a "murder."

The following analysis will investigate the paradoxical status of van Gogh's telltale flock of crows as a retroactive trace of an event that its inscription anteceded by half a century. Following Resnais, numerous artists have invoked *Wheatfield with Crows* as a premonition of the camps. Most notable in this context is the poet Paul Celan, who made the German translation of Cayrol's narration for *Night and Fog*, and the artist Anselm Kiefer, whose paintings and installations are replete with van

Gogh's wheat stalks, sunflowers, crows and crooked paths.[28] We also find an intriguing variation of this motif in two stop-animation films made by William Kentridge. The first, *Zeno Writing* (2002), is an adaptation of Italo Svevo's 1923 novel *La coscienza di Zeno* (Zeno's Confessions) set in Trieste on the eve of the First World War and transposed by Kentridge to Johannesburg during the apartheid era. One of the charcoal drawings for projection shows an expanse of scrubby flatland with a low horizon punctuated by stub-like fence poles under a sooty sky dotted with diagrammatic dashes and hyphens. Set into motion, as Rosalind C. Morris has observed, these annotations turn first "into the diacritical (meta-textual) marks used to indicate metrical stress" and then "into those tiny 'v's that signify birds in a children's drawing—and even the luxuriant painted surfaces of a work like Van Gogh's *Wheatfield with Crows*,"[29] though, we may add, in a patently anemic version, like the fields after a fire. Ten years later, Kentridge returns to this motif in *The Anatomy of Melancholy* (2012), where calligraphic brushstrokes spread across the pages of Robert Burton's eponymous study from 1621, which is turned into a flipbook through stop-animation. Racing through the pages, the inky stains suddenly come to life and transform into a ragged crow swiftly beating its wings.

Kentridge's short films highlight two interrelated elements to be unpacked in the analysis below. The first concerns the relation between the still and the moving image, a topic to which already Artaud devoted considerable attention. For Artaud, who extolled van Gogh's ability to paint "things of inert nature as if in throes of convulsions," the startled crows possess a raw kinetic energy, arrested in flight yet on the verge of bursting into motion.[30] Consistently paradoxical, Artaud on the one hand describes van Gogh's fields and fowls as "beating" and "swirling," and on the other as "peaceful" and "pacified." The second feature accentuated by Kentridge concerns the graphological nature of van Gogh's dashes of black pigment, which hover indeterminately between the typographical and pictographical, between scrawls and figures, notations and animate beings. Incidentally, in my native language, sprawling or illegible handwriting is referred to as "crowfeet." Interpreted as van Gogh's self-penned epigram, this landscape in turmoil arrested at the moment of death may then be read as an updated version of Poussin's "Et in Arcadia Ego," with the funeral procession of crows heralding the dawn of modern landscape painting.

The next section will continue to expand upon the formal and thematic affinities between *Wheatfield with Crows*, the contaminating logic of Cayrol's Lazarean art, and the montage constructed in *Night and Fog*. From Resnais, the remainder of the chapter then moves on to consider the presence of van Gogh's crows in a series of films and video essays made by Jean-Luc Godard from the mid-1980s to the turn of the century. Introduced in reference to the Nazi extermination camps in the first chapter of *Histoire(s) du Cinema* (1988–1998), the black birds, in a manner similar to Kentridge's *The Anatomy of Melancholy*, come unstuck from the space of the canvas and spread as a polyvalent leitmotif across the series, linking Étienne-Jules Marey's chronophotographic studies of aerial locomotion and the lethal bird attacks staged by Alfred Hitchcock to the air raids over Guernica, Germany and Japan. As we shall see, the motif undergoes further transformations in a series of feature films released by Godard during the ten-year production of *Histoire(s)*. Here, it is instead the shrill barks of the crows that come unstuck, abruptly disjointed from their image. Finally, the coda returns us to *Histoire(s)* and the ghostlike presence of van Gogh with which Godard's genealogy of the moving image, and this chapter, is brought to a close.

Another Planet

Let us consider once again the three camera movements that open *Night and Fog*. First, the high-angle view craning down behind the concrete posts; second, tracking backwards to frame the scenery through strings of barbwire; and third, tracking sideways from left to right from the fields into the camps. "In whichever direction one travels—downward, backward, laterally—one is pulled from an apparently harmless present, as if by an irresistible gravitational force, into the black hole of some terrible memory," as Joshua Hirsch observes.[31] This black hole has at least three denotations.

The first is the lacuna in the archive. There are images from before the event (the first ghettoes established in the expanded Reich) and there are images from after the event (the Liberation), but the event itself, the extermination by gas taking place over the course of five years, is missing. Put differently, the defining event of twentieth century Western culture went unrecorded by the cinema. Second, this black hole was instigated when Hitler in 1937 called for the creation of "a *volkloser Raum*, a space empty of people."[32] In *Remnants of Auschwitz: The Witness and the Archive*, Giorgio Agamben argues that the camp, rather than an isolated historical anomaly, constitutes the secret nomos of the political space of modernity. "It is not simply a matter of something like a desert, a geographical space empty of inhabitants" Agamben writes, but a judicial no-man's-land "that, once established in a determinate geographical space, transforms into an absolute biopolitical space, both *Lebensraum* and *Todesraum*, in which human life transcends every assignable biopolitical identity."[33] *Night and Fog* chronicles the arc of the construction and dismantling of this space of exception in three phases. Beginning with its genesis, a photograph of four prospectors leisurely striding waste deep through a grassy field carrying maps and land surveying equipment. A space is cleared and a city constructed. Then, a population is created: amassed in ghettos, deported, and "shaved, tattooed, numbered" upon arrival. As we see an overhead shot of the congested campground, the voiceover declares: "First view of the camp: another planet."[34] Historians and survivors have since named this other planet "the metropolis of death," "cadaverland" and "the other kingdom."[35] As seasons shift, a society is formed within its remits, while "the real world, the world from before, with its peaceful landscapes," still visible through the electrified fences, is transformed into an illusion. Finally, the opening of the camps and the emaciated prisoners as Cayrol inquires: "Will everyday life know them again?" The unfolding of this arc begins and ends with images of the "strange grass" that now covers this outlandish terrain.

Third, the dark hole is the interval created through montage in the jarring contrasts between the grim black and white of the archive and the saturated Eastman-colors of the present. Like the canvases traversed by the camera in *Van Gogh*, zooming and tracking shots animate the archival records, whereas the present, where both the people and the crime are missing, is rendered as a series of still lifes of discarded objects and disused machinery. Film critic Serge Daney characterized the syncopated alterations between movement and stasis, then and now, past tense and present place in *Night and Fog* as a "seismography."[36] More precisely, the rumblings of what Smithson called "a substrata of disaster" are picked up in the shatter zone between three antithetical landscapes: the pacified and verdant present; the vision of a people rooted in the soil of the homeland; and the actual landscapes produced by Himmler's policy of "Productive Annihilation" with its mountains of human hair, fields of crushed and incinerated bones, and "the ceiling *ploughed* by fingernails" in the gas chamber at Majdanek.[37] If van Gogh turned landscape into a suicide note, the harvest reaped in the camps, where human corpses were processed into blankets, fertilizers, soap and lampshades, proffered the death certificate of landscape as a support for political or aesthetical idealism. Through the lens of deferred action one may then, as Jacob Wamberg has argued, discern in the "deliriously blooming countryside" of *Wheatfield with Crows*, or what Artaud describes as "[a] slow generative nightmare," an omen of the totalitarian experiments of the twentieth century, of the grinding of bodies in its gulags and camps, and of the exploitation of the iconography of wreaths of wheat, furrowed fields, stacks of grain and sickles so prominent in Communist and National Socialist propaganda.[38]

From an art historical standpoint, *Wheatfield with Crows* also conveys the sensation of facing a foreign planet in a different sense. Two years ahead of Artaud's attempt to grasp van Gogh's otherworldly means of perception, Meyer Schapiro defined the particular achievement of *Wheatfield with Crows* as an inversion of perspectival conventions. Instead of propelling the gaze toward a vanishing point on the horizon, Schapiro observes, the three forking paths converge in the foreground, "as if space had suddenly lost its focus and all things turned aggressively upon the beholder."[39] The middle path in the field is abruptly cut short, and flanked by two diverging paths, offering neither entrance nor exit. Moreover, the swirling masses of wheat appear to swell in size as they recede, an impression further augmented by the surging crows that "advance from the horizon toward the foreground, reversing in their approach the spectator's normal passage to the distance; he is, so to speak, their focus, their vanishing point."[40] Turned inside out, the Euclidean vectors of linear perspective, and their intimation of depth, distance and direction, turn on the viewer who becomes "the object, terrified and divided, of the oncoming crows."[41] This is the formal explanation for Artaud's "impression of being seen as if from the other side of the grave."[42] Notably, in order to apply geometric rules of proportion while working in the open air, van Gogh used a wooden frame strung with lengths of thread during most of his professional life. He referred to this draftsman's tool as his "little window" or "spy-hole."[43] On some of his paintings, the contours of the intersecting wires may still be discerned as vague pencil traces on the canvas. In analogy to the modernist master narrative on landscape painting, then, van Gogh's artistic development can be summarized as one of learning to master the craft of perspective, and of disclaiming and dismantling it in his last pictures.

The mise-en-scène of *Night and Fog* repeatedly invokes the monitored visual field of monocular perspective by quoting its two basic modus operandi: the grid and the vanishing point. The derelict architecture of the camps itself remains as a collapsed perspectival machine, incarnated by the gridded fence and the vanishing point at the end of the railroad ties. The grid, as we have seen, is established in the first series of shots of the meadows. It is also highlighted in the black-and-white photograph of the Polish town of Lublin, with its medieval castle and Old Town framed by barbwires (Fig. 4.2). The vanishing point is intimated by the ground-level tracking shots over the rails leading to the main entrance to Auschwitz. Steadily pushed along the dolly tracks running parallel to the overgrown train tracks, the disembodied gaze of the camera retraces the train's arrival to the ramp.[44] In the terminology of early cinema, this is a phantom ride, relentlessly pulled toward a point of vanishing.

In common with the image of the rails converging at the gatehouse, which had already been established as an icon of the camps already in a photograph taken by the Red Army at Auschwitz in January 1945, *Wheatfield with Crows* has been interpreted as a terminal point, not only of an artistic life, but also of a dominant mode of Western painting. Both mark at once an irrevocable rupture and a beginning: the latter the birth of modernist painting; and the former, as Serge Daney among others have argued, the birth of modern cinema.[45] This beginning can also be understood as the aftermath of a certain philosophy of history, since one-point perspective was not only a technology for controlling space, but also time,

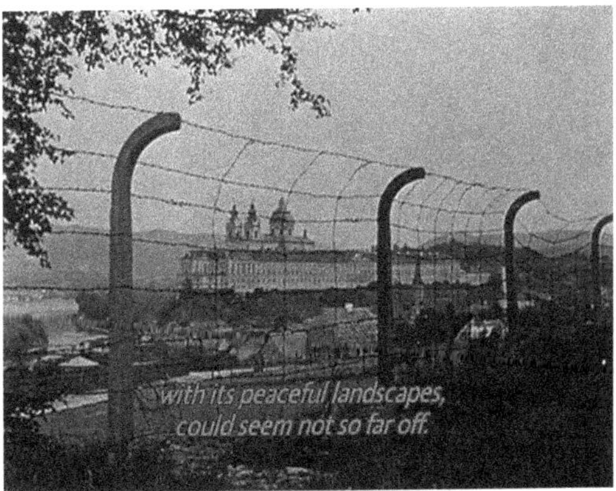

Fig. 4.2 *Night and Fog* (Alain Resnais, 1956)

plotted out along causally determined sightlines between the fixed eye of the beholder, securely positioned on the outside looking in as if through a pane of glass, and the vanishing point. In *Wheatfield with Crows*, on the contrary, the viewer's gaze is sucked under the profuse impasto layers, "swallowed alive, simultaneously in nature and in paint," as Simon Schama writes.[46] Splitting apart the perspectival order, the forking paths in the wheatfield herald the moment, according to André Bazin's canonized essay "The Ontology of the Photographic Image," when painting was emancipated from mimetic tasks (the pseudorealism of renaissance perspective) and reclaimed its aesthetic autonomy, whereas the documentary work was passed over to the novel medium cinema.[47] It is in this context that van Gogh's auspicious birds make their first appearance in Jean-Luc Godard's *Histoire(s) du cinema*.

The Symptom(s) Among Us

If "[p]erspective was the original sin of Western painting,"[48] as Bazin proclaimed in 1945, the original sin of cinema, according to Godard's *Histoire(s) du cinema*, was its failure to bear witness to the camps. Modulating Adorno's disavowal of poetry after Auschwitz, for Godard it marked instead the endpoint of documentary, the moment when cinema failed its historical responsibility to save reality.[49] "It is Godard's view that once art entered the realm of abstraction and lost figurative contact with the historical real" James S. Williams explains, "it was left to cinema." Hence, in adherence to Bazin, "it is only for Godard during those rare moments when the cinematic image recovered its documentary status and allegiance to the real that cinema honored its moral function and redeemed itself."[50] Or, as Godard himself laconically puts it, "just as painting succeeded in reproducing perspective, cinema should have succeeded in something, too, but was unable to, due to the application of sound. But there are traces of it."[51] *Histoire(s)* may thus be understood as a rescue operation, undertaken to recover such scattered traces.

Among its multitude of interlocutors, one work, though cited only with a single clip, holds a privileged position with regard to Godard's exegesis on the relation between the cinematographic trace and the extermination camps in *Histoire(s)*. This is the stern critique of the use of archival images that was formulated in *Shoah*, Claude Lanzmann's monumental film on the Nazi camps that premiered in 1985, the same year as Godard began working on his videographic essay. According to

Richard Brody, the equally monumental undertaking of *Histoire(s)*, unfolding over eight chapters and 226 minutes, "is most clearly understood as Godard's response to *Shoah*, his counter-*Shoah*."[52] From this perspective, the parenthesized "s" in the title also marks the gravitational center around which Godard's project revolves: "Histoires du cinema, avec des s. Avec de SS," as stated in the first chapter. In the numerous elaborations of the title flashing on the screen throughout the series, the "(s)" always stands by itself, disjointed from the other words. Amidst "the signs among us," which is the title of the final chapter, it is the privileged sign; not only as an acronym for the event of the Shoah, or of Lanzmann's film, but the very word Shoah: the "everlasting name" established by the Old Testament verse cited as the epigraph to *Shoah*, and the primacy of language (oral testimony) over images (photographic documents) that this word has come to imply within the discourse of Lanzmann's work. After completing *Histoire(s)*, Godard even approached Lanzmann with a proposal for a conversational film where the two adversaries, polemically cast by Godard as "partisans of the image and partisans of the text," were to debate the premises of their respective projects.[53] While this collaborative project never materialized, the dispute between Godard and Lanzmann has attracted extensive critical attention, most notably by Libby Saxton in her nuanced study *Haunted Images*.[54] We shall explore the implications of this controversy in greater depth in the final chapter. For the purpose of the present discussion, however, let us proceed by identifying the two-pronged tenet on which Godard's project rests. First, its commitment to the evidentiary nature of the cinematographic trace; and second, its reliance on such traces as an epistemological resource to reactivate and rescue the past by means of montage. These two principles, which Godard inherits respectively from André Bazin and Walter Benjamin, also inform the methodology of the atlas of pictorial memory that was constructed by Aby Warburg.

At the outset of a book-length study devoted to *Histoire(s)*, Michael Witt writes that, "[i]f Warburg, as Giorgio Agamben has argued, can be considered the founder of a hitherto 'unnamed science whose contours we are only beginning to glimpse,' Godard is his successor and has a word for that science: 'cinema,' or better in the context of *Histoire(s)*, 'video' – literally 'I see.'"[55] Video, from the Latin verb *videre*, 'to see,' we should further note, shares its etymology with evidence, which gives primacy to acts of seeing and appearing. "Evidence," as Thomas Keenan points out, "is a matter of appearance, of sight, of what manifests itself in the realm of visibility."[56] It was precisely cinema's failure to see and to serve as evidence, the overriding argument of *Histoire(s)* goes, that foreclosed its future. Based on a conception of the image as a documentary trace, the methods of montage practiced in the *Mnemosyne* atlas and in *Histoire(s)* both depend on acts of remediation. Whereas the former displaced artworks through the medium of photographic reproductions pinned on black panels, the latter relentlessly transfigures, disfigures and degrades the cinematic image through the transformative power of video. These displacements aim to create what Warburg called a *Zwischenraum*, or what Deleuze in his discussion on Godard defines as "the *interstice* between images, between two images: a spacing which means that each image is plucked from the void and falls back into it."[57] In Alan Wright's characterization of the stratified and saturated frames of *Histoire(s)*, which applies with equal pertinence to the seismography of Western visual culture that Warburg aimed for, "the cinematic image replicates the elemental quality of liquid or luminous waves, seismic tremors and subterranean echoes."[58]

Understood as a *Mnemosyne* for the post-cinematic age, both in its vastly ambitious scope and in its methodology, the multilayered superimpositions, wipes, and dissolves of *Histoire(s)* construct what Didi-Huberman has called, "a *montage* totally organized around the economy of the *symptom*."[59] It is one particular symptom that concerns us here: the crows unleashed by van Gogh. In common with the *Mnemosyne*, then, *Histoire(s)* will be considered here as a tool for retracing the itineraries of what Karl Sierek describes as, "migrating, bird-like images."[60] Like the *Mnemosyne*, finally, the eclectic constellations of *Histoire(s)*, and its dense yet fragmentary interlacing of quotations, allusions and wordplay, are notoriously challenging to paraphrase. My contention below, however, is that by following van Gogh's crows as they morph and migrate from the first chapter to the last, we will also be able to unpack a series of interrelated arguments that guide and direct Godard's project in its entirety.

Before embarking on this investigation, let us first note that Godard had already cited the opening sequence of *Night and Fog* in his 1964 film *A Married Woman* (Une femme mariée). For their final rendezvous, the film's adulterous lovers, Charlotte and Robert, meet in a movie theater at Orly airport. As Charlotte enters the theater, Godard cuts to a poster of Alfred Hitchcock, a significant figure, as we shall see, in relation to the winged creatures of *Histoire(s)*, who appears to give her a reproachful sideways glance. Once inside, the curtains rise and we hear the familiar overture ("Even a peaceful landscape, even a meadow in harvest with crows circling overhead") before we see the screen, in black and white, and the camera craning down behind the fence. As the voiceover recounts the mundane toponyms of the concentrationary universe ("Strüthof, Oranienburg, Auschwitz, Neuengamme, Belsen, Ravensbrück, Dachau"), the couple impatiently leave the theater. In *Histoire(s)*, however, Godard will only cite *Night and Fog* indirectly, either by quoting the quotations previously made by Resnais's—like the close-up of the Sinti girl peeping out through the boxcar doors of a train debarking from the Westerbork transit camp, or the boy with raised arms in the Warsaw Ghetto—or by rendering explicit Resnais' allusion to *Wheatfield with Crows* in the opening scene.

The conjecture of cinema and the Nazi camps is established halfway into the first chapter, "Toutes les histoires (All the [hi]stories)," with a low-angle color photograph of the rails leading toward the gatehouse of Auschwitz, recalling the almost identical frames in *Night and Fog* and *Shoah*. Soon after we are shown the first photograph of deportees in striped camp garments, and then, accompanied by rattling trains and blowing whistles, the conductor who drives the transport in *Shoah* leaning out of the locomotive to gaze back at his phantom passengers, slicing his hand across his throat when the road sign Treblinka appears behind his shoulder. Amidst murky and monochrome footage of masses marching to war, emaciated deportees, executions and corpses, van Gogh's crows suddenly appear in a close-up framing a small section on the left side of the canvas, which then rapidly dissolves into black-and-white film footage of a procession of bare feet trudging over drab ground, suggestive of wartime deportations and death marches. Flickering back and forth between the crows and the trampling feet, van Gogh's dazzling colors flash through the scratched and granular archive image. This montage emulates the first transition in *Night and Fog* from the deserted camp grounds in crisp early autumnal colors to the monochrome Nazi newsreels chronicling the round-ups, ghettos and embarking convoys. More precisely, Resnais first makes an abrupt cut from a tracking shot moving sideways at walking pace along the rows of oxidized fence posts ("A strange grass covers the paths once trod by the inmates. No current runs through the wires. No footstep is heard but our own") to a low-angle shot of troops marching in the opposite direction at the

Nuremberg rallies. Then, from an overhead image of the railcars arriving at their final destination, another cut returns us to a ground-level shot dollying over the weed-infested rails as the voiceover ponders the futility of its search ("Today, on the same tracks, the sun shines. We go slowly along them, looking for what?")[61] The crosscuts between *Wheatfield with Crows* and the procession of deportees (the phantom footsteps retraced by Resnais' camera) thus condense the first ten minutes of *Night and Fog* into a single elliptical configuration. Numerous images, both documentary and fictional, of the extermination campaigns follow, concluding with a clip from *The Passenger* (Andrzej Munk, 1963), an unfinished, semi-documentary film shot on location in Auschwitz. The slow-motion excerpt shows a uniformed guard standing by the electric fence with belching chimney stacks in the background, which then slowly fades into a more tightly cropped close-up of the crows that hover above the middle path in the field. Isolated from the broad sweep of wheat and sky, they appear less as figures than as a series of contorted waves (Fig. 4.3).

A parallel, though equally prominent, theme is also established in the first chapter, one that associates the crows not with the smoke rising from the crematoria but with fire descending from above. Throughout, references to aerial attacks abound. Initially, this imagery is quoted from a handful of Hollywood classics: the dust-cropper sequence in *North by Northwest* (Alfred Hitchcock, 1959); the aerial acrobatics in *Only Angels Have Wings* (Howard Hughes, 1939); and Rita Hayworth performing

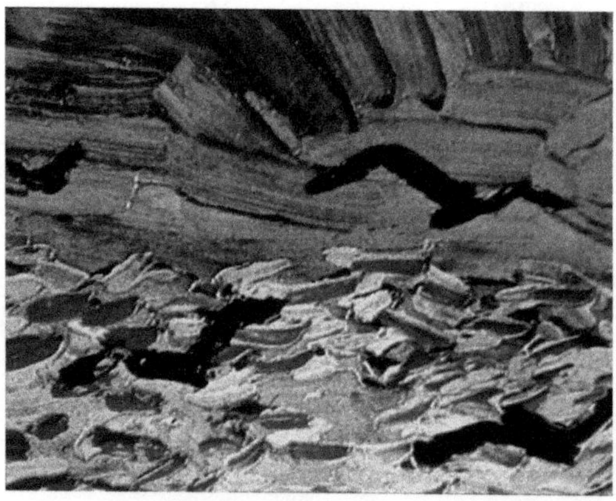

Fig. 4.3 *Histoire(s) du Cinema* (Jean-Luc Godard). Chapter 1A "Toutes les histoires" (1988)

"Put the Blame on Mame" in *Gilda* (Charles Vidor, 1946). While the latter film was in release, the first atomic bomb to be detonated in peacetime was named "Gilda" and decorated with an image of Hayworth. Following the first image of Hitler cited in the series, which is accompanied by the screeching sound of a blitzkrieg attack, feature films give way to documentary footage of ruined cities, dive-bombers and looping warplanes. Two motifs, which will return in the subsequent chapters, explicitly align aerial warfare with bird flight. The first is a slow-motion sequence in black and white where a silhouetted aircraft arcs a blank sky followed by a vertical shot of a bomb being dropped, which is slowed down to a still. This sequence is echoed a minute later by another black-and-white slow-motion shot, this time of birds swarming an overcast sky while the voice states that "[f]orgetting extermination is part of extermination." The second motif is a still photograph of eight military planes flying in opposite directions, two of them colliding in a violent blast. The saturated colors of black aircraft, cobalt sky, and the fiery reds and yellows of the explosion precede the first close-up of van Gogh's crows and blustery sky, which precisely echo the color scheme of the burning aircraft a few seconds earlier.

These two forms of industrialized mass murder by fire, in the camps and from the air, become more closely integrated toward the end of the chapter. Another quote from *The Passenger*, showing the Auschwitz orchestra, is followed by a reference to Pablo Picasso's mural-sized canvas of the destruction of an unprotected Basque market town by the Nazi Luftwaffe in 1937: "It is because this time alone the only veritable popular art form rejoins painting, that is: art. That is: what is reborn from what was burned. We have forgotten that village, its white walls and olive trees, but we remember Picasso, that is: Guernica." What we are shown is not the painting, however, but a grainy newsreel snippet of a small aircraft dropping a bomb. Significantly, Picasso's canvas was dissected in the last of Resnais' cycle of films on famous painters, *Guernica* (Alain Resnais and Robert Hessens, 1950), which opens with an aerial photograph of the devastated city, thereby highlighting the graphic similarity between wartime reportage and the white-gray-grisaille gradations of Picasso's canvas.

The first chapter of *Histoire(s)*, which is also the longest in the series, concludes with a montage that interlaces this triad of motifs: birds in flight, aerial bombardments, and death camps. A sequence from Roberto Rossellini's *Germany, Year Zero* (Germania anno zero, 1948) showing the ruins of Berlin is followed by footage of Max Linder feeding seagulls, and then, in the very last words spoken in the first chapter, we hear a female voiceover reading a factual account of the effects of Zyklon B in the gas cambers. Van Gogh's crows, along with the numerous birds that flutter through "Toutes les histoires," thereby harness two forms of extermination: the gassing and burning of civilians in the rural provinces of Greater Germany, and the incineration of the urban centers of the Third Reich by the Allied air forces. As portended by Artaud, the black fowls in the wheat at once stir up a "terrestrial storm" and descend as a "heavy menace of a suffocation from above."

In a different context, Paul K. Saint-Amour has argued that the carpet-bombings of German and Japanese cities turned the urban population into anxious decipherers of the "cryptic skywriting" performed by overhead aircraft.[62] The prospect of annihilation by a faceless executioner from above triggered, "a pre-traumatic stress syndrome whose symptoms arose in response to an anticipated rather than an already realized catastrophe."[63] Not only did the apprehension of impending disaster "make every bird look like the next bomber," Saint-Amour writes, it also "suggests the power of aerial bombardment, as both a practice and a sustained threat, to rend chronology itself."[64] The capacity to rend chronology and causality is also a defining characteristic of the symptom as developed by Didi-Huberman in his reading of Warburg's *Pathosformel*. Cognate with Saint-Amour's notion of the ominous signs in the sky spotted by non-combatants as anticipatory or proleptic symptoms,[65] the significance of van Gogh's auspicious crows can only be construed after the fact, as traces deposited on the canvas and reactivated at a later date. The convoluted temporality of the symptom also informs the double betrayal for which Godard indicts the cinematic image in *Histoire(s)*. Not only did cinema fail to show the camps, thereby abdicating from its documentary duty to save and honor the real; it also ignored the "warning shadows" ("le montreuer d'ombres") that Godard spots in a series of films from the interwar years.[66] From this perspective, the crows are symptomatic both of the clairvoyant capacity of cinema, and of our inability, or unwillingness, to read its signs. While the two close-ups of the carrion birds in the second half of the first chapter mark the single direct citation of *Wheatfield with Crows* in *Histoire(s)*, these frames establish a form that will recur with the persistence of a symptom throughout the series.

The crows have already returned in the opening credits of the second chapter, "Une histoire seule (A solitary [hi]story)," which is punctuated by a series of raucous squawks. Becoming increasingly frequent and aggressive, the amplified caws serve as an audial cue to set off Bernard Herman's soundtrack to *Psycho*, soon followed by the first photograph of Alfred Hitchcock, overprinted with the words: "a death industry." A dysphemism for the dream industry, as well as an allusion to Hitchcock's slow artistic "death" in this industry, Godard possibly also had another connection in mind when using this phrase, usually reserved for the extermination camps. In the summer of 1945, Hitchcock was flown in from Hollywood to act as a counselor to the editing team of a documentary compiled from the material shot during the Liberation, including the footage from Bergen-Belsen that is the source for the final section of *Night and Fog*. As the voiceover explicates, however, the "death industry" is here primarily to be understood as the automation of optical media, which proffered forensic evidence of a different kind of crime: "At the dawn of the twentieth century techniques decided to reproduce life. So photography and cinema were invented," Godard explains, "preparing to strip reality of its identity, so they began mourning this murder. It is with the colors of mourning, black and white, that the cinématographe came into existence." More precisely, as demonstrated toward the end of the chapter, the cinematograph came into existence with the flapping of black wings against a white background.

First, we see a spinning octagonal disk, then a sequence of twelve photograms of a bird in various stages of flight. As the disk begins to rotate, the wings are propelled into motion within the dark frame (Fig. 4.4). This black bird is one of the numerous animal species toward which the French physiologist Étienne-Jules Marey aimed his chronophotographic gun in the early 1880s. Through the contraption of a portable rifle with a photographic lens in the barrel and a crank-driven cylinder behind it, Marey was able to fire a dozen consecutive shots in one second from a single point of view. Each shot penetrated the rotating disk with light at a regular interval, thereby splicing up the trajectory of aerial locomotion into a sequence of discrete stages. With the aid of a zoetrope (literally "wheel of life"), a revolving drum perforated by narrow slots, the arc of frozen positions could then be resynthesized into a seamless reproduction of life in motion. From the moving plate of Marey's serial-shot camera, Godard cuts once more to the procession of bare feet, the same image that was superimposed together with van Gogh's crows in the previous chapter. Encircled by a dark iris, the grainy footage is now affiliated with the flickering bird trapped in the black frames of Marey's apparatus. Through this associative leap, van Gogh's crows are conscripted into a

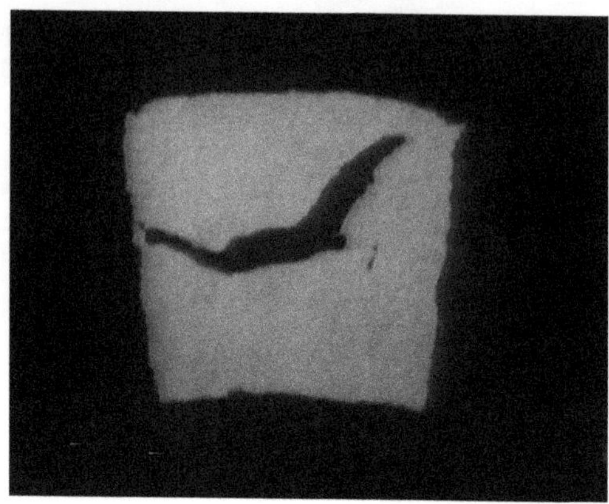

Fig. 4.4 *Histoire(s) du Cinema* (Jean-Luc Godard). Chapter 1B "Une histoire seule" (1989)

particular genealogy of the moving image. Perched on the threshold of virtual movement, the successive wing beats signify the animation of the image and the birth of cinema. In fact, as Schapiro had already pointed out in his analysis of *Wheatfield with Crows*, the crows dispersed by van Gogh across the canvas space, in common with the photograms on Marey's single disk, can be read as a time study: "as a moving series they embody the perspective of time, the growing imminence of the next moment."[67] Migrating into a new terrain, the crows thus accrue an additional layer of meaning, which at the same time casts new light on the copious imagery of aerial attacks in the first chapter.

The incentive for Marey's segmentation of wing strokes was to decipher the secret of aerodynamics.[68] Supported by the French War Department, Marey's chronophotographic studies were not conducted then with a future dream industry in mind, but in order to enable man to conquer the air. The scientific origin of the moving image is sardonically commented on in chapter 3B, "Une vague nouvelle (A new wave)," Godard's requiem for the French New Wave, where Marey's bird returns, this time superimposed with a photograph of Georges Franju holding a white dove (Fig. 4.5) and overprinted with text "fake legends." To paraphrase Friedrich Kittler, cinema did not emerge from a quest for art or peace, but as a by-product of military technology.[69] The parallel development of aviation and cinema is central to the film histories written by Kittler and Paul Virilio, whose groundbreaking studies attracted considerable attention at the time Godard was working on *Histoire(s)*. As Kittler comments in regard to the time studies reproduced

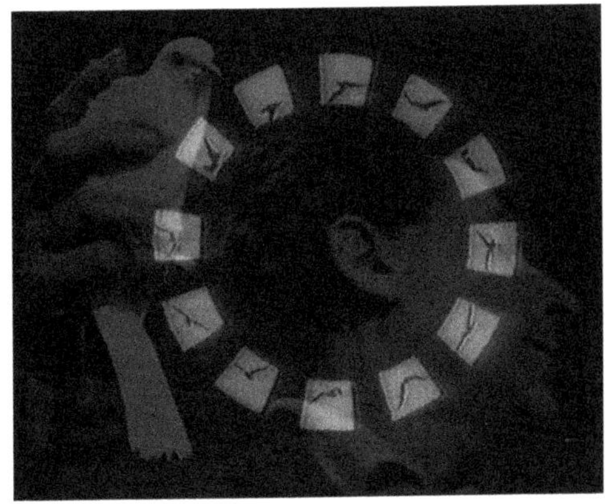

Fig. 4.5 *Histoire(s) du Cinema* (Jean-Luc Godard). Chapter 3B "Une vague nouvelle" (1998)

in Marey's *La machine animale* (1873): "where eyes had always seen only poetic wing-flaps could begin the analysis of the flight of birds, the precondition for all future aircraft constructions."[70] In his late lecture series *Optical Media*, Kittler further tracks the symbiotic relation of ballistics and linear perspective in a continuous line of descent from the conflation of the crosshairs and the vanishing point established in a theoretical treatise written by Albrecht Dürer in the sixteenth century, to the lethal implementation of Marey's gun during the World Wars when film cameras, machine guns and bomb hatches were mounted together on aircraft.[71] Seen in this light, the dark shadow propelled into motion by Marey augurs the predatory birds of the twentieth century.

Chapter 3A, "La monnaie de l'absolu (Currency of the absolute)," continues to expound upon this martial genealogy of the moving image. Following archival footage of corpses lined up in a mass grave and scattered in a grassy field, Godard cuts to the startled crows that ascend from the jungle gym bars on the schoolhouse playground in Hitchcock's *The Birds* (1963). Through his own technology of videographic decomposition of movement, Godard distorts the trajectories of the fluttering birds so that the wing flaps leave a series of afterimages, hovering as semi-transparent shadows in the air. These flickering configurations highlight the similarity between Hitchcock's crows and the proto-cinematic birds targeted by Marey. Then, in a superimposition, a second shadow appears amidst the crows: that of the bomb-carrying aircraft previously observed in the first chapter (Fig. 4.6). Graphically matched with the killer birds, the silhouetted plane joins their attack, swooping down on

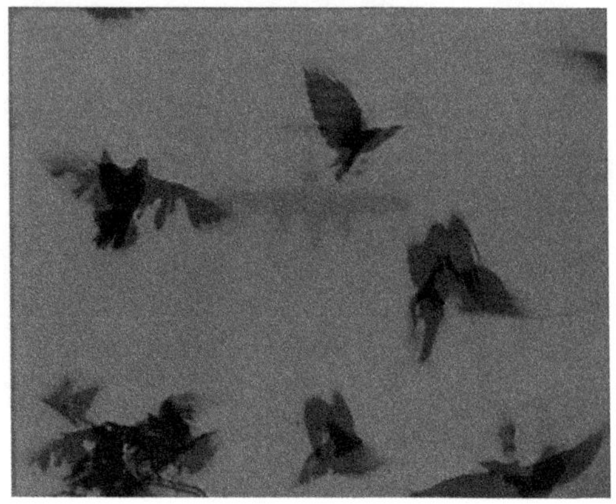

Fig. 4.6 *Histoire(s) du Cinema* (Jean-Luc Godard). Chapter 3B "La monnaie de l'absolu" (1998)

the fleeing schoolchildren in a garish constellation of documentary footage and Hollywood artifice. Of course, the original sequence was already a composite image: an amalgamation of real crows filmed in a wind tunnel, hand puppets, and mechanical birds with motorized wings, like those constructed by Marey for his three-dimensional zoetrope, superimposed over studio footage of the children running on a treadmill in front of a back-screen projection of Bodega Bay.[72] This concoction of artifice and nature also informs the soundscape engineered for *The Birds*, mixing birdcalls with electronic noises generated by a trautonium, anticipating Godard's use of the screeching caws as atonal sound bites, which will be more closely considered in the next section.

The montage of the birds and the aircraft is followed by what may be the most concise, if characteristically elliptical, summary of the various theorems that propel Godard's project: "With Manet begins modern painting: that is, the cinématographe. That is, forms making their way toward speech. Precisely: a form that thinks. Cinema was first made for thinking. This would soon be forgotten. But that's another story. The flame will go out for good in Auschwitz." Thereby, a new series of interlaced ideas cluster around the flapping wings, identified as the elementary form of the "shadows coming to life" in cinema, an artform indelibly linked for Godard, via van Gogh's flurry of impasto strokes, to painting. If the flame (cinema's potential to think in forms) was extinguished in Auschwitz, it had already been forgotten with the introduction of synchronized sound. Sound and dialogue were able to take over, Godard suggests, because we did not want to hear what these forms were telling us. In support of this claim, the chapter culminates with a medley of highlights from neorealist cinema accompanied by a sentimental ballad that extolls Italian as the universal language. The montage concludes with a close-up of the talking crow, encircled by a black iris, from Pasolini's *Hawks and Sparrows* (1966), the film that marked Pasolini's farewell to neorealism. For Godard, neorealism, the progenitor of the French New Wave and the apotheosis of Bazin's ontology of cinema, was able to recover the formal language of silent cinema due to the simple fact that sound and image were not recorded simultaneously on location. Emancipated from discursive restraints, the pictorial legacy of Italian art briefly resurfaced on the screen, and cinema was able to reclaim its affinity with painting.[73] Notably, all the birds that appear in this chapter are, in common with those gathering for their final attack in *The Birds*, silent.

This theme is expanded further in chapter 4A, "Le contrôle de l'univers (The control of the universe)," which pays homage to Alfred Hitchcock, "our century's greatest creator of forms." Reiterating the trope from Chapter one ("We have forgotten that village, its white walls and olive trees, but we remember Picasso, that is: Guernica"), Godard postulates that while we have forgotten the plots of Hitchcock's films, for example why Janet Leigh checks in at the Bates Motel or why Cary Grant's bus stops in the desert, we remember the distinct forms around which they pivot: a glass of milk, a shattered wine bottle, a key dropping through a grate, a turning windmill, or the fluttering wings of crows.[74] That is to say, while we remember the forms, we are oblivious to the historical circumstances out of which they arose. "Forms tells us what is at the bottom of things" Godard intones, chiming with Warburg's credo that forms, in particular those stirred up by the devastation brought on by "elemental man," not only transmit memory, but also, once divorced from any particular function within a plot, lead a life of their own. "There are only black lines crossing a blond painting," Godard continues, showing us a publicity photograph of Marilyn Monroe in pastel colors slashed open by a series of rapid superimpositions of the startled crows in *The Birds* (Fig. 4.7).

In the final chapter, *Les Signes parmi nous*, images of the ghettos, deportations, *muselmänner* and charnel houses, many of them previously cited by Resnais, abound. While Godard borrows the chapter title from a fable by Charles-Ferdinand Ramuz, *Les Signes parmi nous* also patently invokes Cayrol's *Lazare parmi nous*.[75] This allusion is sustained not only by the numerous citations from *Night and Fog*, but in

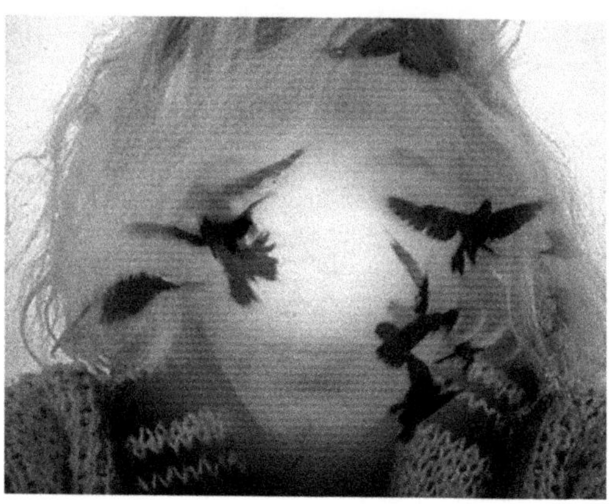

Fig. 4.7 *Histoire(s) du Cinema* (Jean-Luc Godard). Chapter 4A "Le contrôle de l'univers" (1998)

a key scene, repeated several times in *Histoire(s)* as well as in a series of Godard's feature films from this period, that offers a concise metaphor for the Lazarean poetics formulated by Cayrol. This image already appears in the first chapter, cut together with footage of an emaciated prisoner from *Night and Fog*. In this brief clip, excerpted from Boris Barnet's *By the Bluest Seas* (1936), a woman unlocks her necklace when suddenly the string breaks and the shimmering pearls drop to the ground and roll around her feet. In *Foreign Bodies* (Les Corps étrangers, 1959), Jean Cayrol writes: "Every minute contradicts the next. Like a broken necklace whose beads are running at my feet. How to put it back together? How to string the memories in order of size?"[76] In the context of *Histoire(s)*, this implies two things. First, that with the introduction of the camps, something was irrevocably broken, leaving a world beyond repair. Second, the image is emblematic of Godard's philosophy of history as montage, conceived as a method to unstring images and sounds and break up continuities so that the fragments may sparkle in new constellations. More famously, this Lazarean principle is expressed in the often repeated dictum that Godard accredits to the epistles of Saint Paul: "The image will come at the time of the resurrection." As the director unambiguously states, "montage is the resurrection of life."[77] The final chapter also concludes with a conspicuously Lazarean figure condemned to endless wanderings, quoted via Francis Bacon from a painting by van Gogh. Before we attend to the last superimposed frame of *Histoire(s)*, however, the next section will follow the call of the crows as it resounds in a series of films from what prematurely has been called Godard's late period.

Landscape with Crows in Late Godard

In the string of films that Godard released while working on *Histoire(s)*, van Gogh's crows are heard, and occasionally seen, on numerous occasions. Usually, their shrill caws abruptly pierce a placid, bucolic scene, like those heard over images of gilded cloudscapes, sunrises and full moons in *Hail Mary* (Je vous salue, Marie, 1985). Hence, they continue to remind us of the desynchronized image and audio tracks in the opening shots of *Night and Fog*, and the discord between what we see (the peaceful countryside) and what we hear (Cayrol's Lazarean testimony). In the desolate woodland settings of *King Lear* (1987), squawking crows repeatedly stab the ambient soundscape of chirping birds and purling brooks, until we are introduced to a close-up of the dabs of black paint on *Wheatfield with Crows* toward the end of the film. So frequent are these raucous barks in Godard's films from this period that Richard I. Suchenski has suggested that they function "as a sort of indirect authorial signature,"[78] though one that appears to be as inscrutable as the scrawls with which van Gogh signed off his epitaph.

So how are we to decipher this signature? Above all, it directs our attention to the relation between sound and image. The scene from *King Lear* noted above is exemplary of the equal emphasis placed by Godard on the cutting of images and on the cutting of sounds. Like the cropped frames extracted from van Gogh's canvas, the shrieks appear as cutouts: dissonant, disembodied and displaced. These amplified sound bites mark not only a sudden tear in the pastoral fabric, then, but a rupture in the very fabric of cinema. In *Nouvelle Vague* (1990), barking crows are superimposed over a lyrical shot that frames the lower section of a tree trunk and the shaded ground below. The canopy creates apertures of light that flicker in the grass as the interlacing branches and leaves gently sway in the breeze. Often heard over such painterly and contemplative compositions, the squawking crows actualize another recurring thesis in Godard's work, namely that cinema, due to its capacity to convey the transformative power of light, is more closely affiliated with painting than with photography. For Godard, what primarily distinguished cinema from painting was its instant popular appeal: "Painting has never been popular. If Van Gogh were popular his paintings would go on tour."[79] The simplicity and directness of silent cinema and its promise of a universal language was foreclosed by a series of interlaced events: the World Wars, the triumph of Hollywood, and the advent of television. In a conversation with Serge Daney, Godard articulates this idea through an allegory modeled on *Wheatfield with Crows*:

> Everyone can like a van Gogh, but then someone invented a way to spread van Gogh's crows everywhere (albeit in somewhat less terrifying form), so that everyone loved them and felt close to them. Cinema was like the earth. Then came television which was the invention of the plough. If you don't know how to use it, the plow is a bad thing. If you don't know how to till the earth or grow this or that kind of wheat.[80]

For Godard, the capacity of cinema to open up toward a yet unseen space beyond the bounded frame, Vicki Callahan writes, "was taken away by synchronous sound, narrative and naturalistic illumination (the light which leads us to believe there is no other space to investigate)."[81] From this perspective, the croaks are not so much cries of warning as of mourning, funeral lamentations for the new continent briefly glimpsed in silent film. Indeed, Godard has consistently referred to cinema in spatial terms: as a foreign, uncharted terrain ("The cinema was a place, a territory … a place without history"); subsequently conquered by Hollywood and obliterated by television ("I'm in occupied territory. I'm in the resistance," or, "I feel like an occupied country. Change lies between the images"); yet still calling out to be discovered ("there is a land that is out of focus, and this out of focus is the real cinema.")[82]

Laments on homeland and landscape abound in Godard's work from this period. They loom particularly heavy in *Germany Year Nine Zero* (Allemagne année 90 neuf zéro, 1991) where the piercing sound of a crow repeatedly punctuates Lemmy Caution's aimless wanderings through the ruins of post-communist Berlin. In the last exterior shot of the film, which frames the ominous silhouette of the InterContinental Hotel at dusk, the barren trees and winter sky are swarming with crows. Jeffrey Skoller glosses this tableau as, "an urban version of Van Gogh's last painting."[83] Most elaborate in this regard, however, is *JLG/JLG—Self-portrait in December* (JLG/JLG—autoportrait de décembre, 1994). A portrait of the artist in self-imposed exile, it is now the director who assumes the role of a lonely wanderer, roaming the banks of Lake Geneva near his home in Rolle, Switzerland. *Self-portrait in December* is a portrait without a face, as Godard mostly remains off-screen or obscured in shadows. Instead it shows us waves lapping on the shore, deserted fields, solitary trees and sulking forested paths, concluding with the green fields of spring. Notably, the second part of the film's title, "in December," affiliates it with the genre of landscape rather than portraiture, for whereas seasons are irrelevant for a self-portrait, they are essential to a landscape. Once more, these rural scenes are repeatedly shattered by the off-screen sound of a barking crow. "Not only is the crow conspicuously absent on the screen, but its sounds are conspicuously disjunct, too loud to be part of the landscape," as Nora M. Alter has observed.[84] Along the same lines, Christopher Pavsek notes that "[t]he sound is obviously non-synchronous and non-diegetic, and foregrounds itself through its absolute out-of-placeness in the shot."[85] Instead of synchronizing image and sound, then, Godard deploys the audio track like a superimposition, isolated as a *sonimage* (sound image), or what Michel Chion, in a coinage that perfectly paraphrases the slashes of black paint gesticulated by van Gogh, has termed a "sound shot."[86]

The notion of a sound shot returns us to Artaud's pamphlet. For Artaud, *Wheatfield with Crows* is an eminently audible painting: "I hear the wings of the crows striking cymbal blows loudly over an earth whose torrent it seems van Gogh can no longer contain."[87] Something escapes the scene, an unruly and uncontainable energy indexed by the flight of the crows. If the crows have indeed been startled by the blast of the gun, as Anne Carson has deduced, the flock "makes audible the sound of a soul being deserted by its body."[88] Rather than denoting some spiritual dimension, as has often been assumed, the nature imagery so prominent from *Hail Mary* to *JLG/JLG* summons the presence of earthly and corporeal matter that silent cinema so lucidly had exposed, a presence recovered, albeit briefly, by the filmmakers of the Italian neorealism, Godard argues, precisely because the image and audio tracks were not recorded simultaneously on location. For Godard, the landscape, as the director relays in a conversation with Hal Hartley, is,

> like the body. And words and action in movies are the spirit or the mind. And these days the body is almost completely forgotten. In the beginning the body—nature—was more part of the action. It has no meaning today if you put Clint Eastwood in the mountains in Nevada. It has nothing to do with the story. It has just been decided by agents or lawyers. And before the war, and just after the war, it still had a meaning. Now it has disappeared. On TV you can't show landscapes. You just can't. Even a postcard is better. [Landscapes] are too close to painting. And TV has nothing to do with painting. It's just transmission. And you can't transmit a landscape, happily enough.[89]

From this perspective, the harsh croaks mark the separation of nature from spirit and of body from mind, a divorce inflicted by the synchronization of sound and image. The postlapsarian terrains roamed by the vagrant figures in *Germany Year Nine Zero* and *JLG/JLG* are not merely evocative of the receding utopias of communism or childhood, then, but ultimately of the utopia, literally the *non-place*, projected by early cinema.

Phantoms of the Road

When flying over the *Spiral Jetty*, coiling in the red algae of the Great Salt Lake in Utah, Robert Smithson is suddenly assailed by a vision of the extinct waters as "an unbroken field of raw meat with gristle."[90] While the artist at first yearns "to retreat into the cool rooms of reason," a Euclidian space of "dispassionate abstractions" and "the assurance of geometry,"[91] he quickly dismisses this thought: "But no, there was Van Gogh with his easel on some sun-baked lagoon painting ferns of the Carboniferous Period."[92] And, in the helicopter shot that concludes the film *Spiral Jetty* (1970), there is Smithson trudging down the spiral, his body almost obliterated by the searing sunlight blazing in the lake.

Histoire(s) concludes with a similar vision. In the very last image of the final chapter, Godard returns to van Gogh, this time by way of the solitary wanderer in *Painter on the Road to Tarascon* (1888). Notably different from his other self-portraits, van Gogh here depicts himself as a full-bodied figure equipped with canvas, easel and a bucket of brushes on his way to another workday in the fields. Whereas the artist is shown from head to toe, he is, like so many of van Gogh's peasants and reapers, overtly faceless. Lacking discernable features, the head is rendered in the same earthly palette as the bark on the tree behind him. It is not van Gogh's original that Godard shows us, however, but the second version in a series of seven studies based on this painting made by Francis Bacon in 1957. In contrast to the stark geometry of the original, with its lateral bands of gravel footpath, yellow field, and flat horizon, edged by bluish mountains according to the rules of atmospheric perspective and framed by the vertical axes of the artist and the trees, Bacon tilts the entire scene to the extent that the paint appears to be sliding off the canvas. Trailed by his own shadow, which is rendered, crow-like, as an anamorphic black blotch by van Gogh, the artist appears, in Bacon's phrase, "like a phantom of the road."[93] In Bacon's *Study for a Portrait of Van Gogh II*, the figure is all shadow, whereas the road, smeared in thick strokes, more closely resembles the flowing paths in *Wheatfield with Crows*. The shadows multiply in the final superimposition of *Histoire(s)*, when Bacon's study slowly merges with a murky black-and-white portrait of Godard.

Ernst van Alphen has noted that whereas van Gogh tended to paint his own face as if a landscape, in "yellow strokes that give it the texture of a cornfield" or in "little dots and strokes that are as colorful as a pasture in spring," Bacon, conversely, renders the space that surrounds van Gogh as a body.[94] Blurring "[t]he conceptual categories of inside and outside, or innerness and outerness," the body "disunites and, decomposing, invades and contaminates the surrounding space."[95] In fact, van Gogh's "body is not bodily at all," van Alphen continues, whereas "[t]he road, on the contrary, is extremely body-like. The red, pink and white strokes of paint turn it into a meat-like surface."[96] This contamination furthermore causes the enframing apparatus to collapse, thereby invalidating the figure and ground differentiation that defined the "Landscape with…" formula:

> The bodily landscapes and the ferine bodies in these paintings form one continuity. Van Gogh's deathly appearance is stressed, perhaps even caused, by the bodily landscape, which is not distinct enough to frame him. The landscape is in fact a bodyscape, and a bodyscape cannot frame the body into a whole because, as the expression already suggests, it is part of that which has to be framed."[97]

Bacon even adds the perspectival lines, applied by van Gogh through his wooden scaffold of intersecting strings, in crude black strokes, which hover like a cage-like contraption in midair, mockingly evoking the framework that can no longer hold the body in place. Paradoxically, it is the thickly smeared road rather than the figure that seems to move, slipping away under the feet of the crumbling body, which appears to be leaking or melting into the ground.

Painter on the Road to Tarascon belongs to a handful of van Gogh's lost works. In 1937, when Hitler first had professed the need to clear a "peopleless space," the Nazi Party mounted its *Entartete Kunst* exhibition in order to publicly expose the contaminating influence on the German *volk* exerted by degenerate modern art. The renaissance of Germania not only required that its expanding territories should be eradicated of sub-human elements, but also that its cultural institutions should be purged of non-Aryan images. While thousands of artworks were burned, others, like van Gogh's *Self-Portrait Dedicated to Paul Gauguin* (1888), were auctioned to raise foreign currency for the Reich. While the latter ended up in the Harvard Art Museums, *Painter on the Road to Tarascon* remained stored in the basement of the Kaiser-Friedrich Museum in Magdeburg. Heavily bombed by British and American air forces in the spring of 1945, setting fire to the Kaiser-Friedrich Museum, the painting is believed to have perished in the flames. In a literal sense, Bacon's study of van Gogh thus resurrects what was destroyed by fire. The final superimposition in *Histoire(s)* thereby also affirms the credo formulated by André Malraux in his last book, *Lazarus* (1974), cited already in the first chapter of *Histoire(s)* in relation to the bombing of Guernica, that art is "what is reborn from what was burned."[98]

Above all, van Gogh's phantoms and crows are indicative of the capacity of forms to survive. It has long been verified that *Wheatfield with Crows*, contrary to common belief, was not, in fact, van Gogh's last painting. Furthermore, recently unearthed evidence has also cast the circumstances surrounding the artist's alleged suicide into doubt. In their biography *Van Gogh: The Life*, Steven Naifeh and Gregory White Smith deduce from a series of indices that he was more likely shot by mistake by a local teenager who, inspired by Buffalo Bill's traveling Wild West Show, was known to play with a malfunctioning gun in the field where van Gogh worked.[99] The retroactive notion of *Wheatfield with Crows* as the artist's suicide note nonetheless highlights its paradoxical status as an impossible witness, and as a proleptic symptom of the malicious forces that loomed on the horizon of the twentieth century. As we have seen, the enigmatic scribblings above the tempestuous wave of wheat stalks belong neither fully to the realm of letters nor figures. The crows inhabit neither foreground nor background, neither sky nor field. Suspended in flight, between arrival and departure, we cannot tell if they are "flying toward us" or "flapping away,"[100] or if they return from out of the past or advance toward us from the future. Perforating the canvas, they remain in perpetual flight, eluding whatever regime—the perspectival apparatus, chronophotography, or biographical models of interpretation—that seeks to pin them down and keep them in place.

Notes

1. Robert Smithson "Art Through the Camera's Eye" [c. 1971] *Robert Smithson: The Collected Writings* ed. Jack Flam (Berkeley, Los Angeles, and London: University of California Press 1996) 371–375, 375.
2. Quoted from the essay written by Suzanne Liandrat-Guigues and Jean-Louis Leutrat for Alain Resnais' *Reperages* (Paris: Chêne 1974) n.p.
3. In reference to the discussion on *Dust Breeding* in the previous chapter, we may here take note of an earlier image of New York flooded by pollution. In 1920, the same year that he photographed Duchamp's dust-coated *Large Glass*, Man Ray emptied the contents of an ashtray on a floor and photographed it face down. He called it *New York*, a miniature city made of ash, cigarette butts, and burned matches.
4. James Monaco *Alain Resnais* (New York: Oxford University Press 1979) 147.
5. See project website http://www.centrecath.leeds.ac.uk/projects/conmem/ (accessed 1 August 2018).
6. Griselda Pollock and Max Silverman "Introduction" *Concentrationary Cinema: Aesthetics as Political Resistance in Alain Resnais's Night and Fog (1955)* (New York and Oxford: Berghahn Books 2011) 1–54, 2.
7. The earthward crane shot that opens *Night and Fog*, "announces the contamination of past and present, inside and outside and the ordinary and the extraordinary." Max Silverman "Horror and the Everyday in Post-Holocaust France: *Nuit et brouillard* and Concentrationary Art" *French Cultural Studies* Vol. 17 No. 5 (2006) 5–18, 8.
8. Two essays, "Les Rêves lazaréens" and "Pour un romanesque lazaréen," were published together in a small volume under the title *Lazare parmi nous* in 1950. Jean Cayrol *Lazare parmi nous* (Paris: Editions de la Baconnière 1950) 39. "Les rêves-paysages étaient les plus fréquents; c'étaient surtout d'immenses panoramas avec des lointains à l'infini." My translation.
9. Primo Levi quoted by Giorgio Agamben *Remnants of Auschwitz: The Witness and the Archive* [1999] trans. Daniel Heller-Rosein (New York: Zone Books 2000) 101.
10. The term "concentrationary universe" was coined by the French author David Rousset, a former inmate of the concentration camps in Neuengamme and Buchenwald. Rousset was also the first to use the term "gulag" in the French language in reference to the Soviet labor camps.
11. Georges Bataille quoted by Bruno Chaouat "In the Image of Auschwitz" *Diacritics* Vol. 36 No. 1 (Spring 2006) 86–96, 93.
12. Wajcman cited by Libby Saxton in *Haunted Images: Film, Ethics, Testimony and the Holocaust* (London and New York: Wallflower Press 2008) 4.

13. "Do faces no longer expressive of anything internal mean that the camps have brought about the end of face?" Nicolas Losson and Annette Michelson ponder in their discussion of the footage of the emaciated prisoners that was filmed by the Allied forces during the Liberation in the spring of 1945. Earlier in the same essay, Zoran Music, a former inmate of Dachau, provides an account of the glut of decomposing corpses that recalls the landscapes envisioned by Bosch or Turner: "silvery white snow on the mountains, the white spots of flocks of seagulls landed on the lagoon and decomposing out on the water, in the storm's dark field." Nicolas Losson and Annette Michelson "Notes on the Images of the Camps" *October* Vol. 90 (Autumn 1999) 25–35, 32–34.
14. Eric Klingerman *Sites of the Uncanny: Paul Celan, Specularity and the Visual Arts* (Berlin and New York: Walter de Gruyter 2007) 154.
15. André Bazin "Painting and Cinema" *What Is Cinema?* ed. and trans. Hugh Gray (Berkeley, Los Angeles, and London: University of California Press 1967) 164–169, 169.
16. Letter to Theo van Gogh, *The Complete Letters of Vincent van Gogh* (London: Thames & Hudson 1958) 614a, Vol. 3, 232.
17. The paintings from "The Wheatfield" series included by Resnais are, in chronological order: *Enclosed Wheat Field with Rising Sun* from May 1889; *Wheat Fields After the Rain (The Plain of Auvers)* from July 1890; and *Enclosed Wheat Field in the Rain* from November 1889.
18. While a few scattered crows can be spotted in several of van Gogh's wheat fields—*The Sower* (June 1888); *Field with Stacks of Grain* (July 1890); *Wheat Stack Under Clouded Sky* (July 1890) and *The Reaper, After Millet* (1889)—they entirely take over the composition in *Wheatfield with Crows.*
19. Antonin Artaud "Van Gogh, the Man Suicided by Society" [1947] *Antonin Artaud: Selected Writings* ed. Susan Sontag (New York: Farrar, Straus and Giroux 1976) 481–512, 489, 490.
20. Ibid. 489–490.
21. Ibid. 507.
22. Gilles Deleuze *Cinema 2: The Time-Image* [1985] trans. Hugh Tomlinson and Robert Galeta (Minneapolis: University of Minnesota Press 1989) 209.
23. Artaud 487, 488, 503, 508.
24. Ibid. 489–490, 508.
25. Ibid. 500. With regard to *Wheatfield with Crows*, Peggy Phelan similarly notes that, "these crows have lost the purpose, the plot, the destination … the ground flies and fades into water but the crows are still, suspended in flight with no space." Peggy Phelan "Not Surviving Reading" *Narrative* Vol. 5 No. 1 (January 1997) 77–87, 85.

26. Artaud 489.
27. Such crows appear, for example, in Caspar David Friedrich's *Chasseur in the Forest* (1814) and *Tree of Crows* (1822). We may also recall Vasily Vereshchagin's painting *The Apotheosis of War* from 1871, which renders the aftermath of the Russian conquest of Turkestan as a giant pyramid of human skulls circled by crows.
28. Paul Celan alludes to *Wheatfield with Crows* in several of his poems, most explicitly in "Unter ein Bild," which is written as an extended caption to the painting. Anselm Kiefer has maintained a lifelong dialogue with Celan as well as van Gogh, and often fuses the influence of the two. In 1963, Kiefer was awarded a student travel stipend for a project that aimed to retrace the steps of van Gogh and revisit the locations painted by his predecessor. Matthew Biro *Anselm Kiefer and the Philosophy of Martin Heidegger* (New York: Cambridge University Press 1998) 7. For a discussion on Kiefer and Celan in relation to Resnais' *Night and Fog* and van Gogh's *Wheatfield with Crows*, see Andréa Lauterwein *Anselm Kiefer/Paul Celan: Myth, Mourning and Memory* (London: Thames & Hudson 2007) 143–146.
29. Rosalind C. Morris "Drawing the Line at a Tree-Search: The New Landscapes of William Kentridge" *October Files: William Kentridge* ed. Rosalind Krauss (Cambridge and London: The MIT Press 2017) 113–146, 131.
30. Artaud 488.
31. Joshua Hirsch *Afterimage: Film, Trauma, and the Holocaust* (Philadelphia: Temple University Press 2010) 49.
32. Agamben *Remnants of Auschwitz* 85.
33. Ibid. 85–86.
34. If we take Agamben's advice, we should not consider this "other planet" as a rupture in history, but instead ask what measures have been taken to make it come into existence. "The legal equivalent of outer space," is also how one of the lawyers in the George W. Bush administration described the extra-judicial prison camp in Guantánamo. Cited by Yosefa Loshitzky *Screening Strangers: Migration and Diaspora in Contemporary European Cinema* (Bloomington and Indianapolis: Indiana University Press 2010) 138.
35. Otto Dov Kulka *Landscapes of the Metropolis of Death: Reflections on Memory and Imagination* (London: Penguin Books 2013); Michael Dorland *Cadaverland: Inventing a Pathology of Catastrophe for Holocaust Survival* (Waltham: Brandeis University Press 2009); David Rousset *The Other Kingdom L'univers concentrationnaire* [1946] (New York: Reynal and Hitchcock 1947).
36. Serge Daney cited by Georges Didi-Huberman *Images in Spite of All: Four Photographs from Auschwitz* trans. Shane B. Lillis (Chicago: University of Chicago Press 2008) 130.

37. From Paul Celan's translation of Cayrol's narration to *Night and Fog*, cited by Klingerman, 167. My emphasis.
38. Jacob Wamberg "Wounded Working Heroes: Seeing Millet and Van Gogh Through the Cleft Lens of Totalitarianism (Adding Reflections from Kiefer and Baselitz)" *Totalitarian Art and Modernity* eds. Mikkel Bolt Rasmussen and Jacob Wamberg (Aarhus: Aurhus University Press 2010) 36–104, 71. Artaud 499. In a letter written in July 1890, Van Gogh describes his three final canvases in similar terms, expressive at once of "sadness and extreme loneliness" and "the health and restorative forces that I see in the country." In a letter from July 1890, as quoted by Wamberg 70.
39. Meyer Schapiro "On a Painting of Van Gogh" [1946] *Modern Art. 19th & 20th Centuries. Selected Papers* (New York: George Braziller 1978) 87–99, 87.
40. Ibid. 89.
41. Ibid.
42. Artaud 505.
43. Steven Naifeh and Gregory White Smith *Van Gogh: The Life* (New York: Random House 2011) 293.
44. Sylvie Lindeperg *Night and Fog* [2007] trans. Tom Mes (Minneapolis and London: University of Minnesota Press 2014) 77.
45. "It took me time to develop this idea that 'modern' cinema, born with me, was a cinema of an *awareness* of the camps, an awareness that changed the way films were made." As quoted by Lindeperg 250.
46. Simon Schama *Simon Schama's Power of Art* (London: BBC Books 2006) 350.
47. André Bazin "The Ontology of the Photographic Image" [1945] trans. Hugh Gray *Film Quarterly* Vol. 13 No. 4 (Summer 1960) 4–9, 9.
48. Ibid. 7.
49. As the epigraph for his book length study of the four photographs from Auschwitz-Birkenau taken by a member of the Sonderkommando, Didi-Huberman cites the following lines from the first chapter of *Histoire(s)*: "even scratched to death a simple rectangle of thirty-five millimeters saves the honor of all the real." *Images in Spite of All: Four Photographs from Auschwitz* [2003] trans. Shane B. Lillis (Chicago and London: The University of Chicago Press 2008) 2.
50. James S. Williams *Encounters with Godard: Ethics, Aesthetics, Politics* (Albany: State University of New York Press 2016) 61.
51. Godard interviewed in 1988. "Godard Makes [Hi]stories. Interview with Serge Daney" *Jean-Luc Godard: Son + Image 1974–1991* ed. Raymond Bellour (New York: The Museum of Modern Art and Harry N. Abrams 1992) 159–167, 167.

52. Richard Brody *Everything Is Cinema: The Working Life of Jean-Luc Godard* (New York: Metropolitan Books 2008) 511.
53. Godard in a letter to Claude Lanzmann and Bernard-Henri Lévy from 18 March 1999. Cited by Bernard-Henri Lévy "Is Jean-Luc Godard Antisemitic? Not a Gala Dinner (Third Episode, 1999)" *Huffington Post* November 18, 2010 https://www.huffingtonpost.com/bernardhenri-levy/post_1285_b_785058.html (accessed 2 August 2018).
54. Saxton *Haunted Images* 46–67. See also Sylvie Lindeperg *Night and Fog* 105–111.
55. Michael Witt *Jean-Luc Godard, Cinema Historian* (Bloomington and Indianapolis: Indiana University Press 2013) 3.
56. Thomas Keenan "Getting the Dead to Tell Me What Happened: Justice, Prosopopoeia, and Forensic Afterlives" *Forensis: The Architecture of Public Truth* (Berlin: Sternberg Press 2014) 35–55, 43.
57. Deleuze *Cinema 2* 179. For a comparative analysis of the interstice in *Histoire(s)* and the *Mnemosyne* atlas, see Dimitrios S. Latsis "Genealogy of the Image in *Histoire(s) du Cinema*: Godard, Warburg and the Iconology of the Interstice" *Third Text* Vol. 27 No. 6 (2013) 774–785.
58. Alan Wright "Elizabeth Taylor and Auschwitz: *JLG* and the Real Object of Montage" *The Cinema Alone: Essays on the Work of Jean-Luc Godard 1985–2000* eds. Michael Temple and James S. Williams (Amsterdam: Amsterdam University Press 2000) 51–60, 59.
59. Didi-Huberman *Images in Spite of All* 134.
60. Karl Sierek quoted by Latsis 781.
61. The low-angle shot of marching troops at the Nuremberg Nazi Party Congress is cited from *Triumf des Villens* (Leni Riefenstahl, 1935), whereas the concluding shot of the newsreel montage, the overhead image of the train arriving in the night and fog, is illustrated with a clip from Wanda Jakubowska's feature film *The Last Stage* (1948). The question that impels the roving camera in *Night and Fog*—"looking for what?"—is resumed in Sergei Loznitsa's slow, observational documentary *Austerlitz* (2016). Unfolding as a series of static, black-and-white tableaux over ninety-four minutes, Loznitsa frames tourists, equipped with audio guides, information flyers, cameras, smartphones and selfie sticks, visiting Dachau and Sachsenhausen. Rather than an exploration of the site, *Austerlitz* is a study of gestures and attitudes (strolling, pausing, yawning, posing, removing sunglasses, swinging water bottles). Foremost, it attends to the gestures of looking, though we rarely see what these casual visitors from another world are actually trying to discern as they peer through the gates and windows, or what their snapshots intend to preserve. While there is little audible dialogue, the T-shirts provide a glaring commentary to the leisure activity, ironically framed by the *Arbeit Macht Frei* gateway sign, of spending a summer

day in the camp. The T-shirt prints fall into four main categories: toponyms (NY, LA, Paris, Notre Dame, Malibu, Berlin, Chicago, England); blockbuster franchise (Jurassic Park, Batman); brand names (Nike, Lidl, Henri Lloyd, Reebok); and slogans ('dream,' 'today is your lucky day,' 'just don't care,' 'cool story bro'). One T-shirt simply has an image of a white camera printed on black cloth.

62. Paul K. Saint-Amour "Air War Prophecy and Interwar Modernism" *Comparative Literature Studies* Vol. 42 No. 2 (2005) 130–161, 142.
63. Ibid. 131.
64. Ibid. 139.
65. See also Paul K. Saint-Amour "Bombing and the Symptom: Traumatic Earliness and the Nuclear Uncanny" *Diacritics* Vol. 30 No. 4 (2000) 59–82.
66. Among these clairvoyant films, Godard highlights *Nosferatu* (Friedrich Wilhelm Murnau, 1922), *La règle du jeu* (Jean Renoir, 1936), *The Great Dictator* (Charlie Chaplin, 1940) and *To be or not to be* (Ernst Lubitsch, 1942). See Daniel Morgan's discussion in *Late Godard and the Possibilities of Cinema* (Berkeley and Los Angeles: University of California Press 2013) 67, 179. See also Witt 124. "When Langlois projected Nosferatu and in the small village where Nosferatu lived you already saw the ruins of Berlin in 1944, a projection took place." "Godard Makes [Hi]stories. Interview with Serge Daney" 159.
67. Schapiro 89.
68. Marta Braun *Picturing Time: The Work of Etienne-Jules Marey (1830–1904)* (Chicago: The University of Chicago Press 1992) 31–41, 49–62.
69. "The entertainment industry is, in any conceivable sense of the word, an abuse of army equipment." Friedrich Kittler *Gramophone, Film, Typewriter* [1986] (Stanford: Stanford University Press 1999) 96–97.
70. Ibid. 123–124.
71. Friedrich Kittler *Optical Media: Berlin Lectures 1999* [2002] (Malden, MA and Cambridge, UK: Polity Press 2010) 58, 186–187.
72. Tony Lee Moral *The Making of Hitchcock's The Birds* (Harpenden, UK: Oldcastle Books 2013).
73. For a close analysis of this chapter of *Histoire(s)*, see James S. Williams *Encounters with Godard* 53–81.
74. "We have forgotten why Joan Fontaine leans over a cliff, and what Joel McCrea went to do in Holland; we have forgotten what Montgomery Cliff keeps eternally silent about, and why Janet Leigh stops at the Bates Motel, and why Theresa Wright is still in love with Uncle Charlie; we have forgotten what Henry Fonda is not entirely guilty of, and exactly why the American government hires Ingrid Bergman. But we remember a handbag, a bus in the desert, a glass of milk, the wings of a windmill, a hairbrush; but we remember a shelf of wine bottles, a pair of

glasses, a ring of keys. Because with these Hitchcock succeeded where Alexander, Julius Cesar, Napoleon and Hitler failed, in taking control of the universe." For two close readings of this sequence, see Jacques Rancière "Godard, Hitchcock, and the Cinematographic Image" *For Ever Godard* (London: Black Dog Publishing 2007) 214–231; and Trond Lundemo "The Index and Erasure: Godard's Approach to Film History" 380–395 in the same volume.

75. As Godard explains to Daney: "'*Les signes parmi nous*' is a novel by Ramuz that I've always wanted to do: a peddler arrives in a little village above the Vevey and announces the end of the world. There's a terrible storm for a few days, then the sun comes out, and the peddler is kicked out. The peddler is cinema!" "Godard Makes [Hi]stories. Interview with Serge Daney" 167. This parable is also recounted in the last chapter of *Histoire(s)*.
76. Jean Cayrol *Foreign Bodies* [1959] trans. Richard Howard (New York: G.P. Putnam's Sons 1960) 76, as quoted by Hirsch in *Afterimage* 45. The scene of the broken necklace further resounds with Walter Benjamin's idiom of the historian who "stops telling the sequence of events like the beads of a rosary" from his "Thesis on the Philosophy of History." Here Benjamin outlines the methodology for an alternative historical materialism, one that does not subdue events by stringing them together into a causally determined sequence, but instead seeks to ignite the "chips of Messianic time" through montage. Walter Benjamin 1940 "Theses on the Philosophy of History" *Illuminations: Essays and Reflections* trans. Harry Zohn (New York: Schocken Books 1968) 253–264, 263. As Godard remarks: "Making history means spending hours looking at these images and then suddenly bringing them together, creating a spark. This makes constellations, stars that come together or move away, as Walter Benjamin saw it." Godard cited by Didi-Huberman in *Images in Spite of All* 140.
77. Godard cited by Saxton 50.
78. Richard I. Suchenski *Projections of Memory: Romanticism, Modernism, and the Aesthetics of Film* (New York: Oxford University Press 2016) 282 n. 162.
79. Godard cited in Witt 113.
80. "Godard Makes [Hi]stories. Interview with Serge Daney" 162.
81. Vicki Callahan "'Gravity & Grace': On the 'Sacred' and Cinematic Vision in the Films of Jean-Luc Godard" *For Ever Godard* 188–199, 199.
82. "Godard Makes [Hi]stories. Interview with Serge Daney" 160, 164; *Changer d'image—Lettre à la bien-aimée* (Jean-Luc Godard, 1982); *Jean-Luc Godard: Interviews* ed. David Sterritt (Jackson: University Press of Mississippi 1998) 189.

83. Jeffrey Skoller *Shadows, Specters, Shards: Making History in Avant-Garde Film* (Minneapolis and London: University of Minnesota Press 2005) 79.
84. Nora M. Alter "Mourning, Sound, and Vision: Jean-Luc Godard's JLG/JLG" *Camera Obscura* 44 Vol. 15 No. 2 (2000) 74–103, 75.
85. Christopher Pavsek "What Has Come to Pass for Cinema in Late Godard" *Discourse* Vol. 28 No. 1 (Winter 2006) 166–195, 182.
86. "Sonimage" was the name of the production company that Godard founded together with Anne-Marie Miéville in 1973. Michel Chion *Audio-Vision: Sound on Screen* 1990 (New York: Colombia University Press 1994) 42–44.
87. Artaud 508.
88. Anne Carson "Writing on the World: Simonides, Exactitude and Paul Celan" *Arion* Vol. 4 No. 2 (Fall 1996) 1–26, 23.
89. "'In Images We Trust': Hal Hartley Interviews Jean-Luc Godard" *Filmmaker* Vol. 3 No. 1 (Fall 1994) 14, 16–18, 55–56. Here cited from https://cinemagodardcinema.wordpress.com/interviews/hartly/ (accessed 2 August 2018).
90. Robert Smithson "The Spiral Jetty" [1972] *Robert Smithson: The Collected Writings* 148.
91. Ibid.
92. Ibid. 149.
93. John Russell *Francis Bacon* (London: Thames & Hudson 1971) 91.
94. Ernst van Alphen *Francis Bacon and the Loss of Self* (London: Reaktion Books 1992) 144.
95. Ibid. 147, 162.
96. Ibid. 143.
97. Ibid. 144.
98. Significantly, Malraux, who joined the republicans during the Spanish Civil War and later the resistance movement in France during the Second World War, was also the first French novelist to write about the Nazi camps. See James S. Williams' discussion of the Malraux citation in *Encounters with Godard* 204.
99. Steven Naifeh and Gregory White Smith *Van Gogh: The Life* (London: Profile Books 2011) 870–873. The circumstances of van Gogh's death have also been explored in the amalgamated form of film noir mystery and labor-intensive remediation in the animated film *Loving Vincent* (Dorota Kobiela and Hugh Welchman 2017).
100. Schama *Simon Schama's Power of Art* 347.

CHAPTER 5

Persistence of Vision

Mnemotechnics have always relied on the visualization of space, storing time by means of spatial images. From the memory palace of ancient Roman rhetoric and the memory theater of the Venetian Renaissance to Pierre Nora's dichotomy of *lieux* and *mileux de mémoire*, the long spatial turn taken by memory studies is one that has gradually moved from virtual to physical space. As we saw in the second chapter, the two founding fathers that laid the ground for the study of collective memory in the 1920s both took recourse to cartography, charting the process of recollection through complex spatial networks. For Maurice Halbwachs, memories are first grafted onto the terrain and then summoned up from it, as visible landmarks come to serve as placeholders for shared imaginations of the past. Our physical surroundings provide not only a medium for the storage and retrieval of memory, Halbwachs argued, but also a social framework that binds collectives together over time. The atlas of pictorial memory that was compiled at the same historical moment by Aby Warburg subverts the territorializing logic of Halbwachs' mnemonic topography by turning the axis around. Rather than settling a community's relation to the past, Warburg conceived of memory as a volatile force, potentially dangerous, rippling below the domain of common heritage. These early forays into the topographies and undercurrents of collective memory were to cross paths with a very different campaign to redraw the map, guided by the geopolitical concept of *Lebensraum*, the ultimate aim of which was the systematic destruction of the memory of European Jewry. Whereas Warburg's library was rescued from

H. Gustafsson, *Crime Scenery in Postwar Film and Photography*,
https://doi.org/10.1007/978-3-030-04867-9_5

the Nazi takeover in 1933, smuggled out of Hamburg and shipped to London, Halbwachs was arrested by the Gestapo in 1944 and killed in Buchenwald shortly before the war's end. The oft-mentioned confluence of memory studies and the atrocities of the Second World War may thus be said to have predated the revelations of the Nazi camps and their belated entry into the awareness of the outside world.

Unacknowledged during the war, demolished by the perpetrators before they fled the scene, and suppressed in the memory of those who survived them, the camps were long to remain, to paraphrase Nora, a *non-lieux de mémoire*. Since no public memories of the camps were formed outside the system while they were in operation, the collective memory of the killing campaigns was from the outset a confrontation with a place after the event. This confounded relation between *imagines* and *loci*—the ability to form mental images and the location from where they may be retrieved, following the two key principles stipulated by the ancient *ars memoriae*—would emerge as a key concern during the rise of cultural memory studies in the early 1990s, reflected in its prevailing paradigms of post-memory, trauma and secondary witnessing. What these terms foremost convey is a fundamental uncertainty about the provenance of memory, as memories are no longer properly confined to the interior of the consciousness of the individual subject, but seem to be lurking somewhere on its fringes.

Post-memory studies seek to grasp the conditions of possibility for the persistence of a "vicarious past," in James E. Young's phrase, an afterlife facilitated by the transmission of "surviving images," according to Marianne Hirsh.[1] It was precisely the itineraries of this *Nachleben* that Warburg had set out to trace across the panels of his *Mnemosyne* atlas. In common with the convoluted logic of post-memory, the survival of pagan antiquity investigated by Warburg thus poses a challenge to how the temporal structure of memory commonly has been understood. For instance, in her posthumously published book *The Life of the Mind*, Hannah Arendt describes the act of recollection as a fully conscious, causal and controlled process in which the faculty of imagination transforms a sensation into an image:

> Mnemosyne, Memory, is the mother of the Muses, and remembrance, the most frequent and also the most basic thinking experience, has to do with things that are absent, that have disappeared from my senses. Yet the absent that is summoned up and made present to my mind—a person, an

> event, a monument—cannot appear in the way it appeared to my senses, as though remembrance were a kind of witchcraft. In order to appear to my mind only, it must first be de-sensed, and the capacity to transform sense-objects into images is called "imagination."[2]

In the play of presence and absence outlined by Arendt, what has disappeared from the senses reappears in the mind. The model of historical memory implemented by Warburg, however, may indeed be described as "a kind of witchcraft," suggested by his description of the *Mnemosyne* atlas as "a ghost story for the fully grown-up" and of the researcher of pictorial memory as a "necromancer."[3] This has also been the crucial point emphasized by Giorgio Agamben in his enduring commentary on Warburg, commenced in 1975 after a yearlong study in the Warburg Institute Library in London, and most recently expounded in his book length essay *Nymphs*, written almost four decades later. While insisting, like Arendt, that "memory is impossible without an image," recollection requires that images are returned to, and reanimated by, the senses.[4] Here, Agamben refracts Warburg's notion of imagistic memory through Walter Benjamin's conception of the historical index, the epiphanic and flash-like actualization of the past in the present that allows us to glimpse them together, if only for an instant. Irretrievably lost if not recognized at this critical and chiasmatic point in the present, in the now of recognizability that Benjamin understood as a moment of awakening, the image of the past is always in danger of disappearing. Following Agamben, the task to bring images back to life, to summon the ghosts in order to break their spell, is tantamount to the task of redeeming the past that Benjamin attributes to the historical materialist. In the labor of post-memory, the process described by Arendt would thus appear to be cast in reverse, as memories have to be re-sensed in order to be imagined. For what is passed down from one generation to the next is not so much a memory as its ruin, conveyed through silences, symptoms and gestures. Yet somehow, or somewhere, this experience needs to be confronted. Post-memory does not only expand the field of memory, then; it literally requires fieldwork, as memories have to be relocated before they can be recollected.

This point merits a return to the question of *loci*. The mnemonic potential of locations finds its most emphatic expression in the idea of "rememory" coined by Toni Morrison in her novel *Beloved*, according to which mnestic residues of past events linger on at the sites where they once occurred, as "a picture floating around out there."[5] Though the place of the event may itself have been completely eradicated with the passage of time, the picture of it, Morrison insists, "is still there" and "if you go there and stand in that place where it was, it will happen again; it will be there for you, waiting for you."[6] As was noted in the introductory chapter, rememoration turns the basic premises of the art of memory as developed by Greco-Roman rhetoricians on its head. Mental images are not projected and impressed on space, as in the virtual palaces envisioned by Cicero and Quintilian, or the collective frameworks described by Halbwachs, but await us, "[r]ight in the place where it happened." Furthermore, memories do not "appear to my mind only," as Arendt asserts, but are instead summoned to reappear through the stimuli of a bodily encounter, resuscitated in the process of being relocated.

Can we even speak of a memory prior to a technique of recall, or is memory rather, as Plato argued in his dialogue *Meno*, the result of a mnemonic activity?[7] With regard to the various arts of memory to be considered below, the analysis will once more take recourse to the interstices conjectured by Warburg in his *Mnemosyne* atlas to act as an interlocutor between the numb traces lodged on the far side of a generational gap postulated by the theorists of post-memory, and the rememories that remain, according to Morrison, like disembodied spirits floating over the terrain. While the encounter with a rememory appears to be at odds with the deferred symptoms transmitted by post-memory, these two methods of recall nevertheless converge in the anticipation that the memories of past lives may still be retrievable, if someone merely is willing to go looking for them.

Ghost Stories

If "[m]emories are intransmissible," as Jean Cayrol contends, the custodian of the traumatic experiences made by a former generation needs to obtain new images, developing a picture of the scene of a crime that took place before his or her own conscious experience.[8] Such a reciprocal process of relocation and recollection can be identified as a recurring trope in the vast array of artistic engagements with family chronicles ruptured by the genocidal campaigns of the Second World War that came into prominence during the so-called memory boom in the early 1990s. Retracing the itinerary of a previous generation, seeking to mark out a memory on the very site where it has been buried, the three projects addressed in this section all push eastward.

The first is Chantal Akerman's film *D'Est* (From the East, 1993), shot on three successive journeys in 1992 and 1993 in the wake of the collapse of the Soviet Bloc. Embarking from East Germany in late summer, traveling across Poland, the Baltics and Ukraine, Akerman's road movie reaches Moscow in the dead of winter. Beginning with a series of rustic tableaux of peasant life, the camera starts to track leftward after half an hour, and never stops. As seasons change, the quiet fields are overtaken by the muffled hum of heavy traffic. Structurally, *D'Est* thereby inverts the trope of early cinema's travelogues and city symphonies where the process of modernization typically was staged as a journey from agrarianism into industrialized urbanity. Akerman's languorously paced traveling shots, some of them continuing for more than ten minutes, instead venture into the heart of an exhausted modernity. The entire film is a record of an aftermath, a negative force field that slowly saturates the mobile frame of Akerman's tracking camera; the only thing, it appears, that is moving in this post-Cold War setting.

D'Est is a film of bystanders, of anonymous crowds inertly waiting at bus stops, on tram platforms and in the transit halls of train stations; extras in a drama long since abandoned by its protagonists. Passing in and out of frame, most of them ignore the camera, while others return its unblinking stare. Indiscriminately recording everything that passes before its lens, the camera remains resolutely uninvolved, making no attempt to intervene or interpret. Yet, adhering to Benjamin's idea of the optical unconscious, these recordings captured something that Akerman claims she only recognized belatedly while editing the material. For whereas the protracted traveling shots become increasingly crowded as the journey proceeds, the apprehension that something is missing from these eastern communities gradually impinges on the viewer. Griselda Pollock explains:

> Absence was disclosed by what the film silently and persistently filmed. Visibility of an everydayness that had carried on with its relentless rhythms and seasons and work made absence—that of the Jewish world of Europe which had been so integral to these landscapes—unbearably tangible. … In *D'Est* the lack of cuts or joins itself builds the growing awareness in the viewer of the tragic dimension of the missing presences that the filmmaker 'found,' in the negative as it were, as the readymade of the landscape before which she merely placed her camera and rolled the film.[9]

For Akerman, as Alisa Lebow has observed, "there seems to be no eluding the imprint of the past"; a past that remains "merely a trace, unseen, yet persisting in its effects."[10] As the winding cues elicit an afterimage of former line-ups and deportations, the dead of the Moscow winter is also disclosed as the dead calm of the eye of a storm that only ostensibly has abated. Absence persists as a visible symptom, stored in the footage and augmented by the relentlessly deictic camera, pointing in every direction to call attention to what is no longer there. The result is a kind of reversed spirit photography that summons the ghosts of the gulags and pogroms in the "bloodlands" of the East.[11] Notably, *D'Est* premiered the same year as Jacques Derrida published his musings on the dissolution of communism in Eastern Europe and its ghostly afterlife in *Specters of Marx*. Pertinent to the phenomenology of the long take in *D'Est*, Derrida writes that, "[t]he subject that haunts is not identifiable, one cannot see, localize, fix any form, one cannot decide between hallucination and perception, there are only displacements; one feels oneself looked at by what one cannot see."[12] Since we are not drawn into an action or argument in this film devoid of characters, narration and audible dialogue, the incongruity between the excess of description and the dearth of information conveys the disconcerting sensation that the East is vacantly staring back at us.

The matrix of bearing witness, historical narrativization and site-specificity looms heavily in our second journey into the East. Mikael Levin's photo-essay *War Story* (1997) is a post-reportage project with an autobiographical twist, retracing the itinerary of the photographer's father, Meyer Levin, who traveled with the Allied armies from Paris to Prague in the final year of the war while working as a correspondent with the Overseas News Agency.[13] The journey begins in Paris, continues through Belgium and Germany, then follows the dead-end trail that leads to Ohrdruf, the first Nazi concentration camp to be liberated by the American forces on their way east, witnessed first-hand by Meyer Levin, stopping at Buchenwald and Dachau before reentering the Autobahn, passing through the Ardennes and the Alps, until arriving at its final destination in the former ghetto quarters of Theresienstadt. Part road book and part re-photographic survey, *War Story* places news reportage and late photography side by side, bluntly contrasting the decisive moments of the original trip—excerpts from Mayer's autobiography *Europe: The Witness*, newspaper clippings, cable dispatches and the photographs taken by Mayer's jeep-mate Eric Schwab—with the uneventful everydayness of the present. Approximating the vantage point of the original photographs while never completely matching their frames, a previous scene of carnage and drama populated by soldiers and deportees is placed alongside a contemporary scene of mundane complacency with an occasional tourist or passerby. In the interstice, *War Story* advances the simple descriptive tasks that re-photography performs: to mark a place and register the changes that have occurred in the interim. The decades that have passed thus install a parallax effect, a displacement not primarily caused by a different position in space but in time so that the two diverging lines of sight measure up the blind field in between. This dead zone is echoed in the empty plots of land and the desolate stretches of grass and tarmac captured by Levin's camera.

The narrative-driven prose of the original travel journal, the "story" retraced by the son, is counterpointed by the empty street corners, sidewalks and disused train tracks, the sloping footpath that leads up a steep hillside to the mass burial pit of Nordlager Ohrdruf and the cobblestoned road that leads to Buchenwald, and finally the blind alleys and impasses of the ghetto quarters in Theresienstadt. The late traveler literally remains behind the curve. Occasionally intercalated with a more enchanting prospect, like the rock of Lorelei in the mist-cladded woodland of the Rhine Valley, Levin reminds the viewer of an aesthetic and symbolic tradition meticulously repressed in his photographs. Leaving the premises of the Dachau compound, he even includes an image of a sign that invites visitors to explore the castle gardens and to take in the "splendid view" of the Bavarian Alps from the Schloßberg. This scenic discourse is inverted in the austere inventories of the campgrounds, portended by the stony field in Buchenwald that appears on the cover of *War Story*. It is a Kieferesque landscape, strewn with pebbles and stalks of dry weed with a high, unbalanced horizon against a pallid sky. Due to the slightly off-kilter skyline, marked by a pitch-black forest, the ground appears to loom up, as if the camera trembles from a seismic disturbance. Throughout, Levin maintains a limited range of inky tonalities; often heightening the contrasts to the point where the buildings, forests and memorial sites turn impenetrably opaque whereas the sky is bleached out into a uniform white.

In his study *Spectral Evidence: The Photography of Trauma*, Ulrich Baer calls attention to a structural parity between the nondescript and overgrown killing fields portrayed in *War Story* and the purpose that these sites were made to serve, "designed to obliterate the contrast between human beings and their surroundings and thus to level the symbolic distinction between figure and ground that is equally necessary for vision, experience and knowledge."[14] The deliberately flat and uninviting impression of Levin's compositions, Baer argues, thereby marks the site of what Cathy Caruth in a seminal text of trauma studies has referred to as an unclaimed experience.[15] Rather than seeking to recover a memory, *War Story* marks these sites, which were constructed precisely for the purpose of destroying memory and experience, Baer argues, by blocking our access to them. While the extended formats and perspectival cues of Levin's compositions cater to a classical landscape template, our awareness of the historical significance of these sites, the scarcity of visible evidence that they evince, and the "inhospitable" and "affectless" quality of the photographs themselves, together yield an effect of "non-belonging" where "absence becomes the referent."[16] Cognate with the experience of trauma, commonly defined by its resistance to narrativization and its refusal to develop into an image, *War Story* gives form to a failed transmission. Yet, in a Godardian-inflicted phrase, Baer also understands photography as a "medium of a *salvaging*, *preservation* and *rescue* of reality" that confers upon its future viewer "the burden of imagining."[17] This gives rise to a push-and-pull effect where the viewer is at once excluded from the scene, but also beckoned to abridge the distance.

More problematically, Baer argues that this effect is endemic to the photographic medium as such, which, determined by the irrevocable pastness of its indexical grain, automatically positions the beholder as a belated witness. The double negative of the muted spatial depth and the ontological given according to which "[e]ach photograph, by virtue of the medium, inevitably turns the viewer into a latecomer at the depicted site" is allegorically conveyed in a photograph taken over the shoulder of a local farmer who holds up a photograph of the advancing US troops taken in the spring of 1945 against the current backdrop half-a-century later (Fig. 5.1).[18] While the *mise en abyme* composition mimics a trope commonly associated with the romantic vistas of Caspar David Friedrich, the *rückenfigur* in 1995 is not entranced before the forces of nature but instead reframes "the present-day landscape as a scene of reading for memory."[19] As the photograph from 1945 in effect blocks out a section of the present view, Baer further notes, "Levin thus exposes in and as his father's story a central blind spot that results from the struggle to link sight and knowledge."[20] Looking at someone looking, but also at a prior act of viewing in 1945, belatedness is doubly relayed, cognate with the experience of inter-generational memory and secondary witnessing.

Instead of resorting to the Barthian tenet that "all photographs melancholically announces the death of the photographed subject," I want to argue that the "spectral evidence" of *War Story* exudes from the creative act of a reencounter, an activity resolutely situated, in common with the traveling shots of *D'Est*, in the present.[21] Dramatizing the encounter between the late witness and the postwar topography by photographing the print from 1945 in situ, the original is returned to the site from which it emanated, to its birthplace, so to speak. Mapped onto the

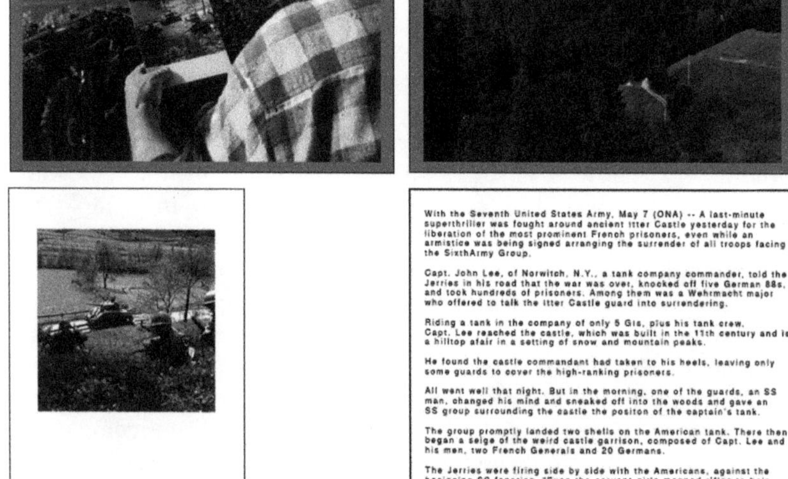

Fig. 5.1 Mikael Levin Untitled (Itter) from *War Story* 1995. Courtesy of the artist

current environment, the particular form of re-photography performed in *War Story* thus elicits a time wrap or ellipsis that hinges on the bifurcated nature of the index as defined by Charles Sanders Peirce, as at once a trace of the past and a gesture in the present. The intricate montage of texts and images crafted by Levin produce a system of interstices that acts against the foreclosure of the past, embalmed and entombed in the photograph. Rather than summoning the specter of death that according to Barthes looms behind every photograph, these constellations compel the viewer to become attentive to the image's capacity to summon an afterlife. For Levin's *War Story* is also, to borrow Warburg's phrase, "a ghost story for adults." In other words, spectrality is not simply given as a result of the automatic inscription conducted by the photographic apparatus, but activated in the process of retracing. Hence, we may also understand the confrontation with the present in *War Story* as an act of resistance against the enduring threat that the traces of the past shall fade from legibility.

Friedrich's *rückenfigur* and towering forests have remained a prominent reference in the art of the Israeli-born and London-based photographer Ori Gersht.[22] The project with which I want to conclude this ensemble of eastward voyages, *The Clearing* (2005), encompasses a series of works set in the dense woodland surrounding Kolomyia in southwestern Ukraine, formerly eastern Poland. The Heideggerian-inflicted title has a duplicitous designation, referring at once to the concept of the clearing (*Lichtung*) with its dual meaning of a clearing in the forest and of bringing something to light, and to the campaigns to clear the eastern territories of Greater Germany and render them *Judenrein*. Between 1941 and 1942, almost the entire Jewish population, among them members of Gersht's family, was massacred by the mobile firing squads known as the *Einsatzgruppen* in front of local spectators. Traveling through the region, Gersht perceives the forests, fields and farmsteads through a distorting blur caused by long exposure times and slow shutter speeds. The impression is that a soaking mist, suggestive of a whitewashing, intervenes between the spectator and the scenery, as if the sites themselves were intentionally trying to cover up or erase something.

One group of photographs in this series is called *Liquidation*, alluding at once to the extermination campaigns and to the liquidation of referentiality engendered by Gersht's smeared-out color fields. A similar effect was attained in *White Noise* (1999–2000), photographed through the window of a passenger train going from Krakow to Auschwitz and Belzec. Capturing impressions from a journey un-witnessed by a previous generation of passengers in bolted boxcars, the wintery surroundings are rendered as a turmoil of marred outlines and impaired vision. As one reviewer noted, "it is hard to know whether the cause of these aberrations was the hand that held the camera shaking uncontrollably, or the view itself is being convulsed in some kind of seizure or earthquake."[23] The comment brings to mind a passage from Jean-François Lyotard's *Le Différend* where the philosopher reflects on the long-term consequences of the perpetrators' systematic destruction of archival records of their deeds: "Suppose that an earthquake destroys not only lives, buildings and objects but also the instruments used to measure earthquakes directly and indirectly. The impossibility of quantitatively measuring it does not prohibit, but rather inspires in the minds of the survivors the idea of a very great seismic force."[24] Following Lyotard's parable, new instruments to measure the ripples and repercussions emitted from the past are in demand.

On the three journeys considered above, the camera is deployed as such a seismographic instrument in order to detect the otherwise imperceptible groundswells of a "great seismic force." Reconfiguring the notion of the photographic bond with its referent, as the referent exists here as an absence (in Akerman), an in-between (in Levin) or in the out-of-focus (Gersht), these works solicit new forms to fathom the spatial and temporal distances that define the phenomenon of post-memory. Through the protracted rhythm of the measured traveling shots of *D'Est*, the gaps staked out between 1945 and 1995 in *War Story*, and the delayed exposures of *The Clearing*, the camera is not merely utilized as a tool to passively receive and register these aftershocks, but to actively stir the ground, to disturb its slumber and shake up a memory. Taken together, the eminently formal approach crafted by these artists calls attention to the intrinsic relation between memory and form. Or rather, to remembrance *as* form, whether in the juxtapositions of montage, in long takes and traveling shots, or in the afterimages that emerge from the persistence of vision.

In the remainder of this chapter, I want to develop and expand upon each of these elements as they present themselves in three films made by

Daniel Eisenberg between 1981 and 1997. A second-generation survivor of the Second World War, Eisenberg's father spent two and a half years in the Soviet labor camp system, while his mother spent two years in the slave labor and concentration camps. They met by chance at Dachau at the end of the war. Eisenberg has described the evasive and oblique manner in which his parents responded to his inquiries about these experiences as "a screen between memory and its expression."[25] As we shall see, his films also caution us that places are themselves liable to congeal into screen memories, and that events are susceptible to be forgotten on the very sites where they once occurred.

Loosely grouped together as the Postwar Trilogy, each film in this cycle configures its own particular proximity between place, memory and the medium of cinema. As the trilogy gradually expands in scope and complexity, from the first short film to the final, full-length feature, each film also actively disengages itself from the strategy of the previous one in order to mark a new point of departure for yet another foray into the past. The following analysis will address the fundamental duplicity that marks the postwar terrain stalked by Eisenberg, one that both alerts us to the risk of reifying the past, and to the possibility of its redemption. In other words, it aims to shed some light on the manners in which space, the first prosthetic memory according to the ancient *ars memoriae*, may at once serve to cover up and conjure back the past.

Crossing Paths

The first film of the Postwar Trilogy, *Displaced Person* (1981), is comprised from four apparently unrelated sources: newsreel footage from *Die Deutsche Wochenshau* shot during Hitler's visit to Paris on the dawn of June 25, 1940; a sequence of two boys riding a bike in New York taken from an American Newsreel from the 1930s; a radio lecture given by Claude Levi-Strauss in 1978; and a string quartet by Beethoven. Eisenberg has recounted the original impulse of *Displaced Person* as an unsettling experience of déjà vu when attending a screening of Max Ophüls' compilation film *The Sorrow and the Pity* (1969):

> In *Displaced Person*, there is an image early in the film, of Hitler's entry into Paris on June 1940, when he steps out of his limousine and passes the gates of La Madeleine. He momentarily stops and looks up before

> going forward. When I first saw that image in *The Sorrow and the Pity* in a classroom in 1972, a shudder went through me. Not for any remarkable reason, but for the simple fact that just a few months prior to seeing the image I had stopped at that very spot, on my first trip to Europe. … Seeing that image in the classroom jolted me into a realization of the ghostliness of that European landscape, a place where so many traumatic and historical events occurred that neither the landscape nor the calendar could sufficiently narrativize them without superimposing them, conflating them, or compressing them into an assemblage of ironic details and fragments… and in some strange way Hitler and I had crossed paths in time.[26]

Recalling Morrison's notion of rememory, a picture is found, albeit recognized retrospectively, on location. More specifically, the mnemonic cue that triggers Eisenberg's project, the gesture of pausing before La Madeleine, invokes the seminal source of what Marcel Proust termed an involuntary memory: the "shudder" that runs through the author of *In Search of Lost Time* upon tasting the *petite madeleine* soaked in lime-flower tea, which releases a wave of submerged memories.[27] As we shall see, in *Displaced Person* this shudder also registers on a formal level.

The film's title alludes not only to the intersecting paths of the filmmaker and the Führer, but also to the displacements that the archival images and sounds are subjected to. Scavenged from an exhibition print of Ophüls' film, Eisenberg has manipulated the German newsreel footage with the aid of an optical printer, repeating and interrupting the brief fragments of women greeting the Führer at the train station and of his sightseeing tour through the defeated city in different variations and combinations. Re-cropping the aspect ratio of the original images, pulling the focus, chopping up subtitles, motions and gestures, it is as if the archival footage was itself beset by nervous tics and convulsions.

The particular historical juncture that Eisenberg locates at the gate of La Madeleine, and the compulsive reworking of the brief strip of film that it engenders, calls for a closer consideration of the formal relation between memory and cinema. "There is no need to shoot film anymore, just to repeat and stop," Agamben has concluded on the basis of the compilation techniques developed in the films of Guy Debord.[28] These two interventions also constitute what Agamben describes as the transcendental conditions of montage. The first one is stoppage, which obstructs time and pulls the image out of the narrative flow of meaning; the second is repetition, which restores possibility to the past by repeating it otherwise and thus rendering "it possible anew."[29] To interrupt and to repeat thus entails "the power to 'decreate' facts" and to give back possibility to what was.[30] For Agamben, this definition applies to memory as well as cinema, as both are able to "transform the real into the possible and the possible into the real."[31] The proximity between cinema and the process of recollection, which actively re-arranges and re-edits impressions of the past, is further highlighted in *Displaced Person* through the ruptures and gaps between the images, as the grainy snippets of newsreel footage, stopped and repeated in the film, are interspersed with black leader, the strips of opaque emulsion joined to the head or tail of a reel of film.

We may therefore say that in *Displaced Person*, displacement is the operative principle of its particular form of mnemotechnics. The archival excerpts are not quoted so much as torn away, unmoored and transposed into a new space. Splicing the archival footage with black leader foregrounds not only the cuts between images, and hence their unlinking and non-linearity; it also instantiates an open-endedness, a reversibility of beginning and end. Such anachronistic breaks and ruptures were imperative to the methodology developed by Aby Warburg. It was precisely in this *Zwischenraum*, the interval or interspace facilitated by the black felt-covered panels of the *Mnemosyne* atlas, that the mnestic energies embedded in the image were to be ignited. As Pasi Väliaho has pointed out, "[o]ne of the Atlas's striking features is that the sphere of potentialities is harnessed in the black intervals … [t]he black gaps between the actual images become temporally oriented intervals, verging on the abyss of time, which each image emerges from and falls back into."[32] In the final pages of *The Surviving Image*, Didi-Huberman dwells at length on the intermediary function of the black intervals as "an indicator of empty spaces, of *missing links*, of memory gaps."[33] The *Mnemosyne* may thus be conceived as a particular form of memory theater, a medium or milieu for images to interact, but also, significantly, as a "dynamic environment"[34] where the zones of black cloth set images adrift, "floating around" as Morrison writes, rather than stringing them together along the itinerary of a preconceived argument as originally intended by the architects of ancient rhetoric. This is also where the theory of post-memory intersects with Warburg's *Mnemosyne.* In both cases, the space of potentiality resides in gaps and ruptures, in the lapses of memory and the lacunae between the images. The afterlife of memory is not facilitated by continuity (whether of oral tradition, or lineages of influence and imitation), but through the construction of new and unexpected pathways in the process of editing disparate elements together.

In an interview with Frances Guerin, Eisenberg has described *Displaced Person* as a deliberate attempt to free images from the discursive constraints of the archive in order to allow us to "enter them through the present, whereas most of the narrative-driven images can be only accessed through a reference to the past."[35] The re-sensing of the archive performed through the loops and repetitions of *Displaced Person* further stands as a counterpoint to the official commemorative architecture on parade in the Nazi newsreel. As Hitler and his entourage of artists and architects pass from one monument to the next—the Paris Opera, La Madeleine, the Pantheon, Notre Dame, the Arc de Triomphe and the Eiffel Tower—the sleeping capital is transformed into what Eisenberg calls "a theme park of Western culture."[36] Hence *Displaced Person* cautions us about the merging of memory and topography, and about accessing a place in the past tense. Such theme parks, or screen memories, will also be explored in the two films to follow, where the problem of memory in more explicit terms is posed as a problem of locality.

In common with *Displaced Person*, the second part of the cycle, *Cooperation of Parts* (1987), begins with a train journey. This one, however, marks a gesture of pulling out of the archive. The voiceover describes a black-and-white photograph of Eisenberg's parents as they board a train out of Germany in 1949, but what we see is instead the exterior platform at Calais/the Gare de Lyon, Paris in the present, shot in color. The photograph described is never shown. In fact, nothing "personal" is shown. In *Cooperation of Parts*, it is not found footage that will be subjected to displacement, but the filmmaker himself. The film was shot in the spring and summer of 1983 on a journey from Paris and Berlin to his parents' birthplaces in Poland. With two decades of hindsight, Eisenberg has explained this journey as "an attempt to find an image of the past to which I knew full well I had no access."[37] *Cooperation of Parts* also transmits images inaccessible to the deportees, locked in boxcars, whose journey it retraces in a sequence early in the film shot through the window of a passenger train en route to Dachau. As the train gathers speed, the view of the Polish countryside dissolves into an agitated blur. Eisenberg continues: "My intention in filming was not to recuperate images from my parents' experience, but instead, to establish my own presence in the world, through the inscription of my own body into these spaces."[38]

The gestural and impressionistic camerawork in *Cooperation of Parts* conveys not so much images as a frantic quest for them. Shot with a hand-cranked 16-mm camera that roams across facades, fields and forests, the film is deliberately "hard on the eyes."[39] "What crimes have been committed here…here…here" the narrator asks as the roving viewfinder randomly points at different sections of the graffiti-sprayed wall in Berlin separating West from East. While having abandoned the archive, the film, in its compulsive gestures of collecting, observing and assembling, nonetheless appears beset by an "archive fever." As the voiceover declares: "I'm taking this all in. Accumulating evidence, facts, figures. Finally it can be put down in the columns." This obsessive yet random inventory is also a search for a remedy against what the narrator calls "a phantom pain. Something unseen yet intensely present."

As in *Displaced Person*, the implications of the title *Cooperation of Parts* are both biographical and formal. On a personal level, it refers to the phantom limbs—echoed in the dismembered figures on ornamental friezes in Berlin—that at once haunt and constitute the autobiography of the second-generation survivor. On the formal level, it invokes the tenuous constellation of "parts"—images, occasionally interrupted by stretches of black leader, verbal commentary, quotes from the filmmaker's conversations with his parents and proverbs written directly on the screen—whose potential meaning is always elusive, shifting and polymorphic. Scurrying around at a frantic pace, the camera appears to be afflicted by a kind of tremor that prevents a clear and focused perception. Rather than being monitored by the eye or mind, it registers the movements of a body interacting with the site. A corollary to these juddering images is provided by a subtitle that refers to the wartime experience of the filmmaker's mother: "It was through her, not through her conscious intention that these things passed," which is followed by a remark on the voiceover: "It is like a shockwave felt through several generations." This sense of a visceral transmission of trauma passing through the filmmaker is most palpably conveyed in the sequences filmed at the empty campgrounds at Auschwitz-Birkenau. The scattered views of the fields and fences, the watchtowers and dormitories, the gravel paths, the rails and the row of ovens, seem intent on disturbing the intolerable stillness that now reigns over the site, once crowded and teeming with activity. Contrary to the method of ancient mnemotechnics, however, the blurry, off-kilter imagery foremost indicates the failure to align an image to a location in order to make it serve as a cue for recollection. The transgenerational "shockwave" indexed by the camera on site further resonates with Warburg's intuition of the image not as a fixed and formal unity, but rather as a medium for the transmission of psychic intensities and paroxysms across time.

In a short essay called "Making It Safe" Eisenberg reflects at length on the fraught relation between memory and location by making a comparison between his visit to the compound at Auschwitz-Birkenau in 1983, which he describes as an experience of intense solitude and austerity, and a more recent return to the site, almost twenty years later. At the time of his revisit, Eisenberg notes, the campground had been transformed into "a theme park" for "the tourism industry."[40] The paths had been covered with asphalt, the lake of ashes framed by memorial stones, and the barracks remade into exhibition rooms. In this context, Eisenberg draws extensively on Pierre Nora's critique of how official commemorative culture and curatorial politics tend to solidify the past into a set of stable landmarks that premediate our encounter and response. From Nora's point of view, by anchoring a memory to a place, we in effect abdicate from the responsibility to remember. While Nora situates the transition from *milieux* to *lieux de mémoire* in the rupture between pre-modern societies and modern nation-states, his argument basically reiterates Plato's appraisal of the externalization of memory in *Phaedrus*. Once stored outside the mind, the philosopher warns, our faculty of memory will rapidly deteriorate. If Eisenberg's essay corroborates this view, the formal complexity of his films modifies Nora's straightforward dichotomy by unrelentingly reminding us that the conditions for remembering are always subject to technology.

As we turn now to the final act of the Postwar cycle, *Persistence* (1997), shot in the newly unified capital Berlin, the makeover of the past into a spectral theme park of memory unfolds before the camera's lens. In marked contrast to the freehand and manual-wind camera in *Cooperation of Parts*, however, *Persistence* facilitates an altogether different mode of encounter, soliciting a slower process of observation, habituating a prolonged and patient gaze more akin to the rigor and repose of a painter's easel, or the automated stare of a surveillance camera. Here, the filmmaker is no longer concerned with the inscription of his body into the spaces he confronts, but with the inscriptions of time on the city and with the afterimages that linger on the fabric of the built and demolished environment.

The Angel and the Archive

The single most widely reproduced image of the devastation in the aftermath of the Allied air raids over German cities during the final years of the war was shot by the former press photographer Richard Peter from the rooftop of Dresden's city hall in September 1945. Known as the "Angel of Dresden," it depicts an angelic sandstone sculpture positioned on a promontory on the Rathaustrum who, with a slightly raised arm and an open palm, gestures toward the immense sea of debris below. Facing away from the viewer, this solitary survivor is framed by Peter as the famous ruin-gazer of Caspar David Friedrich's romantic sublime.[41] This *rückenfigur*, however, does not tower above a sea of clouds but overlooks a manmade desert after the dust clouds have settled. In the eyewitness account of Kurt Vonnegut, who was a prisoner of war in Dresden in February 1945 when tons of explosives and incendiaries were unloaded over the city, the firestorm "ate everything organic" leaving "nothing but minerals."[42] The Angel of Dresden calls to mind another back-turned witness to catastrophic history portrayed by Walter Benjamin in his last known work, posthumously published as "Theses on the Philosophy of History." Written in 1940, during the interim of his release from a French internment camp and his flight from the Gestapo, Benjamin's critique of historical materialism is allegorized through the figure of the Angel of History, inspired by Paul Klee's *Angelus Novus* (1920), a monoprint once owned by Benjamin. In his ninth thesis, Benjamin presents us with the following interpretation:

> This is how one pictures the angel of history. His face is turned toward the past. Where we perceive a chain of events, he sees one single catastrophe which keeps piling wreckage upon wreckage and hurls it in front of his feet. The angel would like to stay, awaken the dead, and make whole what has been smashed. But a storm is blowing from Paradise; it has got caught in his wings with such violence that the angel can no longer close them. The storm irresistibly propels him into the future to which his back is turned, while the pile of debris before him grows skyward. This storm is what we call progress.[43]

These often-quoted lines allude to the wind that was described by Hegel in his *Elements of the Philosophy of Right*. Just like "the movement of the winds preserves the sea from that stagnation which a lasting calm would produce," Hegel ruminated, war is a rejuvenating force that propels the spirit ever forward on its journey from East to West.[44] Benjamin's Angel of History is, on the contrary, a paralyzed witness hurtled backward into the future by the Hegelian wind of progress. The connection between the Angel of Dresden, lamenting the aftermath of the firestorms, and the Angel of History was not lost to the German author W.G. Sebald when he presented his theses on "the natural history of destruction" in a series of lectures held in Zurich in the late autumn of 1997, published two years later under the title *Luftkrieg und Literatur*. In the concluding paragraphs of the second lecture, which deals with Alexander Kluge's account of the destruction of Halberstadt during the last days of the war, Sebald quotes Benjamin's reading of Paul Klee's angel.[45] The melancholic gaze of the angel is further aligned with a vivid image recalled from the author's childhood, as he laconically remarks that "few things were so clearly linked in my mind with the word 'city' as mounds of rubble, cracked walls and empty windows through which you saw the empty air."[46] In contrast to Benjamin's backward-looking angel, however, Sebald argues that the population of postwar Germany, built on top of the rubble of the Allied bombings, had no choice but to look ahead. The ground zero of 1945 thus erected a screen that effectively blocked any retrospective gaze into the nation's past.

A few months before Sebald delivered his lectures on the carpet-bombings of Germany, Eisenberg had completed the last part of his Postwar Trilogy. *Persistence* was shot in the immediate aftermath of the fall of the Berlin Wall, as East and West were to reunite into the federal republic of Germany. The first intertitle in the film, "The Angel of History," is followed by a close-up of the victory column in Tiergarten shot with a telephoto lens from a moving train car in the distance (Fig. 5.2). In an act of *détournement*, the female goddess of victory at the top of the column, originally erected to commemorate the Prussian Wars of Liberation, is turned into Benjamin's male angel who transfixes history's towering heap of debris, intent to extract from this wreckage the memory not of triumph, but of the nameless and oppressed buried beneath it. In the opening shot of *Persistence*, the barren trees in the surrounding park swirl by while the gilded statue remains focalized as the trembling center of the image. Optically processed to emulate the flicker effect of proto-cinematic devices, the traveling shot establishes a sense of urgency about this particular moment, or breach, in time. In the stroboscopic flashes, the "angel" appears to tremble, as if shaken by the storm that has blasted him out of paradise. From the Victory Column, the film

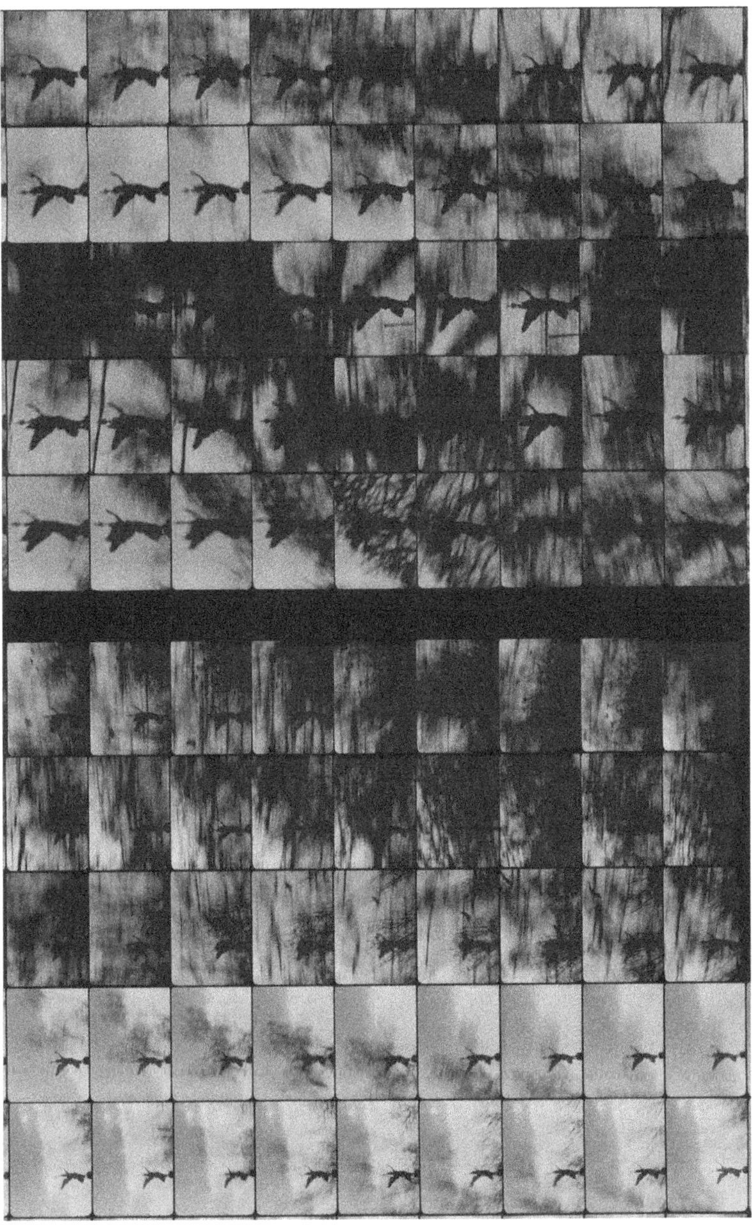

Fig. 5.2 *Persistence* (Daniel Eisenberg, 1997). Courtesy of the artist

cuts to an airborne view circling above Berlin in 1945. Shot in vivid and saturated Kodachrome color stock by US Signal Corps cameramen, and retrieved by Eisenberg from the Department of Defense archives, the glacial stillness is interrupted by the sudden appearance of life and movement within this mortified world. With its raised vantage point and acidic colors, Eisenberg detects a deliberate act of aestheticization in the reconnaissance footage, arguing that the military cameramen "were referencing classical landscape painting with deep focus and very far perspective points."[47] The airborne view of the bombed-out city in color is then followed by a sequence in black and white quoted from Roberto Rossellini's *Germany, Year Zero* where the twelve-year-old boy Edmund explores the same ruins on the ground.

In common with its two predecessors, the final part of the Postwar cycle elicits a formal correspondence between topography, technology and remembrance. The title in full, *Persistence: Film in 24 absences/presences/prospects*, highlights the material basis of cinema, since film doesn't capture but creates movement, twenty-four frames per second. It was long a generally held belief that it was through the optical phenomenon known as the persistence of vision that the projection rate tricked the brain into reassembling a seamless flow from the flicker of single frames. The illusion of motion was predicated on the persistence of a retinal impression that lingered across the gaps between discrete images. While the theory of the afterimage as the explanation for filmic animation has long been debunked and replaced with what physiological optics names the *phi*-effect, it nonetheless propelled the scientific experiments that would lead to the invention of cinema. The footage of the angel, which returns as a leitmotif throughout *Persistence*, calls attention to the filmstrip and the process through which vision is first broken down into flashes and then resynthesized by the projector. On the screen, and in analogy to Benjamin's theses, "we see a chain of events" where there is, in reality, merely an inert "pile of debris."

Let us return for a moment to Agamben's commentary on Warburg, whose main research question was focused on the phenomenon of persistence (*Nachleben*). In *Ninfa*, the Italian philosopher's most sustained engagement with Warburg to date, Agamben extrapolates an analogy between the physiological and the historical afterlife of images. That is to say, between the persistence of ghostly traces of light, the afterimages that linger on the retina, and the persistence of the mnestic charge of images:

> The after-life of images is not, in fact, a given but requires an operation and this is the task of the historical subject (just as it can be said that the discovery of the persistence of retinal images calls for cinema, which is able to transform it into movement). By way of this operation, the past—the images passed down from preceding generations—that seemed closed up and inaccessible is reset in motion for us and becomes possible again.[48]

Agamben's key intervention here is to connect what Warburg called *Pathosformeln*, the life and movement fossilized in the image, with Benjamin's concept of the historical index as "a threshold between immobility and movement."[49] In Benjamin's version of historical materialism, standstill is the privileged mode for seizing the past as it "flits by" and "flashes up at a moment of danger."[50] Rather than mooring an image to a particular moment, the historical index designates the critical point where the past and the future come together to form a legible constellation, charged with time up to the point of explosion, flaring up yet frozen.

In *Persistence*, the constellation of past and present converges in the two proclamations of *Stunde Null* in 1945 and 1989. These zero hours were conceived both as low points of history and as new beginnings, based on the bedrock of oblivion. Congruent with the displacements of the city itself—designated as East after the war and as West after the wall—the chiasmus of postwar and post-unification Berlin is delineated in the clashing movements of the camera traveling in reverse directions. Early in the film, Eisenberg cuts from a close-up panning shot, lasting two minutes, which patiently scans the broken mortar and masonry on the city's battered and crumbling facades in 1991, to a lateral traveling shot moving in the opposite direction recorded on the streets of Berlin in 1945. The latter footage, filmed by the Signal Corps, displays what Sebald in his youth came to consider as the "natural condition of all larger cities": blue sky seen through blasted portals, gutted buildings, fire-scorched walls and armature jutting out of mounds of rubble.[51] And, equally surreal, the gestures of everyday life carried out by the workers, children and women with strollers in the midst of this destruction. The spatial hermeneutic developed in *Persistence* also anticipates the method of Jacques Austerlitz, the eponymous protagonist of Sebald's last novel, whose compulsive study of urban architecture by proxy is a labor of post-memory, painstakingly seeking to reconstruct his autobiography from traces collected in train stations, former ghettos, and film archives across Europe. Incidentally, *Austerlitz* contains a reflection on the afterimages stirred by the luminous "trails of light" left by moths in the night air. However, as the narrator points out, these are "merely phantom traces created by the sluggish reaction of the human eye, appearing to see a certain afterglow in the place from which the insect itself, shining for only the fraction of a second in the lamplight, had already gone."[52] The afterimages transfixed by Eisenberg's camera transpire instead in the public spaces of urban and ideological renewal. Hence, the filmmaker's own predicament—caught between the persistence of his curiosity and his parents' resistance to recall the past—is now played out on the large demolition and construction site of Berlin.[53] This territory, replete with symptoms, déjà vus, and historical ironies, was also the ground zero of the memory boom in the early 1990s. Along these lines, the film posits an analogy between historicization and urban planning as parallel processes of strategic displacements, aimed at manipulating time and our perception of it.

The found and newly filmed footage lingers on the derelict houses and vacant spaces opened up in the urban fabric. Andreas Huyssen has referred to such disused lots, remainders of the Nazi destruction of the city's Jewish community, of the bombing raids in 1944–1945, and of the dismantled Wall, now sold off as souvenirs to tourists, as "the voids of Berlin."[54] These barren zones also open history up for examination. In a formulation that once more brings Warburg to mind, Eisenberg describes the collapse of the regimes in Eastern Europe as, "a seismic rearrangement of social, historic and political forces that allowed subconsciously suppressed memories (historical and personal) to rise to the surface."[55] Such dormant memories seem particularly susceptible to resurfacing from the neglected patches of urban wasteland sought out by the camera. Over the course of the film, this substrate also begins to impinge on the sonic environment. At first, the inventory of Berlin is accompanied by a low ambient soundscape of rustling leaves, chirping birds, footsteps, the murmur of voices, car horns and trolley cars. As the film progresses, however, the timbre and texture of the aural and acoustic space takes on a more menacing drone of industrial white noise, rattling trains and rumbling jet engines, or maybe of bombing raids in the distance.

The first scene to follow the constellation of the victory column, the aerial footage from 1945 and the excerpt from *Germany, Year Zero* in the film's overture, was shot by Eisenberg in July 1991. It shows the

Elisabethkirche while it still remained in a ruined state after the firebombing. Enveloped in the shades of dense vegetation and bathed in dappled pools of light, with its perimeter walls overgrown with ivy, this sylvan site conforms to the staple conventions of the picturesque. In keeping with the method of the former films, the narration is displaced over the current images as the voiceover reads a text dating back to May 1983 and the making of *Cooperation of Parts*. Elisabethkirche is revisited at the end of *Persistence*, now in the process of reconstruction. The Postwar Trilogy thus ends with Berlin being restored to its prewar—its pre-socialist and pre-Nazi—condition. Between the ruin and resurrection of Elisabethkirche, *Persistence* takes the Grand Tour through the ruins of Berlin, new and old, real and fake: the sea of rubble left after the air raids; the artificial ruins built by Frederick the Great on Ruinenberg to grace the view from his summer palace in Potsdam; and the dumpsites of abandoned military hardware piled up at former military bases. This further suggests that ruination, to paraphrase Sebald, is the natural condition of Berlin. The fashion for counterfeit neoclassical ruins indulged by Frederick the Great was later resumed by Albert Speer and implemented on a grand scale in his *Theory of the Value of Ruins*, designing the capital of the Third Reich with its future ruination in mind.[56] Bombed and razed by the Allied forces, Berlin did not crumble into the ivy-clad and awe-inspiring spectacle of imperial power envisioned by Hitler and his architect, however, but collapsed instead into a hideous and shapeless mass of destruction that Sebald describes as "a landscape of low mounds of rubble the color of cement."[57] Primarily, however, it is toward the mundane traces of ruination in the yet undeveloped tracts of the city that Eisenberg's camera directs our attention.

Approximately one-third into the film, there is a protracted sequence of static shots of half-demolished buildings in Berlin-Mitte, each one being marked by the imprint of a neighboring structure formerly attached to it. Accompanied only by ambient sound and continuing for five minutes, these images foreground the palimpsestic texture of the brickwork, etched with the trace of an erasure reminiscent of the chalk outlining of a victim's body at a crime scene. The facades are not scrutinized only for their forensic value, however, but to ignite a movement at a standstill, summoned through the stubborn persistence of the gaze. On one occasion, the viewfinder remains fixed for several minutes on a tall block across a railway platform as trains arrive and depart and passengers pass in and out of the frame (Fig. 5.3). The shot recalls a famous scene from a New York subway station in Chantal Akerman's *News from Home* (1976) where the opening and closing of the sliding doors similarly reframe and cut the image as trains arrive and depart at the platforms. The scope of Eisenberg's exterior frame, however, is of a different character. Recorded with the measured indifference of a surveillance camera, or the fixed frame of an easel painting, this view, which at first appeared overtly inert, gradually comes to life with ephemeral movement: the branches stirred by the breeze, the leaves trembling and light and colors changing as the clouds pass.

Through its persistence of vision, the film seeks to crystalize the past and the present into a single spatial configuration. In the multiple temporal registers superimposed over the course of *Persistence*, like the images of the Elisabethkirche, first as a picturesque ruin and later as a construction site, time appears to be moving in several, and sometimes contrary, directions. This method further entails a process of sifting through strata of gazes, distinguishing its various layers as well as the ruptures between them. As Eisenberg has remarked, an image not

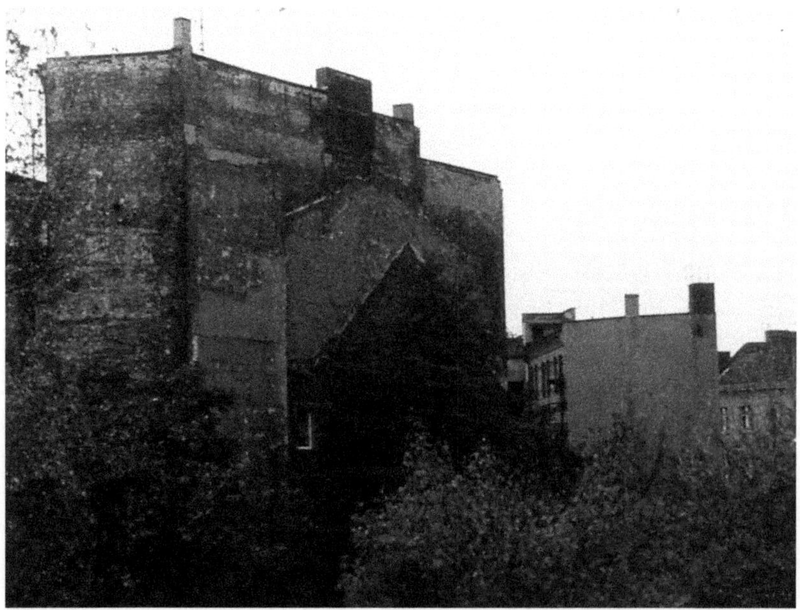

Fig. 5.3 *Persistence* (Daniel Eisenberg, 1997). Courtesy of the artist

only documents "what is seen, but a way of seeing."[58] To remember through images is therefore also to venture into a field of crossing sightlines. Questioning each image by introducing yet another point of view, *Persistence* brings a host of observers to bear on the collapse of the Eastern Bloc and the disintegration of the GDR: from the elevated viewpoint of the Roman goddess in Tiergarten to the airborne view of the Signal Corps and the adolescent gaze in *Germany Year Zero*; from the prospect of Ruinenberg set up by Frederick the Great to the surveillance machine of the Stasi; and from the tourists of former East Berlin to the visionary gaze of the Communist idols, whose monumental heads are the only faces to appear in the film. The succession of visual regimes, each defined by its own set of rules to capture, expose and interpellate, unearthed in *Persistence* brings to mind Paul Virilio's remark, quoted by Jonathan Crary as the epigraph for his study *Techniques of the Observer*, that "[t]he field of vision has always seemed to me comparable to the ground of an archaeological excavation."[59] Our final inquiry therefore concerns the relation between the ocular and epistemic formations embedded in the matrix of memory sites trailed throughout the film: the museum, the ruin and the archive.

The stratigraphy of the gaze undertaken in *Persistence* also implicates the film's own conditions of seeing. Early in the film, we see a man dressed in a trench coat from the viewpoint of a surveillance camera as he enters the Old National Gallery. Once inside, the visitor studies a series of paintings by Caspar David Friedrich: *Cross in the Mountain*, *Klosterruine Eldena* and *Woman by the Window*. As he adopts the posture of Friedrich's brooding *rückenfigur* in front of these landscapes, the voice-over reads a transcript from a fictional surveillance file in the Stasi archive. The *mise en abyme* composition that concludes the first sequence from the gallery, where a panning shot directs the gaze of the cinema viewer to glance over the shoulder of the gallery viewer, who in turn attempts to peer over the woman by the window and into the landscape beyond, sets up a series of framing and obstructing devices. While commonly interpreted as a surrogate viewer and as a cue to augment our immersion into the pictorial space of the canvas, Friedrich's back-turned figure does not so much pull us into the scene as it marks our constitutive absence from it. In his study *Caspar David Friedrich and the Subject of Landscape*, which Eisenberg brought with him to Berlin in 1991, Joseph Leo Koerner understands the *rückenfigur* as a kind of a *memento mori*, one that reminds us that, "we are neither the center nor the origin of our vision."[60] Transfixed before the scene, poised on an edge or a threshold, Friedrich's faceless observer conveys the authority of the original witness. Our own act of looking, then, is marked as a following and coming after. Blocking our path of vision, he makes us aware that we have arrived at the scene too late. Hence, the *rückenfigur* may stand as a cipher for the post-mnemonic condition and the insurmountable gap between generations.

In a second scene from the gallery, which appears halfway through the film, the camera tries to overcome this condition, tracking from left to right and then back again in an attempt to peer over the shoulder of the *rückenfigur* who now stands before Friedrich's *Morning in the Riesengebirge* (Fig. 5.4). Significantly, the observer blocks out the center of the composition, the towering cliff crowned with a crucifix, leaving only the flanking, mist-shrouded hills visible. The scene is framed by footage shot by the Signal Corps. First, immediately preceding it, is a series of vertiginous images taken from the point of view of an aircraft as it attacks military vehicles in the countryside. In each shot, the aircraft

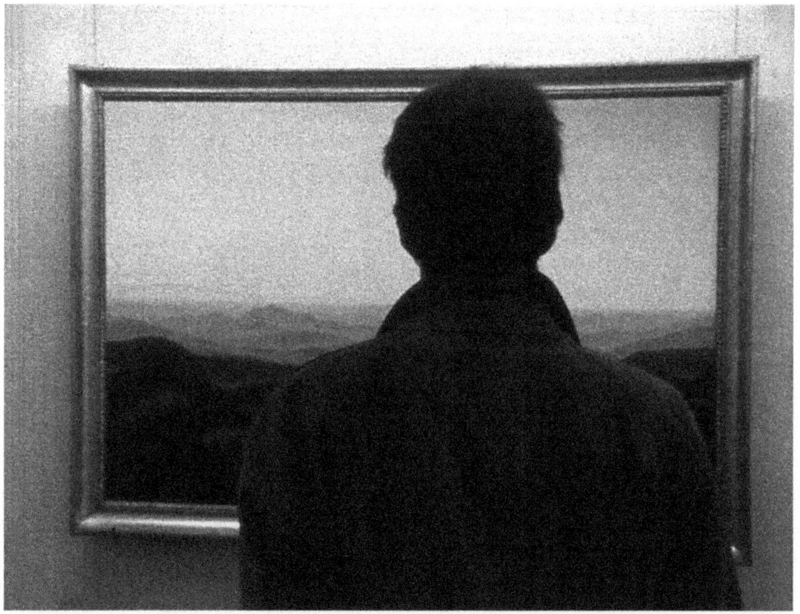

Fig. 5.4 *Persistence* (Daniel Eisenberg, 1997). Courtesy of the artist

plunges toward its target, opens fire and then ascends in a graceful and gravity-defying arc. Second, following the over-the-shoulder shot of the left side of the canvas, a graphic match cuts from Friedrich's softly undulating horizon to a rural hamlet framed by a military cameraman. With merely a slight shift of viewpoint, the scenery changes: as the viewfinder tilts down, it reveals that the fields and ditches in the foreground are scattered with dead soldiers. We may recall that it was a similar alignment of gazes that caused the shudder out of which the Postwar cycle germinated, the realization that the filmmaker and the Führer had "crossed paths in time." In the German newsreel dissected in *Displaced Person*, the camera follows Hitler close behind, framing him as an imposing *rückenfigur* whose gaze lays claim to the city's landmarks, one by one.

Following the final shot of the gallery visitor standing before Friedrich's mountains, *Persistence* ventures into the former Stasi Headquarters on Normannenstraße, introduced by a slow panning shot inspecting the contents of a glass case filled with cameras used by the state security service. The evacuated power centers and memory institutions traversed in the film thus accrue a palimpsest of looking relations that suggest, in turn, that the deposits of succeeding political regimes are stacked together with the sediments of ensuing scopic regimes. With each passage, a new way of seeing regulating the relation between observer and observed has to be adapted. The intertitles enforce this theme in a series of variations: "With instructions for viewing"—"The rules of dispassionate observation"—"From the archive of everyday observations"—"From: the Archive of Former Views / To: the Museum of Former Views," and so forth. The former population of the GDR, referred to by the voiceover as an "army of keen but objective observers," is now to be reeducated into tourists of their own recent past.

The scenes from the gallery explicitly ask us to consider the conditions of possibility for looking back into the past. To return once more to Sebald, we can recognize that this question also occupies a central place in his writings. In fact, the *rückenfigur* returns as a salient trope in all of his novels: a lonely wanderer, mountaineer or passenger, who looks "down on the earth from a great height,"[61] whether from a tall cliff, the terrace of a medieval fortress or an airplane. Significantly, for Sebald this high-angled gaze is always inextricably linked to the faculty of human memory and the limits of knowledge.[62] In German, we should further note, *rückblicke* refers to reminiscences, a backward glance or flashback. It remains ambiguous, however, whether Friedrich's isolated observer peers into the future or the past. In truth, as Koerner points out, its gaze is fixed on "the unpainted surface of the canvas."[63] Placed centrally in the image, the *rückenfigur* evokes an originary experience that it at the same time conceals. Unlike the figures that occupied the landscapes of Lorrain and Poussin, it is not part of a narrative or myth. It is, in fact, not part of the setting at all, but present only as its witness. Or maybe rather, as a trace of the unseen. And contrary to the tiny *repoussoir* figures that bracketed the edges of the Ideal Landscape—to frame, indicate scale and direct the viewer's gaze—Friedrich's solipsistic witness, emblematic of the sovereign subject born out of Western enlightenment, occupies the center of a world that gathers around its posture.[64]

The intersecting trails of the ruin and the archive in *Persistence* finally also invite us to reflect upon the birth of another subject, heralded by the goddess of victory in Tiergarten saluting the unification of Germany after the defeat of Napoleon. As Peter Fritzsche has shown, the Wars of Liberation marked the inaugural moment of the first official archives in the German Confederation. The purpose of these repositories was to establish a prehistory for the nascent nation founded on the heritage of the Holy Roman Empire. The archive, then, does not primarily seek to salvage the past but to settle the conditions for a new beginning. Whether in the wake of triumph or defeat, "[w]ars trigger archives," as Wolfgang Ernst has pointed out.[65] Over the course of the twentieth century, the regional archives assembled after the Wars of German unification were followed by the Reichsarchiv in the wake of the First World War, the racial archives of the Third Reich, and the Stasi archive of the GDR. Before the archive, however, came the ruin. It was during the late eighteenth and early nineteenth centuries that the gothic cathedrals, castles and abbeys dotting the Rhineland rose from the mist of time and began "to speak for the nation."[66] The inventories of these medieval relics, Fritzsche writes, "were the first steps toward the creation of a German archive."[67] Reclaimed as landmarks for mapping out the contours of the still virtual entity of an integrated nation, the ruin spurred the ensuing archival activity of the German state, seeking to track the genealogy of a *Volk* and a *Vaterland* with a common past and a shared future. The succeeding archives did not only aspire "to create a bounded national subject," but also to calibrate its gaze into the past as well as the future.[68]

The ruin, or to be more precise, the archive in ruins, is also the inaugural site for the various arts of memory that have been explored in this chapter. First, the private files and family records burned by German Jews and left-wing dissidents during the rise of the Nazi regime. Second, the "earthquake" or "seismic force" that Lyotard spoke of: the unprecedented destruction of incriminating evidence, state-centered as well as domestic, at the end of the war, assisted by the Allied incineration of German cities. In place of the archive, once more, stood the ruins, or sometimes merely the absence thereof. In the journeys undertaken by the second-generation survivors of Eastern European Jewry considered above, however, the lacunas, blind spots and silences that riddle the terrain also provide an opportunity, as Fritzsche suggests, to reflect upon "the absence of a common past and the enormous violence entailed in the attempts to produce it."[69]

It is not only the topography and toponyms of Berlin that are in a state of flux and redefinition in *Persistence*, but also the conditions for seeing and remembering. As old sites of memory are dismantled, new ones are established. In a striking reversal, the Stasi headquarters have now become a state museum.[70] Another scene shows the shiny surgical instruments neatly arranged as a still life in a glass cabinet at the Human Experimentation Laboratory at Sachsenhausen. Thus, former sites of terror are transformed into present sites of culture, and instruments of oppression into souvenirs. Repeatedly in these inventories of Berlin's new *lieux de memoire*, the camera tracks into the dark corners of a room where it then remains, as if trapped or unable to find a way out.

Rather than the "measureless plains" of memory once roamed by Augustine, the memorials and construction sites tracked by the meandering camera in *Persistence* gradually come to appear as a maze of dead ends.[71] Once more, then, Eisenberg cautions us about the formalization of memory and the risk of reducing history to a series of images fixed in space and frozen in time. Yet, the final act of the Postwar Trilogy may also, in common with Warburg's atlas, be understood both as a seismograph and "a belated memory palace," seeking to salvage the symptoms and anachronisms that erupt across the postwar terrain before they are covered over and lost in time.[72] As for Benjamin, the image of the past is always in peril, always on the verge of congealing into rigorous forms. And in keeping with Benjamin's notion of memory as the antidote to the sequential accounts of traditional historicism, Eisenberg's art of memory is determined to set spaces in motion. Instead of mooring *imagines* to *loci*, the possibility of memory resides in the gaps and fractures that open up between them.

Facing East

Persistence concludes at the Marx-Engels-Forum, one of the few monuments to be spared after the reunion. The penultimate image in the film is a frontal view of the authors of the *Communist Manifesto* facing East, where the parliament of the GDR and the Soviet Union no longer stand. After posing for a group photo, a crowd of tourists clears off and reveals the graffiti spray-painted on the platform: "wir sind unschuldig." For the last image, the camera switches position to a counter-shot filmed from the rear, turning the founders of the socialist movement into a pair of *rückenfiguren* overlooking the post-communist cityscape (Fig. 5.5). On the back of the platform there's a second inscription: "Beim nächsten mal wird alles besser." The effect is all the more startling since the last shot is also the first counter-shot in the entire film, which up until this moment has unfolded in establishing and exploratory shots. Recalling Marx's famous riff on Hegel's statement that history repeats itself, the first time as tragedy, the second time as farce, the image also conveys a more subtle irony, as the two philosophers do not only peer into a future they couldn't foresee (the New Hotel Stadt Berlin in

Fig. 5.5 *Persistence* (Daniel Eisenberg, 1997). Courtesy of the artist

Alexanderplatz) but also straight into the Fernsehturm.[73] In fact, it has been there all along, looming behind the "Angel" in Tiergarten, like a spear piercing through him. *Fernseh*, of course, translates as "far-sight," or tele-vision: the ability to see across distances in time. Abolishing the temporal delay of the cinematic image, it is also the medium that transmits, in "real-time," the historical events and their anniversaries, as they unfold one after the other at an ever-accelerating pace.

Eisenberg's own efforts to observe time in *Persistence* are ironically counterpointed on the soundtrack by the repeated announcement of Greenwich Mean Time, the global time standard reported from the Royal Observatory in London. The Hegelian dramatization of time as the progressive development of Universal Reason, where "revolutions are the locomotives of history"[74] and the State its true protagonist, and the triumphant proclamations of the "end of history" after the collapse of the Berlin Wall are, in fact, two sides of the same coin. Both perpetuate a spatial image of a rectilinear temporality, a time imbued with a goal and direction. Anticipating Francis Fukuyama's thesis that Western liberal democracy marked the end station "of mankind's ideological evolution,"[75] Hegel writes in his *Lectures on the Philosophy of World History* that "[w]orld history travels from east to west: for Europe is the absolute end of history."[76] The task of an authentic revolution, Benjamin insisted, is precisely to estrange time from such teleological accounts of history as merely a means to an end.[77] The arts of memory crafted from *Displaced Person* to *Persistence* actively seek to de-suture the very form of historical thinking by continually displacing any vantage point from where the past may resolve into a unified view so, as Eisenberg says, "that the past can be read with a very different set of possibilities. The past still has possibilities."[78] In the final ironic reversal of the Postwar Trilogy, Marx and Engels now overlook the urban landscape after communism, the Cold War and the Berlin Wall. The *rückenfiguren* remains, numb and static, whereas the scenery continues to change.

Notes

1. James E. Young "The Holocaust as Vicarious Past: Art Spiegelman's *Maus* and the Afterimages of History" *Critical Inquiry* Vol. 24 No. 3 (Spring 1998) 666–699; Marianne Hirsh "Surviving Images: Holocaust Photographs and the Work of Postmemory" *The Yale Journal of Criticism* Vol. 4 No. 1 (2005) 5–37.

2. Hannah Arendt *The Life of the Mind* (New York: Harcourt Inc. 1978) 85.
3. E.H. Gombrich *Aby Warburg: An Intellectual Biography* [1970] (Oxford: Phaidon 1986) 287; Philippe-Alain Michaud *Aby Warburg and the Image in Motion* (New York: Zone Books 2004) 236.
4. Giorgio Agamben *Nymphs* 2007 (London, New York, and Calcutta: Seagull Books 2013) 9.
5. Toni Morrison *Beloved* 1987 (London: Vintage 2007) 43.
6. Ibid.
7. Howard Caygill "Meno and the Internet: Between Memory and the Archive" *History of Human Sciences* Vol. 12 No. 2 (1999) 1–11.
8. Cayrol quoted in Emma Wilson "Material Remains: *Night and Fog*" *October* Vol. 112 (Spring 2005) 89–110, 93.
9. Griselda Pollock "Chantal Akerman: Moving Between Cinema and Installation" *Impure Cinema: Intermedial and Intercultural Approaches to Film* eds. Lúcia Nagib and Anne Jerslev (London and New York: I.B. Tauris 2013) 227–248, 233.
10. Alisa Lebow "Memory Once Removed: Indirect Memory and Transitive Autobiography in Chantal Akerman's *D'Est*" *Camera Obscura* 52 Vol. 18 No. 1 (2003) 34–83, 36, 49.
11. Timothy D. Snyder *Bloodlands: Europe Between Hitler and Stalin* (New York: Basic Books 2010).
12. Jacques Derrida *Specters of Marx: The State of the Debt, the Work of Mourning and the New International* (1993) trans. Peggy Kamuf (New York and London: Routledge 1994) 136.
13. Mikael Levin *War Story* (Munich: Gina Kehayoff Verlag 1997).
14. Ulrich Baer *Spectral Evidence: The Photography of Trauma* (Cambridge and London: The MIT Press 2002) 18.
15. Cathy Caruth *Unclaimed Experience: Trauma, Narrative and History* (Baltimore and London: Johns Hopkins University Press 1996).
16. Baer 66, 76.
17. Ibid. 24.
18. Ibid. 181.
19. Ibid. 97.
20. Ibid. 100.
21. Ibid. 119.
22. For a discussion on Gersht's dialogue with Friedrich, see Yoav Rinon "Manifest Time: The Art of Ori Gersht" *Ori Gersht: History Repeating* ed. Lucy Flint (Boston: MFA Publications 2012) 211–223.
23. Adrian Searle "Secrets of the Forest" *The Guardian* 20 December 2005 http://www.theguardian.com/artanddesign/2005/dec/20/photography.secondworldwar (accessed 2 August 2018).
24. Jean-François Lyotard *The Differend: Phrases in Dispute* 1983 trans. Georges Van Den Abbeele (Minneapolis: University of Minnesota Press 1988) 56.

25. Daniel Eisenberg "Making It Safe" Unpublished Conference Talk presented at "Imaging the Unimaginable: The Iconicization of Auschwitz" University of Florida, Gainesville, November 2007, n.p. http://www.danieleisenberg.com/alltexts/2014/7/28/university-of-florida-gainesville-november-2007 (accessed 2 August 2018).
26. Daniel Eisenberg, Unpublished artist's talk, Middlebury College, November 10, 2003 http://www.danieleisenberg.com/alltexts/2014/8/18/unpublished-artists-talk-middlebury-college-daniel-eisenberg (accessed 2 August 2018).
27. Marcel Proust *Swann's Way: Remembrance of Things Past* 1913 trans. C.K. Scott Moncrieff and Terence Kilmartin (New York: Random House 1989) 48. Nora M. Alter also notes this pun in her analysis of the soundtrack of *Displaced Person*: "Proust's now infamous 'Madeleine' biscuit, the smell or taste of which unleashed memories of a lost time, has transformed into an equally powerful mnemonic device as an architectural structure of La Madeleine. In both instances, the linguistic signifier of the proper name 'Madeleine', whether a cake or a church, serves as a memory trigger. The 'Madeleine' brings back past time, a history, and forces it into the present day consciousness." Nora M. Alter "Sound Scores: Musical Armature in *Displaced Person*" *Postwar: The Films of Daniel Eisenberg* ed. Jeffrey Skoller (London: Black Dog Publishing 2010) 48–61, 49.
28. Giorgio Agamben "Difference and Repetition: On Guy Debord's Films" *Guy Debord and the Situationist International: Texts and Documents* ed. Thomas McDonough and trans. Brian Holmes (Cambridge: MIT Press 2002) 313–319, 315.
29. Ibid. 316.
30. Giorgio Agamben "Cinema and History: On Jean-Luc Godard" *Cinema and Agamben: Ethics, Biopolitics and the Moving Image* eds. Henrik Gustafsson and Asbjørn Grønstad (New York and London: Bloomsbury 2014) 25–26, 26.
31. Agamben "Difference and Repetition" 316.
32. Pasi Väliaho *Mapping the Moving Image: Gesture, Thought and Cinema circa 1900* (Amsterdam: Amsterdam University Press 2010) 155.
33. Georges Didi-Huberman *The Surviving Image: Phantoms of Time and Time of Phantoms* [2002] trans. Harvey L. Mendelsohn (University Park: The Pennsylvania State University Press 2017) 317.
34. Ibid. 326.
35. Frances Guerin "Archives and Images as Repositories of Time, Language, and Forms from the Past: A Conversation with Daniel Eisenberg" *The Moving Image* Vol. 12 No. 1 (Spring 2012) 112–118, 113.
36. Eisenberg Unpublished artist's talk n.p.

37. Eisenberg "Making It Safe" n.p.
38. Ibid. n.p.
39. Guerin 117.
40. Eisenberg "Making It Safe" n.p.
41. Richard Peter's iconic photograph was originally titled "Blick von Rathausturm nach Süden." The figure in the foreground is August Schreitmüller's sandstone sculpture "Die Gute," which is not an angel, as commonly assumed, but an allegorical depiction of Goodness.
42. Kurt Vonnegut *Slaughterhouse Five, or, the Children's Crusade: A Duty-Dance with Death* [1969] (New York: Dial Press 2009) 128, 227.
43. Walter Benjamin "Theses on the Philosophy of History" [1940] *Illuminations: Essays and Reflections* trans. Harry Zohn (New York: Schocken Books 1968) 253–264, 257–258.
44. Georg Wilhelm Friedrich Hegel *Elements of the Philosophy of Right* [1820] ed. Allen W. Wood and trans. H.B. Nisbet (Cambridge: Cambridge University Press 1991) 361.
45. W.G. Sebald *On the Natural History of Destruction* (1999) trans. Anthea Bell (London: Penguin Group 2003) 68. In Alexander Kluge and Oskar Negt's *History and Obstinacy* (Geschichte und Eigensinn, 1981), Klee's *Angelus Novus* is reproduced alongside Benjamin's interpretation in the ninth thesis.
46. Sebald *On the Natural History of Destruction* 74.
47. Guerin 114.
48. Agamben *Nymphs* 24.
49. Ibid. 26.
50. Benjamin 255.
51. W.G. Sebald *Vertigo* [1990] trans. Michael Hulse (London: Vintage Books 2002) 187.
52. W.G. Sebald *Austerlitz* [2001] trans. Anthea Bell (London: Penguin Books 2002) 131.
53. Along the lines of this spatial metaphor, and drawing on Hayden White's *The Modernist Event*, Eisenberg writes: "Holocausts of one kind or another remain traumatic in public and private memory because they are still sites of contention. And it's because present generations can't agree on the meaning of such events that these historical 'sites of contention' become active construction zones for artists, writers, and filmmakers," Eisenberg Unpublished artist's talk n.p. Developing his trope of "the artist-as-archivist," Hal Foster similarly remarks that the task is "to turn belatedness into becomingness," and "'excavation sites' into 'construction sites'." Hal Foster "An Archival Impulse" *October* Vol. 110 (Fall 2004) 3–22, 22.
54. Andreas Huyssen "The Voids of Berlin" *Critical Inquiry* Vol. 24 No. 1 (Autumn 1997) 57–81.

55. Daniel Eisenberg "Notes for Persistence" 1997 n.p. http://www.danieleisenberg.com/alltexts/2014/8/18/notes-for-persistence-in-berlin-film-festival-daniel-eisenberg (accessed 2 August 2018).
56. "By using special materials and by applying certain principles of statics, we should be able to build structures which even in a state of decay, after hundreds or (such were our reckonings) thousands of years would more or less resemble Roman models." Albert Speer *Inside the Third Reich* [1969] trans. Richard and Clara Winston (New York: Macmillan 1970) 66.
57. Sebald *On the Natural History of Destruction* 36.
58. Eisenberg "Notes for Persistence" n.p.
59. Paul Virilio *Negative Horizon: An Essay in Dromoscopy* (London: Continuum 2006) 29; Jonathan Crary *Techniques of the Observer: On Vision and Modernity in the Nineteenth Century* (Cambridge and London: MIT Press 1990) 1.
60. Joseph Leo Koerner *Caspar David Friedrich and the Subject of Landscape* (New Haven: Yale University Press 1990) 277.
61. W.G. Sebald *The Emigrants* [1993] trans. Michael Hulse (London: Random House 2002) 145.
62. "If we view ourselves from a great height, it is frightening to realize how little we know about our species, our purpose and our end," the narrator ruminates in *The Rings of Saturn*. On a later occasion, he notes that the sovereign hindsight of the historian "requires a falsification of perspective. We, the survivors, see everything from above, see everything at once, and still we do not know how it was." W.G. Sebald *The Rings of Saturn* [1995] trans. Michael Hulse (London: Vintage Books 2002) 92, 125.
63. Koerner 271.
64. There is, of course, a great variety of *rückenfiguren* in Friedrich's work, many of whom resemble the *repoussoir* figures in earlier landscape paintings. In fact, the more imposing figures I am alluding to here, like *Woman by the Window*, *Woman before the Setting Sun*, or *Wanderer above the Sea of Fog*, are, relatively speaking, rarer.
65. As quoted in Peter Fritzsche "The Archive" *History and Memory* Vol. 17 No. 1–2 (Spring–Winter 2005) 13–44, 24.
66. Ibid. 19.
67. Ibid.
68. Ibid. 18.
69. Ibid. 39.
70. We may recall that it was such an institutional passage that provided the starting point for Jacques Derrida's reflections on the violence of the archive, where he ponders the institutional makeover of Freud's house in London into the Freud Archives, which was also the venue of the

conference where Derrida first presented his lecture in 1994. Jacques Derrida "Archive Fever: A Freudian Impression" trans. Eric Prenowitz *Diacritics* Vol. 25 No. 2 (Summer 1995) 9–63.

71. Augustine *The Works of Saint Augustine: A Translation for the 21st Century. The Confessions* ed. John E. Rotelle and trans. Maria Boulding (New York: New York City Press 2002) 254.
72. Christopher D. Johnson *Memory, Metaphor, and Aby Warburg's Atlas of Images* (Ithaca: Cornell University Press 2012) 10.
73. In *The Eighteenth Brumaire of Louis Napoleon*, Marx writes: "Hegel remarks somewhere that all great world-historic facts and personages appear, so to speak, twice. He forgot to add: the first time as tragedy, the second time as farce." Karl Marx *The Eighteenth Brumaire of Louis Napoleon* [1852] Karl Marx and Friedrich Engels *Selected Works in Two Volumes: Volume 1* (Moscow: Foreign Languages Publishing House 1962) 247. The comment has accrued an additional irony with the passing of the new anti-communist law in Ukraine in 2015, ordering that all communist monuments be demolished and 25 cities and 1500 streets renamed. Furthermore, the leader of the Ukraine Institute of National Memory, an amateur historian by the name of Volodymyr Vjatrovytj, has officially been appointed to construct a new national history from the sources of the National Archive, including the archive previously belonging to the KGB, now under the custody of the Memory Institute.
74. Karl Marx *The Class Struggles in France: From the February Revolution to the Paris Commune* [1895] (Newtown: Resistance Books 2003) 102.
75. Francis Fukuyama "The End of History?" *The National Interest* (Summer 1989) 3–18, 4.
76. Georg Wilhelm Friedrich Hegel *Lectures on the Philosophy of World History. Introduction: Reason in History* 1837 trans. H.B Nisbet (New York: Cambridge University Press 1975) 197.
77. Giorgio Agamben "Time and History: Critique of the Instant and Continuum" [1978] *Infancy and History: On the Destruction of Experience* (London: Verso 2007) 97–116, 99. See also Ronald Beiner "Walter Benjamin's Philosophy of History" *Political Theory* Vol. 12 No. 4 (August 1984) 423–434.
78. Guerin 118.

CHAPTER 6

The Testimony of Trees

Three pieces of bark arranged on a white sheet of paper. This is how *Écorces* (Bark), Georges Didi-Huberman's latest intervention into the polemical conversation on images and the Nazi death camps, begins. The author contemplates these scraps, which he has collected in the birch forest of Birkenau, in an attempt, quoting Hofmannsthal, "to read something that was never written."[1] Their monochrome texture—the black lenticels that streak the white papery crust—evokes at once scribbling and black-and-white photography, and thus marks the indeterminacy of these tokens, suspended between text and texture; meaning and materiality; words and images. "The bark is irregular, discontinuous, rough," Didi-Huberman notes, and he refers to them as "fragments of time."[2] As such, they imply a loss of context and continuity. They are vestiges of what can never be grasped in its totality, the visual traces of a disappearance.[3] They belong, in short, to the category of the visual that Didi-Huberman calls symptoms.

The distinction between symbol and symptom is a crucial one in Didi-Huberman's work on the image in general, and in his reading of Warburg's *Mnemosyne* atlas in particular. Whereas the symbol, following the iconological tradition developed by Erwin Panofsky, transmits an intrinsic meaning handed down by tradition that guides the interpretation toward synthesis and closure, the symptom introduces an element of dissemblance that disturbs this linear transmission. In *Confronting Images*, he describes it as an obstacle to, or an incision in, "the 'normal' regime of the visual world, a regime wherein we think we know what we

H. Gustafsson, *Crime Scenery in Postwar Film and Photography*,
https://doi.org/10.1007/978-3-030-04867-9_6

are seeing."[4] Rupturing the signifying process, the symptom is a deterritorializing force that "breaks up all discursive unity,"[5] and that unsettles the position of the viewer as a subject of knowledge.

In *Écorces*, the scopic regime in question is the state museum at Auschwitz-Birkenau, visited by the author on a day in June 2011. Didi-Huberman strolls on the compound amidst the crowds of tourists and pilgrims, and through the barracks now converted into exhibition spaces and national pavilions. Under the diligent zeal of curators and conservationists, he notes, the renovated campground has undergone a complete makeover, from a site of barbarity to a site of culture, as if one could be clearly separated from the other. Transformed into an open-air museum, complete with gift shops, signposts and guided tours, Didi-Huberman concludes that Auschwitz is forgotten on site. He responds by making an inventory in nineteen single-word captions—"bark," "barbwire," "floors," "flowers," and so on—supplemented by as many black-and-white snapshots. They show, among other things: a locked gate; a gravel path; a wall made of cement mixed with wood and sand; the surface of a lake; the bricks that remain of a perimeter wall; a concrete floor covered with lichen. Resisting our inquisitive gaze, he refers to these surficial deposits as "the bark of history."[6]

The argument in *Écorces* builds on the art historian's lifelong interest in the involuntary or accidental form, the stain, shard or stigma, and in images produced by contact. This follows, in turn, from his study of the early Italian Renaissance and its two most revered and contested relics, which are also the exemplary contact images: The Veil of Veronica and the Shroud of Turin. In common with the pieces of bark, "[w]hat strikes one immediately" he writes, "is the triviality, the extreme humility, of the objects themselves, which have nothing to show but the tatters of their material."[7] More precisely anticipating *Écorces*, a notion of the bark of history is also articulated in his monograph on Warburg. "The symptom," Didi-Huberman states in *The Surviving Image*, "refers to that which falls, not to that which signifies," or what he in a later passage describes as "the endless fraying of a vast polymorphous fabric. There is no core. There are only overlappings, endless folds."[8]

While the pieces of bark may appear as a deliberately oblique point of entry for commencing a work of memory, *Écorces* has some notable predecessors in French post-structuralist thinking. Maurice Blanchot famously described language as "a bit of bark," a material fragment "in which the reality of the earth continues to exist" and as "a piece barely detached from its subterranean surroundings."[9] In his introduction to *Paper Machine*, Jacques Derrida points out that *biblion* did not initially refer to "book" but to the material support for writing, derived from *biblios*, the Greek word for, "the internal bark of the papyrus and thus of paper, like the Latin word *liber*, which first designated the living part of the bark before it meant 'book'."[10] In the concluding paragraphs of *Écorces*, Didi-Huberman makes the very same etymological reflection. Before writing or drawing, then, there is the tablet, the ground of primal matter from which words and images are conjured. Wood pulp, we may add in light of the titular metaphor of Didi-Huberman's essay, is not only the material base of paper, but also of photographic film.

For Didi-Huberman, the strips of bark torn from the tree still maintain some relation to the living surroundings from which they have been separated. Yet, their survival, their potential to "*start an afterlife* which sustains our memory,"[11] depends on the historical subject who is willing to pay them attention. Highlighting the tension between the visible surface of the image and the invisible (back)ground from which it has been cut, *Écorces* finally also calls to mind the proposition made by Jean-Luc Nancy in *Au Fond des Images*, previously considered in the chapter 3 with regard to the dynamics between the cut and the continuum in the work of Sophie Ristelhueber. For Nancy, the image is at once cut out *within* a ground and torn away *from* it.[12] Congruently, for Didi-Huberman, the frayed edges of bark show the marks of this tearing.

It was precisely the edges of the cut, the aimless and accidental framings, which Didi-Huberman called attention to in his close reading of four photographs made by a member of the *Sonderkommando*, the "special units" of Jewish prisoners whose task was to dispose of the corpses at Birkenau in August 1944.[13] He has referred to these clandestine photographs as "tiny extractions from such a complex reality, brief instants in a continuum that lasted five years," and as "stolen shreds, bits of film," or, more provocatively, as images "snatched from a vast hell."[14] On the compound, he encounters them again, mounted on three black memorial slabs with white inscriptions in Polish, English and Hebrew explaining their significance. He notes that the photographs have been reframed and retouched, and that the obscure elements—the dark zones of the doorway and the birch trees—that obstructed the view in the original images have been removed. Cleared of these bewildering features, the danger and urgency involved in bearing witness to this historical moment is cropped out. Rendered legible by the conservationists, the images do not only convey the impression that the scene was easily accessible to the camera, they also imply that history itself can be fixed and finalized as a lucid image, and thus safely confined to the past. Moreover, he notes that the fourth photograph, the one which merely showed the trees cast against the sky, is missing. In a gesture to redeem this omission, he seeks out and repeats the random shot toward the treetops.

The Land of Extermination

With *Écorces*, Didi-Huberman returns to the vexed debate stirred by a divisive exhibition called *Mémoire des camps* that took place in Paris ten years earlier, and to the violent reactions provoked by his catalogue essay, "l'images malgré tout."[15] His understanding of the clandestine photographs as acts of resistance, as visual testimonies, and as "*survivors*,"[16] was first attacked by Claude Lanzmann, the director of *Shoah*, in an interview in *Le Monde*, and followed by Gérard Wajcman in *Les temps modernes*, the journal edited at the time by Lanzmann. In his article, Wajcman accused the art historian not only of corroborating the logic of Holocaust deniers, who demand that the event is yet to be proved, but, primarily, of "Christianizing the Shoah" by means of images.[17] Didi-Huberman's conversation with Lanzmann, however, goes further back, beginning with a brief essay on *Shoah* with the title "Le lieu malgré tout," the *site* in spite of all, written in 1995, which predates his book length polemical retort in *L'images malgré tout*, *images* in spite of all, by almost a decade.[18] The site, then, comes before the image, not only in terms of chronology, but also, I want to argue, as a common ground between the two adversaries. Both have expressed their determination to work "from the ground up," insisting that site-specificity facilitates a move away from abstract concepts toward concrete singularities.[19] In this sense, the physical location grounds their critique of mimetic representation. Furthermore, Lanzmann precisely delineates the symptomatic force at work on these sites when he recalls from his journey to Poland how "[t]he persistence and the disfigurement of places coexisted, wrestled with each other, impregnated each other."[20] Finally, the inventory undertaken in *Écorces* does not only repeat the "cinematic gesture" of Sam Fuller at Falkenau and George Stevens at Buchenwald and Dachau in 1945, or that of Alain Resnais ten years later, "*walking* on the site of horror, camera in hand,"[21] but also the founding gesture of *Shoah*.

"I was the first person to return to the scene of the crime," Lanzmann states in his memoirs *The Patagonian Hare*, published the same year as *Écorces*.[22] Recalling his initial reaction upon arriving at the sites of the first extermination camps in Poland that had been dismantled, plowed under and planted over with saplings of pine trees long before the end of the war, he writes that he instinctively adopted "the strange gait of a surveyor," as if the sites themselves compelled him "to postpone the moment of understanding."[23] Lanzmann writes:

> I knew that during my stay here I would visit the sites, pace them and survey them as I was later to do at Chelmno, but I needed to say as little, to ask as few questions, as possible; to remain on the surface, to move lightly over the land of extermination.[24]

Altering between slow-paced pans and traveling shots, emulating the formal approach of the travelogues and phantom rides of early cinema, the surveying camera in *Shoah* seems to be governed less by authorial style or intention than by the physical parameters of the sites themselves. Along these lines, Lanzmann has stressed the visceral impact of each minute detail on site, every steel rail and stone, including "the lone, charred, twisted tree framed against the white sky next to the Little Farm House, which had been turned into an experimental gas chamber; I had allowed it to seep into me, to imprint itself on me."[25] The film's power surges from this rigorous inscription and relentless accumulation of tangible facts, prompting a confrontational mode of collision, contact, and contamination: "The journey to Poland was like a journey through time," Lanzmann continues: "Here, the nineteenth century existed, one could *touch* it."[26] Thus, it is a different 'in spite of all' that impels his quest: that everything still existed "as though nothing had happened," that it "dared to exist," as Lanzmann puts it, and that life went on now as it had then, in spite of all.[27] He sums up the essence of this menacing presence touched and transmitted by *Shoah* as, "the old medieval Christian anti-Semitism of the Polish peasants."[28] The austere survey undertaken by Lanzmann does not only seek to retrace the event, then, but to grasp and encompass it in its entirety, to touch it and to internalize it. Hence, it was not envisioned as "a film *about* the Shoah, but a film that *is* the Shoah."[29] The result, in his own words, is "an arid and pure film" which "tells the truth" and "teaches everything."[30]

The epistemological metaphor pursued by Didi-Huberman in *Écorces* points in the opposite direction, as when he refers to the pieces of bark as "the impurity" that falls from the thing.[31] Mounting a defense for historically "useless images,"[32] he never ceases to caution the reader that testimony, in whatever form, is always flawed and frayed. Knowledge is available for us only as a vestige, in the meager threads of what remains to be seen. Straying off the beaten paths of the Auschwitz-Birkenau Museum, annually trampled by more than one million visitors, it is the adjacent camps and crematoria at Birkenau that were added to the original compound at Auschwitz in 1941 and almost completely destroyed in the final days before the Liberation, that attracts his attention. Instead of a museum, Didi-Huberman describes these demolished structures as the site of an archaeological excavation. Dynamited and burned down as Soviet troops were approaching, the only thing that remains of the crematorium is the cement floor. It was precisely because it was considered insignificant as proof that it was spared. Hence, its survival is conditioned by its lack of evidentiary value. According to Didi-Huberman, this is also why the floor deserves, and demands, our attention.

Assuming the role of Benjamin's ragpicker on the former campground, sifting through the scattered refuse in order to salvage it from its "enshrinement as heritage,"[33] Didi-Huberman also adheres to Benjamin's model of the dialectical image that appears in a flash and "flits by" never to be seen again.[34] Acknowledging that the tenuous constellation of fragments assembled by the historical materialist will never resolve into a complete picture, the goal is not to bridge the past and the present, but to ignite a tension between them that allows us to glimpse them together, if only for a fleeting instant. In other words, it is not the past that flits by, but a sudden actualization in the present. This flash-like cognition only attains legibility at a particular moment. Irretrievably lost if not recognized in the present, the image is always in danger of disappearing.

Such an epiphanic flash, emanating from the volatile clash between the past and the present, is also recalled by Lanzmann in his memoirs. Before reluctantly making the journey to Poland after years of research, convinced that nothing remained there to be seen, Lanzmann describes himself as, "a harmless bomb—the detonator was missing."[35] It was during an aimless drive through the countryside that the detonator suddenly materialized at the moment he recognized the name of a village spelled out in black letters on a road sign: "Treblinka became real, the shift from myth to reality took place in a blinding flash, the encounter between a name and a place wiped out everything I had learned."[36] In its relentless and explosive confrontation between "a name and a place," *Shoah* aims to summon what Lanzmann calls a "hallucinatory intemporality."[37] Rather than a general ban on images, Lanzmann's famous repudiation of "images without imagination" commends images *with* imagination.[38] While the archival image positions the spectator at a temporal remove, Lanzmann has described the arduous task that he commenced in 1973, and that would absorb him for the next twelve years, as inflicting a "suspension of time."[39] *Shoah*, he insists, thereby effects an "abolition of all distance between past and present."[40]

Shoah's suspension of time is encapsulated by the film's epigraph, quoted from the Book of Isaiah: "I shall give them an everlasting name." This name converges, in turn, with the director's sovereign act of nomination. "'Shoah' was a signifier with no signified, a brief opaque utterance, an impenetrable, unbreakable word," Lanzmann has explained: "Shoah is now a proper noun, the only one, and hence untranslatable."[41] To this reasoning one may object that in Hebrew, the word "Shoah" simply means "catastrophe." This is also the meaning of the Arabic word "Nakba," which refers to the expulsion of the Palestinian population and the destruction of their homesteads in 1948, an event narrated by the state of Israel as the War of Independence. Consequently, no sign, whether verbal or visual, can lay claim to the singularity that Lanzmann insists on, as each sign at once illuminates and obscures that to which it refers. As the author of *Écorces* would urge us, this is not an incentive to abandon signs, but instead to relentlessly work on them, and to combine and construct images into new constellations.

The spots and tears on the thin and flaky pieces of bark studied by Didi-Huberman, which are neither words nor images yet redolent of both, highlight the at once material and elusive nature of signs. Significantly, the pieces of bark are also signs handed to us by what scholars of the Middle Ages called the Book of Nature. Considered as documents, they are ambiguously situated between nature and culture. As the next section will show, trees have traditionally played a privileged role in the cultural imaginary of Germany as mediators between a people and a place. In the aftermath of the Second World War, however, the iconography of the German forests was subjected to an extensive revision in a broad array of artistic forms, often in ways that instigate a close affinity between trees and testimony. It is to this genealogy of iconoclastic tree art that we now turn.

A Green Silence

"I regard the trees as you interrogate mute witnesses," Didi-Huberman ruminates, "the sole survivors, if you think about it, which still live here."[42] The dead are there, the author insists, in the swarm of white flowers that now covers the perimeters of the incineration pits, in the lake where the ashes were dumped, and in the sap of the birches.[43] The trees, the lake and the flowers remain not only as survivors of the event, but also as agents of its erasure, or what Paul Celan, in a poem inspired by *Night and Fog*, called "a green silence."[44] Though the shallow-rooting habits of the white-barked birch tree enable them to survive in nutrient-poor soil, however, their lifespan is relatively short. The trees that Didi-Huberman photographs in 2011 might not even have grown there in 1944.

This apparently futile gesture of interrogating trees, and of bestowing the role of a witness to the vegetative life of trees and flowers, has a long line of precursors. The transition in *Night and Fog* from verdant landscapes to killing grounds had already been prefigured in the first informational film about the camps, known under the austere title *German Concentration Camp Factual Survey*.[45] Assigned to supervise the editing of the footage shot by British and Soviet film units at Bergen-Belsen in April 1945, it was Alfred Hitchcock who suggested that the film should begin with a brief montage of rustic tableaux showing the surrounding countryside in full bloom, with its farmhouses, fruit trees, grain fields and orchards. This prologue did not only serve to suspend the moment of revelation, but also to stake out the spatial proximity of civil life and death camp.

With this gesture, Hitchcock established a salient trope to be repeated across the rich body of artistic work that has enacted the primal scene of the moment of opening the camps. Perched on the edge of the campground, the forest marks a site where voracious nature, fertilized by the ashes, is entangled with the German humanist traditions exploited by Nazi propaganda. This cultural legacy had already been implicated in the title of Resnais' film, quoting the *Nacht und Nebel* decree that called for the abduction and disappearance of resistance fighters in the occupied territories. In another euphemism coined by the Nazis, the captives were to be *vernebelt*, transformed into mist.[46] The phrase *Nacht und Nebel* is already a quotation, however, derived from *Das Rheingold*, and borrowed, in turn, by Richard Wagner from the nation's most acclaimed poet and playwright, Johann Wolfgang von Goethe. Resnais alludes to this etymology by way of an archival image that shows Goethe's Oak on the Ettersberg, a short walk from Weimar, where the author reputedly penned "Wanderer's Night Song." The oak tree was originally located in the middle of the beech forest that was cleared in 1937, but which remained as the name of the camp that would take its place, Buchenwald, with Goethe's solitary oak now occupying its center.[47]

Another famous oak, this one from the hand of Caspar David Friedrich's, appears in the opening sequence of Alexander Kluge's 1979 film *Die Patriotin*. Kluge provocatively begins by playing Hans Eisler's leitmotif from *Night and Fog* over images culled from Curtis Bernhardt's *Die letzte Kompanie* (1930), which was part of a cycle of patriotic Weimar films that, in the aftermath of the defeat of the First World War, nostalgically venerated the victories of Frederick the Great. This compilation of sounds and images does not merely invoke the score from Resnais' film but also its ground-level tracking shots, as Bernhardt's camera wanders through a waterlogged battlefield in Prussia, swept in mist and strewn with the bodies of slayed German soldiers. From here, Kluge cuts to Friedrich's *Oak Tree in Snow* (1827) and a close-up of the mysteriously red pond where its roots coil (Fig. 6.1). Following the Wars of Liberation, the coniferous woods painted by Friedrich often served as a symbol for the nation's resilience and rebirth after the French occupation, most conspicuously in *Chasseur in the Forest* (1814) where a forlorn Napoleonic soldier faces an imposing wall of fir trees. Within

Fig. 6.1 *Die Patriotin* (Alexander Kluge, 1979)

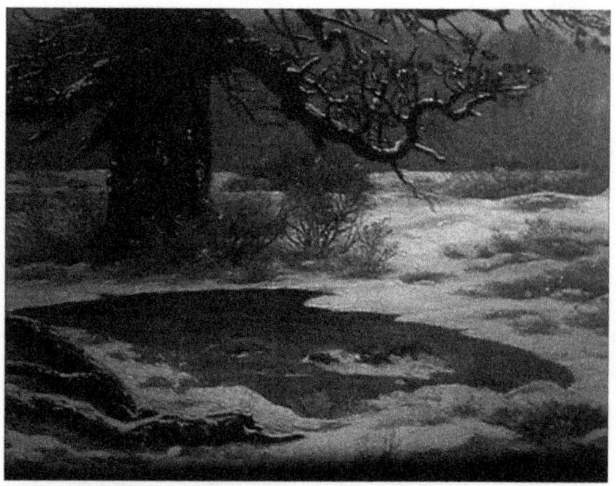

the context of Kluge's film's, the red water that nourishes the oak tree alludes to the Nazi doctrine of a people unified by ties of blood and soil. The close-up also introduces the blood-soaked earth excavated by the film's protagonist, a frustrated history teacher who turns into an amateur archaeologist, determined to dig out material traces from the earth in order to undermine the official narrative of her nation's past. Another tree painted by Friedrich concludes the film's dialogue with *Night and Fog*: a close-up of the single leafless tree that appears out of the mist in *Riesengebirge Landscape with Rising Fog* (1819–1820).

According to Christopher S. Wood's study of Friedrich's predecessor Albrecht Altdorfer, trees did not only metonymically serve as the distinguishing feature of the German nation, but also as the point of origin for the genre of landscape painting itself. Marking the natal moments of the autonomous landscape, when the setting advanced from being a mere backdrop to become a subject in its own right in the early sixteenth century, trees, rather than the mythical and historical figures that soon would inhabit the sceneries of Lorrain and Poussin, conspicuously occupy the foreground of the canvas. Hence, Wood points out, landscape painting was vertical before it became horizontal, adapting its format to the upright shape of trees prior to its lateral orientation along the surface of the earth.[48]

In the postwar installations of the Teutonic forest under consideration here, the distinction between natural setting and historical subject is often deliberately collapsed. From the late 1960s and onwards, Georg Baselitz frequently portrayed his trees either as injured, with their branches broken and bleeding, sometimes with strips of bandage tied around them, or as inverted, like the birch trees he sketched or painted upside down in 1972.[49] The arboreal theme has also remained a lifelong pursuit for the artist Anselm Kiefer (whose surname, incidentally, translates as "pine tree"). A kindred spirit to Gabi Teichert, the schoolteacher in Kluge's *Die Patriotin*, Kiefer has described his idiosyncratic fusion of history and landscape painting as an, "archaeology in reverse."[50] In Kiefer's vast panoramas, the locus of the forest interior becomes an overdetermined site of ethnocentric myths and demented idealism; a theater of collective memory where the brooding silence of the woods resounds with voices from the past. Often, figures and phrases from Germanic myth and folklore literally come out of the woodwork as Kiefer inscribes the roots and branches with the names and portraits of the nation's cultural titans. Occasionally, trees do not only provide a recurring motif in his work but also its raw material, as in his woodcuts and wood carvings, or, more recently, in the diorama *Winterwald* (2010) where a glass-encased forest has been stuffed with thorny bushes whose dried branches are entangled with long ribbons of wartime newsreels.

While lacking the material gravity of Kiefer's densely textured and clotted canvases, Marcel Odenbach conveys a similar effect in a large collage titled *You Can't See the Forest for the Trees* (2003). When viewed from a distance, the canvas offers a cohesive view of a birch wood. If the spectator moves in closer, however, the trunks and leaves will disintegrate into a patchwork of shredded newsprint and sheet music used for the silver birches and scraps torn from magazines dyed green for the forest floor. Hence, the sylvan domain turns out to be densely populated, as the faces of politicians, soldiers and celebrities emerge from its shaded lairs to peer back at us. Resnais' film remains the seminal reference in such investigations of the arboreal screen as a site of exchanged glances. In *Night and Fog* (1991), Lorie Novak literalizes this notion, using the nocturnal forest as a screen for her re-photography of a slide projection of Margaret Bourke-White's iconic image of prisoners gazing out through the barbwire fence at Buchenwald. For her video and sound installation *The Watch Man* (2007), Shona Illingworth instead aligns the counterpoint structure utilized by Resnais with the concept of screen memory, interspersing the fragmentary testimony, filmed in black and white, of a former British soldier who witnessed the liberation of Bergen-Belsen, with dazzling flashbacks in color of towering trees and branches spreading overhead.

For the last two artists that I wish to include in this ensemble of tree art, the forest is engaged less as an idea or art historical trope than as an indexical marker. First, in a short 16-mm film simply titled *The Forest* (2005) made by Ori Gersht.[51] The film is part of a more extensive project called *The Clearing* (2005), which was addressed in the previous chapter, and shot in the remote woodland interiors of southwestern Ukraine where members of Gersht's family hid after the area had been declared *Judenrein* following the campaigns of the paramilitary death-squads known as the *Einsatzgruppen*. For more than 13 minutes, the camera tracks through the woods as one tree after another sporadically topples over and crashes into the undergrowth with a thundering roar, stirring a cloud of leaves and dust that twirl in the air in the brief silence that follows. As the ambient sounds of the canopy gently swaying in the breeze and the murmur of cicadas resume, the camera continues its trajectory, and then pauses anew when another splintering crack tears the silence. The ensuing rhythm of pans and pauses, turmoil and tranquility, recalls Bishop Berkley's famous conundrum: "If a tree falls in a forest and there is no one there to hear it, does it make a sound?" As the artist has explained: "When I was looking at the landscape in the Ukraine I was seeing all these houses and trees that were there 60 years before and are living there now with total indifference to the human horrors that took place but somehow *bear within them* the memory of those events."[52]

The summoning of trees, whose foot, stem and crown are suggestive of a human figure, as witnesses finds its most explicit and uncompromising exponent in the "guilty trees" portrayed by the Dutch artist Armando, who spent his youth in close vicinity to the Amersfoort Transit Camp in Utrecht that was built by the German occupiers in 1938. In a series of paintings, photographs and texts called *Guilty Landscape*, Armando short-circuits the metaphorical approach to assess the silent complicity of the forest edge, perched on the edge of history, as both witness and culprit, bystander and perpetrator. "They grow up and keep still. Whatever happens," the artist explains: "The trees in the front must have seen a thing or two. Those behind them can hardly be blamed, they could never see anything. But the edge, the seam of the forest, that has seen it."[53] In an essay called "Touching Death," Ernst van Alphen highlights Armando's insistence on the causal link between sign and signifier: "The guilt of the trees resides in the invisibility of the violence and the evil that took place at their feet, an invisibility they 'caused.' Thus they betray the indexical meaning of their presence." As active forces of disfiguration and dissemblance, the trees thus remain, van Alphen writes, as "symptoms of the event."[54] In other words, van Alphen here precisely corroborates Didi-Huberman's understanding of contact images as symptoms.

As the exposition above has shown, *Écorces* may be construed as part of a long lineage of latecomers to the scene that has called upon the trees to act as perennial witnesses. A number of the themes engaged by the artists addressed in this section—the disfiguring force of the forest, the exchange of glances, the blurring of figure and ground, and, more generally, the crisis of mimetic representation after Auschwitz—was concisely expressed in a brief essay written by Didi-Huberman more than a decade before the *Mémoire des camps* exhibition. While apparently unrelated to the revelations in the spring of 1945, I want to argue that this short piece, called "The Paradox of the Phasmid," may be read as a parable of the opening of the camps. Written after a visit to the vivarium of the *Jardins des Plantes*, Didi-Huberman here reflects on how the biotopes staged in the glass cases entice a "mimetic play."[55] The trapped animal falls prey to the inquisitive gaze of the visitor who patiently awaits a slight tremor, a quiver or breath, to reveal the living figure of a reptile or arthropod against the ground of its enclosure. It is a particular species, however, that attracts his attention: the phasmid, the walking stick or stick bug, which assumes the guise of a leaf, twig or a piece of bark.

For Didi-Huberman, the phasmid is exemplary of the event of dissemblance, as it holds the unsettling surprise that the miniature forest is, in fact, the animal it supposedly was hiding. Introducing an indistinction between figure and ground, imitation and original, the insect's body *is* the scenery. Consequently, "the forest you are strolling through is the animal that will soon devour you." In common with the game of hide and seek played by Resnais' camera in *Night and Fog*—craning down from the open fields through the barbwire, tracking past a screen of trees to reveal a crematorium, or over the weeds that cover the tracks—the paradox of the phasmid reflects the paradox of the death-infested rural East: the stench that permeated the air for years; the undulation of the ground caused by decomposing bodies; the rivers and lakes saturated with ashes; the crushed bones used as fertilizers and spread across fields and meadows; and the movements of the earth which to this day continue to unearth teeth and bone in the forests surrounding the camps, like an endless harvest. It is precisely what Didi-Huberman here refers to as "the menacing quality of *place*" that is so powerfully conveyed in *Shoah*.

In *Le lieu malgré tout*, his first commentary on *Shoah*, Didi-Huberman commends the film for showing and augmenting the silence of the locations, and he refers to the wooded glades that open up at the end of each overgrown path pursued by Lanzmann as symptoms.[56] *Shoah* does not only aim to show this silence, however, but also to expand it across the temporal and spatial distances that it traverses. Ultimately, it aims to expose the true nature of the places it confronts, and to make the *genius loci* of the East reveal itself in what Lanzmann describes as "a hallucinatory, timeless moment."[57] The next section will address the subtle shifts from the indexical to the metonymical and metaphorical in *Shoah* as they unfold through a series of graphic matches and traveling shots across the lands of extermination.

Debarked

Shoah begins by establishing a link between asphyxiation and forestation as the first witness, Simon Srebnik, walks down a wooded path in Chelmno toward a clearing in the woods and the site of the first camp where Jews were gassed. From the forest clearing in Chelmno, where nothing remains to be seen but the bare outline of the perimeter walls, the film cuts to a clearing in the woods of Ben Shemen in Israel. Here, Motke Zaïdel, who escaped the killing squads in the Ponari forest of Vilna in 1944, notes that while the trees in Israel may resemble those of Lithuania, the Eastern woods were "denser," the trees "taller and fuller." The contrast is highlighted in the next scene as a measured pan moves across the pine forest of Sobibór. Framed low, an impenetrable coniferous mass engulfs the screen, followed by Jan Piwonski's account of how the Germans in the early winter of 1943 had started to plant saplings of pine trees in order to liquidate the traces of the mass graves. "That screen of trees?" Lanzmann asks, followed by another pan across a long row of tall pines. Piwonski responds that, "when he first came here in 1944, you couldn't guess what happened here, that the trees hid the secret of a death camp." As further testimonies ensue, we learn that this strategy was implemented across the occupied territories. "Woven into the barbed wire were branches of pine trees," Franz Suchomel, a former SS guard at Treblinka, recalls: "It was known as 'camouflage.' There was a Camouflage Squad of Twenty Jews. They brought in new branches every day." Throughout the film, the searing gaze of the camera struggles to pierce this screen, peering through the boughs and branches that cover the road sign spelling "Treblinka" (Fig. 6.2), or through the dark foliage of the wooded parkland that shelters Villa Wannsee.

Pushing eastward to clear a living space for German settlers and farmers, the author of *Mein Kampf* narrated the territorial campaigns of *Generalplan Ost* as a German version of Manifest Destiny. "The launching of the offensive in the East and the working up of the "Final Solution" was organically conjoined," Lanzmann explains as he paraphrases the protocols of the Wannsee conference:

> The East was not only the great reservoir of Jewry; in the hallucinatory German *Weltanschauung* it was also the place of absolute indefiniteness, of the shapeless, the vague. *Everything is possible in the East*; people are exterminated in the East, people are deported from West to East.... *The East is unsurpassed slaughter country.*[58]

Fig. 6.2 *Shoah* (Claude Lanzmann, 1985)

The First Era of *Shoah* concludes with a handheld camera racing down the forested path that was used by the first gas vans in Chelmno, followed by an abrupt cut to the towering skyline of the Ruhr district, enveloped in steam and exhaust fumes. The transition from the soaring forests of Greater Germany to the industrial heartland of the Federal Republic announces the full-scale industrialization of death that will be the subject of "The Second Era." The final scene in the film shot on the grounds of Auschwitz-Birkenau makes this gesture in reverse. Following a montage of tall smokestacks, cooling towers, and oozing vents in the Thyssen steel mills, Lanzmann cuts from a low-angle shot framing three fire exhaust pipes to the scorched branches of a solitary tree in Auschwitz-Birkenau cast against a pallid sky (Fig. 6.3). The graphic match is abridged by the white noise of the factory plants, which blends into the ambient sound of rustling weeds as the camera tilts down along the stem to the soil where its roots are buried. The ground consists of nothing but rusty spoons, leftovers from the camp's vanished labor force. Recalling an earlier shot where a protracted lateral pan measures up the petrified forest of chimney stacks at Auschwitz, the vertical descent along the charred tree marks a final disclosure, literally a defoliation, of the bewildering mass of trees that first confronted the filmmaker in Poland. Meanwhile, the silent life of plants continues its work of obliteration. The final setting of the film is the weed-infested ghetto quarters at the heart of Warsaw where a new forest of scrub and brushwood rises, marking the enduring ignorance and neglect of the East.

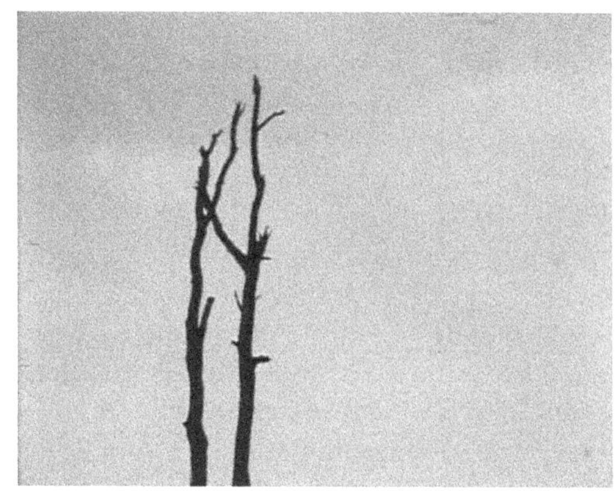

Fig. 6.3 *Shoah* (Claude Lanzmann, 1985)

The horizontal and vertical gestures of the camera—panning across the forest and tilting down along the stem—delineate the two-point axis around which *Shoah* pivots. In linguistic terms, these axials are commensurate to metonymy (the part substituting for the whole) and metaphor (one thing substituting for the other). In terms appropriate for our discussion here, they mark the crossing point of territory and testimony. This chiasmatic structure is established at the intersection of the lateral gaze of the surveyor who scans the lay of the land to measure up distances and spatial relations, and the vertical gaze of the archaeologist who digs, drills and excavates in order to make a place yield its secrets.[59] The next section seeks to grasp the proximity of these two axials, drawing not only from Lanzmann and Didi-Huberman, but also from Giorgio Agamben's attempt to locate the place of testimony in what remains his most contested work, *Remnants of Auschwitz: The Witness and the Archive*.

The Place of Testimony

Let us reiterate the statements made by Georges Bataille and Gérard Wajcman, previously addressed in Chapter 4, that the image of the human body cannot be untangled from the assault it suffered in the gas chambers. This observation may also apply to the image of trees, as their anthropomorphic quality cuts both ways. Not only were the bystanders as indifferent as the forests facing the killing ground, the process of dehumanization also took recourse to a speech act that equated people with lumber. “The Germans even forbade us to use the words ‘corpse’ or ‘victim.’ The dead were just blocks of wood,” a witness from the massacres in the Ponari forest recalls early in *Shoah*. This ban calls to mind the photograph of rigidified human torsos stacked among the logs in a pile of firewood shown in *Night and Fog*. As Emma Wilson has noted with regard to this image, the “obscene similarity between flesh and wood” evinces how “the divide between living and dead, and between once animate and always inanimate matter is eroded.”[60] Such a transgression is implied also in *Écorces*, as bark connotes both skin and paper, and thus suggests how one came to be transformed into the other under Himmler’s decree of “productive annihilation.” Again, an archival image reproduced in Resnais’ film comes to mind, the one that shows shreds of human skin used as drawing paper.[61]

For Giorgio Agamben, this eroding boundary between the animate and inanimate marks the “place of testimony” and the zone where the protagonist of his study *Remnants of Auschwitz* dwells. Known in the camp under the German word for Muslim, the *Muselmann* was a prisoner in the final stage of malnutrition, reduced by starvation and dysentery to a vegetative state of existence, deprived of speech and agency. Hence, for Agamben, the “complete witness” is unable to bear testimony. Challenging the common understanding of testimony as a first-person eyewitness account, to testify, for Agamben, it means to speak for someone who can no longer speak. Prior to any content communicated, it is the act of speaking the unspeakable, or of imagining the unimaginable, that concerns him.

Two interrelated points in Agamben’s account of the structure of testimony are pertinent for our discussion. First, that it contradicts the argument that was formulated a year previously by Jacques Derrida in *Demeure: Fiction and Testimony*. For Derrida, “testimony is always autobiographical: it tells, in the first person, the sharable and unsharable secret of what happened to me, to me, to me alone.”[62] Agamben, conversely, seeks to displace subjectivity by instantiating a shift from the first person to the *Muselmann*, for whom autobiography and subjective pronouns such as “I” or “me” have lost all meaning. With recourse to etymology, Agamben reminds us that testimony, derived from the Latin *testis*, does not, in fact, refer to a first, but to a third person, a disinterested witness.[63] Second, and in contrast to the obligation to speak in *Shoah* and the “everlasting name” inscribed by its title, Agamben stresses the contingency of speech, "as a capacity not to be."[64] The intermediary role of the witness and the potentiality of speech can only be harnessed in relation to silence. Auschwitz is the negation of this contingency, seeking to produce "the final biopolitical substance" by separating, once and for all, "conscious life from vegetative life."[65] In a signature move that can be traced across all aspects of Agamben's writing, it is through the limit-figure of the *Muselmann*, who introduces a zone of indistinction between the human and the inhuman where one no longer can be clearly separated from the other, that this binary ontology may be deactivated.

This third, anonymous position is also at the heart of Didi-Huberman's poetics of montage. As he writes in *L'images malgré tout*, the image appears in the confrontation between two points of view, clashing "*under the gaze of a third*."[66] Elsewhere, he elaborates further on the intervention of a third as the product "of an interval, a caesura-effect, and thus a montage-effect, in the expected distribution of roles between the one who looks and the one who is looked at."[67] In cinematographic terms, the gaze of a third breaks up the symmetry of shot and counter-shot, the first rule of narrative cinema. It is in this third, subject-less space that the remnant, investigated by Agamben, and the trees, interrogated by Didi-Huberman, dwell. The sheets of bark that have curled off the trunk and dropped to the ground in the *hors-champ*, the off-screen space of the camp, introduce such a third perspective. To interrogate trees, then, is also to "bear witness to a missing testimony," as Agamben puts it, and to act as a witness to witnessing.[68]

The considerations on testimony offered by Agamben and Didi-Huberman are indebted to Lévinas' phenomenology of the look of the third person that intervenes between the Self and the Other.[69] In both cases, furthermore, this condition is facilitated through an engagement with a silent interlocutor, the *Muselmann* in the former, and the exterior layer that encases the tree trunk in the latter. The flat pieces of bark, the silent witnesses or "fragments of time" scrutinized in *Écorces*, can only bear testimony indirectly and involuntarily, as they possess neither a voice nor a will to serve as evidence. They are, to borrow Marc Bloch's phrase, "witnesses in spite of themselves."[70] From this voicelessness it follows that testimony will always remain incomplete and fragmented. As for Agamben, the witness is what remains between death and survival.

The place of testimony marks a point where the inventorial report of a survey forms a chiasmatic relation with an archaeological excavation.[71]

These two methods coalesce in the concept of the index, as at once a trace of the past and as deixis, an act or gesture situated in the present. It is precisely this deictic dimension that Didi-Huberman highlights in his reading of the four photographs of the incineration pits and birch grove. These clandestine images are foremost expressive of their own act of enunciation, and of the moment of danger that their making entailed. Their fortuitous framings mark, in Didi-Huberman's words, "pure 'utterance,' pure gesture, pure photographic act without aim."[72] For this reason, "they require *archaeological* work. We must dig again in their ever so fragile temporality."[73] This work, he continues, demands "a vantage point that is able to see what has survived together with what has disappeared."[74] Or, put differently, to perceive in the vestiges that remain the destruction that they have outlived.

The argument in *Remnants of Auschwitz* hinges on the key role that the deixis—the grammatical shifters or indicators of enunciation—plays in Agamben's philosophical project as a whole. For Agamben, the deixis marks the act in which language is put to use, the event in which it *takes place*. This is also the phenomenon investigated by the archaeologist. The *archē* is therefore not the historical site of an original event that can be traced back through linear time. Conversely, what the archaeologist seeks to uncover is "the non-place of the origin," and how the very notion of an origin has come to be retroactively constructed over time.[75] Agamben's conception of archaeology is thus purposefully counterintuitive, as it deals with appearances and enunciations. Instead of an excavation into the interiors of the earth, it is engaged with exteriorities, or what Agamben refers to as, "the *outside* of language, the brute fact of its existence."[76]

The testimonies of *Shoah* also emerge from a non-place. First, because no one survived the gas chambers; and second, since the name "Auschwitz" was unbeknownst to the majority of the victims killed there. Hence, the film's foundation, as Lanzmann says, is "immemorial,"[77] extending beyond any record of human memory or knowledge. The *non-lieux* in Poland are also enveloped in a *non-temps*, or with a phrase culled from the glossary of modern cinema, a *temps morte*.[78] The former members of the *Sonderkommando*, the key witnesses in *Shoah*, bear testimony from the grave, Lanzmann explains, for "they too were fated to die—which is why I call them 'revenants' rather than survivors."[79] The place of testimony is established in the first scene where

Simon Srebnik enters the frame in a rowboat on the Narew River flanked by lush foliage, as if carried by the oarsman Charon across Styx.[80] He utters these bewildered words, the first to be spoken in *Shoah*, as he comes before the clearing in Chelmno:

> It's hard to recognize, but it was here. They burned people here. A lot of people burned here. Yes, this is the place. No one ever left here again... No one can describe it. No one can recreate what happened here. ... Even I, here, now. ... I can't believe I'm here. ... It was silent. Peaceful. Just as it is now.

Invoking the dual meaning of the revenant, as someone who returns *from* the dead and *to* a place, *Shoah* begins by asserting the index in its dual sense, both as an archaeological trace dug up from the past and as an event in the present, instantiated, on site, through the deictic shifters: "Even I, here, now." Literary critic Shoshana Felman takes note of the rhetorical significance of the deixis in *Shoah* when she writes that the film "calls us into what it cannot show, but what it nonetheless points to."[81] In common with Didi-Hubermn and Agamben, then, the place of testimony uncovered by Lanzmann is one where the horizontal axis of the survey and the vertical axis of an archaeology converge. This place, however, has a more specific designation and authority in Lanzmann's work. "Every time I discovered someone still alive, I was absolutely stunned, it felt almost like something unearthed during an archeological dig," Lanzmann recounts in his memoirs.[82] The poignant line that concludes the opening credits of *Shoah*—"I found him in Israel"—introduces Srebnik as such an archaeological recovery. Felman elaborates further on the key significance of this line for the film as a whole: "Something is found, here, in Israel, which embodies in effect a point of arrival in Lanzmann's journey, as well as the beginning."[83]

Israel also frames the film in terms of chronology. While rarely addressed in this context, *Shoah* was conceived as the middle part of a trilogy, preceded by *Pourquoi Israël* (Israel, Why, 1973) and followed by *Tsahal* (1994). These two films, which will be discussed in more depth below, were respectively made to celebrate the twenty-fifth and the fiftieth anniversary of the War of Independence and the declaration of the state in 1948. Inaugurated by the Eichmann trial in Jerusalem and culminating with *Shoah*, what Fellman has dubbed "an Era of Testimony" thus also holds a territorial dimension, one that begins and ends in Israel.[84] As Lanzmann unambiguously states in his memoirs: "the state of Israel was born of the Shoah," therefore, "a causal relationship connects these two key events."[85] It is this causally determined relation that Lanzmann seeks to unearth in his films. The next section will continue to probe such acts of speaking and pointing, and their capacity to connect one event to another, in light of Didi-Huberman's concept of the contact image.

Touching Ground

The longest single testimony put on screen by Lanzmann unfolds in his most recent, and final, journey into the past, *The Last of the Unjust* (2013). The film combines outtakes from *Shoah*—an interview conducted in 1975 with Benjamin Murmelstein, the last leader of the Jewish council in Theresienstadt—with newly shot footage of the filmmaker, now in his late eighties, on site in the present, as he retraces the itinerary of the first deportations. Invoking the ending of The First Era of *Shoah*, the first part of the journey undertaken in *The Last of the Unjust* concludes with a tracking dolly moving down through the columns of trees along the path that leads to the first deportation camp, set up deep within the lush woods of Nisko in southern Poland. Interviewed on his rooftop terrace in Rome, Murmelstein begins the conversation with the following parable:

> The past we are talking about had repercussions for the whole of Europe. As with a forest, you see, when it is destroyed. Its destruction has climatic repercussions on a whole region. Even far from where it stood. Similarly, the absence of Judaism from the East … has climatic repercussions on the whole world. Here in Rome too.[86]

In Lanzmann's films, the forest does not only serve as an index and a metaphor for this absence and destruction, but also, as we shall see, for the resurrection of the lost world of the Jewish nation.

The theological framework that has galvanized the critical discourse on the visual legacy of the gas chambers, staking the monotheistic ban on images in the Old Testament against what Wajcman called "the Christian passion of the image,"[87] had been fortified in the dispute between Lanzmann and Jean-Luc Godard that preceded

Didi-Huberman's intervention. Again, it was Wajcman who set out the stakes, pitting "Saint Paul" Godard against "Moses" Lanzmann.[88] Three years later, Godard was joined by Didi-Huberman who, by elevating the *Sonderkommando* photographs into religious relics, assumed, "the mantle of Saint Paul announcing to the world the coming of the Image."[89] The controversy surrounding the *Mémoire des camps* exhibition finally also coincided with the inflamed critical reception of *Remnants of Auschwitz* in France.[90] Thus, a third interlocutor with the apostle entered the stage, as Agamben made clear that his conception of the remnant was derived from Christian teleology and Paul's letters to the Corinthians.[91] These binaries—of Logos versus Icon, Judaism versus Christianity, and monotheism vs. idolatry, or, as Didi-Huberman puts it in *Écorces*, of essence versus appearance and substance versus semblance—seem to have mired the debate in a double bind where each side has accused the other of symbolically repeating the crime of the Nazi regime. Either by insisting on visible evidence, and thus accepting the revisionist logic of those who insist that proof remains to be presented, or by refuting all images, and thereby corroborating the perpetrators' plan to bury all evidence together with the dead.

These two contested figures—the apostle Paul who declared himself to be neither Jew nor gentile, and the *Muselmann*, a Jew named as a Muslim—return us to the core of the controversy: the poetics and politics of montage. In *Les temps modernes*, Wajcman cautioned the reader of the danger endemic to the profusion of images and the unbound semiosis of reckless and illegitimate comparisons that it might stir. In such a "dizzying whirlwind," Wajcman explains, the Nazi regime can be compared to the State of Israel and the stateless Palestinians regarded as "the true Jews of our time."[92] This criticism was deliberately been provoked by Jean-Luc Godard in his reading of the *Muselmann* as a cipher for the historically reversible roles between oppressors and oppressed across the conflict zones of Eastern Europe, Palestine, Beirut and Sarajevo.[93] Agamben has similarly been detracted not only for nominating the mute *Muselmann* as the "complete witness" of the Shoah, but for abstracting the logic of the Nazi *Lager* into a general norm of governmentality, positioning the camp "as the hidden paradigm of the political space of modernity, whose metamorphoses and disguises we will have to learn to recognize."[94] It is worth bearing in mind that this controversy had already been sparked by the allegorical approach taken by Resnais in *Night and Fog*, which associates the camps with the current French colonial war in Algeria. In common with Didi-Huberman, Godard and Agamben, Resnais has been attacked for obscuring the historical specificity of the gas chambers and for undermining the singularity of the Shoah. In the sphere of images, where any sign may take the place of another, everything is also potentially like something else. From this perspective, the ban against images may more properly be understood as a prohibition against making comparisons, of articulating relationships between distant and disparate things, and of suggesting that victims and aggressors may change places over the course of history. Conversely, one may argue that to prohibit comparisons is an effective means of depoliticizing the crimes of the Nazi regime and to attribute to them the status of an ultimate and timeless evil.

The Christian paradigm of the image, which is elaborated at length by Didi-Huberman in *Confronting Images*, is not a "passion of the image," however, but of the vestige.[95] That is to say, not a passion of photography per se, but of the imprint. This passion had originally been conveyed by the pious artists of the early Renaissance whose task it was to summon God *in spite of* his silent withdrawal from the world.[96] This signature phrase, "in spite of all," which returns as a leitmotif across Didi-Huberman's writing, can be traced back to an essay from 1984 called "The Index of the Absent Wound." The topic under consideration is the Holy Shroud of Turin, and the hermeneutic tradition of interpreting the stains on this piece of linen serge. To the devote beholder, Didi-Huberman explains, it is the very absence of figuration that verifies that, "*contact* has taken place. The noniconic, nonmimetic nature of this stain guarantees its *indexical* value."[97]

Thus, Wajcman is partly right when he in the concluding paragraphs of his critical appraisal in *Les temps modernes*—notably, one of the few passages that Didi-Huberman does not comment upon in *L'images malgré tout*—proposes that the secret cipher of the art historian's reading of the four photographs from Auschwitz is, "the Holy Shroud, the linen certifying the body of Christ through his image."[98] It is also in light of Didi-Huberman's essay on the Shroud of Turin, and what he there calls "the logic of the index,"[99] that Mary Ann Doane offers her commentary on the double status of the photographic image as both trace (the film touched by light, like damp soil impressed by a foot) and deixis (the frame that directs our attention and asserts "there!"). "The dialectic of the trace (the 'once' or pastness) and deixis (the now or presence) produces the conviction of the index," Doane explains, "the two understandings of the index collude to buttress an almost theological faith or certitude in the image."[100] "Deixis," as Doane further notes with reference to Roman Jacobson's understanding of the deictic shifters, "is the moment when language seems to *touch ground*."[101] In visual terms, the deixis is, as Didi-Huberman might say, the moment when the image touches the eye by alerting the viewer to the acts of looking and appearing.

Significantly, it was through the intervention of the medium of photography that the stains on the linen serge in Turin could be disclosed, on a photographic negative, as an *Imago Dei*. In its dual status as religious relic and photographic index, the shroud aligns faith and forensics, constituting, in Philippe Dubois phrase, the "first crime photograph."[102] The miraculous transformation from index to icon, from stain to figure, and from dissemblance to semblance, is also unpacked by Didi-Huberman in analogy to the forensic restaging of a crime scene. Not only is the blood, and thereby the body, of Christ summoned from the stained piece of cloth, but also the scene of the Passion and the entire narrative of the Gospels. It is the aim of this logic, which asserts the spiritual superiority of the index over the icon, he concludes, to overwhelm the index with its "iconic and symbolic dimensions."[103]

It is precisely such an overwhelming, I want to argue, that takes place in the films of Lanzmann, as they summon from the brute and nonsensical materiality of the ground a metaphysical narrative order. Not that of the Passion or the Gospels, but of the Exodus. Hence, despite its formal rigor and stern critique of photographic archives, *Shoah* is heavily invested in the ontology of the index. "The power of index is immense. Its metonymic force transforms an object into the evil it signifies," as Margaret Olin has noted in her discerning commentary on the spatial rhetoric of *Shoah*.[104] Olin describes this as a process of tainting the ground by implicating it in the murderous regime as complicit to the deed. Lanzmann's camera is equally attentive to the residues of the past—the train yards, campgrounds and ghetto quarters—as it is to the apparently contingent and random details of the present: a passerby, a buss queue, a street corner or traffic light, sights and details that appear to hold no relation to the Final Solution other than their spatial proximity. In these long, lingering takes, an auratic presence gradually advances that transcends the quotidian content of the imagery, investing every field, building and vacant lot with a quiet menace that at any moment may cause the entire geography to relapse into its former condition, its true self: the judicial *non-lieux* that first rendered its Jewish population stateless by the Nuremberg laws and then speechless in the camp.[105] The task undertaken by Lanzmann is to reverse this trajectory. Contrary to the archaeologies undertaken by Didi-Huberman and Agamben, Lanzmann's is not oriented toward a third person, but toward a first: not toward a threshold, but toward an essence and origin. The deixis does not only touch the ground of what can no longer be a home for the Jewish people, as one witness attests on a railway platform in Berlin, it also clears the ground for a homecoming.

Martyr's Forest

Against the archive, Lanzmann posits the monument, urging that *Shoah* should not be regarded as a documentary, but, in a phrase that he borrows from Wajcman, as "a 'monument' that is part of what it monumentalizes."[106] Monuments, moreover, feature prominently in all of Lanzmann's films. Prompting to be read in accordance with the Latin *monere*, which means both "to remind" and "to warn," they perform a vital function to bridge not only the past and present, but also, I propose, to form a bond between testimony and territory and to tie a people to a place. The penultimate section will retrace these monuments as they appear over the course of four decades of filmmaking. Once more, trees play a decisive role, acting as mediators between the land of extermination and the land of resurrection.

The concluding scene of *The Last of the Unjust* is set in the Roman Forum, and framed, quite literally, by the Victory Arch of Titus. The archway was built to commemorate the military commander who oversaw the siege of Jerusalem and the destruction of the Second Temple in 70 AD, the event that marked the onset of the third diaspora. It is through this portal that Lanzmann and Murmelstein enter the scene, and as they continue to stroll back and forth on the cobbled road, it looms in the background, framing their conversation. The topic of their final talk is Murmelstein's life in exile despite, as the opening credits put it, "his deep desire to go to Israel and his pure love for that land." This exile is set in its proper perspective by the archway at the vanishing point of the film's final image. Recalling Murmelstein's parable of the destroyed forest, the past indeed has "repercussions on the whole world. … Here in Rome too."

The relief inside the Arch of Titus, which depicts a procession of soldiers carrying away the spoils from the Second Temple and the captives brought in chains to Rome, was the subject of the seventh plate of Warburg's *Mnemosyne* atlas. The *Pathosformel* of this frieze returns as the model for the bas-relief on the eastern side of the Warsaw Ghetto Monument, designed by Nathan Rapoport to commemorate the uprising that took place in the ghetto in the spring of 1943. It is only the Nazi helmets and bayonets looming behind the procession of prisoners that indicate its recent historical significance.[107] This monument appears in two of Lanzmann's films. Most recently in *Sobibor 14 octobre 1943 16 heures* (2001), which combines an interview with Yehuda Lerner, a survivor of the uprising in the Sobibór camp, recorded in 1979 and on-location footage shot twenty years later. The film opens with an extended panorama of Warsaw, followed by a second panning shot that moves from a somnolent park and comes to a full stop as it frames Rapoport's monument. Barely visible behind the garish postcard rack of a souvenir vendor, the monument attracts no interest or visitors. From here, the next panning shot takes us to the monument at the Umschlagplatz, the square in Warsaw from where Jews were deported to Treblinka. It was built to resemble an open freight car, and tramcars continue to pass before it as the camera pauses at length to show the lintel in the shape of a gravestone above the entrance gate. A forest of broken trees, symbolizing the shattered Jewish nation, appears in relief on the lintel. A counterpoint to the destroyed forest is offered in the final image of the film; a silent, lateral pan that moves across the soaring autumnal forest of Sobibór, its dark mass unruffled by the wind.

Rapoport's monument is mobilized with a more defiant effect in the final minutes of *Shoah*. A measured panning shot paces across the dilapidated ghetto quarters until it comes to a pause on the western side of the monument where a bronze frieze of men, women and children armored with grenades, rifles and daggers faces the open square. The camera zooms in close on the faces of the resistance fighters. Then, in a graphic match, it cuts to a close-up of the replica of the monument that was built on the large plaza at the Yad Vashem memorial in Jerusalem. It zooms out and resumes its panning motion across the Jerusalem Forest and toward the Holy City in the distance.[108]

The Yad Vashem memorial is also where Lanzmann's first film, *Pourquoi Israël*, begins and ends. In a gesture that prefigures the geography to be charted in *Shoah*, the camera scans the names inscribed on the stone floor of the memorial hall: Auschwitz, Mauthausen, Bergen-Belsen, Dachau. For its epilogue, three hours later, the film takes us into The Hall of Names where a clerk enumerates all the Lanzmanns who perished in the camps. After the last name, the director simply instructs: "Cut!" In between, *Pourquoi Israël* unfolds as a Grand Tour through the sprawling immigrant nation, showcasing all its major landmarks. Lanzmann even acts as a tour guide for a young immigrant family from Kiev, taking them to the Wailing Wall and Masada. "I haven't been here in two thousand years," the man from Kiev confides to Lanzmann, a statement later corroborated by an archaeologist who explains to the filmmaker, "we carry two thousand years of history in our genes." *Pourquoi Israël* also contemplates the new memorials that are spreading across the territory of the young state. A lyrical montage accompanied by a solitary, pastoral flute shows how saplings of pine trees are being planted in the sandy dunes, one for each of the six million names in the Yad Vashem archive. The ceremony is followed by a panorama of the steeply wooded valleys and traveling shots through the lush forests with sun flares breaking in the lens, concluding with a silent close-up of a sign that reads: "Martyrs Forest. In sacred memory of six million Jews. Victims of the European Holocaust" (Fig. 6.4). The full-frame shot of the memorial inscription in Hebrew and English prefigures the explosive "encounter between a name and a place," detonated by the Treblinka road sign, that would become the modus operandi of Lanzmann's subsequent work. The living memorial of

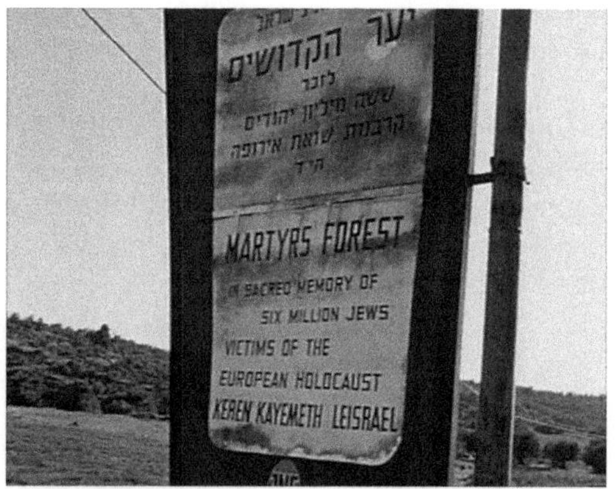

Fig. 6.4 *Pourquoi Israël* (Claude Lanzmann, 1973)

Martyrs Forest thus commemorates what the forests in Poland, the "*non-sites of memory*" scrutinized in *Shoah*, conceal.

Martyrs Forest was part of the massive afforestation campaigns launched in the aftermath of the Arab-Israeli war in 1948. Symbolically, saplings were sown to commemorate the dead, to serve as a proxy for returning immigrants, and to lay the roots of the nation by reinstating the natural reserves that had been cleared during the Ottoman Empire. They were also part of a strategy to prevent return, systematically planted on the grounds of the Palestinian villages that had been deserted and destroyed during the war. Due to their rapid growth, their far-branching root system and the acidity of pine needles, the forestations did not only cover the traces of former farmsteads and cemeteries, they also eradicated the undergrowth of nutrients and water and the possibility for grazing and olive groves, the basis for the agrarian economy of the Palestinian population.

Tsahal, the concluding part of the trilogy, takes its title from the Israeli defense force and tackles how the army was shaped between the Six-Day War in 1967 and the Yom Kippur War in 1973. Toward the end of the film, a montage of helicopter shots circle over Jerusalem, Masada, and the hilltop settlements. The panoramic sweep of the country is accompanied by the voice of Ehud Barak as he ponders the historical destiny of his people: "We carry in our blood the genes of the Maccabees and of those Zealots who died in Masada." Linking the Holy City to the new settlements, and the fortress on Masada to the State of Israel, the aerial panorama displays the territory of the state as a monument in its own right.

Across the geographies charted in Lanzmann's films, the relation between the surveyor and the territory undergoes a transformation. Throughout *Shoah*, the camera paces back and forth across tracks buried in mud, debris in the undergrowth, and the crematoria sunken into the earth. In the final scene showing the Polish countryside, a low-angle camera slowly pans across a field edged by dark woods and frozen over with an icy shell. The travelogues through Israel advance a different iconography: that of the frontier and the pastoral. They exhibit the open horizons of the coastline and desert; the pioneer spirit of Kibbutzim and the settlements, with chanting voices and elegiac hymns playing over images of rolling sand dunes and forest reserves; and the combat-training zones in the desert cast against full moons and glorious sunsets.

The intricate conjunction of a survey and an archaeology that undergirds Lanzmann's project had already been inaugurated by the two incentives that impelled *Pourquoi Israël*. First, to cover the territory and to stake out its sovereign borders; second, by the question that Lanzmann pursues throughout the film: "Who is a Jew?" Lanzmann's insistence on this question may be understood as a response to the thesis promulgated by his mentor Jean-Paul Sartre in "Anti-Semite and the Jew," which argued that the Jew exists only as an image derived from anti-semitism, and thus, that the Jew is a phantom summoned and nourished by a passionate hatred that ultimately lacks an object. Challenging Sartre's claim, Lanzmann has defined anti-semitism as "the metaphysical hatred against a people who is the origin and knows it and wills it."[109] This ancient hatred is the nexus, or more correctly, the *archē* in its double sense of a commencement and a commandment, which connects the ghettoes, gulags and camps of the East with the imminent threat of annihilation by the Arabs, encroaching upon the borders of the Israeli state.[110] Thus, two historical records converge: the two thousand years of exile from the homeland and the destruction of a previous generation in Europe. The intervening millennia are left vacant, as if the land itself had been exiled, biding its time, awaiting the return of its rightful owners and its re-entry into history. It is not merely the Second Commandment, with its ban against graven images, which derives from the book of Exodus; exile and return also provide the master plot of Lanzmann's films. It is a narrative about origins and ownership, bloodlines and biological heredity, and about Israel as the embodiment of the Jewish world. Conflating ethnic identity and state territory, it is a recognition and confirmation of a world according to a vision, an image of "a people who is the origin and knows it and wills it."

In her preface to the published screenplay of *Shoah*, Simone de Beauvoir writes that, "[t]he greatness of Claude Lanzmann's art is in making places speak."[111] The compliment paraphrases the working title of *Shoah*, "Site and Speech." Neither places nor trees, however, possess a voice. Like images, they appear rather to be enveloped in a protruding muteness. To confront images, then, is also to confront silence. Unremarked by Didi-Huberman, the birch tree has earned the nickname "the Watchful tree" due to the eye-shaped impressions on their bark. Such a capacity to return our gaze is also a key characteristic of symptoms, as understood by Didi-Huberman. Like the black lenticels that rip the white bark, they do not establish eye contact, much less a communion. Instead, their mute stare "places us in question, interrogates our own capacity to forget."[112] A capacity, we should add, inexorably entangled with our urge and desire to remember.

Coda: *A Land and Its People*

"What kind of times are these, where a discussion about trees is itself almost a crime, because it involves keeping silent about so many misdeeds!"[113] So pondered Bertolt Brecht during his exile in Denmark two years before the outbreak of the Second World War. This was not the first time that Brecht set the lyrical musing on trees against a politically committed art: "One cannot write poems about trees when the forest is full of police." Or: "Delight at the apple tree in blossom /And horror at the house-painter's speeches. / But only the second / Drives me to my writing desk."[114] The house-painter was Brecht's sobriquet for the Führer, referring to his early, and unsuccessful, career as a landscape painter. On another occasion, however, when asked what he considered his most radical act during the war, the playwright and poet responded that it consisted in writing a paean to an apple tree growing in a garden in Berlin.[115] The latter comment acknowledges the capacity of landscape to transform our sense of time, and to restore a moment from where it is possible to discern the horizon of an indeterminate future. It is, however, to the interlaced acts of silencing and speaking about crimes and misdeeds that these concluding remarks now turn, considered in light of two pairs of trees brought to a face-to-face encounter.

First, a palm tree that gently leans before a crescent bay, enticing our gaze across the calm waters to a distant shore. Then, the bulky trunk and massive leafy foil of an olive tree that fills the screen in a blurry close-up (Fig. 6.5). These are the two photographs, made a century apart, which introduce the brief sequence titled "Palestine" in Jean-Luc Godard's *Film Socialisme* (2010). It follows after a series of passing references to Jaffa, Haifa, and Mandatory Palestine, along with the key date 1948, during the first half hour of the film, and it is announced by a voice declaring: "The photograph of a land and its people, at last." Curiously, however, the two photographs that are shown contain no people, only trees.

Godard quotes these two images, and the spoken line that introduces them, from the photographic collection *Les Palestiniens: La photographie d'une terre et de son peuple de 1839 à nos jours* compiled by the Palestinian historian and poet Elias Sanbar, whom the director had befriended in

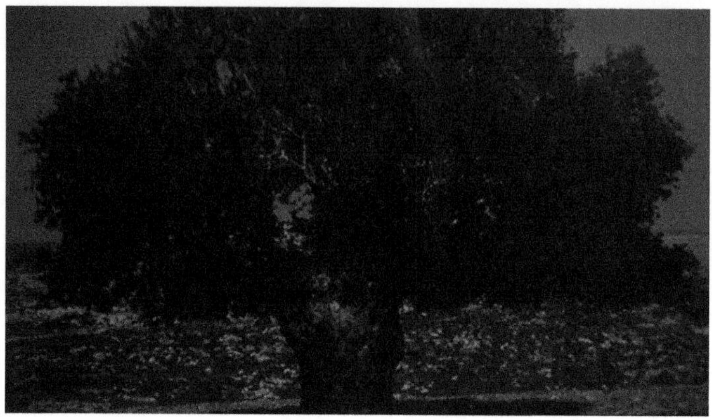

Fig. 6.5 *Film Socialisme* (Jean-Luc Godard, 2010)

Jordan in 1969 during the making of what would later become *Ici et ailleurs* (Here and Elsewhere, 1970–1974).[116] Sanbar also appears on screen in *Film Socialisme* to recount how the invention of the Daguerreotype hurled a pilgrimage of photographers to record the sites of the biblical lands. The first image—the palm tree before Haifa Bay—was photographed by Félix Bonfils in 1880. In his book, Sanbar gives it the caption "charms of paradise lost."[117] Emblematic of the orientalist pictorialism promulgated by French and British travel agencies at the time, the work of Bonfils evinces two conflicting yet affiliated visions of the land: on the one hand, as the blank slate of a New World; on the other, as a "gigantic antique Necropolis" and "a phantasmagoric museum."[118] Following Sanbar, this vision of the land as at once a new beginning and a relic of a pre-historic world of shepherds, nomads and ruins served to inscribe a double disappearance of the indigenous population, and as a moral incentive to resettle and redeem the land after centuries of neglect.

The second image—the close-up of an olive tree—was made by the French photographer Joss Dray in 1989. It is the penultimate photograph in Sanbar's book and reproduced as a diptych facing, on the opposite spread, the Separation Wall's vertical mass of concrete. Dray's photograph highlights the transformation of the olive tree from a token of peace in ancient Mediterranean culture to become a ubiquitous and highly potent political totem deeply imbricated in a struggle that is as much symbolic as it is strategic.[119] On both sides of the conflict, trees, groves and forests have provided a visual form to articulate a people's rootedness and perseverance in the land. The tree-planting ceremonies performed by Israelis and Palestinians alike thus entail a ferocious struggle over images and identities, staking out mutually exclusive claims to a living bond between a land and its people. "Much as I liked pine trees they looked like intruders," the West Bank author and activist Reja Shehadeh remarks in his elegiac travelogue *Palestinian Walks*, "forcefully claiming the land where they struck root. Like the olive trees their roots remained close to the surface, knotted and smoothed like knuckles, scrambling for the same piece of ground, making it hard for them to coexist."[120] On another occasion, Shehadeh instead finds himself "looking at an olive tree, and as I am looking at it, it transforms itself before my eyes into a symbol of the samidin, of our struggle, of our loss."[121] However, as Shehadeh immediately adds, at that moment he is also "robbed of the tree," which has been galvanized before his eyes, or rather, through his gaze, into an apotheosis of oppression and resistance. This transformation is indicatory of the longings and laments that landscapes arouse, and the demands that looking activates.

For the last set of images to be considered in this study, we turn once more to the work of Ori Gersht. Before embarking into the primeval woods of Eastern Europe to shoot *The Forest*, Gersht had turned his viewfinder toward the trees of his native country in order to examine how they had been mobilized, on both sides, to stake out competing claims to an ancestral land. The first of these works was begun in 2003 and given the title *Ghost*. Each image in the series portrays a single tree from the remains of an ancient olive grove in Galilee, survivors of the Ottoman Empire, the British Mandate, and the expansion of Israeli settlements after the Six-Day War in 1967, the year when Gersht was born in Tel-Aviv. Withered and gnarled over centuries, some of these specimens appear completely hollowed out, as only the outer crust of the bark remains, folded around the empty core of an absent trunk. When making the photographs, Gersht deliberately flooded the film with the searing light of the midday sun. When developing the prints in the darkroom, the process was reversed in order to salvage the almost obliterated inscriptions, buried in light and unearthed from the nearly black negatives. Moving in and out of visibility, the ethereal figures that reemerged appear like spectral apparitions, transmitted from a distant past. The oscillation between overexposure and underexposure, erasure and evocation, disappearance and reappearance, that takes place on the sensitized surface of the photographic film thus parallels the physical manipulation of memory on the ground, serving as an intimation of the landscape's capacity to make us remember as well as forget, as irreconcilable memories inevitably cohabit on the same site.

Two years later, *Ghost* was accompanied by a second series called *Mark* (2005). This time, Gersht photographed cypress trees planted as commemorative markers of Israeli soldiers killed in battle. Viewed together, Gersht's ghosts and marks elicit two markedly distinct images of a body holding its ground: twisted and tormented in the first case; stoic and defiant in the second. The anemic and asymmetrical olive trees and the dark, dense and spire-like evergreen cypresses, which Greek and Latin poets associated with the underworld, nonetheless converge in their funeral, dirge-like connotations. From this perspective, Gersht's solitary trees seem fraught with a more sinister meaning. Rather than an elegiac reminder, they elicit the menacing premonition that they will remain "the sole survivor," as Didi-Huberman writes in *Écorces*, "who still lives here."

Maybe every landscape, given time, has that impact on us, positioning us as witnesses to our own absence. And maybe then, as a young W.G. Sebald reflected in his first published poem, it is the landscape that silently watches us as we vanish.[122] Like the long exposures utilized by Gersht, prolonged looking fosters the impression that the objects that surround us, in their stunned silence, start to gaze back, reversing the relation between seeing and seen, image and beholder, as in the sensation famously described by Paul Klee, "that the trees were looking at me, were speaking to me. … I was there listening."[123] We may be reminded here of the filmmakers of the *Fûkeiron* movement considered in the introductory chapter, the group of Japanese artists and intellectuals who traversed and transfixed the quotidian landscape of postwar reconstruction in static long shots and slow-paced pans. The photographer Nakahira Takuma has explained the phenomenological notion underlying this project in the following terms: "You cannot help but recognize that the more you look at this landscape, the more you are being seen. The question is how to endure the enemy's gaze."[124] This is not the only pertinent question, however, that arises from the sensation of being subjected to the landscape's gaze.

Following Sartre's intuition that seeing only occurs when you see yourself being seen, landscape presents a privileged site for an ethical encounter. Instead of distancing us from the Other (whether an indigenous population, a labor force, or nature as such) or exposing us to the demanding gaze of an ancestor or intruder (calling for vigilance, sacrifice or retribution) the very passivity of the landscape, which asserts nothing but its duration, may be taken as an invitation. Along the lines of Lévinas' proposition of an ethics based on the Other's gaze, in this scenario it is not the transcendental and self-reflective subject that asserts itself before the world viewed, to gather and grasp it within its gaze, but conversely, the landscape that asserts itself before us, gazing back at us, calling us into question. Like the watchful trees interrogated by Didi-Huberman, the pockmarked deserts, shrapnel scars, cratered roads and swarming crows that have been considered throughout this book all face us with such eye-like cavities. The voids and silences that they convey urge the viewer to conjure up something that the images themselves do not reveal.

This calls for a final remark on the etymological link between bark and language that concludes *Écorces*, one that previously had been noted by Blanchot and Derrida. The skein of abstract inkblots or photographic grains discerned by Didi-Huberman in the shreds of bark, and the discourse on the unsayable and unimaginable nature of the Nazi crimes against which these modest tokens are advanced, find their most concise expression in an aphorism penned by Giorgio Agamben: "Where language stops is not where the unsayable occurs, but rather where the matter of words begins. Those who have not reached, as in a dream, this woody substance of language, which the ancients called *silva* (wildwood), are prisoners of representation, even when they keep silent."[125] To be a prisoner of representation, we may say, paraphrasing Baudelaire, is tantamount to walking through a forest of symbols in the midst of which we are only able to see our own images. This forest is a site of struggle for recognition and legitimacy, for forging bonds and binaries by rooting a people to a place. The edge of the forest, conversely, marks the no-man's-land where traces proliferate.

Poised at the limit of representation, suspended between the sensible and the legible, the trace is first and foremost an index of what Agamben above refers to as the wood-like substance of language. For the moment when language fails, when it stutters or falls silent, is also the moment in which we may glimpse language as such. That is, the event of language taking place. At once eluding and enabling enunciation, both warranting and withdrawing from meaning, the trace is what establishes the conditions for something to appear and signify, or not to. Like landscape, language does not belong to us. Rather, it comes to us from the outside, and as we pass through it, it beckons to us, soliciting our attention and articulation. Like the threadbare pieces of bark, the oblique evidence photographed by Didi-Huberman on site—the wall, the lake and the cement floor—marks the limit where representation stops and the matter of words begins. In common with the miscellany of surface exteriors—stained, striated, bruised or rubbed—that have been considered throughout this study, they delineate the threshold where imagining and remembering becomes possible, and where the gestures of retracing begin.

Notes

1. Georges Didi-Huberman *Écorces* (Paris: Les Éditions de Minuit 2011) 9. All translations from this essay are my own. Echoing Hofmannsthal's characterization of astrology, Heinrich Himmler referred to the genocide as, "the most glorious page in our history, one not written and which shall never be written." As quoted by Joshua Hirsch *Afterimage: Film, Trauma, and the Holocaust* (Philadelphia: Temple University Press 2010) 12.
2. Didi-Huberman *Écorces* 10, 68–69.
3. I'm paraphrasing here Didi-Huberman's remark that we need "to look at what remains (visible) while summoning up what has disappeared: in short, to scrutinize the visual traces of this disappearance." Georges Didi-Huberman *Confronting Images: Questioning the Ends of a Certain History of Art* [1990] trans. John Goodman (University Park: The Pennsylvania State University Press 2005) 50.
4. Ibid. 28.
5. Ibid. 169.
6. Didi-Huberman *Écorces* 64.
7. Didi-Huberman *Confronting Images* 188.
8. Georges Didi-Huberman *The Surviving Image: Phantoms of Time and Time of Phantoms* [2002] trans. Harvey L. Mendelsohn (University Park: The Pennsylvania State University Press 2017) 192, 274.
9. Maurice Blanchot "Literature and the Right to Death" [1948] *The Work of Fire* (Stanford: Stanford University Press 1995) 327–328.
10. Jacques Derrida *Paper Machine* [2001] (Stanford: Stanford University Press 2005) 6.
11. Georges Didi-Huberman "Opening the Camps, Closing the Eyes: Image, History, Readability" *Concentrationary Cinema: Aesthetics as Political Resistance in Alain Resnais's Night and Fog* eds. Griselda Pollock and Max Silverman (New York and Oxford: Berghahn Books 2011) 84–125, 116.
12. Jean-Luc Nancy *The Ground of the Image* trans. Jeff Fort (New York: Fordham University Press 2005) 7.

13. To briefly recap the history of these images: A camera was smuggled into the camp by the Polish resistance movement to members of the *Sonderkommando*, the unit whose task it was to exhume the gas chambers, burn the bodies and bury the ashes. In August 1944, a member of the *Sonderkommando* known as Alex took four snapshots of the activities outside Crematorium V. At the time, the ovens were overloaded due to the mass deportations of Hungarian Jews, and corpses were burned outdoors in the grassland bordering on the fence and forest. This strip of film was smuggled out of the camp in a tube of toothpaste.
14. Georges Didi-Huberman *Images in Spite of All: Four Photographs from Auschwitz* trans. Shane B. Lillis (Chicago: University of Chicago Press 2008) 33, 38, 47.
15. Georges Didi-Huberman "Images malgré tout" *Mémoire des camps: photographies des camps de concentration et d'extermination nazis (1933–1999)* ed. Clément Chéroux (Paris: Marval 2001) 219–241.
16. Didi-Huberman *Images in Spite of All: Four Photographs from Auschwitz* [2003] trans. Shane B. Lillis (Chicago and London: The University of Chicago Press 2008) 46.
17. As quoted by Didi-Huberman *Images in Spite of All* 165, from Gérard Wajcman "De la croyance photographique" *Les Temps Modernes* Vol. 56 No. 613 (2001) 47–83.
18. Georges Didi-Huberman "Le lieu malgré tout" *Vingtième Siècle. Revue d'histoire* No. 46 Numéro spécial: Cinéma, le temps de l'Histoire (April–June 1995) 36–44. Reprinted as "The Site, Despite Everything" trans. Stuart Liebman *Shoah: Key Essays* ed. Stuart Liebman (Oxford and New York: Oxford University Press 2007) 113–123.
19. Lanzmann has explained that the "issue of the site is so important" because he "did not make an idealist film." Hence, he describes *Shoah* as "a film from the ground up, a topographical film, a geographical film." Marc Chevrie and Hervé Le Roux "Site and Speech: An Interview with Claude Lanzmann About *Shoah*" trans. Stuart Liebman *Shoah: Key Essays*, ed. Stuart Liebman 35–49, 38–39.
20. Claude Lanzmann *The Patagonian Hare*: A Memoir [2011] trans. Frank Wynne (London: Atlantic Books 2012) 475.
21. Didi-Huberman "Opening the Camps, Closing the Eyes" 111.
22. Lanzmann *The Patagonian Hare* 477.
23. Ibid. 485, 472.
24. Ibid. 477–478.
25. Ibid. 489.
26. Ibid. 475, my emphasis.
27. Ibid. 472.
28. Chevrie and Le Roux 44.

29. Lanzmann *The Patagonian Hare* 411
30. Didi-Huberman *Images in Spite of All* 127.
31. Didi-Huberman *Écorces* 69.
32. Didi-Huberman *Images in Spite of All* 47.
33. Walter Benjamin *The Arcades Project* trans. H. Eiland and K. McLaughlin (Cambridge and London: The Belknap Press of Harvard University Press 1999) 472
34. Walter Benjamin "Theses on the Philosophy of History" *Illuminations: Essays and Reflections* trans. Harry Zohn (New York: Schocken Books 1968) 253–264, 255.
35. Lanzmann *The Patagonian Hare* 473.
36. Ibid. 473.
37. Lanzmann cited by Michael D'Arcy "Claude Lanzmann's *Shoah* and the Intentionality of the Image" *Visualizing the Holocaust: Documents, Aesthetics, Memory* eds. David Bathrick, Brad Prager, and Michael David Richardson (Rochester: Camden House 2008) 142.
38. Chevrie and Le Roux 40. Notably, Lanzmann's final film, *The Last of the Unjust*, does not discard or refute archival images. On several occasions, it shows drawings in charcoal or watercolor made by the Jewish inmates of Theresienstadt. These visual testimonies are juxtaposed with excerpts from the Nazi propaganda film *The Führer Gives a City to the Jews* (1944) which brazenly embellishes the "model ghetto," showing its population at work and leisure, attending concerts, card games and soccer games, or, in its most staggering cynicism, entering and walking out of the municipal bathhouse.
39. "Le monument contre l'archive?" Claude Lanzmann in dialogue with Daniel Bougnoux, Régis Debray, Claude Mollard, Louise Merzeau, Philippe Petit, Veronique Hervouet, Maurice Sachot, and Robert Dumas *Les cahiers de médiologie* No. 11 (2001) 271–279, 272. My translation.
40. Chevrie and Le Roux 45.
41. Lanzmann *The Patagonian Hare* 506–507.
42. Didi-Huberman *Écorces* 69.
43. Ibid. 62.
44. Paul Celan "Stretto" [1958] *Paul Celan: Selections* ed. Pierre Joris (Berkeley, Los Angeles, and London: University of California Press 2005) 67. This poem was written by Paul Celan after he had translated Jean Cayrol's voiceover narration for *Night and Fog* into German.
45. For the seventieth anniversary of the Liberation, this film was restored and released together with a documentary called *Night Will Fall* (Andre Singer, 2014) chronicling the history of the footage from Bergen-Belsen. For a detailed discussion on the formal choices made during the

editing process, see Nicolas Losson and Annette Michelson "Notes on the Images of the Camps" *October* Vol. 90 (Autumn 1999) 25–35.

46. Robert E. Conot *Justice at Nuremberg* [1983] (New York: Carroll & Graf Publishers 2000) 300.
47. Goethe's Oak plays a key role in two novels written by survivors from Buchenwald: Ernst Wiechert's *Der Totenwald: Ein Bericht* (Forest of the Dead, 1947) and Pierre Julitte's *L'Arbre de Goethe* (Goethe's Oak, 1965). On 24 August 1944, the oak tree was hit by a stray incendiary bomb and claimed to have burned all night, interpreted as an omen of the end of the Nazi regime. The remaining stump was cast in concrete and preserved on the site.
48. Christopher S. Wood *Albrecht Altdorfer and the Origins of Landscape*. Revised and Expanded Second Edition (London: Reaktion Books 2014) 208.
49. I am referring here to two works, both from 1972: the birches sketched upside down on a sheet torn from a book on French art history in *Birken (Paysage)*, and the oil painting *Fingermalerei-Briken*.
50. Matthew Biro *Anselm Kiefer and the Philosophy of Martin Heidegger* (Cambridge: Cambridge University Press 1998) 122.
51. "The Forest" is also the name of an art installation at Polin: The Museum of the History of Polish Jews in Warsaw. Serving as a prologue to the exhibitions, the visitor is invited to walk through a series of glass screens onto which digitally animated trees are projected, illustrating the legend of how the first Jews came to Poland (in Hebrew, *Polin*). Fleeing prosecution they entered a primeval forest with Hebrew words carved on the trees. I am indebted to Isabel Gil for this reference. A video is available here http://culture.pl/en/video/the-legend-of-the-arrival-of-the-jews-in-poland (accessed 2 August 2018).
52. Ori Gersht interviewed by Camilla Jackson, Senior Curator at The Photographers Gallery in London. My emphasis. Available at the gallery homepage http://crggallery.com/exhibitions/ori-gersht-the-forest/ (accessed 2 August 2018).
53. Ernst van Alphen *Caught by History: Holocaust Effects in Contemporary Art, Literature, and Theory* (Stanford: Stanford University Press 1997) 128.
54. Ibid. 132.
55. Georges Didi-Huberman "The Paradox of the Phasmid" (1989) trans. Alisa Hartz, n.p. Available at http://underconstruction.wdfiles.com/local--files/imprint-reading/huberman_paradox.pdf (accessed 2 August 2018).
56. "It *shows silence* and also augments it, that is, gives it form, constructs it, giving to the sites the power to return our gaze /…/ he often makes a detour so that a truth incapable of being conveyed in signs comes to

light as a symptom, if only in a pan shot of an empty clearing in the forest." Didi-Huberman "The Site, Despite Everything" 118, 120.

57. Lanzmann quoted by Didi-Huberman in "The Site, Despite Everything" 122.
58. Claude Lanzmann "From the Holocaust to 'Holocaust'" *Shoah: Key Essays* 27–36, 35.
59. Lanzmann returns to this notion several times in his conversation with Marc Chevrie and Hervé Le Roux: "Making images from reality is to dig holes in reality. Framing a scene involves excavating it. … the truth is constantly attested to at different levels, one must dig for it. … this idea of drilling [for truth], of archeology". Chevrie and Le Roux 42–44.
60. Emma Wilson "Material Remains: *Night and Fog*" *October* Vol. 112 (Spring 2005) 89–110, 101.
61. Chris Marker, who assisted Jean Cayrol in writing the narration for *Night and Fog*, resumes this theme five years later in his essay film on Israel, *Description of a struggle* (Description d'un Combat, 1960): "Signs. At first the land speaks to us in signs. Signs of land. Signs of water. Signs of man. … Signs have but a short life. This tire dump in Jaffa has now disappeared. And this man standing in the waters of Tiberias can hardly be there now. For lasting signs are carved in the bark of trees. And the skin of man." Following the footage of inscriptions carved into bark, the film shows a series of close-ups of the identification numbers tattooed on the skin of former camp inmates.
62. Jacques Derrida *Demeure: Fiction and Testimony* [1998] ed. and trans. Elizabeth Rottenberg (Stanford: Stanford University Press 2000) 43.
63. Agamben is here discussing the two Latin words for "witness," the first being *testis* (a third party) and the second *superstes* (a person who has survived an ordeal). Primo Levi, Agamben's primary interlocutor in the study, "is not a third party; he is a survivor [*superstite*] in every sense." Giorgio Agamben *Remnants of Auschwitz: The Witness and the Archive* [1999] trans. Daniel Heller-Rosein (New York: Zone Books 2000) 17.
64. Ibid. 145.
65. Ibid. 85, 156.
66. Didi-Huberman, *Images in Spite of All* 151. Didi-Huberman has on several occasions reflected on the domain of the third person with recourse to a quote from Deleuze: "Emotion does not say 'I'. You said it yourself: you are beside yourself. Emotion is not of the order of the ego but of the event. It is very difficult to grasp an event, but I do not believe that this grasp implies the first person. It would be better to use the third person like Maurice Blanchot when he says that there is more

intensity in the sentence 'he suffers' than 'I suffer'." Gilles Deleuze "Painting Sets Writing Ablaze" *Two Regimes of Madness: Texts and Interviews 1975–1995* ed. David Lapoujade, trans. Ames Hodges and Michael Taormina (New York: Semiotext(e) 2006) 181–187, 187.

67. I am quoting here from a lecture held by Didi-Huberman at the Symposium of Haus der Kunst in Munich on 9 June 2012, on the occasion of the opening of the exhibition "Image Counter Image." The lecture addresses the work of Harun Farocki, whom Didi-Huberman refers to as "a filmmaker in the third person." Notably, the reflection on the intervention of a third is followed in the lecture by two linguistic remarks respectively made by Aby Warburg and Emile Benveniste, both of which pertain to Agamben's notion of the deixis addressed in my chapter. The lecture is available at https://www.youtube.com/watch?v=qQq5BOP96TM (accessed 2 August 2018).
68. Agamben *Remnants of Auschwitz: The Witness and the Archive* [1999] trans. Daniel Heller-Rosein (New York: Zone Books 2000) 34.
69. For a discussion, see William Paul Simmons "The Third: Levinas' Theoretical Move from An-archical Ethics to the Realm of Justice and Politics" *Philosophy and Social Criticism* Vol. 25 No. 6 (1999) 83–104.
70. Marc Bloch *The Historian's Craft* [1954] trans. Peter Putnam (Manchester: Manchester University Press 1992) 51.
71. In the opening paragraphs of *Remnants of Auschwitz*, Agamben describes his investigation as a foray into the "new ethical territory" opened up in the wake of Auschwitz, following the lead of Primo Levi whom he later denominates as "the cartographer of this new *terra ethica*, the implacable land-surveyor of *Muselmannland*." The metaphor of a survey, however, is soon to be followed by that of an archaeology. Agamben *Remnants of Auschwitz* 69.
72. Didi-Huberman *Images in Spite of All* 37–38.
73. Ibid. 47
74. Ibid. 51.
75. Giorgio Agamben *The Signature of All Things: On Method* [2008] trans. Luca D'Isanto and Kevin Attell (New York: Zone Books 2009) 84.
76. Agamben *Remnants of Auschwitz* 139.
77. "Le monument contre l'archive?" 272. My translation. This interview is also discussed and quoted by Didi-Huberman in *Images in Spite of All* 93–94.
78. The process of retracing the place of testimony in *Shoah* comprises two intertwined acts: unerasing and reinscription. In Joshua Hirsch's analysis of the opening scene, Srebnik "begins to reverse the effects of this attempted erasure by remembering it, by rewitnessing it, by recognizing the site of the erasure now made almost unrecognizable by its

own erasure. The process of unerasing memory, in other words, begins with the memory of the erasure itself." Hirsch *Afterimage* 77. Gertrud Koch further notes that Lanzmann's insistence on "the concrete course of events" and "the phenomenological physiognomy of fact" presents the ground for retracing: "physical materiality must be present before the symbolic formation of language or signs can take place on its basis." Gertrud Koch "The Angel of Forgetfulness and the Black Box of Facticity: Trauma and Memory in Claude Lanzmann's Film 'Shoah'" trans. Ora Wiskind *History and Memory* Vol. 3 No. 1 (Spring 1991) 119–134, 131.

79. Lanzmann *The Patagonian Hare* 424
80. Benjamin Murmelstein, the last of the elders in Theresienstadt and the protagonist of *The Last of the Unjust*, also takes recourse to Greek mythology, comparing his testimony to Orpheus' descent into the underworld. Along these lines, Lanzmann's filmed dialogue with Maurice Rossel, the Red Cross official who wrote a favorable report about Theresienstadt, was given the title *A Visitor from the Living* (*Un vivant qui passe*, 1999).
81. Shoshana Felman "In an Era of Testimony: Claude Lanzmann's *Shoah*" *Yale French Studies* No. 79 (1991) 39–81, 72
82. Lanzmann *The Patagonian Hare* 427.
83. Felman 57.
84. For a discussion on the turn from an era of testimony to an era of forensics, see Eyal Weizman *The Least of All Possible Evils* (New York and London: Verso 2011) 112–113.
85. Lanzmann *The Patagonian Hare* 389
86. Lanzmann paraphrases Murmelstein's parable in a later interview: "I thought the destruction of Judaism in Eastern Europe was like the destruction of a forest. Once a forest is destroyed, the climate conditions are altered for kilometers around." Chevrie and Le Roux 42–43.
87. Didi-Huberman *Images in Spite of All* 71.
88. Gérard Wajcman "*«Saint Paul» Godard contre «Moïse» Lanzmann*" *Le Monde* December 3, 1998 https://editions-verdier.fr/2014/03/06/le-monde-jeudi-3-decembre-1998-par-gerard-wajcman/ (accessed 2 August 2018).
89. Wajcman quoted by Didi-Huberman *Images in Spite of All* 53.
90. See, for example, the book length critique presented by Philippe Mesnard and Claudine Kahan at the time of the *Mémoire des camps* exhibition, *Giorgio Agamben: à l'épreuve d'Auschwitz: témoignages/interpretations* (Paris: Kimé 2001). See also Philippe Mesnard "The Political Philosophy of Giorgio Agamben: A Critical Evaluation" *Totalitarian Movements and Political Religions* Vol. 5 No. 1 (Summer 2004) 139–157.

91. The Italian philosopher would continue to pursue the Christian theological concept of the remnant in his next book, *The Time That Remains: A Commentary on the Letter to the Romans* [2000] trans. Patricia Dailey (Stanford: Stanford University Press 2005). While the argument in *Remnants of Auschwitz* is consistent with the set of ideas developed by Agamben across his oeuvre, it would become his most contested work, especially in France where its critical reception coincided with the debate on the *Mémoire des camps* exhibition. It may not be without significance, in this context, that Paul has been accused of introducing anti-semitism to Christian theology.
92. Wajcman "De la croyance photographique" 62–63. My translation.
93. Henrik Gustafsson "Remnants of Palestine, or, Archeology After Auschwitz" *Cinema and Agamben: Ethics, Biopolitics and the Moving Image* eds. Henrik Gustafsson and Asbjørn Grønstad (New York: Bloomsbury 2014) 207–232.
94. Giorgio Agamben *Homo Sacer: Sovereign Power and Bare Life* [1995] trans. Daniel Heller-Roazen (Stanford: Stanford University Press 1998) 123.
95. Once more, we may note the influence of Lévinas' notion of the trace and its imbrication in a Judeo-Christian tradition that posits that God can only be represented negatively as a material vestige: "To be in the image of God does not mean to be an icon of God, but to find oneself in his trace… He shows himself only in his trace as is said in Exodus 33." Emmanuel Lévinas "The Trace of the Other" *Deconstruction in Context* ed. Mark C. Taylor (Chicago and London: Chicago University Press 1986) 345–359, 359.
96. Bruno Chaouat "In the Image of Auschwitz" *Diacritics* Vol. 36 No. 1 (Spring 2006) 86–96. Chaouat criticizes Didi-Huberman for interpreting the *Sonderkommando* photographs within the discourse of the Christian art of the Italian Renaissance, as explored by Didi-Huberman in his study of Fra Angelico a decade earlier. Chaouat summarizes: "the art historian and the Christian artist yearn for the image *In Spite of Everything*, be it for the invisible image of God as arch-Image or for Auschwitz as the limit of human imagination" 93. Didi-Huberman, however, does not posit Auschwitz as a unique event that demarcates such a limit. Imagination is always limited, or rather, it is the limit that any historical investigation has to expand. Memory work thus always means to work with the liminal.
97. Georges Didi-Huberman "The Index of the Absent Wound (Monograph on a Stain)" trans. Thomas Repensek *October* Vol. 29 (Summer 1984) 63–81, 67 and 68.
98. Gérard Wajcman "De la croyance photographique" 83. My translation.

99. Didi-Huberman "The Index of the Absent Wound" 81.
100. Mary Ann Doane "The Indexical and the Concept of Medium Specificity" *Differences* Vol. 18 No. 1 (2007) 128–152, 140
101. Ibid. 134. My emphasis.
102. Philippe Dubois *L'Acte photographique et autres essais* (Paris: Nathan Université 1990) as quoted in Luce Lebart "The Man of the Shroud: The 'First Crime Photograph'" *Images of Conviction: The Construction of Visual Evidence* ed. Diana Defour (Paris: Le Bal/Éditions Xavier Barral 2015) 61–79, 63.
103. Didi-Huberman "The Index of the Absent Wound" 81. One may, as Bruno Chaouat has argued, trace a direct lineage from the disconcerting "blotches of paint" (Chaouat 2) analyzed by Didi-Huberman in his 1995 study of the Italian Renaissance painter Fra Angelico, to the dark and blurry zones that spread across the clandestine photographs of the incineration pits, as well as the cracked floors of the crematoria and the pieces of bark studied in *Écorces.* Dissemblance, or what Didi-Huberman refers to as the "excessively *material*" (*Fra Angelico* 4) aspects of the pigments that cloud and obscure Fra Angelico's images, is thus established as the privileged means for figuring the divine. Affiliating Peirce's semiology with the discourse of Medieval theology, such blotches and stains are designated by Didi-Huberman "as indexes of the mystery" (*Fra Angelico* 7). Furthermore, the operation through which the "figureless" comes to be invested with the "powers of signification" (*Fra Angelico* 3) spurs what Didi-Huberman describes as an "undecidable play of *it's that* and *it's not that*" (*Fra Angelico* 8). This idea returns in his discussion of the photographs taken by the *Sonderkommando*, and the conflicting responses that they have triggered, locked in the epistemological double bind of either asserting "yes, that's it!" or, contrarily, "no, that's not it, because it is unimaginable" (*Écorces* 40). My argument here is that this transfiguration of the indexical into the iconic, and of the invisible into the visible, is the modus operandi of Lanzmann's films. Georges Didi-Huberman *Fra Angelico*: Dissemblance & Figuration [1990] trans. Jane Marie Todd (Chicago and London: The University of Chicago Press 1995).
104. Margaret Olin "Lanzmann's *Shoah* and the Topography of the Holocaust Film" *Representations* No. 57 (Winter 1997) 1–23, 17.
105. In his *Passagen-Werk*, Benjamin makes the following distinction between aura and trace: "The trace is appearance of a nearness, however far removed the thing that left it behind may be. The aura is appearance of a distance, however close the thing that calls it forth. In the trace, we gain possession of the thing; in the aura, it takes possession of us." Benjamin *The Arcades Project* 447.
106. Lanzmann cited by Georges Didi-Huberman in *Images in Spite of All* 93.

107. For a discussion, see James E. Young "The Biography of a Memorial Icon: Nathan Rapoport's Warsaw Ghetto Monument" *Representations* No. 26 Special issue: Memory and Counter-Memory (Spring 1989) 69–106.
108. I am drawing here from Margaret Olin's analysis: "The ending of *Shoah* conforms to an official Israeli discourse that understands the Holocaust primarily in its role as the foundation of the Israeli state." Olin adds: "The view of Jerusalem gives closure to the dialogue between Israel and Poland." Olin 13.
109. Claude Lanzmann *La Tombe Du Divin Plongeur* (Paris: Gallimard 2012) 367. My translation.
110. Jacques Derrida "Archive Fever: A Freudian Impression" trans. Eric Prenowitz *Diacritics* Vol. 25 No. 2 (Summer 1995) 9–63, 1.
111. Simone de Beauvoir, Preface to *Shoah: The Complete Text* (New York: DaCapo Press 1995) iii.
112. Didi-Huberman *Confronting Images* 159.
113. Bertolt Brecht "To Those Born Later" *Poems 1913–1956* eds. John Willett and Ralph Manheim (London: Eyre Methuen 1976) 318.
114. Bertolt Brecht "Bad Time for Poetry" [1938] *Bertolt Brecht: Poetry and Prose* eds. Reinhold Grimm and Caroline Molina y Vedia (New York and London: Continuum 2003) 95.
115. Another apple tree, this one standing in an orchard in Hamburg, became the subject of the final entry into the diary of Aby Warburg. On the very day of his death in late October, Warburg noted that new buds were sprouting on the withered branches, and that the tree, long assumed to be dead, had "suddenly turned green again, revived." Didi-Huberman *The Surviving Image* 338.
116. For a discussion on these two photographs in *Film Socialisme*, see Roland-François Lack "A Photograph and a Camera: Two Objects in *Film Socialisme*" *Vertigo* No. 30 (Spring 2012); and James S. Williams *Encounters with Godard: Ethics, Aesthetics, Politics* (Albany: State University of New York Press 2016) 200–201.
117. Elias Sanbar *Les Palestiniens: La photographie d'une terre et de son peuple de 1839 à nos jours* (Paris: Hazan, 2004) 208. My translation.
118. Ibid. 13. My translation.
119. Since 1967, approximately 800,000 olive trees have been cut down on the West Bank, depriving Palestinian families living in the area of their primary means of income. On December 10, 2014, we may further note, a Palestinian minister died after a confrontation with the Israeli army during a symbolic olive tree planting ceremony near Ramallah.
120. Reja Shehadeh *Palestinian Walks: Notes on a Vanishing Landscape* (London: Profile Books 2008) 45–46.

121. As quoted by Barbara McKean Parmenter *Giving Voice to Stones: Place and Identity in Palestinian Literature* (Austin: University of Texas Press 1994) 87.
122. The poem, "For how hard it is," was written by W.G. Sebald at an age of 22 and published in a student paper in Freiburg. It also introduces the posthumously published volume *Across the Land and the Water*: Selected Poems 1964–*2001* ed. and trans. Iain Galbraith (London: Hamish Hamilton 2011).
123. Maurice Merleau-Ponty "Eye and Mind" trans. Carleton Dallery *The Primacy of Perception and Other Essays on Phenomenological Psychology, The Philosophy of Art, History and Politics* ed. James M. Edie (Evanston: Northwestern University Press 1964) 167.
124. See the roundtable discussion "On Landscape (1970): Nakahira Takuma, Adachi Masao, and Nakahara Yūsuke (moderator)" *From Postwar to Postmodern: Art in Japan 1945–1989. Primary Documents* eds. Doryun Chong, Michio Hayashi, Kenji Kajiya, and Fumihiko Sumitomo (Durham: Duke University Press 2012) 233–238, 234.
125. Giorgio Agamben *Idea of Prose* [1985] trans. Michael Sullivan and Sam Whitsitt (Albany: State University of New York Press 1995) 37. In Late Latin it is *silva* and in Ancient Greek *hyle*. Both terms have a double denotation: on the one hand, wood, grove or timber; on the other, the creative force of primal matter. Notable in relation to Agamben's interest in liminalities and thresholds, *silva* is also the derivation of the Old English *syl*, meaning foundation or threshold.

Index

H. Gustafsson, *Crime Scenery in Postwar Film and Photography*,
https://doi.org/10.1007/978-3-030-04867-9

B

C

H

Y

Z